The Ethical Economy of Conflict Prevention and Development

Nijhoff Law Specials

Volume 68

The titles published in this series are listed at the end of this volume.

The Ethical Economy of Conflict Prevention and Development

Towards a Model for International Organizations

Ralf Bredel

Martinus Nijhoff Publishers
Leiden • Boston

Cover design:
Ralf Bredel: "Conflict" (2004)
Acryl on Canvas
160x110 cm

A C.I.P. Catalogue record for this book is available from the Library of Congress.

The views expressed herein are those of the author and do not necessarily reflect the views of the United Nations Industrial Development Organization.

Printed on acid-free paper.

ISBN-13: 978 90 04 15305 9
ISBN-10: 90 04 15305 5

Printed and bound in The Netherlands.

For Tim &
Moritz

CONTENTS

Part Two. The Social Economy of Conflict Prevention

Part Three. The Ethical Economy of Conflict Prevention

FIGURES

PREFACE

A classical novelist once wrote: 'Thou know that the ages will pass, and humanity will proclaim by the lips of their sages that there is no crime, and therefore no sin; there is only hunger? Feed men, and then ask of them virtue!' By the time he wrote those paradigmatic sentences, our novelist had carefully explored this issue in a series of pertinent books. His preoccupation was with the deeds of the individual, as well as the complementary responses of conscience and iusticia. With regard to both he made his feeding appeal. This appeal conflicted with the common assumptions of the day. He did not believe that an individual's ethical record was independent from that same individual's welfare status. Quite to the contrary, he believed that one's welfare status had a causal effect on his or her ethical choices. The troubles of ethical choice would not evolve only after the dilemmas of welfare had been solved. By alleviating people's hunger, one could expect a direct improvement in their criminal and ethical record as well. As welfare thrived conscience would flourish and iusticia could lean back and rest.

What may have been a revolutionary in those days is widely accepted today. Most of us share the view that there is a connection between the wants people experience and the fears they encounter. Recent development debates often highlight the effect of people's welfare status on the crimes they commit as individuals and the conflicts that arise at the group level. In his own words, our novelist thus expresses an ideal that has kept parts of the development community revolving for some time. Looking at development debates, the present understanding differs from traditional thought in two major ways: Firstly, in previous decades the development community has been operating on the assumption that development cooperation was a moral responsibility of the aid-givers. The present understanding introduces the notion that development cooperation can develop an ethical potential for the aid-givers as well as for the recipients. Thus, it may contribute to prevent conflict in the developing world. Ultimately, this could also lead to a change in North-South debates, which often feature the traditional moral understanding of development cooperation. Secondly, as we explore the concept of positive ethical effects for recipients of development cooperation, we come to realize that the biggest challenges to conflict prevention today are not posed by individual perpetrators commanding comfortably over a number of passive followers. This describes our typical understanding of war crimes. Instead, group actions and various dynamics draw whole assortments of people into collective violence. Looking to the twenty-first century, civil war, genocide and terrorism may loom larger within the specter of key threats than traditional interstate conflict.

In some sense, addressing the ethical challenges in group action and group conflict poses a serious challenge to traditional ethical thought, which normally focuses on individual deeds. After all, moral conscience remains individual, and so does the addressee of ethical claims and norms. At least in the first place, one would expect this challenge to occur. However, practically this is hardly the case. There is indeed much debate about the ability of development to prevent conflict. So-called long-term conflict prevention strategies of international organizations have been thriving for some time. In as much as those strategies contribute to prevent conflict, they also provide an *end-of-pipe* ethical gain. But a comprehensive debate about an active role of ethical norms in the prevention of conflict is missing. One can certainly debate the worth of development efforts and long-term conflict prevention strategies that include direct ethical strategy, i.e. some sort of ethical education. Because, we may suspect that ethical behavior cannot be learned like other skills and developed as such. But it would be necessary that development debates clarify their relationship with ethics. The present book endeavors to contribute to this process of clarification. Some progress in terms of such clarification more recently relates to our understanding of *human rights*. Development practitioners today wish to express that human rights underlie and motivate development efforts, contrasting with the previous practice of keeping human rights separate from the development agenda. Thus, notions of a human rights-based approach to development have become prominent, especially in the work international organizations. This is an important step in as much as depoliticizing human rights issues helps to install and promote a genuine human right to development. Above all, this right finds expression in the *International Bill of Human Rights*. On the other hand, there is a need to ensure that a human rights-based approach to development really clarifies or even increases the role of ethics in interventions for development and conflict prevention. For example, one of several criticisms to be examined later in this book concerns the fact that a human rights-based approach to development only serves to identify recipients of development cooperation as rights holders. To a lesser extent, it might serve to identify them as ethical duty bearers. Therefore, unwillingly such efforts could also serve to dissolve an active role of ethical norms in conflict prevention. Finally, such norms might require definition and implementation through ethical interventions in the conflict prevention arena. Ethical interventions might need to join development interventions on par. In fact, while our novelist invoked the idea of virtue, which is more than a result of economic relief, there is no comparable ethical sensitivity in present development debates.

So are we being over-optimistic if we deem conflict prevention to be an ethical concept? A pragmatist might say that the present status of development debates, i.e. a rights-based approach with some incremental end-of-pipe ethical gains, discharges of ethics' own adjustment to a reality of group action, and collective rather than individual deeds. Because, if there is anyway no active role of ethical norms in those debates, there is also no challenge on ethics to adapt. Also, to some extent the problems of ethics can be seen to evolve after the economic groundwork has been put in place. The root causes, effects and interventions that relate to conflict and its prevention often fall squarely in the economic dimension. With this in mind, we are increasingly drawn toward the promise of a political economy of conflict. Alongside this promise, an *economic paradigm* has gained momentum within conflict prevention debates, especially in the operations of international organizations. In a positive fashion, this evolving economic paradigm supersedes earlier conflict prevention strategies, which were typically short-term and structured along political diplomacy and preventive deployment. It, therefore, gives rise to a category of genuine long-term conflict prevention strategies. For all its promise, true ethical interventionism could be farther from reach than before.

The key question concerning the evolving economic paradigm in conflict debates is the issue of scope. What are the limits of a political economy of conflict prevention? Since the arrival of the new millennium, more rudimentarily since the end of the Cold War, policy makers and academics have been willing to extend the promise of a political economy of conflict. Thus, apart from threats arising from socio-economic failure and poverty, the aforementioned categories of group conflict have found inclusion. A political economy of conflict prevention may hence also apply to civil war, genocide, terrorism and transnational crime. Within the latter group of threats, the evolving economic paradigm abandons more traditional assumptions as to the primacy of ethnic, racial and religious factors. Instead, the fundamental role of economic features is highlighted. By incorporating religious factors, one could even envision a political economy of terrorism. Ultimately, a political economy of conflict holds a lot of promise, because of the diversity of the problems that it seeks to solve.

The purpose of this book is to carefully reexamine the evolving economic paradigm in conflict debates. While looking closer at the political economy of conflict, it argues the need to assimilate into our thinking distinct social and ethical economies of conflict prevention. An ethical economy of conflict prevention clarifies and criticizes the role of ethical norms in present long-term conflict prevention strategies. Before that, a social economy of conflict prevention reconsiders the interplay of economic with structural and cultural factors in conflict. Especially cultural factors, such as ethnicity, race and religion, have been rated lower on the agenda of conflict factors recently, as the political economy of conflict is stressed.

As one engages in distinct political, social and ethical economies of conflict prevention, one also needs to give credit to the evolving economic paradigm. After all, that paradigm has been supportive in maintaining the multilateral idea of economic development cooperation. The latter continues to establish a counterweight to an obscure understanding of economic cooperation, sometimes invoked to justify bilateral involvement in countries with poor human rights records. The key expectation of this special version of cooperation has been that economic integration and development will necessarily provoke progress on the political human rights agenda. According to the multilateral idea, economic development cooperation helps to implement a human right to development. At the same time, there is sense that such cooperation implies no guarantees for improvement on the political human rights agenda. Only the most carefully designed intervention may prompt an end-of-pipe ethical gain in the political human rights and conflict prevention arena.

Part of the attractiveness of the evolving economic paradigm in conflict debates is the unified account of conflict it offers, the integration of seemingly disparate categories of conflict. Notwithstanding such unifying potential, there are several economic models that impact on the evolving economic paradigm. As homogeneous as this evolving paradigm is in demanding that conflict features a political economy, there is wide variety amongst economic models with respect to the precise nature of this political economy. A critique of the evolving economic paradigm focuses on the strongest economic model. Otherwise, it may end up playing in the hands of those economic models that in fact sustain the evolving economic paradigm. We shall see that a so-called *horizontal inequality* approach to conflict promises to be such a strongest economic model. Certainly, this establishes a premise that can be attacked on principal grounds. There is a certain risk that proponents of the evolving economic paradigm will exit to other models in the first place. But this risk cannot be avoided. At the same time, there is a need to stress the following fact: Different from a social economy, the ethical economy of conflict prevention can be applied to most economic models that are granted a paradigmatic status. Therefore, the critique that emanates from this ethical economy will need to be considered by any political economy of conflict prevention.

An ethical critique of the evolving economic paradigm cannot limit itself to complaints about a lacking active role of ethical norms in conflict prevention debates. Instead, this critique observes a simple but consequential rule. This rule sets that both perpetrators of conflict and development practitioners *cannot not* supply some sort of ethical statements in conflict debates. We must follow this rule even as one engages in an economic debate that superficially excludes explicit ethical norms. Inseparable from the political economy, we need to conceive of *built-in* ethical economies of conflict and conflict prevention. Inadvertently, we may adopt some paradoxical ethical norms, if we restrict ourselves to the evolving economic paradigm in conflict debates. These ethical paradoxes are neither rooted in, nor do they render questionable the human rights-based approach to and end-of-pipe ethical gain of development. Both are fairly explicit components of the evolving economic paradigm. As such, they are most appreciable. Different from that, the ethical paradoxes just mentioned are implicit and unintentional. An attempt to surface these ethical implications channels them into two major ethical models designed as *ethical welfarism* and *ethical modernism*. In view of these models' ethical paradoxes, one may well wish to close Pandora's box. One may wish to return to the original thesis, according to which the evolving economic paradigm simply lacks a link with active ethical norms. But that shall be impossible. Upon recognizing that there are some ethical paradoxes in the evolving economic paradigm, the latter could also be at odds with one of its most fundamental endeavors. Therefore, only on first approximation it might carry its name on account of a pivotal role of economic factors in conflict. It might comply with an economic paradigm in a yet deeper sense. Superficially, a tendency to reduce conflict prevention strategies to technical imperatives and economic interventions only allows for a quasi-causal approach to the root causes of conflict. To the extent that this approach must be convenient, it could also serve to identify the evolving economic paradigm as an 'economical paradigm'.

The goal of an ethical critique is to remove some of this convenience. But the final objective of such a critique is to advise on some way forward. Thus, in the end a rethinking of the ethical economy of conflict prevention will provide a useful tool for international organizations, when implementing long-term conflict prevention strategies and a human rights-based approach to development. On the way to realizing this objective, the book is organized as follows: The idea of distinct albeit linked political, social and ethical economies of conflict prevention and development suggests three major parts.

Part One examines the political economy of conflict prevention and development. The objective of this part is to employ the horizontal inequality approach, as a potentially strongest basis for the evolving economic paradigm.

A comprehensive grasp on the subject starts from a period of economic thinking that is typically referred to as 'political economy' in a classical sense of the word. Thus, chapter I reexamines three basic schools of thought, those being classical liberal, Keynesian and Marxian economics. A formidable discussion of these schools serves several purposes: Firstly, although this is sometimes ignored, early political economy features a direct link to conflict debates. To different extent, all three schools assign elements of conflict to economic operations. The chapter takes an innovative approach to political economy in probing the systematic place of Adam Smith's and John Stuart Mill's account of competition, John Maynard Keynes' theories of underemployment equilibrium and effective demand, as well as Karl Marx's law of the falling rate of profit for a comprehensive political economy of conflict. Secondly, while discussing classical political economy, focus is on those tenets that help define a number of key propositions of the horizontal inequality approach. We argue that to this endeavor classical political economy is preferable to more recent models in development economics that take departure in classical political economy's three major schools. Thirdly, the same schools are related to a number of explicit ethical theories and norms. In two ways, awareness of those norms benefits the project of this book: On the one hand, those norms rule out common belief that economics are free of ethical implications. On the other hand, they are of help when surfacing a number of ethical paradoxes of the evolving economic paradigm in conflict debates. Finally, political economy's three schools have been the basis for three schools in international relations that deal with processes of international organization and institutional integration goals. A glimpse at those schools fits with the overall goal of relating this book to the work of international organizations today. These schools also provide the backdrop for clarifying the specific place of human rights-based approaches to development within the work of those organizations.

Chapter II offers a systematization of the horizontal inequality approach in conflict debates. Thus, it uses the scaffold laid out in chapter I. Originally proposed by Oxford scholar Frances Stewart, this approach has solicited wide appreciation recently, especially from international organizations in the development field. Concretely, the horizontal inequality approach allows for defining long-term conflict prevention strategies. The chapter identifies and discusses some main propositions at the bottom of this approach. While giving preference to economic factors, the horizontal inequality approach also recognizes symbolic factors, i.e. ethnicity, race, religion, and others more. Those factors are assigned a distinct, co-fueling role in economic conflict. The actual strength of horizontal inequality approaches is demonstrated as rooted in such comprehensiveness, which supersedes either-or distinctions.

Part Two moves on to a critique of the evolving economic paradigm. Thus, it centers the social economy of conflict prevention. Two chapters are designed as complementary critiques under this social economy. While pursuing separate structural and cultural critiques of the horizontal inequality approach, both chapters are concerned with one particular category of conflict, which a political economy of conflict prevention often leads to ignore. This category comprises cases of *hidden conflict.* A question weighed in the realm of these conflicts is whether to upgrade hidden conflict on the international development and conflict agendas, also diverting some attention from open conflict situations.

Chapter III establishes a structural critique of the horizontal inequality approach. It focuses on a social reality that is frequently enough at odds with simple dichotomies. Preference for dichotomous structures, e.g. rich and poor, privileged and underprivileged, better-off and worse-off, is pictured as a basic characteristic of the horizontal inequality approach. Against this dichotomous approach, the chapter demonstrates that multi-grouped social settings can lead to suppress rather than escalate potential for conflict.

Chapter IV is tailored to a complementary critique on cultural grounds. Cultural elements in conflict are essentially composed of symbolic factors, i.e. ethnicity, race, religion and others more. The chapter pleads for a new appreciation of these factors. It takes up a particular strength of the horizontal inequality approach, which makes it partly superior to other economic models. In a fairly detailed manner, this approach assigns cultural factors a co-fueling role in group conflict. Ultimately, the chapter turns this supposed strength against the horizontal inequality approach. Thus, deviating from its promise to offer a most comprehensive conflict model, horizontal inequalities have been restricted to politico-economic factors. The chapter pioneers in that it considers the same category of inequalities for cultural factors. The consequences of such application are far-reaching. What originally strengthens the economic side in conflict, also serves to reinforce the cultural side in an unprecedented manner. The broader implication is that potential for open conflict decreases rather than increases.

Part Three realizes the ethical economy of conflict prevention. The part features a series of contemplations that come together in one major point, being a number of ethical paradoxes of the evolving economic paradigm in conflict debates. It also advises on a way out of these paradoxes.

Chapter V deals with value judgments. Value judgments are different from ethical norms and associated paradoxes. But they influence the questions we pose, the answers we seek and the actions we take. The chapter starts off by identifying implicit ethical statements that primary actors form when embarking on economic conflict. These statements form primary value judgments. From there, the chapter moves on to value judgments economic models bear. This analysis applies to international organizations, to the extent that more recently their development cooperation has come to evolve on the basis of a comprehensive assessment exercise that precedes development strategies and interventions. Economic models, such as the horizontal inequality approach, are employed to arrive at practical assessments. Concretely, these models are integrated into particular assessment tools that are applied to the country level.

Chapter VI moves on to strategies and interventions for development and conflict prevention. The evolving economic paradigm founds those strategies and interventions. Here, ethical norms and paradoxes become real. The chapter brings into application said rule that development practitioners *cannot not supply ethical statements* in conflict debates. We must follow this rule even as one engages in a purely economic discussion that superficially excludes explicit ethical norms. A prime goal is to render these implied ethical norms explicit, so as to respond to a built-in threat. Given their implicit nature, these norms leave ethics with no option to react, essentially because they are never stated explicitly. The process of rendering explicit these norms finds support from the side of ethics in a line of thought that has been referred to as 'ethical realism'. An ethical realism-centered angle identifies and links ethical welfarism and ethical modernism as two particularly problematic ethical norms relevant to the evolving economic paradigm. Both ethical models are originally designed. The economists-philosophers consulted in designing ethical welfarism range from quantitative and qualitative act-utilitarians, such as Jeremy Bentham and John Stuart Mill respectively, to different outcome moralist's like Amartya Sen. The economists-philosophers consulted in designing ethical modernism are such seemingly adverse authors as Karl Marx and Karl Popper, i.e. the formers holism, technological determinism and anti-interventionism, and the latter's piecemeal social engineering approach and technological interventionism. In as much as it implies ethical welfarism, the evolving economic paradigm culminates in a number of concrete ethical paradoxes. To the extent that it implies ethical modernism, that paradigm collides with a concept of autonomy for which Immanuel Kant remains the main reference.

A critique of both ethical models leads over to a debate of ways forward, especially for international organizations actively engaged in long-term conflict prevention strategies. Chapter VII broaches human rights-based approaches to development for their potential to surface ethical norms in development cooperation, in such way as to remove their ethical paradoxes. Thus, it separates from economic pondering. The chapter concludes with an outline of specific requirements of a spelled-out ethics of conflict prevention. Development cooperation that also deserves the name of ethical interventionism may need to absorb of such an ethics.

Finally, we must not close this introduction without returning to our novelist and the questions he invoked as a consequence of the ones that opened this preface. Eventually, this is also the point to disclose his identity. The author who wrote the sentences mentioned there was no one less but Fyodor M. Dostoevsky. The remarks are taken from the famous 'Grand Inquisitor Legend' in *The Brothers Karamazov*. As a consequence of those remarks, the Russian writer was struggling with the question whether 'freedom and bread' were inconceivable after all. From the perspective of the ethical economy of conflict prevention this question may finally not be as absurd as it seems now, as we have just come to think about development as freedom.

PART I

THE POLITICAL ECONOMY OF CONFLICT PREVENTION

Introduction

From Samuelson-Swan, Harrod-Domar and Prebisch, back to Smith, Keynes and Marx, and beyond

Through the mid-nineteenth century the term political economy stood for economics in general. After that it has only been used in specific occasions to indicate that the scope of economics ought to be wider than restricted to macroeconomics. The term points to the fact that in various cases economics is a social science that takes on board political issues. One such issue is the topical issue of conflict. Where economics is willing to contemplate issues of conflict, it theorizes a political economy of conflict. Where it follows up on those contemplations in practice, it realizes a political economy of conflict prevention. Most broadly speaking, a political economy of conflict seeks to establish a strong relationship between economics and conflict. It appreciates that changes or manipulations in each domain will influence the other domain in a direct way. Thus, a political economy of conflict rules out one option. According to this option, interventions in the individual spheres of economics and conflict influence the other sphere rather coincidentally. Generally, evidence of a strong relationship between both will derive much easier when conflict accounts for the independent variable. Clearly, a certain degree of existing conflict will always obstruct economic performances. However, a political economy of conflict focuses on economic operations as a prime characteristic and normal state of society. Hence, it assigns conflict the role of a dependent variable. From here it goes out to observe how close aspects of conflict are associated with economic operations. While doing so it considers two main options: According to a first option, conflict comprises a rare possibility of economic operations, an emergency to occur in those few cases where something goes terribly wrong in the economy. According to a second option, conflict accounts for an intrinsic moment of economic activity.

A prime question concerns individual branches of economics, from which a political economy of conflict will borough. The focus of this study is on those kinds of conflict mentioned in the preface, i.e. civil war, genocide and terrorism. It is a sad truth that often those categories of conflict occur or have a root in the developing countries. Thus, it seems logical to employ development economics in order to arrive at a political economy of conflict. Chapter II analyzes the horizontal inequality approach (h.i.-approach) to conflict. Located in the field of development economics, this approach provides important input to a political economy of conflict. At the same time, it serves to put some restrictions on three pertinent schools in development economics, as well as traditional conflict models aligned with them. Those schools have been neo-classical growth theory, Post-Keynesian growth theory and Dependencia analysis. Particular restrictions relate to those schools' direct impacting on a political economy of conflict. They also relate to the extent to which they help understanding the h.i.-approach. As for the first point, the three schools have mainly been concerned with issues of economic growth, rather than tailored to a study of conflict. To the extent that they integrate a conflict lens, i.e. through a related conflict model, they have offered rather categorical and incommensurable perspectives on a political economy of conflict. Also, one cannot avoid the view that in some cases economics has been employed to prove that certain conflicts are real, rather than to analyze conflict through a neutral lens. This applies particularly to some branches of Dependencia analysis. In all these senses, the three models fall short of an integrated approach to conflict, as is the h.i.-approach.

As for the second point, the advantage of an integrated approach like the h.i.-approach is that it assimilates particular elements of the mentioned three models into its own analysis. Generally, this would justify a first chapter that only systematizes those models. However, the explanatory power of those models in relation to the h.i.-approach increases under one precondition. It does, when the h.i.-approach is related to these models' theoretical origins, rather than their latest conceptual outgrowths. For to main reasons: Firstly, in a way the h.i.-approach provides so overall an economic theory of conflict that there is limited worth in relating it to specific tenets of different models in development economics. Secondly, mainly at their theoretical origin conflict has been esteemed as an intrinsic moment of economic activity. Also, some important ethical theories and suggestions for the process of international organization have been developed with direct reference to these origins. In present models, there is much preoccupation with technical questions, e.g. technology adaptation, reverse engineering, and the like. The micro nature of these discussions partly deviates from broad issues such as economic conflict. In detail, the theoretical origins of present models in development economics are provided in three schools of early political economy, i.e. liberal, Keynesian and Marxian economics. Chapter I reexamines those schools, rather than repeating present growth models. With those schools we are back to the term political economy in an original sense of the word. Although this is sometimes ignored, development was also the first and foremost concern of classical political economists from Smith and Ricardo, to Mill and Marx. Only the neo-classical marginalist revolution of the 1870s subtracted both distributional equity and economic development to leave only allocational efficiency in economics.[1] With Keynes economics was back on track. Just as their modern counterparts, the three schools in political economy have been extremely diverse. In the realm of its truly innovative approach, the h.i.-approach will be related to some aspects of each. Such proceeding further justifies from three points:

Firstly, beyond focusing on technical questions, modern development economics has become used to apply abstract economic models, i.e. to be econometrics. Neo-classical growth theory has made use of the Samuelson-Swan model and others

[1] S. Chew and R. Denemark (eds.), *The Underdevelopment of Development: Essays in Honour of Andre Gunder Frank*, Thousand Oaks: Sage Publications (1996).

more. Post-Keynesian growth theory applies, among others, the Harrod-Domar model. To a lesser extent this has been the case with Dependencia analysis, and authors such as Raúl Prebisch. A critique of the use of abstract economic models is not uncommon and necessary today.[2] It goes beyond development economics and concerns economics in general. According to such a critique, the social world requires analysis as an open system. In this open system, the different components of the social realm are highly internally related and subject to mutual influence. Abstract economic models tend to feature a view of the social world as a closed system and people as separable individuals, also implying an undue focus on the identification of event regularities. Results obtained by deductive, a priori economic methods, e.g. econometrics, are transferred to the real world.[3] Often such thinking is rooted in a fallacious understanding of the nature of abstraction. For example for neo-classical writers such as Milton Friedman things are as simple as this that a 'hypothesis is important if it explains much by little, that is, if it abstracts the common and crucial elements from the mass of complex and detailed circumstances surrounding the phenomena to be explained and permits valid predictions on the basis of them alone.' It is accepted that 'truly important and significant hypotheses will be found to have assumptions that are wildly inaccurate descriptive representations of reality, and, in general, the more significant the theory, the more unrealistic the assumptions.'[4] As opposed to this, there is a need for a mode of abstraction conscious to the difference of considering something *as not* having a particular characteristic, as opposed to observing it *not as* assuming that trait.[5] There is a need to distinguish between precisive and non-precisive abstraction.[6] Modern development economics often ignores this point. The h.i.-approach stays away from abstract economic models. Thus, it may not be considered by means of those.

Secondly, an analysis of the h.i.-approach takes place in awareness of the final goal of this analysis. Political economy is employed to make sense of the economic precepts of that approach. But those economic precepts are analyzed in view of their ethical implications. In that sense, chapter II prepares for chapter VI, just as chapter I prepares for chapter II. While defining a logical way forward, such proceeding faces one problem, which is a lack of explicit ethical argumentation in the h.i.-approach. Different from that, political economy relates to various pertinent ethical theories, sometimes even developed by the same writers. For example, John Stuart

---

2 See T. Lawson, *Economics and Reality*, London: Routledge (1997); T. Lawson, 'Connections and Disconnections: Post Keynesianism and Critical Realism', in *Journal of Post Keynesian Economics*, Vol. 22, No. 1 (1999) 3-14; T. Lawson, *Reorienting Economics*, London: Routledge (2003).

3 S. Austen and T. Jefferson, 'Comparing Responses to Critical Realism', Paper presented at the 17th Conference of the History of Economic Thought Society of Australia, University of Western Australia, Perth, Australia, 6-9 July 2004.

4 M. Friedman, 'The Methodology of Positive Economics', in M. Friedman, *Essays in Positive Economics*, Chicago: University of Chicago Press (1953) 3-43.

5 See Aristotle, *Physics* [ca. 350 BC], Oxford and New York: Oxford University Press (1996) 193b22-36; Aristotle, *Metaphysics* [ca. 350 BC], Cambridge MA: Harvard University Press (1969-73) 1077b23-1078a29.

6 R.T. Long, 'Realism and Abstraction in Economics: Aristotle and Mises versus Friedman', Paper presented at the Austrian Scholars Conference No. 10, Ludwig von Mises Insti-tute, Auburn, USA (2004) 6.

Mill was a classical economist, but he also designed utilitarianism as a related ethical theory. By finally looking into the relationship between political economy and ethical theory, chapter I provides a scaffold chapter VI may capitalize on. It does so, in addition to setting up the economic scaffold necessary to understand the h.i.-approach.

Thirdly, the point of departure for analyzing the h.i.-approach is the feedback it has solicited from international organizations. This approach has become a model for international organizations when addressing long-term conflict prevention goals, thus realizing a political economy of conflict prevention. The project of this book is to review and partly revise this model. However, way before that model emerged the three schools in political economy have been the basis for distinct liberal, realist and Marxian models of processes of international organization. For two major reasons chapter I briefly addresses those models: Firstly, to contrast their focus on governing influences between economics and politics, as well as institutional integration goals, with an intervention-centered angle international organizations take on under the h.i.-approach. Secondly, a debate of the three models prepares for chapter VII. That chapter probes human rights-based approaches to development. Human rights-based approaches are considered as a potential remedy for ethical paradoxes in the h.i.-approach and interventions international organizations accept under its auspices. However, for human rights-based approaches to become real, processes of international organization must be thought of as far reaching. These processes go beyond the three basic models. At the same time they were prepared in them.

With this brief outline, a political economy of conflict and conflict prevention may be tackled directly. An economic theory of conflict attracts this name by virtue of inseparable political, historical, methodological, ethical and institutional dimensions.

CHAPTER I

POLITICAL ECONOMY

Political economy's three major schools conceive of economics and conflict through two major options. Some consider conflict as an intrinsic moment of economic activity. Some reject conflict as a rare possibility, an emergency to occur only in those few cases where something goes terribly wrong in the economy. But in a development context they all serve to understand the horizontal inequality approach (h.i.-approach). Degrees of internalization of conflict into economic operations increase systematically, when moving from the liberal school, to the Keynesian and Marxian schools. In all three cases, the extent of such internalization is co-determined by assumptions concerning the governing influences between economic and political activity. Given those assumptions, these schools exceed a political economy of conflict. They also impact on a political economy of conflict prevention. The latter is particularly relevant for international organizations. For example, if conflict was integral to economic operations, and economics drove politics, the relationship between economics and conflict becomes utterly strong. An option for corrective political action vanishes. Long-term conflict prevention strategies of international organizations were at a loss. The below investigation analyzes all three schools in political economy according to two complementary aspects: Firstly, for *degrees of internalization* of conflict into economic operations; secondly, for *governing influences* between the economic and political spheres. The first aspect is dealt with under the 'conflict'-entitled sections. These sections provide input to a political economy of conflict. The second aspect is considered in complementary 'interventions'-named sections. These sections also include provisions related to processes of international organization. As such they impact on a political economy of conflict prevention.

Having established these investigative lenses, one can take a closer look at political economy's three major schools. The abovementioned example moved close to a most radical model. Being the Marxian conception of political economy, that model highlights aspects of conflict in economic operations, and a clear direction of influence between the economic and political spheres, whereby economics determine politics. Before looking into Marx's political economy, the liberal and Keynesian models are considered as two comparatively moderate models. The liberal model provides a good starting point, in that economics are freed from moments of conflict. Also, preference is given to a loose relationship between the economic and political spheres. Between the liberal and Marxian extremes, Keynesian economics approves of a strong relationship between economics and politics. However, it does so with a clear focus on conflict as a political rather than purely economic phenomenon. It also illustrates how politics sometimes employs economics when following up on power goals.

Different from the past, today's world is moving from domestic economies to a globalized economic order, and from import substituting to export-oriented economies. Both nationally and internationally, the economic and political spheres are increasingly intertwined.[1] Governing influences are more complex than before. A separation of both spheres nowadays means applying some category of 'ideal types' in the Weberian sense. The sub-sections on processes of international organization pay reference to this fact. On a broader scale, there is the need for a non-ideological, integrated political economy of conflict prevention today. A final section weighs such a political economy. By borrowing from political economy's three major schools, it shows that an integrated political economy of conflict prevention may dispose of ideological and moral implications, but rarely will it escape ethical implications.

Section 1. Liberal Economics

Liberal economists don't bother with aspects of conflict. This is a very common assumption today. Exploration of liberal models normally stops with this assumption. However, at a closer look, the absence of aspects of conflict must not be misinterpreted as a lack of concern on the part of liberal economists. Rather, the reasons for such absence are built in the ways economic operations are perceived on a broader scale. After all, those reasons need to be understood.

Generally, liberal models seek interpretation by means of one paradigmatic concept, both concerning the relationships between economic activity and conflict, as well as the one between economics and politics. As such, these models are not different from Keynesian and Marxian economics. As for this concept, all interaction between economic agents is seen to be describable by a mode of *competition*. The latter mode replaces any reference to conflict economies. It also bears direct implications for the relationship between economic activity and politics. As the section moves to liberal interventions, it deals with the fact that political interventions are typically deemed unnecessary. Straightforwardly, this fact is deducted from the unlikelihood of economic conflict. Principally, there would be scope for such interventions. Liberal models acknowledge political activity as a set of measures distinctly different from economic activities. However, not only that any influence taking of politics in the economy is considered unnecessary, also, such influence taking could only be detrimental. Ultimately, it may introduce conflict where no conflict existed in the first place. Limitations in the concept of competition have only been explored more recently. This has also led to a partial revision of the classical liberal model, the designation of a compensatory liberal approach, as well as advocacy for particular forms of international organization.

---

1 R. Gilpin, 'The Nature of Political Economy', in C. Goddard et al. (eds.), *International Political Economy. State Market-Market Relations in the Changing Global Order*, London: Lynne Rienner Publishers (1996) 9.

Conflict

Individualism

When classical liberals observe the economic field, they only recognize the exchange of individuals. No group or block for a non-market driven allocation of economic resources is acknowledged in the first place, as this block could also lead a violent re-distribution of resource. For classical liberals in the tradition of Adam Smith's *The Wealth of Nations* of 1776 it all depended on how much one was willing to apply a bottom-up approach to economics. Thus, the individual-centered approach found a strong basis in a microeconomic advance to macroeconomics. It also did so in the way economic activities originally started. At the beginning of economic activities, stood the self-interested and profit-seeking individual, which became so much embraced afterwards. Therefore, individuals started businesses in order to feed their drive. As those businesses flourished, others signed up in the same field. As the flipside of those supply activities, consumers occurred constituting a demand to be satisfied on the market, rather than by people continuing their agrarian lives. Under all circumstances, the exchange relationship between supplying individuals and those demanding would be of a conflict-free nature in this stage.

After all, no principal change to defining features of this exchange relationship was set to occur, when, owing to society's growing demand, efficiency concerns attracted an expansion of businesses and the establishment of a division of labour. Such a division of labour would prompt efficiency gains, in as much as it improved the dexterity of labourers, whose business was being reduced to some one simple operation in a chain of many.[2] Mass production and modified supply patterns notwithstanding, the average wage labourer, who was an individual supplier before, would still be an *individual* consumer on the market. A concern for the problems labourers could experience in securing a living wage went beyond the scope of the classical liberal model.

Why is the individual-centered approach so ultimately important to liberal thought? It is so, because economic *competition* can only take place where consume comprises a number of separate individuals, thus ensuring a conflict-free economic sphere. Certainly, the concept of free competition also requires that the supply side of economic activities is divided into several supplying individuals, so as to rule out artificially high prices due to lack of competition for consumers. However, according to liberal view enduring market distortions, such as monopolies, only occur where they are explicitly granted to individuals or corporations by special law. A closer look into the concept of competition clarifies how competitive behavior is granted to ensure a conflict-free economy, provided there was perfect liberty, in that a number of individual suppliers and consumers existed.

---

2 A. Smith, *An Inquiry into the Nature and Causes of the Wealth of Nations*, Dublin: Whitestone (1776) Book I, Ch. 1.

Competition

Together with classical liberals one needs to assume that, at all times, the prize at which individual suppliers sell their commodities to the market is above the natural price, so as to leave them a profit, the proper fund of their subsistence. Quite naturally, suppliers will try to push up the actual prize as high as possible. But obviously, the actual market prize of their commodities will always be determined by two factors in addition to their aim for profit-maximization. Both of these factors are only guaranteed where the principle of individuality rules:

Individuality of supply, as a first factor, guarantees that a number of suppliers compete on the market, providing that the quantity of commodity *x* brought to the market increases. It ensures that the actual price, or price of free competition, will not be too high above the natural prize and affordable to the consumers, whose demand can be satisfied. Individuality of demand, as a second principle, warrants that consumers not willing to pay more than the natural price of the commodity, compete for the stocks offered, also ensuring that the market price will be above the natural prize, and such that suppliers make a profit. In Adam Smith's words: 'A competition will immediately begin among them, and the market price will rise more or less above the natural price, according as either the greatness of the deficiency, or the wealth and wanton luxury of the competitors, happen to animate more or less the eagerness of the competition.'[3] Competition will be perfect where a large number of producing and consuming individuals exist, and the supplied goods are perfect substitutes. The principle of perfect competition will in these cases not only apply to the market for goods, but equally to the labour and capital markets.

After all, a key point of the classical liberal model is that individual consumers will *always* be individual consumers, and individual suppliers will always be individual suppliers. Applied to the situation of competition this means:

> Rather than want it altogether, some of them will be willing to give more.[4]

In other words, the liberal economic individual will rarely exit to cooperative behavior when following up on economic goals. It will rather compete against other individuals with the same demand, and always accept the risk to go without the commodity. It will never distort purposely the principle of perfect competition. Therefore, the liberal economic individual is far from seeking economic alliances with others, not even to mention the case of a violent redistribution of economic supplies where over-demand pushed up prices.

For classical liberals the promises of free competition were even greater. Beyond there being no *means* for conflict to evolve, there were hardly ever good *reasons* for conflict. This followed from classical liberalism's supply-driven approach to economics, according to which supply creates its own demand, i.e. from Say's Law.[5]

---

3 Ibid. Book I, Ch. 7.

4 Ibid.

5 J.-B. Say, *A Treatise on Political Economy: Or the Production, Distribution and Consumption of Wealth* [1803], Philadelphia: Lippincott, Grambo & Co. (1855).

Therefore, a main argument for why a situation like the one just mentioned would rarely occur has been that production could be increased to any extent, so as to satisfy the effectual demand. If going without the commodity this time, the individual consumer will satisfy his demand next time, as supply increases and prices go down. Minor fluctuations aside, supply and demand will always be in equilibrium. At the same time of re-stating those assumptions, one realizes that classical liberals were everything but ignorant to the issue of conflict. As previously mentioned, the relationship between economics and conflict in liberal thought is hardly about a lack of concern. According to their own premises, liberals could simply *explain away* such phenomena as conflict.

One can even find a glimpse of unease in classical liberal thought. It entails Adam Smith's recognition of those who are never competitive on the market on account of their inability to meet the natural prize of a commodity. For this reason, he also distinguished between effectual demand and absolute demand, with the former meaning buying demand, a notion eventually not to be confused with Keynes' effective demand conception. Then again, Smith's optimistic answer as to why those whose demand located below the threshold of constituting effectual demand would be brought into the boat, was that the real recompense of labour, i.e. the real quantity of the necessaries and conveniences of life which it can procure to the individual labourer and consumer, increases in a still greater proportion than its money price.[6] Generally, unemployment was seen as a phenomenon of too many workers being employed in a particular industry, who could easily be shifted to another sector.

Interventions

Invisible Hand

As for classical liberals, the conditions under which the economic behavior of self-interested individuals can be beneficial to all did not fall under a problem-centered angle. Undeniably, what Smith introduced to the history of political economy, is a concern for *unintended consequences* of economic activity, a lens later carried on by Thomas Malthus, David Ricardo and others.[7] Rather than capturing imperfections and problems that could occur in the market, the notion of unintended consequences has a positive connotation when applied to in Smith's economic thought. It comes to the fore in what is commonly known as the *invisible hand.* As a most important category of unintended consequences of economic activity, the concept of the invisible hand projects that in a context of perfect liberty individuals only need to fol-

---

6 Smith (1776) Book I, Ch. 8.

7 See T. Malthus, *An Essay on the Principles of Population*, London: J. Johnson (1798). Malthus' dealing with population development is pregnant with possible unintended consequences. Suppose that society aids its most needy members by giving them food. As a result, they can survive and reproduce. Helping the poor would, according to Malthus' argument, increase population and in the future lead to even larger numbers on the verge of starvation. Hence, charity would be self-defeating. According to a strict reading of the Malthusian argument, all attempts to improve society are doomed to fail.

low up on their own goals in order to enhance the wealth of society as a whole. According to such belief the individual:

> intends only his own security; and by directing that industry in such a manner as its produce may be of the greatest value, he intends only his own gain, and he is in this, as in many other cases, led by an invisible hand to promote an end which was no part of his intention. Nor is it always the worse for the society that it was no part of it. By pursuing his own interest he frequently promotes that of the society more effectually than when he really intends to promote it.[8]

Smith's argument for this unintended promoting effect is, in fact, rather blurry and even carries signs of transcendental belief. It definitively revolves around one basic principle that confirms the individual-centered approach. According to this principle, individuals are the natural backbone of any economic activity. They are so, not only due to their self-interested nature. But in its local situation each individual 'could judge much better than any statesman or lawgiver can do for him.'[9] As two defining characteristics of economic individuals, self-interest and rational judgment are intertwined. According to John Stuart Mill, the immediate interest of people in the business of their life qualifies them to be better judges than the government of the means of attaining the particular end at which they aim.[10]

A more analytical assessment of the roots of liberal belief in unintended consequences, goes back to those elements of the supply-and-demand theorem Adam Smith did not contemplate explicitly when introducing his invisible hand theory. One of those elements is the so-called 'liberal reward of labour'. Beyond putting his stakes into assumptions about an increased real recompense of labour, Smith was ultimately positive about an ever-growing demand for labour. Therefore, the same principle of over-demand, which in one direction worked to push up the money price of commodities, and put the consuming labourer at a disadvantage, in a second direction effected an increase in the wages and purchasing power of labour, as the demand for labour grew. For classical liberals, it was as simple as this that the scarcity of working hands occasioned a competition among employers bidding against one another in order to get labourers. Voluntarily, they would thus break through the natural tendency of employers not to raise wages. The invisible hand theorem is indeed not banal in as much as it recognizes that the continual increase of national wealth, rather than its greatness in the first place occasions a rise in the wages of labour. But it is banal in as much as it took this steady increase for granted.

Again, the legacy of the liberal model is that it rejects the possibility of economic conflict both as regards the existence of necessary *means* and substantial *reasons*. Especially, the latter assumption must be questioned in view of crucial shortcomings of the invisible hand theorem and the concept of perfect competition. One question mark refers to the perfect rationality of individuals, which classical liberals proclaimed so rigorously. Another doubt concerns the availability of complete informa-

---

8 Smith (1776) Book IV, Ch. 2.

9 Ibid.

10 J.S. Mill, *Principles of Political Economy: With Some of Their Application to Social Philosophy* [1848], Fairfield: A.M. Kelley (1987) 951.

tion to individual suppliers and consumers about all prices on the market at all times, the absence of which necessarily leads to distort prices. Outside the field of general equilibrium theory, the invisible hand theorem receives critical questions from the provisions of game theory. Especially, the *prisoner's dilemma* in game theory serves to challenge the salience of the invisible hand theorem.

A well-known example, the prisoner's dilemma takes two individuals in a rather simple situation, both attempting to maximize their well-being in an individual, non-cooperative manner, and yet making choices that clearly lead to an unnecessarily poor outcome for both. Both individuals are thus suspected of being accomplices in a crime and are held prisoner in separate, non-communicating cells. Both are being offered the following deal: The one who offers evidence against the other one will be freed. If none of them accepts the offer, they are in fact cooperating against the police, and both of them will get only a small punishment because of lack of proof. They both gain. However, if one of them betrays the other one by confessing to the police, the defector will gain more, since he is freed. The one who remained silent, on the other hand, will receive the full punishment, since he did not help the police, and there is sufficient proof. If both betray, both will be punished, but more severely than if they had refused to talk. What will both prisoners do in this situation? If the other prisoner does not confess, then the best course of action is to confess and go free. Even if the other prisoner does confess, it will be better to have done likewise; at least the sentence will be lower. Both prisoners will reason accordingly, and both will confess. At the same time they will end up serving sentences longer than if both had remained silent.

The dilemma rests with the fact that each prisoner cannot make a good decision without knowing what the other one will do. As things are, utility cannot be maximized. Still, when employed to criticize the invisible hand theorem, the dilemma only comprises a vague analogy. First of all, economic individuals are no prisoners, because by definition economic behavior is dependent on some sort of exchange with others, and individuals will agree to this kind of exchange. Also, in the given example it is not the individuals' own choice not to communicate, but rather they are held in isolation. However, as an analogy the dilemma experiences its most severe limitations in the fact that a situation of increased communication would still not lead to enhanced cooperation between economic individuals operating in a Smithian context. In a situation like the prisoner's dilemma, any behavior bears clear consequences. Only such clear knowledge of the consequences makes communication and cooperation meaningful, because upon coordinating their behavior individuals can expect to prompt particular consequences, namely those that are utility maximizing. However, as compared to the prisoners' situation, the invisible hand theorem relies on utility in terms of *unintended* consequences of economic behavior; most of all, because in any situation it is unclear and rather unconvincing to the single individual how cooperative decision finding maximizes its own utility as well as that of others. Even in a situation of unrestricted communication, the Smithian individual would still stick to self-interest. To stay in the above picture: It would rather hang out in its cell and implicate the other individuals.

The above picture still worsens. For classical liberals the individual is the best judge of the means of attaining the ends at which they aim, and coincidentally of the aims of society as a whole. Given this premise, situational egoism emancipates from shortsightedness and introspectiveness. It won't be cured eventually by an authority with a better knowledge of those means and apt to maximize social utility. Purposely, the invisible hand theorem lacks any me. The unintended consequences it expresses are by all means undesignable, non-arrangeable consequences. For liberals the dilemma would actually start where those imprisoned individuals were to sit together to design a masterplan for social welfare maximization.

But then again, classical liberals are utterly comfortable with the undesignable nature of social consequences. Finally, this leads back to liberal perception of the relationship between economics and conflict. Again, the essential point about this relationship is that any moment of conflict can be dissolved in the *competitive* behavior of individuals. According to such understanding, competitive behavior means individuals who consult markets as the only way of satisfying economic needs. It means that both the virtual satisfaction of needs as well as ways of progressing such satisfaction are necessarily *individual*. Correspondingly, the classical liberal model does not recognize non-economic competition, where individuals join hands so as to push through a redistribution of economic resources. Even if there was indeed an equilibrium problem between supply and demand in society and potential for conflict increased, for classical liberals this still did not change the fact that no conflict occurred. Conflict would lack all the necessary means, as provided in processes of group building and group mobilization. On a separate note, this is why the classical liberal model gives an outlook on aspects of hidden conflict, an issue chapter III and IV will deal with.

In the middle of both extremes, i.e. no reasons and means for conflict, a third option has been at the core of the classical liberal model. According to this third option, which eventually assigns conflict with some reasons and means, any effort to making economics the case for conflict is still unrealistic. It is unrealistic in as much as it is bound to be *uneconomic*. The argument that conflict will finally provide currently underprivileged individuals and groups with a commercial advantage is rejected as an optical illusion.[11] Two main reasons are building for this belief: Firstly, in a situation of ever-increasing economic exchange, any behavior threatening to disrupt regular supplies of goods and services needs to be avoided. This is why Richard Cobden saw the free trade principle as a principle 'which shall act on the moral world as the principle of gravitation on the universe - drawing men together, thrusting aside the antagonism of race, and creed, and language, and uniting us in the bonds of eternal peace.'[12] Secondly, apart from disrupting economic exchanges, conflict needs to be financed. David Ricardo's *Principles of Political Economy and Taxation* of 1817 give expression to this point, namely when demanding that conflict be financed from taxes rather than by borrowing, so as to make clear how uneconomic conflict is even before it is launched: 'When the pressure of war is felt at once, without mitigation, we shall be less disposed to get out of it.'[13] Both argu-

---

[11] N. Angell, *The Great Illusion: A Study of the Relation of Military Power in Nations to their Economic and Social Advantage*, New York and London: G.P. Putnam's Sons (1912) vii.

[12] R. Cobden, *The Political and Economic Works of Richard Cobden* [1846], 6 Volumes, London: Routledge (1995) Vol. 3, 362-363.

[13] D. Ricardo, *On the Principles of Political Economy and Taxation* [1817], Cambridge: Cambridge University Press (1951) 186.

ments contemplating the uneconomic nature of conflict were originally designed for the international economic system and international conflict. To a lesser extent, they were quoted to explain domestic economic behavior. But, on the whole, it was this third option that made classical liberals even more optimistic as to the conflict preventive qualities of an economic system applying liberal principles.

Laissez-Faire

A second analytical point concerns *governing influences* between the economic and political spheres. Those influences are important, in as much as the possibility of corrective political action in the realm of flawed economic developments and conflict is decided on their ground. Obviously, this point can be answered as a result of the points above. It is also clear that this answer implies a yes. The liberal idea of rational individuals foresees that there are no principal restrictions on political interventions in the economic sphere. But a completely different story is whether such influence taking is desirable. Here, on the other hand, the liberal model implies a clear no, with two reasons substantiating this no: Firstly, in line with an economic system driven by a mode of equilibrated competition among suppliers and consumers, there seems no *need* for any broader political intervention. Secondly, with individuals who are the best judges of the means of attaining particular economic ends, on account of an immediate interest in the business of their life, there is no *justification* for corresponding interventions. Both reasons together are founding for liberalism's laissez-faire approach to political economy.

Reference to a laissez-faire approach can be found in classical and modern writings. Ultimately, as a consequence of past interferences of governments into economic matters, Adam Smith emphasized a 'system of natural liberty'. According to such a system, the sovereign had only three duties to attend to, i.e. the defense of the country, the administration of justice, and the maintenance of certain public institutions, which it can never be for the interest of any individual to erect.[14] Another classical writing, John Stuart Mill's *Principles of Political Economy* of 1848, dwelled upon past excesses of exaggerating the province of government, a pattern identified all through until the French Revolution. Mill's major criticism of that period was that for the individual under the rule of paternal government it was not enough to do well, to do better. It was necessary to do according to the rules.[15] At the same time, there are elements of deviation between Smith and Mill. Although Mill also recognized that the labourer is always the best selector of means, he did not want to affirm with the same universality that the labourer as a consumer is always the most competent judge in a laissez-faire economic system: 'Is the buyer always qualified to judge of the commodity? If not, the presumption in favor of the competition of the market does not apply to the case; and if the commodity be one in the quality of which society has much at stake, the balance of advantages may be in favor of some mode and degree of intervention by the authorized representatives of the collective

---

14 Smith (1776) Book IV, Ch. 9.

15 Mill (1848) 796.

interest of the state'[16]. However, in the end degrees of deviation between Smith and Mill were minor.

Modern liberals, on the other hand, have been more precise about different levels of political interventions. At the domestic level, the classical angle has largely been endorsed. A profile of negative freedom has been elaborated to indicate what the individual is supposed to be free from, rather than what it is free to do. The task of government is thus seen as the creation of a framework for individuals to pursue their individual economic goals. Only sometimes, this government may use its coercive powers of raising revenue, particularly for the provision of services, which for some reason the market is unable to supply.[17] In their limited dependency relationship, the economic and political spheres are considered equally supportive of one another, and equally dependent upon the survival of the other. In detail, for a laissez-faire economy being supportive of a democratic political system means that in the wish to preserve their liberties, free markets and property rights will ensure that rational, self interested individuals will deploy democratic influences to constrain governments from any attack upon free markets, or property rights.[18]

As for the international system, assumptions of economic liberals since the second half of the twentieth century are similar to the ones endorsed for the national level. As for the economic side, the open world market is seen as the core of the international arrangement, just as the free market is the basis of the domestic structural arrangement.[19] As for the political side, the imperative for governments is to minimize their interference in trade relations. If all states adopted such a minimalist stance, then free trade would flourish and relationships deepen. Just as free trade extends consumption opportunities, producers are provided with additional incentives for specialization in areas in which they enjoy an international advantage.[20]

Compensatory Liberalism

Another group of liberal thinkers has questioned the principle of ensuring the negative freedom of economic individuals as too limited. Thus, a pattern of positive liberty has been invoked. For example, it has been criticized that according to the precepts of negative freedom 'the blind is not interfered by those who could afford to pay for a sight-restoring operation. But because he goes without the operation, what he can do is significantly limited.'[21] Present exponents of a compensatory liberal model acknowledge that economic freedom involves questions of equality of which two types are distinguished, i.e. the right to equal treatment and the right to treat-

---

16 Ibid. 53.

17 A.F. v. Hayek, *Law, Legislation and Liberty*, 3 Vol., Chicago: University of Chicago Press (1979) Vol. 3, 129.

18 B. Jones, *Globalization and Interdependence in the International Political Economy: Rhetoric and Reality*, London and New York: Pinter Publishers (1995) 20.

19 R. McKinlay and R. Little, *Global Problems and World Order*, Madison: F. Pinter Publishers (1986) 33.

20 Jones (1995) 21.

21 L. Crocker, *Positive Liberty: An Essay in Normative Political Philosophy*, The Hague and Boston: Martinus Nijhoff Publishers (1980).

ment as an equal. The latter right is made the focus of attention.[22] On the whole, there is recognition that a pure laissez-faire approach to political economy may actually put the self-sustainability of a society at stake.

Supranational Organizations

A discussion of the role and design of international organizations in international political economy suits the framework of compensatory liberalism. Because, compensatory liberalism allows for regulating action on the international market.

Functionalism vs. Constitutionalism: An influential liberal pondering of institutional questions has been David Mitrany's functionalist approach of the 1960s. That approach has dismissed constitutional approaches, such as associations of nations and federalist systems. In terms of a working peace system, associations of nations were seen to perpetuate the individual index of power applying to World War Two, i.e. the principles of sovereignty and self-reliance. More particularly, functionalism has been a response to the ongoing process of economic globalization and technological transformation in the post-war period. Thus, emphasizing a common index of need, it envisaged the building of comprehensive and solid authorities in selected fields of common life.[23] By no means, functionalism sought to supersede the existing order of nation states. Clearly, this would have been at odds with the objective to link authority to specific activity and imperfections in the international economic system.

Beyond rejecting constitutional approaches, Mitrany dismissed the federalist approach of Carl Friedrich and others.[24] Supporters of the high-sounding federal idea were blamed for their tendency to be so hypnotized by the attraction of the form that they had neglected to study its actual performance. In spite of the need for functional federalism, the barely regional character of formal federations was stressed.[25] Finally, although this was not in the scope of his principle that 'form follows function', Mitrany has criticized yet another important liberal school. In terms of conflict prevention strategies and possible ways of abolishing war as a social institution, the transactional approach of Karl Deutsch had only considered the promises of security-communities.[26] One may also question whether the separation of pluralistic security-communities (e.g. NATO) and amalgamated security-communities (e.g. USA) has met the functionalist criteria that federations should be built as needs-based communities.

Neo-Functionalism and the Theory of Political Unions: A systematic extension of integration goals has been realized by neo-functionalist approaches. These approaches include the idea of supranational political unions. At the same time, neo-

---

22 McKinlay and Little (1986) 27.

23 D. Mitrany, *A Working Peace System*, Chicago: Quadrangle Books (1966) 159.

24 C. Friedrich, 'Nationaler und Internationaler Föderalismus in Theorie und Praxis', in *Politische Vierteljahresschrift*, Vol. 5, No. 2 (1964) 154-187.

25 Ibid. 27.

26 K. Deutsch et al., *Political Community and the North Atlantic Area: International Organization in the Light of Historical Experience*, Princeton: Princeton University Press (1957) 3.

functionalist writers have remained careful when determining final integration goals. But some theoretical shortcomings relating to integration processes in old functionalism have been ruled out. In particular, old functionalism's group theory has been revised, so as to reflect the integrative potential of actual modern practices.[27] The predecessor's basic needs-centered utilitarian approach has been reaffirmed, but not so classical liberal preoccupations on the lack of a formal relationship between political action and economic welfare. The revision of this and other separability doctrines in functionalism toward a theory of interest politics, has allowed for an unbiased view on processes of international integration. Thus, personal political loyalties came to be seen as the result of satisfaction with the performance of crucial functions by an agency or government. Since actors can be loyal to several agencies simultaneously, a gradual transfer of loyalties to international organizations performing most of the crucial functions has been endorsed.[28]

International activities that are located in selected policy fields, e.g. in economics, are at the core of the neo-functionalist integration theory. However, during the last decades the spilling over of engagement in selected policy fields to other policy fields further contributed to the emanation of supranational political unions, such as the United Nations or the European Union. The focus of this investigation remains on international organizations active in the economic development field.

Section 2. Keynesian Economics

An ultimately different political economy of conflict materializes when a Keynesian lens guides our perception of the world. Such difference concerns both the relationship between economic activity and conflict, as well as the one between economics and politics. Keynesian economics combine a number of entry points for a critique of the liberal model. The section opens with a methodological debate of abstractions and simplifications that are an integral moment of liberal 'modeling' of the socio-economic world since the classical economists. Neo-classical economics only radicalizes this trend. The section continues with a critique of the concept of competition from the purview of Keynes' concept of underemployment equilibrium. Directly, this critique broaches the place of economic conflict in Keynesian economics. The section closes with a discussion of various intervention-related aspects, including aspects of international organization.

The liberal model has often been criticized for assumptions such as the perfect rationality of individuals, the availability of complete information on the market to economic individuals, and others the like. All these aspects address one common theme, which is an overload of rather ideal, abstract premises in liberal economic thought. A critique of these aspects has gained maximum momentum recently with Tony Lawson's *critical realism* entitled school of thought at Cambridge University.

---

[27] E. Haas, *Beyond the Nation State: Functionalism and International Organization*, Stanford: Stanford University Press (1964) 30.

[28] Ibid. 21-22 and 47-50.

The target of this school are abstract econometric models.[29] However, the origins of a methodological critique of the liberal model date much earlier. They are exemplarily entrenched in Austrian economics, the target of which were, among others, classical liberal writers such as John Stuart Mill. After all, John Maynard Keynes himself can be viewed as a 'critical realist', especially in moments such as the following, when the methodological basis of macroeconomics came under scrutiny.[30] At those points, we learn that macroeconomics ought to be 'a science of thinking in terms of models joined to the art of choosing models which are relevant to the contemporary world [...] because the material—to which it is applied—is, in too many respects, not homogenous through time [...] The object of a model is to segregate the semi-permanent or relative constant factors from those, which are transitory so as to develop a logical way of thinking of the latter.'[31]

The common basis of most methodological critiques of the liberal model are beliefs into the social world as an open system. In this open system the different components of the social realm are highly internally related and subject to mutual influence. Classical liberals and neo-classical writers are criticized for a misplaced ontology. This ontology features a view of the social world as a closed system and people as separable individuals, implying an undue focus on the identification of event regularities. As a consequence of such thinking, results obtained by deductive, a priori economic methods, e.g. econometrics, are seen to be reliably transferable to the real world.[32] The point against such thinking is clear. The microeconomic foundations of macroeconomics are being rejected, especially the idea that aggregate activities can be deconstructed into individual activities and understood from there. Exemplarily, Ludwig von Mises has criticized the individual-centered approach in liberal thought. This approach culminates in what appears as a separation of complex individuals into non-communicating individual traits, with no exchange among the set of motives each of them carries along. According to liberal doctrines, economic behavior mainly comprises activities of supplying and demanding products on the market. By all means, such behavior is seen to be guided by self-interest. Other aspects of the personality of individuals are neglected, particularly those that could be at odds with personal egoisms and the maxims of rationality. In von Mises words:

> When they distinguished between purely economic motives and other motives, the classical economists referred only to the acquisitive side of human behavior. [...] The approach of Classical economics appears highly unsatisfactory from the point of view of modern subjective economics. Modern economics rejects as entirely fallacious also the argument advanced for the epistemological justification of the Classical methods by their last fol-

29 See T. Lawson, *Economics and Reality*, London: Routledge (1997); T. Lawson, 'Connections and Disconnections: Post Keynesianism and Critical Realism', in *Journal of Post Keynesian Economics*, Vol. 22, No. 1 (1999) 3-14; T. Lawson, *Reorienting Economics*, London: Routledge (2003).

30 J. Jespersen, 'Macroeconomic Methodology: A Post Keynesian Perspective', Paper prepared for the Conference: Debating Critical Realism, Roskilde University, Denmark, 17-19 August 2001.

31 J.M. Keynes, 'Defence and Development', in *The Collected Writings*, Vol. XIX: The General Theory and After, Part II, London: Macmillan for the Royal Economic Society (1973).

32 S. Austen and T. Jefferson, 'Comparing Responses to Critical Realism', Paper presented at the 17th Conference of the History of Economic Thought Society of Australia, University of Western Australia, Perth, Australia, 6-9 July 2004.

> lowers, especially John Stuart Mill. According to this lame apology, pure economics deals only with the 'economic' aspect of the operations of mankind, only with the phenomena of the production of wealth 'as far as those phenomena are not modified by the pursuit of any other object.'[33] [...] Modern economics traces all human actions back to the value judgments of individuals. It never was so foolish [...] as to believe that all that people are after is higher incomes and lower prices. [...] the term well-being [...] does not refer only to concerns commonly called egoistic but comprehends everything that appears to an individual as desirable and worthy of being aimed at.[34]

At the end of the day, liberal negligence of the conflict-prone nature of economic operations could have a starting point in the way individuals are conceived. While individuals are granted a whole set of motives, any exchange relationship between these motives is ignored. In the extreme, liberal failure to grasp of economic activity in a comprehensive sense has been rooted in a fallacious understanding of the nature of *abstraction*. While neo-classical writers, such as Milton Friedman, emerge as a prime target when reviewing such understanding, the latter also applies to the classical economists. For Friedman, things are as simple as this that a 'hypothesis is important if it explains much by little, that is, if it abstracts the common and crucial elements from the mass of complex and detailed circumstances surrounding the phenomena to be explained and permits valid predictions on the basis of them alone.' Moreover, to be important 'a hypothesis must be descriptively false in its assumptions; it takes account of, and accounts for, none of the many other attendant circumstances, since its very success shows them to be irrelevant for the phenomena to be explained.' In sum, 'truly important and significant hypotheses will be found to have assumptions that are wildly inaccurate descriptive representations of reality, and, in general, the more significant the theory, the more unrealistic the assumptions.'[35]

An illustrative criticism of the classical and neo-classical understanding of abstraction refers to an earliest debate in ancient Greek thought. In this debate, Aristotle rebutted Plato's understanding of abstraction in terms of idealization.[36] For Plato, a species could be abstracted from its matter in such a way as to think that the species did not exist in matter. For the purpose of understanding the species, nothing would be lost. Different from that, Aristotle's thinking propounds a mode of abstraction conscious to the difference of considering something *as not* having a particular characteristic, as opposed to observing it *not as* assuming that trait.[37] Medieval scholars such as Pierre Abélard and Thomas Aquinas later revived this mode.[38]

---

33 J.S. Mill, *Essays on Some Unsettled Questions of Political Economy* [1844], London: Longmans and Green (1877) 140-141.

34 L. v. Mises, *Theory and History*, New Haven: Yale University Press (1957) Part 3, Ch. 10, II.

35 M. Friedman, 'The Methodology of Positive Economics', in M. Friedman, *Essays in Positive Economics*, Chicago: University of Chicago Press (1953) 3-43.

36 R.T. Long, 'Realism and Abstraction in Economics: Aristotle and Mises versus Friedman', Paper presented at the Austrian Scholars Conference No. 10, Ludwig von Mises Institute, Auburn, USA (2004).

37 See Aristotle, *Physics* [ca. 350 BC], Oxford and New York: Oxford University Press (1996) 193b22-36; Aristotle, *Metaphysics* [ca. 350 BC], Cambridge MA: Harvard University Press (1969-73) 1077b23-1078a29.

38 See Thomas Aquinas, *Summa Theologica* [1265-1274], New York: Benzinger Bros. (1947) First Part, Treatise on Man, Sec. 85: Of the Mode and Order of Understanding, Prop. 1: Whether our Intellect Understands by Abstracting the Species from the Phantasms, Objection 1; Thomas Aquinas, *On Hu-*

Robert Long has highlighted that the Aristotelian distinction coincides with what is nowadays referred to as precisive and non-precisive abstraction. In a nutshell, 'a precisive abstraction is one in which certain actual characteristics *are specified as absent*, while a non-precisive abstraction is one in which certain actual characteristics are *absent from specification.*'[39]

The liberal model features the idea of an economic field guided by event regularities. It also stresses that individuals act in an informed manner, and that they are coherent as to their various motives. One can seriously consider tracing these ideas to the first or precisive mode of abstraction. All of a sudden, the concept of perfect competition could be at stake, because not only does it fail to specify the existence of information gaps or conflicting motives. Rather, quite explicitly it specified the absence of those traits. The impetus of such a critique must be felt much harder by classical liberals than by neo-classical writers. Because, namely the former went out to claim that their theories be close approximations to reality. For neo-classical writers such as Milton Friedman it is only a theory's predictions not the theory itself that must be squared with reality.[40] Keynes would probably join into such a critique. He would not demand that traits such as the ones just mentioned be specified. But his economic theory seems to insist that their non-existence not be specified either. A critique of the liberal concept of competition from the purview of Keynes' contemplation of underemployment equilibrium evolves from here.

Conflict

Underemployment Equilibrium

In a complex manner, Keynesian economics questions the liberal axiom of a closed macroeconomic system, with macroeconomics being generalized microeconomics. In his *General Theory of Employment, Interest and Money* of 1936 John Maynard Keynes objected a core element of the liberal theory of prices and distribution. This core element concerns the reality of an equilibrium position at which the factors of production were fully employed, always remembering that for Keynes the factors of production were generally identical with labour.[41] Keynes' main concern was with

---

man Nature, Indianapolis: Hackett (1999) 157: 'Abstraction may occur in two ways. First [...] we may understand that one thing does not exist in some other, or that it is separate from it. Secondly [...] we understand one thing without considering another. Thus, for the intellect to abstract one from another thing which are not really abstract from one another, does, in the first mode of abstraction, imply falsehood. But, in the second mode of abstraction, for the intellect to abstract things which are not really abstract from one another, does not involve falsehood [...] If, therefore, the intellect is said to be false when it understands a thing otherwise than as it is, that is so, if the word otherwise refers to he thing understood [...] Hence, the intellect would be false if it abstracted the species of a stone from its matter in such a way as to think that the species did not exist in matter, as Plato held. But it is not so, if otherwise be taken as referring to the one who understands.'

39 Long (2004) 6.

40 Ibid. 14.

41 J.M. Keynes, *The General Theory of Employment, Interest and Money*, London: Macmillan (1936) Ch. 16, II: 'I sympathize, therefore, with the pre-classical doctrine that *everything is produced by labour* [...] It is preferable to regard labour, including, of course, the personal service of the entrepre-

unemployment that was not voluntary or frictional but involuntary. For Keynes, the liberals had neglected to consider the determinants of the volume of employment as a whole. At the same time of criticizing the classical liberal model, he kept the liberal theory of prices and distribution, as a model of analyzing the manner in which the factors of production are combined, and how the value of the final product is distributed between them. In other words, he kept using the concept of equilibrium as an analytical tool, however, outside full equilibrium. For both reasons of a determination to identify the determinants of the volume of employment, and his subscribing to the concept of equilibrium, Keynes can be criticized for having been *precisive*. According to such criticism, Keynes only used a broader scope than the liberals. Particularly, the meaningfulness of using the concept of equilibrium as an analytical tool outside full equilibrium has inspired the critique of critical realists:

> It is the full employment/general equilibrium that methodologically gives no meaning when uncertainty prevails. The Principle of Effective Demand could stand on its own feet without the need of an equilibrium concept. This would have relieved Keynes from the straight jacket of Equilibrium from the very out set of his different ontology [...]. That would have given Keynes an open analytical framework (the process analysis) which would have been theoretically much more satisfactory. Perhaps Keynes should have stuck to what [...] later has [been] called 'economics of disorder'.[42]

However, in terms of realistic and unrealistic pondering in economics it remains a fact that Keynes opened a window on imperfections in the economic system. These imperfections include a possibility to contemplate economic activity with a conflict-centered lens. Keynes saw that there were equilibrium positions besides that of full employment. In rare cases, the latter could prevail. However, for the most part of the economic order, equilibrium would only be achievable at a point far below full employment.[43] In determining the factors that establish actual equilibrium positions, the principle of *effective demand* assumes the center role in Keynes' theory. Most broadly speaking, this famous principle forms the counter piece to classical liberal doctrines that supply creates its own demand, i.e. to Say's Law. An integral component of Say's Law was that the volume of labour employed in the production of increasing supplies would always be pushed to the maximum, or full employment. Conversely, the principle of effective demand opposes the Ricardian idea that the aggregate demand function can safely be neglected. This being said, how does the principle of effective demand add precision to the aggregate demand function, and how does it restrict expectations of a symmetrically increased demand for employment?

Keynes started like the classical liberal economists, in that entrepreneurs take decisions about how much to produce during a defined production period. For any

---

neur and his assistants, as the sole factor of production, operating in a given environment of technique, natural resources, capital equipment, and effective demand.'

42 J. Jespersen, 'Keynes, the Principle of Effective Demand, and Open Systems', Paper for a Lecture at University of Iceland, Iceland, 10 October 2003, 13.

43 A.H. Hansen, 'Mr. Keynes on Underemployment Equilibrium', in *The Journal Political Economy*, Vol. 44, No. 5 (1936) 670.

production volume, the individual supply functions are straightforward to the entrepreneurs. They are so, in as much as they reflect quite precisely the costs incurred in a particular volume of employment. What applies to individual supply functions, also applies to the aggregate supply function, which derives as a result of aggregation of all individual supply functions. At all times, this is only one side of the whole story. Deviating from the classical economists, Keynes saw that in fixing the production volume each entrepreneur is forced to form *expectation* about how much he will actually be able to sell on the market, and about the prices he will yield.[44] In other words, he needs to form assumptions about the size of demand for his products once they reach the market. This owes to the fact that things are not as simple as held in Say's Law, according to which supply creates its own demand. In short, it is never the entrepreneur alone who decides how much to supply. Key problems relate to a deficient aggregate demand function. But why? If aggregate production increases, one would expect that the increased number of labourers necessary to produce this volume will also prompt an increase in aggregate income, and in aggregate consumption accordingly? The Keynesian answer to this question has two parts. Both parts are well known:

Firstly, one needs to remember what Keynes calls the *propensity to consume*. The propensity to consume is explained as a functional relationship between the amount of consumption measured in money-wage units and the amount of income similarly measured. At the same time, income in terms of money wage-units is held to correspond substantially in its variations with the variations in levels of employment. Therefore, writing C_w for amount of consumption in wage-units and Y_w for income in wage-units, Keynes states the propensity to consume as: $C_w = \chi (Y_w)$. Although Keynes recognizes a number of factors, both subjective and objective ones, which might affect the value of χ, Y_w remaining constant, he takes all of them to be of minor importance as compared to changes in Y_w.[45] On the basis of this simple relationship, Keynes signifies a psychological law explaining why the demand for products entrepreneurs expect could be substantially reduced. In detail, this psychological law establishes that 'the psychology of the community is such that when aggregate real income is increased aggregate consumption is increased, but not by so much as income.'[46] Keynes claims that in richer communities the gap between actual and potential production will tend to be wider, because such communities are less prone to use the greater part of their aggregate income on consumption. Consequently, it is also those societies that are in general worse-off in terms of involuntary unemployment on account of limited actual production.

Secondly, in order to grasp of the determinants of actual production and volumes of employment, one needs to weigh another element. Generally, this element is in no disagreement with classical liberalism. It concerns the principal role of investments. At first glance, this role seems to rescue the economic system from entrepreneurs

---

44 J. Hartwig, 'Trying to Make Sense of the Principle of Effective Demand', Paper presented at the Seventh Annual Post Keynesian Workshop, Kansas City, Missouri, USA, 22 June-3 July 2002.

45 J. Viner, 'Mr. Keynes on the Causes of Unemployment', in *The Quarterly Journal of Economics*, Vol. 51, No. 1 (1936) 164.

46 Keynes (1936) Ch. 3, II.

cutting back on the amount of labour as a result of a deficient aggregate demand function, an action that would further decrease demand for consumption. The idea with investments is as follows: In view of an increasing gap between aggregate incomes and aggregate consumption, entrepreneurs would make a loss if their labour force was only employed to satisfy the demand for immediate consumption. To justify an increase in the amount of labour employed, entrepreneurs need to go into investments so as to absorb the excess labour, i.e. labour not used to produce the output consumed by the community at the given level of employment. The liberal idea of the working of such investments was that entrepreneurs' demand for loanable funds to finance investments would be brought into equilibrium with the supply of voluntary saving, in consequence of adjustments to what was called the natural rate of interest. The liberal model subscribes to a loanable funds theory of interest rate determination.[47] At all times, the amount of voluntary saving necessary would be supplied by income-recipients by means of that portion of their incomes not used on immediate consume.

A realist like Keynes finds fault with the classical liberals for their disregard to a gulf between the desire of entrepreneurs to invest and the desire of income-recipients to save, particularly resulting from a tendency to hoard. The firm conviction that hoarding was so abnormal a phenomenon as not to constitute a significant contributing factor to unemployment entangles particularly David Ricardo's economic thought. According to the same thought, unemployment was a phenomenon mainly caused by wage-rigidities. However, for Keynes hoarding was a *real* problem, which also presented a serious barrier to full employment. The details of Keynes' assumed propensity to hoard are beyond the scope of this analysis. It is sufficient to understand the influence of hoarding on the amount of new investments in society. The way the interest rate is being determined in Keynes is clearly incompatible with the liberal idea of a natural rate of interest that guides supply and demand on the market for credit, also ensuring that loanable funds were always available in sufficient size. Instead, Keynes claimed his famous *liquidity preference* theory of interest rate determination. According to this theory, an excessive tendency of income-recipients to hold money, or high liquidity preference, must set a high interest rate in order to overcome the reasons for liquidity preference. The direct consequence of a high interest rate must be a low level of investment expenditures on the part of entrepreneurs. In this situation, Keynes saw no way how interest rate and investment could self-adjust to levels compatible with full employment.

Not only did Keynes anticipate a gap between the desire of entrepreneurs to invest and the desire of income-recipients to save. In Keynes, the inducement to invest is also reduced as the result of a falling schedule of the *marginal efficiency of capital*. What Keynes meant by this is fairly simple. Provided investment in any type of capital is being increased, the marginal efficiency of this capital will be diminished progressively as a consequence of two main reasons: Firstly, because the prospective yield will fall as the aggregate supply of that type of capital increases; secondly, be-

47 G.R. Steele, 'The Money Economy: Mercantilism, Classical Economics and Keynes' General Theory', in *American Journal of Economics and Sociology*, Special Invited Issue: Money, Trust, Speculation and Social Justice, Part 2: Trust and Money (Oct. 1998) 5.

cause pressure on the facilities to produce the capital would cause its supply price to increase.

At the end of the day, for Keynes expectations about a society's aggregate demand were only safe when projections of that society's demand for immediate consume combined with a thorough contemplation of the amount it is willing to devote to new investments, i.e. not to hoard. Those expectations are crucial in as much as they determine the production and employment volumes entrepreneurs decide on at the beginning of each production period. The sum of two quantities, expected consume (D_1) and expected amount of new investments (D_2), forms the *effective demand* (D) in Keynesian economics. The expected effective demand determines the amount of labour (N) entrepreneurs will employ: $D_1 + D_2 = D = \square(N)$. Obviously, the sum of these assumptions achieves considerable distance from the supply-driven approach in liberal political economy. It has been stated correctly that, strictly speaking, the term effective demand is an unfortunate term, in as much as it refers to the output that will be supplied, whereas in general there is no assurance to entrepreneurs that this output will also be demanded.[48] However, the term is valid in as much as it captures in a neat way the distance from supply-centered approaches.

Shifting of Conflict

Keynes was very clear in his belief that the effective demand associated with full employment was just a special case, to be achieved by accident or design. Certainly, it would not be the result of the working of market mechanisms alone. For Keynes, according to the precepts of his realist model, there can be equilibrium positions besides that of full employment. For the most part of the economic order, equilibrium would only be achievable at a point far below full employment. However, in as much as the notion of underemployment equilibrium was the last word in things, one could also be attracted to assume that things were fairly okay. This could be the view of a conflict-centered angle, exploiting the notion of 'equilibrium'. After all, if supply and effective demand are in equilibrium, key economic and social forces appear to be in balance. Also, any protest of those marginalized and forced to live at the social periphery will be weak. As a matter of fact, this is how Keynes himself saw the course of economy, if considered from a narrow domestic perspective:

> It is an outstanding characteristic of the economic system in which we live that, whilst it is subject to severe fluctuations in respect of output and employment, it is not violently unstable. Indeed it seems capable of remaining in a chronic condition of sub-normal activity for a considerable period without any marked tendency either towards recovery or towards complete collapse. Moreover, the evidence indicates that full, or even approximately full, employment is of rare and short-lived occurrence. Fluctuations may start briskly but seem to wear themselves out before they have proceeded to great extremes, and an intermediate situation which is neither desperate nor satisfactory is our normal lot.[49]

---

48 V. Chick, *Macroeconomics after Keynes: A Reconsideration of the General Theory*, Oxford: Philip Allan (1983) 65.

49 Keynes (1936) Ch. 18, III.

The key question is how those fluctuations would wear themselves out. Interestingly enough, Keynes' explanation of domestic economic peace can be combined with a re-interpretation of commonly assumed motives for the establishment of an international liberal order as well as the principles of free trade. Coincidentally, this re-interpretation provides the means for a critique of the liberal model at the global level. Liberals in Keynes' own time were accustomed to applaud a free trade international system as furnishing the fruits of the international division of labour and harmonizing at the same time the interests of different nations. By the way, this was a position Keynes himself had shared for considerable time. It comes to the fore in his *The Economic Consequences of Peace*, where a clear ardor for free trade finds expression on the grounds of its tendency to establish a harmony of interests.[50] Different from that, the Keynes of the *General Theory* endeavors to reveal the 'real' motives behind the liberal doctrine of free trade, and an apprehension of the 'true course of events'. In a most general sense, such correct apprehension implied that countries neglecting the struggle for international markets run the risk of seeing their prosperity drooped. However, according to Keynes, a full account of liberal advocacy for free trade leads back to the wearing out of domestic fluctuations in chronic conditions of sub-normal economic activity and underemployment. Keynes claims that the 'real' intention behind liberalizing international markets is a mitigation of economic distress at home:

> Under the system of domestic *laissez-faire* and an international gold standard such as was orthodox in the latter half of the nineteenth century, there was no means open to a government whereby to mitigate economic distress at home except through the competitive struggle for markets. For all measures helpful to a state of chronic or intermittent under-employment were ruled out, except measures to improve the balance of trade on income account.[51]

In the Keynesian appreciation, international conflict comprises the worst case of a system where domestic economies seek to *shift conflict*. Such shifting of conflict was embraced as the true relationship between liberal economies at home and an international order applying free trade principles. Keynes acknowledges that conflict has always been about those leaders, dictators and others, 'to whom war offers, in expectation at least, a pleasurable excitement', and who thus seek to work on the 'natural bellicosity'[52] of their peoples. But more realistic would be those cases where conflict had a cause in domestic economies' competitive struggle for markets. Thus, it presented an alternative way of one country forcing its wares on another, or repulsing the offerings of its neighbor. The express objective while doing so would be to upset the equilibrium of payments, so as to develop a balance of trade in its own favor. According to such view, international competition comprises the shifting of internal conflict from shortcomings in the liberal concept of domestic competition. International conflict comprises the case of low competitiveness of a country in international spheres.

---

50 J.M. Keynes, *The Economic Consequences of Peace*, London: Macmillan (1919).
51 Keynes (1936) Ch. 24, IV.
52 Ibid.

For the early Keynes, things with domestic underemployment equilibrium were such that international trade comprised a desperate expedient to increase employment at home by forcing sales on foreign markets and restricting purchases. This also meant shifting the problems of underemployment and domestic conflict to neighbors. In this situation, the only possible cure was that nations learned to provide themselves with full employment by applying appropriate domestic policy. In the context of our analysis, this leads back to a second investigative question, which is about governing influences between the economic and political spheres.

Interventions

Socialization of Investment

In the given situation of underemployment equilibrium, Keynesian economics votes for a comprehensive socialization of investments so as to adjust the determinants of effective demand, i.e. people's propensity to consume and inducement to invest.[53] A comprehensive socialization of investments is seen as the only means to secure an approximation to full employment. Clearly, this socialization is assigned to the public authority, also involving a large extension of the functions of government as compared to those foreseen under the liberal model. However, what is the precise meaning of a comprehensive socialization of investments, and how is this socialization supposed to work? Keynes' idea of an *investment multiplier* comes into play at this junction. The idea of the investment multiplier is sufficiently known itself. It may be considered to the extent that it elucidates the governing influences between the economic and political spheres in Keynesian economics.

In as much as the propensity to consume is such that normally aggregate real income increases faster than aggregate consumption ($\Delta Y_w > \Delta C_w$), an increment of investment will be needed to justify the increased aggregate real income associated with full employment ($\Delta Y_w = \Delta C_w + \Delta I_w$). This we said before. However, in as much as a high interest rate emanating from liquidity preference also sets a low level of investment expenditures on the part of entrepreneurs, there is no choice but the increment in investment required to produce full employment stemming from the public authority, thus taking steps to stimulate the investment industry. According to Keynes, such stimulus preferentially takes the form of increased public works on which additional labour can be employed. Narrowly considered, the resulting increase in aggregate income will comprise the real incomes of those employed on public investment, or as Keynes said of those under primary employment. However, beyond that the investment multiplier joins in. According to Keynesian economics, the increased employment in investment will be associated with a stimulus or 'favorable repercussion' on employment in the industries producing for consumption. Simply, because those employed on investment contribute to increase the community's aggregate consumption. Therefore, the increase in primary employment (ΔN_2)

[53] Ibid. Ch. 24, III.

will inevitably lead to a total increase of employment (ΔN) which is a multiple of the primary employment required by the investment itself: $\Delta N = k\Delta N_2$.[54]

The proper form of Keynes' investment multiplier, i.e. an increase in aggregate income due to an increment of aggregate investment, is $\Delta Y_w = k'\Delta I_w$. In presenting this formal argument, Keynes sought to distinguish his multiplier from Richard Kahn's 'employment multiplier', as presented in a 1931 article called *The Relation of Home Investment to Unemployment.* This earlier multiplier had considered the increment of total employment associated with a given increment of primary employment in the investment industries in line with the above formula. Keynes' formal argument against Kahn's multiplier was that the ratio of the increment of employment in one set of industries to the increment of demand that has stimulated it could deviate from that in another set of industries. However, in order to explicate the idea of his investment multiplier in a more generalized form, Keynes allowed an identity between his and Kahn's multiplier ($k = k'$). This also followed quite naturally from Keynes' focus on a theory of employment closely related to income creation.

According to Keynesian economics, the presented multiplier effect can only be achieved on the grounds of public investment, rather than by private investment alone. There are straightforward implications for the governing influences between economics and politics. For Keynesianism, the central controls necessary to cope with the problems of underemployment and inequalities of incomes and wealth require a large extension of the functions of government in the domain of domestic economy. Such extension is still equilibrium oriented, and Keynesian economics would not want to dispose of the Manchester System. Rather, it would fill the gaps in the liberal model. It would seek to cater for the necessary environment for the free play of economic forces to realize their full potential. In a word, once this politically adjusted economic environment was a fact, the advantages of individualism and private self-interest would hold good. As Keynes wrote:

> Our criticism of the accepted classical theory of economics has consisted not so much in finding logical flaws in its analysis as in pointing out that its tacit assumptions are seldom or never satisfied, with the result that it cannot solve the economic problems of the actual world. But if our central controls succeed in establishing an aggregate volume of output corresponding to full employment as nearly as is practicable, the classical theory comes into its own again from this point onwards. If we suppose the volume of output to be given, *i.e.* to be determined by forces outside the classical scheme of thought, then there is no objection to be raised against the classical analysis of the manner in which private self-interest will determine what in particular is produced, in what proportions the factors of production will be combined to produce it, and how the value of the final product will be distributed between them. Again, if we have dealt otherwise with the problem of thrift, there is no objection to be raised against the modern classical theory as to the degree of consilience between private and public advantage in conditions of perfect and imperfect competition respectively.[55]

---

[54] Ibid. Ch. 10, II.
[55] Ibid. Ch. 24, III.

For Keynes, the broader implications of such political adjustment for the *international* economic system and conflict were the following: Once international trade ceased to be what it was, namely a means of mitigating economic distress at home, there would be room for the international division of labour and an unimpeded exchange of goods and services in conditions of mutual advantage.[56] Later, Keynes moved away from this vision of shaping an international harmony of economic interests at home. The reasons for that were rooted in his own time:

First of all, in the wake of Nazism in Germany and Fascism in Italy, Keynes' economic thought leant towards a protectionist line. He, therefore, sympathized with those who would minimize rather than maximize economic entanglement between nations: 'Ideas, knowledge, art, hospitality, travel – these are the things which should of their nature be international. But let goods be homespun whenever it is reasonable and conveniently possible.'[57] Economically, this line adopted elements of neo-mercantilist thinking. In fact, one is strongly reminded of Alexander Hamilton's 1791 *Report on Manufacturers*. As a matter of national economic strength, Hamilton had pledged for far-reaching state regulations that would render the United States independent of foreign trade policies. While emphasizing patterns of economic self-reliance, the primary object of the policy of nations needed to be to supply themselves with subsistence from their own soils. As far as circumstances permitted, manufacturing nations would have to procure from the same source the raw materials necessary for their own fabrics.[58] However, for classical mercantilists like Hamilton, the spirit of implementing a monopoly to the domestic market, thereby enhancing the prosperity of manufacturers, was materially connected with the security of a country. In Keynes' case, a protectionist line was rather a moral matter of rejecting real business with the totalitarians. At that point, the means of securing international peace were considered to be politico-military, i.e. rooted in re-armament.[59]

In fact, for a short while of World War Two Keynes' realism could appear to adopt principles of the evolving realist school in international relations. According to one of its earliest proponents, political realism became the insight that 'to make the harmonization of interests the goal of political action is not the same thing as to postulate that a natural harmony of interests exists.'[60] The latter had so far been expressive of liberal belief. The most crucial doctrine of political realism related to the idea that nation states always strive for power maximization. Thus, the ultimate goal of politics needed to be for *hegemonic stability*.[61] Economics were seen to be of mi-

---

56 Ibid. Ch. 24, IV.

57 J.M. Keynes, 'Let Goods be Homespun', in *New Statesman and Nation*, July 1933.

58 A. Hamilton, *Report on the Subject of Manufacturers* [1791], Philadelphia: Library of Congress (1827) 23.

59 J.M. Keynes, Letter to the *New Statesman and Nation*, 13 July 1936: 'A state of inadequate armament on our part can only encourage the brigand powers who know no argument but force, and will play, in the long run, into the hands of those who would like us to acquiesce by inaction in these powers doing pretty much what they like in the world [...] Can I not persuade you that the collective possession of preponderant force by the leading pacific powers is, in the conditions of today, the best assurance of peace?'

60 E.H. Carr, *The Twenty Years' Crisis 1919-1939*, London: Macmillan (1939).

61 K. Waltz, *Theory of International Politics*, Reading: Addison-Wesley (1979) 194.

nor importance for the achievement of such stability.[62] It would comprise 'low politics' as opposed to security politics assuming the rank of 'high politics'. A more detailed discussion of institutional integration goals adopted by the realist school follows below.

On a broader scale, independent from the circumstances of World War Two, Keynesian economics clearly distinguishes between appropriate means of securing an international harmony of economic interests, and the rather amoral doctrines of political realism. Those means are essentially politico-economic, although it is also true that Keynes never returned to the idea of shaping an international harmony of interests at home, eventually by ways of a 'comprehensive socialization of investments'. A careful distinction between Keynesian economics and political realism is particularly important, for an economic line within political realism has recently gained momentum. This line provides an economic theory of power maximization. At the same time, economic realism has become increasingly aware of the incompatible nature of international economic interdependence and a desire for domestic autonomy in mercantilist doctrines. Certainly, a beggar-my-neighbor approach with the objective of forcing a trade surplus has also been integral to traditional mercantilism. The concept of hegemonic stability remains a main justifying angle to ease the tensions between domestic autonomy and international economic interdependence, both for mercantilism and economic realism. As such, it justifies economic interdependence with reference to security gains from economic dominance abroad. This essentially power-driven moment in economic realism is the all-distinguishing element from the Keynesian account of international economic interdependence. For Keynes, international economic interdependence possessed a relief-character. Increased international economic interdependence aims at mitigating economic distress at home. It comprises an attempt to shift conflict, rather than be conflict- or security-centered in a primary sense. The following sub-section on processes of international organization offers an opportunity to look more closely into economic realism as a security-centered doctrine.

Keynes' own solution for securing an international harmony of economic interests does not share much with economic realism. Still during World War Two it consisted of an 'international clearing union'. The envisaged purpose of such a union was to create an international currency system that allowed countries to pursue domestic policies of full employment, while maintaining equilibrium in the balance of payments between them.[63] After all, no matter how far it had been taken from the liberal equilibrium model, Keynesian economics was still equilibrium-oriented at last. It yet combined with a healthy dose of political interventionism both nationally and internationally.

---

[62] H. Morgenthau, *Macht und Frieden: Grundlegung einer Theorie der Internationalen Politik*, Gütersloh: C. Bertelsmann (1963) 50.

[63] S. Turnell, 'Keynes, Economics and War: A Liberal Dose of Realism', in *Macquarie Economics Research Papers*, No. 7 (2002) 16.

Intergovernmental Organizations

As previously mentioned, for a short while of World War Two Keynes' thinking could appear to adopt principles of the evolving realist school in international relations. However, different from liberal and Marxian economics, there is no direct link between Keynes' economic theory and that school's extension on processes of international organization. This point also applies to a recent offspring of early post-war realism, called economic realism. In all cases, the indication of a realist approach has been to signal a non-abstract, essentially empirical and pragmatic investigation of the international.[64] Particularly in the past, such pragmatic pondering did not hinder theoretical deliberations on human nature. Component elements of that nature were seen to be reflected at the level of the state.

The Principle of Hegemonic Stability and High Politics: Contemporary economic realism derives three crucial propositions from realist approaches. Firstly, a decisive role is assigned to the acting of nation states in the sphere of international relations. Realism has argued this perceived role of the state with reference to the false assumption of historically declining nationalism.[65] A second proposition concerns the striving for international power maximization of nation states. Rooted in the nature of human individuals who predominately act within their self-interest, power- or interest-politics are recognized for the safety they provide. For realists, the more powerful enjoyed wider margins of safety in dealing with the less powerful. They also had more to say about which games is played and how.[66] Finally, in view of an international system of power-seeking nations, the resulting security-dilemma would only be solved by means of a balance of power. As far as international organizations were concerned, this dilemma could be worked out through the predominant influence of one hegemonic national power on these organizations. Strictly, from the view of politics as safety-centered power politics it followed that other fields of interest-guided action were given no systematic consideration.[67] Given its focus on wealth maximization, economics was assigned the role of low politics. In contrast, security questions comprised high politics. Having separated the political and economic spheres so rigorously, the mantle of realism continues to sit slightly uneasily on the shoulders of economic realism today.[68]

An Economic Theory of Power Maximization: Economic realists have revised the original realist agenda. In view of global trade and economic interdependence, economic realists envision that existing patterns of international economic interconnectedness could, with time and determined effort, be converted into significant dependencies that progressively render the dependent societies vulnerable to the influence, and even dictates, of the dominant partner.[69] Beyond confirming the special appeal

---

64 Morgenthau (1963) 48.

65 According to Morgenthau, the French who considers himself a Communist was expected to become a Russian Nationalist to fight for the case of the Soviet Union, etc.

66 Waltz (1979) 194.

67 Morgenthau (1963) 50.

68 Jones (1995) 30.

69 Ibid. 32.

of power-centered approaches to economic realists, one can show how this view determines politics and economics concretely.

Common to all exponents of neo-realist theories is their continued commitment to the principle of hegemonic stability. According to this principle, strong international economic regimes depend on hegemonic power. Thus, fragmentation of power between competing countries is seen to lead to the breaking up of the international economic regime, whereas concentration of power contributes to stability.[70] Technological and economic change are what creates the complex structure of world power today. For the old economy of power applying to World War Two, there was no way of economically 'factoring out' errors in grievous political fields. Different from that, present authors like Paul Kennedy reason against excessive arms spending. Because, above all such spending will hurt the power implications of economic growth.[71] Thus, the balancing of short-term security effects from large defense forces and long-term security implications of rising production are identified as an increasingly crucial issue today.[72] On the whole, economic competitiveness is reviewed in the same context of political competitiveness. The economic position of a state will determine the relative power position of this state in the international system. This is why economic realists have always asserted that international economy and international *political* economy are the same things.[73]

Deviating from traditional realist doctrines of fixing the limits of international power strategies through political and military means, enhanced importance is now attributed to the role of international norms. Those norms politically adjust developments within the international economic order.[74] However, at the core of economic realists' grasp on processes of international organization, an inherited desire for domestic autonomy remains obvious. In application of traditional realist assumptions on the existence of antagonist nations, economic realists are concerned with the incompatible nature of domestic autonomy and processes of international norm-building. Clashes between both are anticipated. The traditional way of mitigating their rivalry has been the concept of hegemonic stability. In resumption of this concept, the recent vanishing of the United States' unrestricted power in international organizations like the Bretton Woods institutions is viewed critically.[75] However, calls for new direction within the international economic system are still being tied to the economic sources of political and military strength.

---

70 R. Keohane, 'The Theory of Hegemonic Stability and Changes in International Economic Regimes 1967-1977', in Holsti et al. (eds.), *Changes in the International System*, Boulder: Westview Press (1980) 136.

71 P. Kennedy, *The Rise and Fall of the Great Powers: Economic Change and Military Conflict from 1500 to 2000*, London: Unwin Hyman (1988) 444.

72 Ibid. 445.

73 D. Rapkin and J. Strand, 'Is International Competitiveness a Meaningful Concept', in Goddard et al. (1996) 111.

74 R. Gilpin, *The Political Economy of International Relations*, Princeton: Princeton University Press (1987) 117.

75 L. Thurow, 'A New Economic Game', in Goddard et al. (1996) 143.

Section 3. Marxian Economics

The same Keynes who pledged for political interventionism in economic affairs had also found strong words against a system of state socialism. For Keynes, it was not the ownership of the instruments of production that the state needed to assume. If the state was able to determine the aggregate amount of resources devoted to augmenting the instruments and the basic rate of reward to those who own them, it would accomplish all that was necessary. Moreover, necessary measures of socialization could be introduced gradually and without a break in the general traditions of society.[76] Then again, the same Keynes who criticized a system of state socialism on political grounds occasionally found positive words for Karl Marx, when contemplating economic substance. In one of few statements about the preceding thinker, key elements of his own economic thought, and particularly the 'puzzle of effective demand', are granted to 'live on furtively, below the surface in the underworlds of Karl Marx.'[77]

As this investigation looks into Marx's radical political economy, it frequently refers to key principles of Keynesian economics. In all these cases, substantial reasons outweigh didactic reasons. Keynes' and Marx's economic theories are compatible with regard to large parts of their business cycle, although some important differences relate to the assumed root of problems incurred in this cycle, or drivers of cyclical crisis. At the same time, Marx's view of the economy integrates more principal problems, which anticipate that economy's decline. Before developing the cyclical ('Conflict I') and decline-related ('Conflict II') elements of conflict, this section puts both in context with each other. It also alludes to some possible contradictions between both that require particular attention. It then prepares the basic economic ground for all aspects of conflict in Marx, i.e. Marx's take on surplus, capital accumulation, etc. A final sub-section, devoted to the governing influences between economics and politics, centers interventions, i.e. Marx's superstructure rationale, or idea of an economic infrastructure that entirely determines politics. This sub-section also offers an opportunity to look into processes of international organization. At all times, this analysis refers to the original writings of Karl Marx, so as to avoid a primarily political interpretation that characterizes the history of 'Marxism'. Political interpretations have much contributed to a superficial picture of the economic basis of Marx's conflict theory. This picture persists today and keeps damaging Marx's ideas. Ironically, the biggest contribution to such a biased view owes to Marx's most passionate admirers, i.e. to political Marxists, rather than to his harshest criticists. Unfortunately, economic shallowness has not been the privilege of politicizing Marxism. Also, political philosophy has been overly attracted by humanistic concepts, such as Marx's account of alienation, when pondering the foundations of revolution. Thus, it has further diverted from the economic basis of Marx's conflict theory. No matter whether Marx's economic theory is ultimately accepted or not, his conflict theory requires exploration in terms of that economic theory.

---

[76] Keynes (1936) Ch. 24, III.

[77] Ibid. Ch. 3, III.

A brief overview of component elements of economic crisis and conflict serves to sharpen an economic debate of Marx's conflict theory. As previously mentioned, there are mainly two such elements. They revolve around Marx's business cycle theory on the one hand, and comprise the economic foundations of capitalist decline on the other. Both elements can be visualized in a simple graph, capturing the various stages of a fictive economy over time (Fig. 1.1). Even before providing specific content to both sets of elements, one can see quite easily that, far from being compatible, both lead to completely different statements as to the course of so-called 'capitalist' economies. As for the cyclical elements, there are some severe setbacks whenever the business cycle enters into phases of contraction. However, the overall course of the economy is expansive, at depression point X still amounting to a fairly sustainable level of economic output or aggregate supply Y_2. As for the other elements, deemed to describe the long-term trend of capitalist economies, the tenor is reckless economic decline. At the same point X, they envision a meager level of economic output Y_1, which is not restricted to a temporary phase of depression.

Both scenarios have one major implication. On first approximation, there could be some severe contradictions in Marx's theory of conflict, provided this theory is indeed considered from an economic angle. Almost automatically, these contradictions are ignored when embarking on a political or philosophical journey with Marx's writings. Hitherto, the above situation of incommensurability only captures a theoretical scenario. It must not pre-conclude that both economic concepts in Marx are indeed incommensurable. Therefore, besides pointing at the limitations of a non- or semi-economic approach to Marx's conflict theory, the present remarks serve to highlight the challenges of an economic debate. For the remainder of this chapter, this challenge is to explain how elements of cyclical crisis can be reconciled with Marx's vision of capitalist decline.

Fig. 1.1: Cyclical Crisis and Capitalist Decline

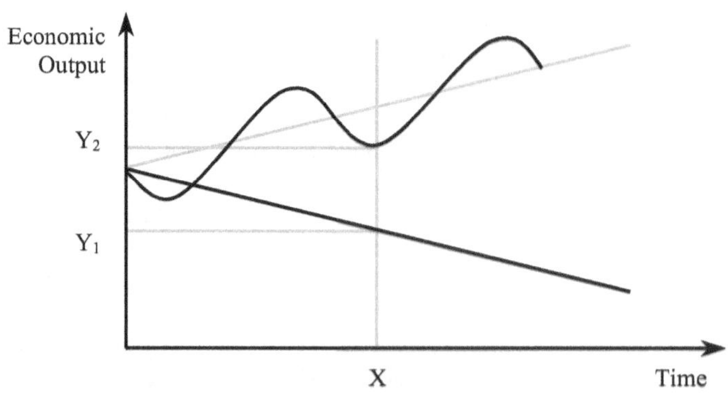

An understanding of different elements of crisis and conflict in Marx's economic theory hinges on Marx's grasp on capital accumulation. However, a deep grasp on Marx's understanding of capital accumulation requires the broader picture of how economies reproduce themselves, because capital accumulation forms only one although prevailing mode of reproduction as far as so called 'capitalist' economies are concerned.

On first approximation, Marx occupies common ground. Before any physical act of production can start, money capital *M* is being transformed into the elements of production *C*, writing *M*→*C*. More particularly, Marx recognized two main elements of production on which money capital is spent, i.e. money capital laid out upon the means of production, namely equipment (constant capital), designated as c; and money capital expended upon labour power, namely wages (variable capital), designated as v. Under capitalism, the total value of goods emanating from the adjoined processes of production V comprises a third portion, namely the profit of the entrepreneur to be realized by selling the goods on the market. This last portion Marx called *surplus*, designated as s, also implying that $V = c + v + s$. Within the whole cycle of economic reproduction, the sphere of production is considered the only sphere where entrepreneurs yield a profit.[78] That is why the surplus constitutes the only source of revenue for the entrepreneur. The mere fact of this surplus being an integral part of capitalist production is seen to make such production an act of *exploitation*, independent of whether wages paid to the labour force are high or low.

Just as Keynes, Marx further described the process of production as necessarily comprising two types of industries, i.e. an investment and a consumption industry. The former, he called Department I of Means of Production, because it produced the equipment demanded by the consumption industry and the investment industry itself. The latter, Marx called Department II of Means of Consumption, for the reason that it produced to satisfy the aggregate demand for consume generated within both types of industries. For both departments Marx assumed $V = c + v + s$, writing $V_1 = c_1 + v_1 + s_1$ and $V_2 = c_2 + v_2 + s_2$ respectively. This being said, Marx further assumed two different models of reproduction with different likeliness to end up in disequilibrium. Only the second model is seen to contain elements of cyclical and structural crisis, because only here capital accumulation is involved:

A first model outside capital accumulation Marx called 'simple reproduction'. In order for simple reproduction to work three basic conditions must be present: Firstly, the means of production Department I produces must be exactly as much as both departments need to replace consumed means of production: $V_1 = c_1 + c_2$). Secondly, the total value of the consumption goods produced by Department II must equal the total value of consumption goods demanded by both departments: $V_2 = (v_1 + v_2) + (s_1 + s_2)$. Thirdly, once both departments have purchased that portion of their own products needed by themselves, they must be able to sell to each other the remainder of their products: $V_1 - c_1 = c_2$ and $V_2 - (v_2 + s_2) = (v_1 + s_1)$. The 'great exchange' Marx's model thus assumes for both types of industries is perfectly compatible with Keynes' principle of effective demand, namely that the sale of some output of each department depends on expenditures derived from income generated

78 Marx objected to the idea that profit could be created in the sphere of circulation (C'→M') through entrepreneurs buying cheap and selling dear, on the grounds that if one man gets more by selling, another must get less by purchase.

in the other department or industry. However, Marx also conceded that for the most part reality looked different.

Particularly, capitalist production does not comply with a model of 'simple reproduction'. Rather, 'enlarged reproduction' or capital accumulation is the goal. According to Marx, it is the very nature of the entrepreneur in his function as capitalist that he seeks to increase his capital. So far as 'he is personified capital, it is not values in use and the enjoyment of them, but exchange value and its augmentation that spur him into action.'[79] In other words, the capitalist's surplus product does not only consist of things destined to satisfy his wants and desires, things that consequently enter into his consumption-fund. Rather, this surplus product or profit is only partly taken in the form of consumption goods. The capitalist characteristically tends to reconvert a portion of his profit into new and additional capital, so that he may in the future reconvert even more profit into capital.[80] By doing so, capitalists execute capital accumulation.

On the whole, enlarged reproduction implies two things: Firstly, that capitalists don't consume their profit completely ($V_2 < (v_1 + v_2) + (s_1 + s_2)$). Secondly, that they will invest a portion of their profit into additional means of production, also meaning that the total value of the means of production Department I produces will be larger than both departments' need for replacement purposes ($V_1 > c_1 + c_2$).[81] Marx's concept of enlarged reproduction can be linked to Keynesian nomenclature. Before that, one needs to note that for Marx things were not as simple as that, that an economic system discharged of capitalist principles could also suspend all forms of enlarged reproduction, and work on the basis of simple reproduction only. Marx was clear about the fact that 'in economic forms of society of the most different kinds, there occurs, not only simple reproduction, but, in varying degrees, reproduction on a progressively increasing scale.'[82] As by degrees more is being produced and more consumed, consequently more products have to be converted into means of production. However, Marx did believe that this process could be administered publicly, rather than being in private hands. In other words, it would not present itself as accumulation of capital, or function of capitalists, as long as the labourers' means of production, and with them their product and means of subsistence, do not confront them in the shape of capital.[83]

A comparison of Marx and Keynes states that both economic thinkers are in agreement about one basic fact. According to both thinkers, entrepreneur-capitalists form profit *expectations* about the size of aggregate demand for their products once they reach the market. According to both economists, the realization of those expectations depends on investments sufficient to compensate for the portion of a soci-

---

79 K. Marx, *Capital Volume One: The Process of Production of Capital* [1867], in Marx and Engels, *The Collected Works of Karl Marx and Frederick Engels*, 50 Vol., New York: International Publishers, London: Lawrence & Wishart Ltd., Moscow: Progress Publishers (1975-2005) Vol. 35, Ch. 24, III.

80 S.S. Alexander, 'Mr. Keynes and Mr. Marx', in *The Review of Economic Studies*, Vol. 7, No. 2 (1940) 124.

81 See Fan-Hung, 'Keynes and Marx on the Theory of Capital Accumulation, Money and Interest', in *The Review of Economic Studies*, Vol. 7, No. 1 (1939) 30.

82 Marx (1867) Ch. 24, III.

83 Ibid.

ety's aggregate income not spent on consume. Unless there are corresponding investments, effective demand will be checked. In this very general form, the rule is also valid for non-capitalist societies. Although Marx did not formalize a theory of effective demand, it is integral to the discussed reproduction models. More precisely, Marx's account of capitalist societies agrees and disagrees with four building blocks of Keynes' economic thought:

Firstly, by counting with periodic changes in aggregate supply due to deficient effective demand, both Marx and Keynes adopt a *partially cyclical* view of the economy. As for Keynes, this cyclical view is entrenched in the schedule of the marginal efficiency of capital. According to this schedule, the prospective yield of any type of capital will fall periodically as the aggregate supply of that type of capital increases. At the same time, there are limitations of viewing Keynes as a business cycle theorist. On the one hand, Keynes was concerned with underemployment equilibrium as a fairly stable phenomenon, being more than a periodic occurrence in the short run. On the other hand, he broke with those emphasizing the inevitability of the cycle, in such that periods of large-scale unemployment were deemed necessary to correct the excesses of periods of prosperity. Here precisely, politics came into play, in that government investment allowed for a multiplier effect in the economy, also altering its current cycle. As for Marx, a cyclical view of the economy is enshrined in the principles of enlarged reproduction and capital accumulation. The following section, looks into the drivers and stages of Marx's business cycle. Needless to say that for Marx, much more than for Keynes, the limits of assigning a full-grown cyclical view to his economic theory are rooted in the premises of capitalist decline.

Secondly, Marx theorizes his very own version of Keynes' *propensity to consume*. He does so, by assuming that the only goal of entrepreneur-capitalists is for the achievement of capital accumulation, as particular form of enlarged reproduction applying to capitalist societies. However, different from Keynes, Marx considered investment and saving as exclusive attributes of the capitalists, whereas workers are mostly bound to consume the total of their income. Therefore, different from Keynes, he localized the most significant feature of the propensity to consume, i.e. the inducement to invest, in the capitalist class, regarding it as the fundamental organic behavior of that class. Keynes himself was concerned with the problem that when aggregate real income increases aggregate consumption increases, but not by so much as income.[84] However, rather than analyzing corresponding behavior as the behavior of a particular class in a particular stage of economic development, he referred to such behavior in terms of a general psychological law. In Marx, on the contrary, the working class is characterized by consume, and only by consume. More precisely, the working class is seen to consume in two ways: While producing, it consumes by its labour the means of production, and converts them into products with a higher value than that of the capital advanced. This part Marx called the working class' productive consumption. On the other hand, the working class turns the money paid to it for its labour power into means of subsistence, this being its individual consumption.[85]

---

84 Keynes (1936) Ch. 3, II.

85 Marx (1867) Ch. 23.

Thirdly, Keynes' idea of a progressively reduced propensity to consume is compatible with Marx. A related question concerns the schedule that guides the inducement to invest of entrepreneurs, also assuming that investment always means the overcoming of some motives for *liquidity preference*. As we saw earlier, the rate of interest plays an important role in this context. Just as Keynes, Marx rejected liberal assumptions of a natural rate of interest, which guides supply and demand on the market for credit in a manner ensuring that loanable funds are always available in sufficient size. Thus, both dismissed the loanable funds theory of interest rate determination. Both are proponents of a monetary theory of interest. Also, both subscribe to the view that interest is not a reward for saving, but for *not* hoarding, which is to say for lending. According to Keynes' liquidity preference theory of interest rate determination, a rather permanent tendency of income-recipients to hold money, or to hoard (high liquidity preference), is to set a high interest rate. This high rate will be necessary to overcome the reasons for liquidity preference. However, inevitably a high interest rate will also result in low levels of investment expenditures on the part of entrepreneurs. In other words, Keynes saw liquidity preference as a continually operating problem. In contrast, Marx considered the possibility of absorption in hoards only as a transitional stage in the accumulation of capital or business cycle. On the whole, interest plays a rather peripheral role in Marx's theory. Later on, we will see that the deeper reasons for this peripheral role are rooted in Marx's concept of capitalist decline. Beyond rooting deficient effective demand in Keynesian underinvestment scenarios, this concept relates such deficiency to technological change patterns resulting from investment precisely.[86]

Fourthly, besides offering different explanations for the determinants of effective demand, neither Marx nor Keynes should be considered as underconsumptionists. Underconsumption theories project that at full employment level there is not enough purchasing power in the hands of consumers to buy up the aggregate supply of consumption goods. A consequent solution is deemed to be to increase the income and purchasing power of the consumers. Although Keynes and Marx would not deny that at given times underconsumption could be a real problem, they both rejected the assumed root and cure proposed.[87] All of this attracts a direct focus on the central role of technological change in Marx. However, before centering those elements that supposedly work for the decline of capitalism, one needs to spell out the cyclical elements of crisis. They arise from capital accumulation, i.e. maladjustments between the consumption and investment industries. Eventually, this can be done by making use of the reproduction models analyzed in this section.

---

[86] D. Dillard, 'Keynes and Marx: A Centennial Appraisal', in *Journal of Post Keynesian Economics*, Vol. 6, No. 3 (1984) 428.

[87] For the relationship between Marx's and Keynes' political economies see also R. Brandis, 'Marx and Keynes? Marx or Keynes: A Reply', in *Journal of Economic Issues*, Vol. 21, No. 1 (1987) 470-473; D. Dillard, 'Dillard on Keynes and Marx: Rejoinder', in *Journal of Post Keynesian Economics*, Vol. 8, No. 4 (1986) 632-636; R. Fichtenbaum and Shahidi H., 'Marx and Keynes? Marx or Keynes: A Comment', in *Journal of Economic Issues*, Vol. 21, No. 1 (1987) 467-470; H. Jensen, 'Marx and Keynes: Alternative Views on Capitalism', in *Atlantic Economic Journal*, Vol. 17, No. 4 (1989) 29-38.

Conflict I: Cyclical Crisis

For Marx, cyclical crisis in the economy results as follows: Under capitalism, individual capital accumulation and profit expectations are rendered necessary preconditions for production to start. Entrepreneurs will only produce if they can expect to sell their commodities on the market. All this concerns the *sphere of production*. However, at the same time capitalism bursts through all restrictions as to time, place and individuals earlier imposed by direct barter in the *sphere of circulation*. It, therefore, splits up the direct identity that in barter existed between the alienation of one's own and the acquisition of some other person's product into what Marx calls the antithesis of a sale and a purchase. The complete metamorphosis of a commodity in the sphere of circulation requires both phases, which are complementary therefore. For Marx, this implies the possibility of crisis, in as much as no one can sell unless someone else purchases. But no one is forthwith bound to purchase, because he has just sold. Crisis is set to occur where the interval in time or split between sale and purchase becomes too pronounced.[88]

Not only theoretically but also practically, Marx saw capitalism to bring about such *realization crisis*. The latter would occur still although each capitalist formed thorough expectations as to the effective demand for his products in the first place. Clearly, such crisis is embedded in the business cycle that both Marx and Keynes assumed to run through the history of 'capitalist' production. In detail, Marx's business cycle recognizes the typical recurring phases, i.e. moderate activity, prosperity, overproduction, crisis and stagnation. Each phase will develop as the necessary result of the foregoing phase. Also, as all phases are subject to cyclical return, one is free to take up the cycle at any point. Everything else means invoking some chicken and egg questions. For ease of reference, one may yet start with the best of cases, that is, a phase of economic boom.

Ultimately, as the result of earlier contraction, three things are in demand during phases of economic boom: Firstly, commodities are in demand. Production is consequently being expanded, and commodities are readily sold, also providing the first part of the required metamorphosis of commodities in the sphere of circulation. On the other hand, money is over-supplied. Thus, consumers are ready to buy the commodities, also ensuring the other part of the necessary metamorphosis of commodities. Secondly, just like other commodities, labour power is in demand in this phase. Unemployment falls as workers labour to handle the increased production volume. Last but not least, credit is in demand with interest rates on the rise as bankers grab their share.

However, as workers realize the demand for their labour power, they also push through improvements in wages and conditions. On this particular point, the late Marx disagreed with David Ricardo. The latter had promulgated a pessimistic theory of wages, according to which worker salaries always have a tendency to be confined

[88] Marx (1867) Ch. 3, IIA.

to the minimum. Ricardo called this idea the 'iron law of wages'.[89] At the same time of rising wages, a raise in interest rates will now serve to slow down the expansion. Debts build up as a result of borrowing for expansion. Stocks are increasingly full as a result of the expanded production.

In this situation, Department I, the supplier of the expanded production, must hit falling rates of profit. Ultimately, it decides to cut back, reduce wages and to lay off workers. Inevitably, the cooling off in Department I leads to maladjustments with Department II. The reduction in wages in the former sector means that sales in Department II fall off and stocks increase. Department II also reduces wages and lays off workers. Department II's demand for products from Department I decreases. As production and incomes decline in both departments, confidence falters and creditors call in their loans. But entrepreneurs with declining order books (Department I) and overstocked shelves (Department II) cannot pay. Loans default, bankruptcies escalate and unemployment leaps. Entrepreneurs not yet bankrupt are anxious to unload their goods at whatever cost, meaning that the price of all commodities along with wages falls. Money is scarce, but people cannot afford to borrow, and interest rates fall. The economy has reached a full state of *cyclical crisis.*

Eventually, the phase of crisis passes over to a period in which activity continues at a very low level. The capitalists have no weapon more powerful for use against the workers than unemployment. As desperate people queue at the factory gates begging for work at lowest levels of wages, and overstocked shelves begin to require restocking, the foundations for recovery are being laid, and opportunities for profit-making are ample. Means of production need repair or replacement, bad debts have been written off, and the cycle starts from scratch. In Marx own words:

> The enormous power, inherent in the factory system, of expanding by jumps, and the dependence of that system on the markets of the world, necessarily beget feverish production, followed by over-filling of the markets, whereupon contraction of the markets brings on crippling of production. The life of modern industry becomes a series of periods of moderate activity, prosperity, over-production, crisis and stagnation. The uncertainty and instability to which machinery subjects the employment, and consequently the conditions of existence, of the operatives become normal, owing to these periodic changes of the industrial cycle. Except in the periods of prosperity, there rages between the capitalists the most furious combat for the share of each in the markets. This share is directly proportional to the cheapness of the product. [...] there also comes a time in every industrial cycle, when a forcible reduction of wages beneath the value of labour-power, is attempted for the purpose of cheapening commodities.[90]

All of this focuses on one question raised already: If the life of modern economies complies with a series of cycles featuring alternating periods of contraction and expansion, why at all would cyclical crisis contribute to erode the foundations of capitalism? For where regular periods of expansion make up for the downward trend

---

[89] D. Ricardo, *The Iron Law of Wages* [1817], in Ricardo D., *The Works of David Ricardo*, London: J. Murray (1881). See also W.J. Baumol, 'Marx and the Iron Law of Wages', in *The American Economic Review*, Vol. 73, No. 2, (1983) 303-308.

[90] Marx (1867) Ch. 25.

during phases of contraction, what could sustain assumptions about the historical decline of capitalism? Thus far, Marx could stand for yet another version of equilibrium-oriented economics. In fact, Joseph Schumpeter has been among the first who questioned the inner coherence of Marx's business cycle and concept of capitalist decline. Schumpeter suspected that 'the ultimate problem remained unsolved' in Marx mind.[91] An authoritative answer as to the compatibility of component elements of crisis and conflict in Marx's political economy depends critically on the overall economic trend of several adjoined business cycles. Clearly, a merging of cyclical elements of crisis with assumptions of the future decline of capitalism cannot be effected with reference to the standard form of the business cycle. The standard form projects a horizontal economic trend line with fluctuating cycles of equal periodicity and amplitude. In some cases, it may even integrate an economic upward trend line, such as present in Fig. 1.1 above. While this is rather easy to see, the situation with Marx is by no means so clear.

An initial screening of Marx's relevant writings identifies sections that seem to rely on the standard or equilibrium type of business cycle, as well as others that elaborate a general downward trend line. Only the latter sections are compatible with assumptions of the historical decline of capitalism. The first option finds support in some less known speeches of Marx. For example:

> [The working class] will sometimes receive something above the minimum, but this surplus will merely make up for the deficit which it will have received below the minimum in times of industrial stagnation. That is to say that, within a given time which recurs periodically, in the cycle which industry passes through while undergoing the vicissitudes of prosperity, overproduction, stagnation, and crisis, when reckoning all that the working class will have had above and below necessaries, we shall see that, in all, it will receive neither more nor less than the minimum.[92]

Certainly, this paragraph leaves it open whether Marx really centered the individual worker and his wage. Marx only refers to workers as a class. In fact, there is a possibility that the indicated equilibrium is gained by an influx of new workers, formerly belonging to the capitalist class, who compensate the constant loss of others, i.e. the victims of non-subsistence wages. In this case, contraction periods did not equal expansion periods, but rather extended beyond them. This option could be linked to 'the corpses upon the industrial battlefield', which Marx also mentions in this context. While thus moving closer to the second option, a general economic downward trend line is indeed entailed in Marx's prominent writings. For example, in the *Communist Manifesto* Marx speaks of 'commercial crises that by their periodical return put on trial, each time more threatening, the existence of the entire bourgeois society.'[93] Eventually, a grasp on unsustainable business cycles is left with three principal options:

---

[91] J.A. Schumpeter, *A History of Economic Analysis*, New York: Oxford University Press (1954) 750.

[92] K. Marx, 'On the Question of Free Trade', Speech to the Democratic Association of Brussels at its Public Meeting of 9 January 1848, in Marx and Engels (1975-2005) Vol. 6, 450-465.

[93] K. Marx and F. Engels, *Manifesto of the Communist Party* [1848], in Marx and Engels (1975-2005) Vol. 6, 477-519.

Fig. 1.2: Cycle-Embedded Downward Trend

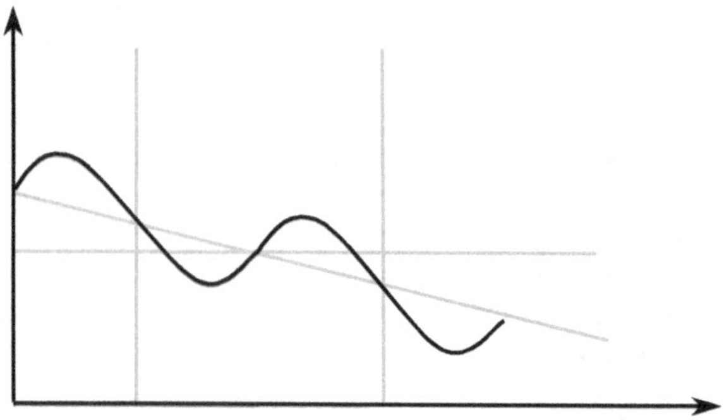

Fig. 1.3: Increased Cyclical Crisis

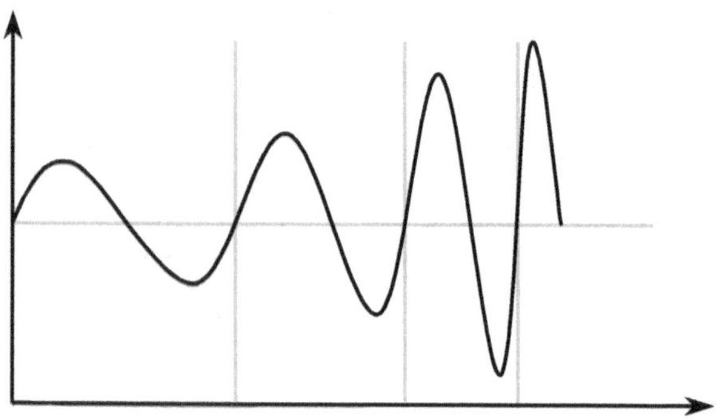

Fig. 1.4: Increased Cyclical Crisis with Cycle-Embedded Downward Trend

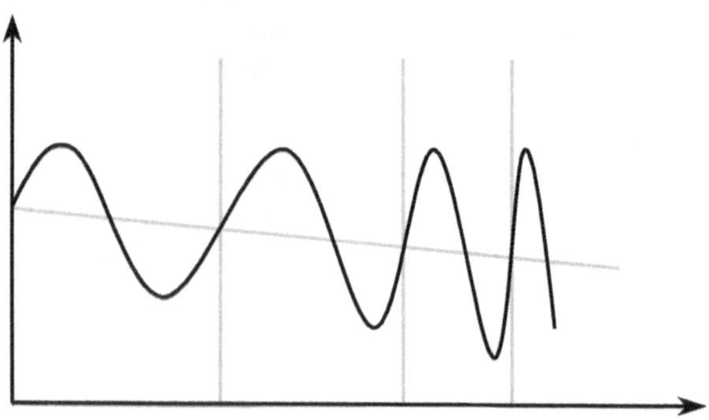

A first option reckons a downward trend in employment and wages, around which cycles of roughly equal periodicity and amplitude fluctuate (Fig. 1.2). A second option features a trend line showing no deviation from the minimum subsistence for workers, around which cycles of increasing amplitude and/or shortened length oscillate (Fig. 1.3). A third option comprises a combination of both. Here, cycles of increasing amplitude and shortened length fluctuate around a declining trend line (Fig. 1.4).[94]

All three options are generally possible. However, without doubt Marx was in favor of the third option. This derives from various remarks in *Capital*, in which Marx assigns to modern industry a course comprising 'decennial cycles and periodic phases, which, moreover, as accumulation advances, are complicated by irregular oscillations following each other more and more quickly.'[95] Only if we assume such a course, long-term trends in Marx's business cycle become compatible with the concept of capitalist decline. But a valid question remains: Why would the downward swing of business cycles weigh more seriously, in that they are not forthwith compensated by subsequent upward swings? In everything that was said before, there is no such element as to justify corresponding assumptions. An authoritative answer to this question needs to look into those principal determinants of Marx's political economy that have no equivalent in Keynes. In a nutshell, those determinants revolve around the role of technological change and other issues.

Conflict II: Decline

The Falling Rate of Profit

While cyclical crisis forms a mechanism that partially recreates the preconditions for profitable capital accumulation, Marx was intent to commit long-term trends in the development of profits to a law, which he called the law of the tendency of the rate of profit to fall. Marx was of the firm opinion that, as capital accumulation proceeded, a falling rate of profit would assert itself as a continuous structural threat, eventually leading to the decline of capitalism. Two conceptual elements were building for this belief: The first element concerns Marx's dealing with technological change. The second element is Marx's labour theory of value, which serves to link technological change patterns with a falling rate of profit. A comprehensive treatment of all elements concerned did not take final form in Marx's writings. Consequently, there has been ongoing debate over the correct interpretation of the indicated law.[96] A careful weighing of all aspects involved is all the more relevant today.

---

94 For a similar systematization see R. Brandis, 'Marx and Keynes? Marx or Keynes', in *Journal of Economic Issues*, Vol. 19, No. 3 (1985) 647-648.

95 Marx (1867) Ch. 25, III.

96 J. Christiansen, 'Marx and the Falling Rate of Profit', in *The American Economic Review*, Vol. 66, No. 2 (1976) 21.

Technological Change

The great importance Marx assigned to the role of technological change within his own theory can be picked from remarks like the following, where a parallel is drawn to Charles Darwin's theory of evolution:

> Darwin has interested us in the history of Nature's Technology, i.e., in the formation of the organs of plants and animals, which organs serve as instruments of production for sustaining life. Does not the history of the productive organs of man, of organs that are the material basis of all social organisation, deserve equal attention? And would not such a history be easier to compile, since, as Vico says, human history differs from natural history in this, that we have made the former, but not the latter? Technology discloses man's mode of dealing with Nature, the process of production by which he sustains his life, and thereby also lays bare the mode of formation of his social relations, and of the mental conceptions that flow from them.[97]

The difference between Marx and Keynes is most striking at the point of contemplations into the impact of technological change on social relations. Some authors have suspected correctly that this is a topic Keynes ignored, or was unable to deal with.[98] In Marx, technology change is doomed to alter social relations in such way as to accelerate the decline of capitalism. In order to understand the role of technology change in Marx's law of the falling rate of profit, let us go back to the very point that gives meaning to capitalism, that is, the economic competition of entrepreneur-capitalists. The ultimate question concerning such competition is how individual capitalists ensure their competitiveness in the market, an issue so much embraced by liberal political economists. They do so, of course, by speeding up the process of individual capital accumulation. Marx occupies common ground when stating that technology change assumes a pivotal role for achieving competitiveness through capital accumulation. Because, only technology change enables the individual capitalist to produce at lower costs than his competitors, due to the introduction of labour-saving machines. What the individual capitalist does is to lay out money capital in an increased manner upon the means of production (equipment, raw material), or constant capital c. At the same time, the portion invested in variable capital v (labour power) sees a decrease.[99] The change in the overall outlay of capital in direction of an, as Marx says, increasingly *organic composition of capital* aims at augmenting the individual capitalist's surplus value s in the equation $c + v + s = V$, where V comprises the value of the final product. However, for this surplus value to materialize, the individual capitalist only takes advantage of the fact that adjustments to new methods of production usually take time. Thus, they allow the capitalist ahead to sell at a price still determined in the market by the prevalence of less

---

97 Marx (1867) Ch. 15, I.

98 P. Burkett, 'Dillard on Keynes and Marx: Comment', in *Journal of Post Keynesian Economics*, Vol. 8, No. 4 (1986) 623.

99 Although Marx was aware that technological innovation could be labour-saving *or* capital-saving, he payed less attention to the latter.

mechanized methods of production.[100] On the macro-level, an immediate side effect of individual capitalists extending the use of advanced machinery must be that the production in Department I, which furnishes Department II with the means of production, is increased beyond levels implied in the principles of enlarged reproduction ($V_1 > c_1 + c_2$).

The fact that Marx considered the technical basis of capitalist economies as *revolutionary* owes to the path of competition-induced innovation they follow. Whereas preceding modes of production have been conservative, capitalism is granted that it never treats the existing methods of production as final.[101] In the same context, Marx applies Mirabeau's famous bonmot 'impossible! ne me dites jamais ce bête de mot' to modern industry. Occasionally, one can even find a positive glimpse in Marx's pondering of technological change. So, for example, where he grants modern industry for compelling society, under penalty of death, to replace the detail-worker of today, grappled by life-long repetition of one and the same trivial operation, and thus reduced to the mere fragment of a man, by the fully developed individual, fit for a variety of labours, and ready to face any change of production, also giving free scope to his own natural and acquired powers.[102]

For Marx, the negative side of advanced technology and machinery under capitalism comprises a number of short- and medium-term effects. These effects come into play yet before technology change contributes to a falling rate of profit in the long-run. For example, Marx criticizes John Stuart Mill's *Principles of Political Economy* for invoking that mechanical invention could lighten the day's toil of the average labourer. Like every other increase in the productiveness of labour, the purpose of machinery under capitalism is signified to cheapen commodities. By no means, it is meant to lengthen that portion of the working day, which the labourer works for himself, eventually expressed in a higher wage. According to the same idea, technology change is only to lengthen that portion the labourer gives, without an equivalent, to the capitalist. For Marx, technology change is synonymous with increased exploitation. A medium-term effect of technology change in Marx comprises the hastening on of the decline of small entrepreneurs, unable to compete with larger firms on the grounds of technological innovation and advanced production methods. Therefore promoting what Marx called the *concentration of capital* under capitalism, such decline was seen to lead to a continuous flow of new recruits and steady increase of the working class.

Beyond the problems of increased exploitation and a constant swelling on of the working class, Marx discussed the labour-displacing and wage-reducing effects of technological change. They all feed directly into the concept of capitalist decline. Before concentrating on a law expressing the increasing misery of the working class, our debate continues with Marx's law of the falling rate of profit. From a strictly economic perspective, this law only impacts on the notion of capitalist decline. It detaches this process temporarily from the broader social implications for the working

---

[100] A. Walker, 'Karl Marx, the Declining Rate of Profit and British Political Economy', in *Economica*, Vol. 38, No. 152 (1971) 363.

[101] Marx (1867) Ch. 15, IX.

[102] Ibid. Ch. 15, VIII.

class. Previous to that, our analysis of the central role of technological change in Marx concludes with a brief comment on a controversial debate in the academic literature.

Although the introduction of new technologies, mainly in the form of labour-saving machines, is deemed inevitable for capitalists who wish to stay competitive, Marx's idea of technology change, strictly speaking, does not comply with a system of *technological determinism*. The latter point has been argued quite frequently.[103] For a system of technological determinism, the driving forces of economic and social change are limited to technological characteristics. In contrast, Marx saw clearly that a proper account of early capitalist societies had little to do with technological change patterns. Rather, a tendency to fully develop the division of labour described those societies. According to Adam Smith's account of early entrepreneurial activities, such division mainly counted on efficiency gains from improvement of the dexterity of labourers whose business was being reduced to one simple operation in a chain of many. In a word, for Marx the origins of capitalism lay not in a change in technology, but in a change in social relations, i.e. in the emergence of a class of property-less wage labourers.[104]

A major role of technology should be confined, therefore, to Marx's view of mature capitalist societies. Only here, automation comes into full swing, in that it supposedly transforms the machine from a means of transmitting human action to the object of labour into the actual doer of the work.[105] However, for this to happen some kind of human decision had to be in place for which technology cannot account by itself. According to Marx, sciences, the original source of technological innovation, had to be pressed into the service of capital. The clue is that those decisions are necessarily human and essentially non-technological in character. Any form of technological determinism experiences its most serious limitations at this point. It has been stated correctly that Marx portrays technology as an enabling factor, rather than as an original cause, autonomous force or determining agent.[106] Machines don't make history. Certainly, in many situations a drive for competitiveness and capital accumulation forces capitalists to subscribe to technological change and labour displacing automation.[107]

---

103 G.A. Cohen, *Marx's Theory of History: A Defense*, Princeton: Princeton University Press (1978). See also J.R. Llobera, 'Techno-Economic Determinism and the Work of Marx on Pre-Capitalist Societies', in *Man*, New Series, Vol. 14, No. 2 (1979) 249-270; W.H. Shaw, 'The Handmill Gives You the Feudal Lord: Marx's Technological Determinism', in *History and Theory*, Vol. 18, No. 2 (1979) 155-176.

104 D. MacKenzie, 'Marx and the Machine', in *Technology and Culture*, Vol. 25, No. 3 (1984) 482.

105 K. Marx, *Outlines of the Critique of Political Economy* [1858], in Marx and Engels (1975-2005) Vol. 29, 5-256.

106 B. Bimber, 'Karl Marx and the Three Faces of Technological Determinism', in *Social Studies of Science*, Vol. 20, No. 2 (1990) 345.

107 For Marx's account of technological change see also P.S. Adler, 'Marx, Machines, and Skill', in *Technology and Culture*, Vol. 31, No. 4 (1990) 780-812.

Labour Theory of Value

If technological change is implemented into existing methods of production for no other reason than to increase competitiveness and to enhance profits, what could possibly justify the link with a falling rate of profit? In order to make this link plausible, one needs to grasp of the special theory of value Marx applied. Again, this can be done in critical distinction from Keynes and the classical liberals. Let us therefore focus on the situation of an increased organic composition of capital in the course of technological innovation: By introducing labour-saving machines, entrepreneurs have increased the constant component of capital. At the same time, the variable component, or portion laid out upon labour power, has decreased. For Marx, this situation created an economic problem rather than an improvement for capitalism. It does so, in light of far-reaching assumptions concerning the value generating power of different types of capital in the process of production, i.e. of constant capital or machinery on the one hand and variable capital or labour on the other.

The assignment of value to different factors of production and segments of the economy within a theory of value was no privilege of Marx. The assignment of such value expresses a rather general desire to discover essential properties and relations beneath the surface phenomena of the market. An integral moment of such pondering has always been the exclusion of certain factors and segments from those functional agents that generate value. A non-functional agent highlighted by the classical liberals was the job of rentiers, or income from rent. Beyond rent, Keynesian economics also considered income on interest as non-functional, thus carrying no value in a strict sense of the word. Only with Keynes one operates in a framework of value generation, which is roughly compatible with the aforementioned factors of production, i.e. labour power and machinery. Although Keynes sympathized with the doctrine that 'everything is produced by labour', he also recognized the value generating nature of constant capital, at least to some extent. Hence, apart from defining machinery as 'the result of past labour, embodied in assets',[108] he granted machinery to yield a return in excess of costs on account of a high rate of interest on money, which normally served to keep it artificially scarce.[109] Beyond that, Keynes also included the services of capitalists into the group of value generating activities.

Different from Keynes, Marx's political economy gives expression to a pure labour theory of value. Beyond excluding all three mentioned non-wage shares—rent, interest and profits—from value generating activities, Marx also saw constant capital as a non-functional agent. Thus, it could only transfer part of its own value to the product which it was used to produce. At the same time, labour was held to possess the unique power of increasing the value of commodities. Of course, once a labour theory of value has been accepted, it is only a small step to link assumptions of an increasingly organic composition of capital induced by technological change, to Marx's law of a falling rate of profit. Simply, because in Marx's equation $c + v + s = V$, the capitalist's surplus s, the basis of his profit, is now dependant on a proportionally increased portion of constant capital c invested in machinery. Together with its

---

[108] Keynes (1936) Ch. 16.
[109] Dillard (1984) 430.

material growth, this portion will not realize a similar growth in value, as variable capital allegedly does. Needless to say that Marx's thus derived *gradual fall of the general rate of profit* hinges on constant degrees of labour exploitation. It depends on an invariable portion of the working day which the labourer gives, without an equivalent, to the entrepreneur. It also hinges on the prerequisite that a gradual change in the composition of capital is not confined to individual spheres of production. Therefore, it must occur more or less in all, or at least in key spheres of production, so as to involve a change in the average organic composition of the total capital of a given society.[110]

On a more general level, Marx's labour theory of value poses two important questions: One question is, of course, whether Marx's labour theory of value is at all plausible. Can this theory be kept today in view of ever-increasing degrees of automation in the presence of fairly sustainable economies, which according to Marxian nomenclature are all capitalist in nature? In fact, why should machines only transfer part of their own value to the product and not generate a surplus value in excess of maintenance and running costs. Most probably, a pure labour theory of value cannot be kept today. Marx's doctrine that constant capital creates no surplus value is partially influenced by his goal to arrive at a falling rate of profit by whatever means.

A question more important for a comprehensive political economy of conflict is the following one: Given that both Keynes and Marx, more or less, applied a labour theory of value, how can it be that they arrived at so ultimately different assumptions concerning the future of capitalism? One side took an essentially reformist approach, while the other promulgated capitalism's near decline. An authoritative answer to this question needs to look at the precise nature of both thinkers' labour theory of value. In the same course, one will find that both thinkers' historical projections strongly relate to a particular definition of 'value generation' within a labour theory of value. In short, Marx defined value as a property of the commodities produced. Keynes theorized value more broadly in relation to income yielded for participation in production.

Marx's definition of value as a property of the commodities produced resembles Adam Smith. It assigns value to commodities *prior* to their exchange for money in the sphere of circulation. More narrowly, a commodity would carry two value-related powers: Firstly, the power to satisfy particular human needs, thus carrying use value; secondly, to be exchangeable for other products, with this power being thought of quantitatively as an amount of exchangeability or command over other commodities.[111] Under all circumstances, this amount would be equivalent to the labour time invested in the production of a commodity. For what is being consumed in labour time is nothing else but labour power, and labour power was seen as the actual generator of value.[112] Since capitalism is characterized by the buying of labour,

---

[110] K. Marx, *Capital Volume Three: The Process of Capitalist Production as a Whole* [1893], in Marx and Engels (1975-2005) Vol. 37, Ch. 13.

[111] D.K. Foley, 'On Marx Theory of Money', in *Social Concept*, Vol. 1., No. 1 (1983) 5-6.

[112] For Marx's labour theory of value see also H. Hollan, 'Class Antagonism, Exploitation, and the Labour Theory of Value', in *The Economic Journal*, Vol. 92, No. 368 (1982) 868-885, P.A. Samuelson, 'The Normative and Positivistic Inferiority of Marx's Values Paradigm', in *Southern Economic Journal*, Vol. 49, No. 1 (1982) 11-18; R.P. Wolff, 'A Critique and Reinterpretation of Marx's Labor The-

from his own particular perspective Marx could claim that capitalism involves the penetration of value relations into production. The persistent contradiction Marx saw entrenched in this act of penetration would find embodiment in a falling rate of profit. It would do so, in as much as it combined with the labour displacing momentum in technology change.[113]

As opposed to this view, Keynes' definition of value generation is not bound to the very act of labour consuming production itself, but to the income generated from production. Such view of value being a payment in exchange for participation in production must result in two consequences: Firstly, not only the labourers' work needed to be considered as value generating, but also entrepreneurs were generating value. They did so, in as much as they gained an income from 'appropriating' the surplus of their labourers' work, i.e. the portion not required for their workers' daily reproduction. The second consequence leads back to the initial question, how two proponents of a labour theory of value could include a reformer and a revolutionary in the face of technology change. Keynes' income based concept of value left him with no choice other than to take the existence and reproduction of labourers and entrepreneurs as exogenously given. There was no room for the possibly contradictory character of this dichotomy.[114] For the same reason, there was no need for a social revolution to alter the existing relations of production. The job of political economy was to inspire gradual reforms where necessary. The other angle on which this reformist approach rests is Keynes' limited attention to technological change patterns. Keynes was hardly concerned with Marx's pondering of an increased organic composition of capital.

In summary, one could add that Marx's law of the falling rate of profit has been synthesized, time and time again, with Keynes' schedule of the marginal efficiency of capital. In a very different sense, this schedule also signals reduced profit expectations of entrepreneurs. However, Keynes' schedule of the marginal efficiency of capital is an integral part of the business cycle, and thus a periodical phenomenon. It recognizes that the efficiency of a given capital can be temporarily diminished, owing to changes in the supply and supply price of that capital. In contrast, Marx's falling rate of profit represents an irreversible trend line within the development of capitalism. The different conceptual location of both concepts, in relation to elements of cyclical crisis in one case and issues of economic decline in the other, must separate both concepts from each other.[115] However, if one accepts Marx's law of the falling rate of profit, what stands at the end of this development?

---

ory of Value', in *Philosophy and Public Affairs*, Vol. 10, No. 2 (1981) 89-120; E. Wolfstetter, 'Surplus Labour, Synchronised Labour Costs and Marx's Labour Theory of Value', in *The Economic Journal*, Vol. 83, No. 331 (1973) 787-809.

[113] For Marx's law of the falling rate of profit see also R.P. Appelbaum, 'Marx's Theory of the Falling Rate of Profit: Towards a Dialectical Analysis of Structural Social Change', in *American Sociological Review*, Vol. 43, No. 1 (1978) 67-80; H.D. Dickinson, 'The Falling Rate of Profit in Marxian Economics', in *The Review of Economic Studies*, Vol. 24, No. 2 (1957) 120-130; M.A. Lebowitz, 'Marx's Falling Rate of Profit: A Dialectical View', in *The Canadian Journal of Economics*, Vol. 9, No. 2 (1976) 232-254.

[114] Burkett (1986) 626.

[115] This point has sometimes been overlooked in literature. See e.g. Alexander (1940) 125.

Vertical Inequalities

The above question turns away from macro-economic indicators, such as the falling rate of profit, and toward the participants in production. As before, Marx's political economy is bound to the law-like character of all developments within and beyond capitalism. It indicates a quasi-law aimed at capturing the increasing misery of the 'proletariat', thus forming the flipside of the falling rate of profit. More particularly, this quasi-law has two faces: A humanistic one, much inspired by the romanticist and idealist tradition, and a physical one, eventually in line with Marx's materialist conception of history. With the first, Marx's account of alienation comes into play. The second refers to the wage-reducing and labour-displacing effects of technology change. It alludes to a situation of increased vertical inequalities.

By proclaiming that the misery of proletariat is expressed in a situation of *alienation*, Marx sought to center defining moments in the worker's relationship to his work. In rather emotional terms, this situation is characterized as the state of workers who do not confirm themselves in their work, but deny themselves, feel miserable and not happy, do not develop free mental and physical energy. Ultimately, the worker 'feels himself only when he is not working; when he is working, he does not feel himself.' His labour does not comprise the satisfaction of a need, but 'a means to satisfy needs outside itself.' At last, 'external labour, labour in which man alienates himself, is a labour of self-sacrifice.'[116] Analytically speaking, there are three aspects of alienation in Marx: Firstly, under the fully developed division of labour, the individual worker is pictured as bound to life-long repetition of one and the same trivial operation, also meaning that he has no relationship to the product as a whole. Secondly, under capitalism the worker does not own the means of production. Allegedly, the product of his work confronts him in the form of capital. Finally, that same product is restricted to become a commodity, the only purpose of which is to be readily sold on the market and to yield the capitalist a profit. Clearly, for Marx aspects of alienation are not restricted to the late stage of capitalism where conflict prevails. Strictly speaking, they are not even restricted to the working class. In Marx, the capitalist class also presents moments of self-estrangement, which it is however granted to be at ease with, because it recognizes them as its own power.[117] Only the working class feels annihilated in estrangement. The privilege of declining capitalism is that only here the labourer's alienation from his work reaches its final guise. According to Marx, the ultimate point of such alienation is reached when, as a result of technological change, all alienation of the intellectual and other aspects of work achieves technical embodiment in the machine, when 'along with the tool, the skill of the worker in handling it passes over to the machine.'[118]

---

[116] K. Marx, *Economic and Philosophical Manuscripts* [1844], in Marx and Engels (1975-2005) Vol. 3, First Manuscript.

[117] K. Marx and F. Engels, *The Holy Family or Critique of Critical Criticism* [1845], in Marx and Engels (1975-2005) Vol. 4, Ch. 4.

[118] Marx (1867) Ch. 15, IV. For Marx's account of alienation see also G.A. Conly, 'Alienation, Sociality, and the Division of Labor: Contradictions in Marx's Ideal of Social Man', in *Ethics*, Vol. 89, No. 1 (1978) 82-94; J. Christman, 'Self-Ownership, Equality, and the Structure of Property Rights' in *Political Theory*, Vol. 19, No. 1 (1991) 28-46; O.J. Hammen, 'A Note on the Alienation Motif in Marx',

Beyond rather humanistic pondering, Marx's law of the increasing misery of the proletariat is expressed in hard economic facts. The first consequence of a constantly falling rate of profit is that capitalists cannot but lower wages below levels corresponding to fluctuations in the business cycle. In the first place, this even seems to imply an increase in productiveness, because according to Marx the conditions of direct exploitation are only limited by the absolute productive power of the working class. At the same time, this means ignoring the indirect effect of such exploitation on the working class' consumer power. By now accounting for the bulk of society, the working class' consumer power reflects a minimum varying within very narrow margins. Marx arrives here at the cost of integrating elements of an underconsumption theory into his political economy of conflict. However, the overall claim for the late stage of capitalism is clear. The more productiveness develops, the more it is seen to be at variance with the narrow basis on which the conditions of consumption rest.[119]

The second physical consequence of a falling rate of profit concerns a non-cyclical increase in levels of unemployment, or Marx's famous *industrial reserve army*. Therefore, the accelerated relative diminution of the variable constituent of capital that goes along with the accelerated increase of the total capital, and moves more rapidly than this increase, is seen to take the inverse form, at the other pole, of an absolute increase of the labouring population, moving more rapidly than that of the means of employment.[120] Marx was of the firm belief that capital accumulation produces, in the direct ratio of its own energy and extent, a relatively redundant population of labourers. At the same time, it produces potential for conflict sufficient to result in the decline of capitalism.[121] In Marx own words:

> [The] absolute contradiction between the technical necessities of Modern Industry, and the social character inherent in its capitalistic form, dispels all fixity and security in the situation of the labourer; how it constantly threatens, by taking away the instruments of labour, to snatch from his hands his means of subsistence, and, by suppressing his detail-function, to make him superfluous. [...] this antagonism vents its rage in the creation of that monstrosity, an industrial reserve army, kept in misery in order to be always at the disposal of capital; in the incessant human sacrifices from among the working-class, in the most reckless squandering of labour-power and in the devastation caused by a social anarchy which turns every economic progress into a social calamity.[122]

---

in *Political Theory*, Vol. 8, No. 2 (1980) 223-242; J. Ring, 'On Needing Both Marx and Arendt: Alienation and the Flight from Inwardness', in *Political Theory*, Vol. 17, No. 3 (1989) 432-448; I. Shapiro, 'Resources, Capacities, and Ownership: The Workmanship Ideal and Distributive Justice', in *Political Theory*, Vol. 19, No. 1 (1991) 47-72; E.G. West, 'The Political Economy of Alienation: Karl Marx and Adam Smith', in *Oxford Economic Papers*, Vol. 21, No. 1 (1969) 1-23.

119 Marx (1893) Ch. 15, I.

120 Marx (1867) Ch. 25, III.

121 See F.M. Gottheil, 'Increasing Misery of the Proletariat: An Analysis of Marx's Wage and Employment Theory', in *The Canadian Journal of Economics and Political Science*, Vol. 28, No. 1 (1962) 107. What Marx needed to show was 'that the demand for labour forthcoming from mechanization *via* capital accumulation is insufficient to compensate for the labour displaced by the mechanization [...] The failure to demonstrate that *absolute* surplus population expands with mechanization [also] invalidates the argument that real wages under capitalism must coincide with subsistence.'

122 Marx (1867) Ch. 15, IX.

Both economic hard facts, i.e. an increase in the number of non-subsistence wages as well as levels of unemployment, require relating to Marx's concept of inequality. Exclusively, this concept grasps of inequalities in terms of classes and social layers. In the context of social life, these classes and layers are part of a vertical structure. Overall, Marx's political economy complies with a concept of vertical inequalities. The following chapter contrasts this vertical concept of inequalities with a concept of horizontal inequalities.

Revolution

The consequences Marx foresaw for the time when social anarchy reached a sufficient size are well known: By more and more completely transforming the great majority of the population into proletarians, capitalism was seen to create the power which, under penalty of its own destruction, is forced to accomplish a *social revolution*. By virtue of the increased concentration of capital, which forces on more and more the transformation of the vast means of production already socialized into state property, capitalism showed itself the way to accomplish this revolution. The proletariat would seize political power and turn the means of production in the first instance into state property. But in doing this, it abolished itself as proletariat, abolished all class distinctions and class antagonisms, and abolished also the state as state.[123] Only then social evolutions would cease to be political revolutions,[124] and so and so forth.

The special flavor in Marx's political economy of conflict is that in bringing about this social revolution both classes are assigned a role they cannot escape. Strictly speaking, this argument is in excess of the precepts of historical materialism. Historical materialism as such only establishes the economic foundations and inevitable nature of all social developments. Although accounting for the conservative or affirmative elements of capitalism, the capitalist class exercises a revolutionary role by virtue of the fact that it 'cannot exist without constantly revolutionizing the instruments of production and thereby the relations of production, and with them the whole relations of society.' Marx's dictum that 'the bourgeoisie, historically, has played a most revolutionary part'[125] must be understood in that sense. With reference to the same idea of capitalism's creative destruction, Joseph Schumpeter has noted occasionally that 'capitalism is being killed by its achievements.'[126]

---

[123] F. Engels, *Anti-Düring: Herr Eugen Dühring's Revolution in Science* [1878], in Marx and Engels (1975-2005) Vol. 25, Part III, Ch. 2.

[124] K. Marx, *The Poverty of Philosophy* [1847], in Marx and Engels (1975-2005) Vol. 6, Ch. 2, Sec. 5.

[125] Marx and Engels (1848) Ch. 1.

[126] J.A. Schumpeter, *Capitalism, Socialism and Democracy*, New York: Harper (1950) xiv. See also J.E. Elliott, 'Marx and Schumpeter on Capitalism's Creative Destruction: A Comparative Restatement', in *The Quarterly Journal of Economics*, Vol. 95, No. 1 (1980) 45-68; J.E. Elliott, 'Schumpeter and Marx on Capitalist Transformation', in *The Quarterly Journal of Economics*, Vol. 98, No. 2 (1983) 333-336; J.B. Foster, 'Theories of Capitalist Transformation: Critical Notes on the Comparison of Marx and Schumpeter', in *The Quarterly Journal of Economics*, Vol. 98, No. 2 (1983) 327-331; O.H. Taylor, 'Schumpeter and Marx: Imperialism and Social Classes in the Schumpeterian System', in *The Quarterly Journal of Economics*, Vol. 65, No. 4 (1951) 525-555.

At the same time of stressing the revolutionary role of the capitalist class in Marx's political economy, the revolutionary role of the working class remains intact. The revolutionary potential of the proletariat revolves around the concepts of *class-consciousness* and *emancipation*. With the first concept, Marx sought to augment the physical preconditions for a social revolution by the necessary theoretical means inside the working class. As class-consciousness grew, it would serve to challenge the ruling intellectual force. Tied to the capitalist class, or ruling material force of society, Marx called this intellectual force ideology.[127] In a related note about the German labour movement, Friedrich Engels once emphasized that the theoretical and the economic sides of conflict form one harmonious and well-planned entity catering for a concentric attack.[128] Therefore, both consciousness of its loss in the proletariat, as well as no longer disguisable, imperative economic need, leads the working class to revolt by emancipating itself. It emancipates itself by abolishing the conditions of its own life. It abolishes the conditions of its own life by abolishing all the inhuman conditions of life of society.[129]

On the other hand, the limitations of any revolutionary role of Marx's proletariat are set. Simply, because this role would never be in excess of the precise state of prevailing economic conditions as effected by both classes. The proletariat's revolutionary consciousness and mental preparedness lacks any anticipatory moment. This follows strictly from Marx's critique of critical criticism:

> Critical Criticism, on the contrary, teaches them that they cease in reality to be wage-workers if in thinking they abolish the thought of wage-labour; if in thinking they cease to regard themselves as wage-workers and, in accordance with that extravagant notion, no longer let themselves be paid for their person [...] Critical Criticism teaches them that they abolish real capital by overcoming in *thinking* the category Capital, that they *really* change and transform themselves into real human beings by changing their '*abstract ego*' in consciousness and scorning as an un-critical operation all real change of their real existence, of the real conditions of their existence, that is to say, of their *real ego*.[130]

Marx's pondering of the real conditions of life leads over to key principles of the governing influences between economics and politics in his political economy. For the duration of this chapter, this has been our second analytical question.

---

[127] K. Marx and F. Engels, *The German Ideology: Critique of Modern Philosophy according to its Representatives Feuerbach, B. Bauer and Stirner, and of German Socialism according to its Various Prophets* [1846], in Marx and Engels (1975-2005) Vol. 5, Part IB.

[128] F. Engels, *The Peasant War in Germany* [1850], in Marx and Engels (1975-2005) Vol. 10, Preface.

[129] Marx and Engels (1845) Ch. 4. For Marx's and Engel's account of social revolution see also A. Gilbert, 'Social Theory and Revolutionary Activity in Marx', in *The American Political Science Review*, Vol. 73, No. 2 (1979) 521-538; O.J. Hammen, 'Alienation, Communism, and Revolution in the Marx-Engels Briefwechsel', in *Journal of the History of Ideas*, Vol. 33, No. 1 (1972) 77-100.

[130] Marx and Engels (1845) Ch. 4.

Interventions

Superstructure

The goal with this second analytical question has been to determine the possibility of corrective political action under circumstances where conflict is built into economic operations. Naturally, if economics drove politics, rather than the other way round, the relationship between economics and conflict became utterly strong. Obviously, according to the doctrines of historical materialism, there is no such thing that could ensure politics an intervening angle in the economic *infrastructure*. In Marx's famous words, 'the mode of production of material life conditions the general process of social, political and intellectual life. It is not the consciousness of men that determines their existence, but their social existence that determines their consciousness.'[131] For example, in the above scenario, elaborating on the revolutionary role of the working class, the theoretical and the economic sides of conflict were said to form one harmonious and well-planned entity for a concentric attack. Purposely, there was no mentioning of the political side in conflict, which Marx called the dictatorship of the proletariat. There was no mentioning of the political side, because in Marx this side is seen to be fully dependent on the economic and theoretical basis of conflict, i.e. on conflict between the productive forces and existing relations of production on the one hand, and ideology critique on the other.[132]

For the same reason why the working class has to wait for the material preconditions for a social revolution, efforts of the capitalist class to mobilize the political superstructure are doomed to fail once the economic basis has been lost. This is also seen to apply to any other ideological means that could be employed for the prevention of conflict, be they legal, religious, artistic or philosophic. According to Marx, it will not help the capitalist class that the political infrastructure and state power have been the organ to enforce its supremacy.[133]

Imperialist Organizations

Marx has inspired authors in the field of processes of international organization, who turn aside major premises at the core of the liberal-realist dichotomy, i.e. supranational versus intergovernmental organizations. Deviating from liberal and realist approaches, Marxist writers refer to such processes in a rather pessimistic vein. Although processes of supranational and intergovernmental organization are conceptually separated from each other, a common tendency to perpetuate 'patterns of subordination' elicits the same criticism. Both in the case of supranational organizations and intergovernmental organizations, distribution fights are seen as an intrinsic con-

---

[131] K. Marx, *A Contribution to the Critique of Political Economy* [1859], in Marx and Engels (1975-2005) Vol. 29, Preface.

[132] For Marx's account of the role of the state, see also J. Sanderson, 'Marx and Engels on the State', in *The Western Political Quarterly*, Vol. 16, No. 4 (1963) 946-955.

[133] F. Engels, *Ludwig Feuerbach and the End of Classical German Philosophy* [1886], in Marx and Engels (1975-2005) Vol. 26, Ch. 4.

stituent. On the other hand, Marxist pondering of international organizations does not form a monolithic bloc. Such pondering ranges from earliest attempts, such as Lenin's rejection of all forms of international organization, to various recent angles affiliated with Dependencia Analysis.

Imperialism Debate: In his *Imperialism* entitled book of 1917, Lenin was the first who extended implications of historical materialism to the international sphere. Thus, he designated international political economy, or 'imperialism', as the highest stage of capitalism and the eve of the social revolution of the proletariat. Narrowly speaking, the book tried to prove that World War One had been an imperialist war between prevailing national classes. Lenin was intent to provide a compilation of facts that could not be disproved.[134] In broader terms, Lenin sought to falsify Karl Kautsky's idea of ultra-imperialism, or concept of a league of nations as persistent form of international organization that rescues capitalism globally. Thus, in his book *National State, Imperialist State and League of Nations* of 1911 Kautsky had argued that the best and most promising means to extend the domestic market is the integration of various nation states into a league of nations with equal rights.[135] In political theory, the dissent between Lenin and Kautsky become known as Imperialism-Debate. Soviet-Communism until the high period of the Cold War in the 1960s widely followed Lenin's anticipation as of 1917.

Dependencia Analysis: Only the 1970s witnessed crucial modifications in the traditional upsurge of Marxist theories. While generally confirming the idea of conflict-driven international relations, Dependencia analysis has stretched the term imperialism beyond its inherited meaning. Since then, imperialism has been identified in relationships across state frontiers, in which there is no formal political subordination of one state by another. Although interconnectedness is still considered in terms of economic relationships, assessments of the political sphere have been detached from the superstructure rationale.[136]

One of the most established advocators of an advanced version of Dependencia analysis, Immanuel Wallerstein has presented his World System school of thought. Being one interdependent system, the world economy is perceived through a tri-modal system, which arranges countries around a three-tiered hierarchy. Precisely speaking, this hierarchy is derived from a core-periphery analysis of the international system, which includes capitalist, semiperipheral, and peripheral countries. In picturing the idea that the wealth of some capitalist countries is necessarily gained at the expense of other countries, Third World countries are referred to as peripheral capitalist, rather than as underdeveloped or developing countries.[137] With his tri-modal system, Wallerstein elaborates on a group of structuralist theories that formed a sub-school of Dependencia analysis in the 1970s. Thus, in his 'Structural Theory of Imperialism' Johan Galtung made notion of go-between nations, which Waller-

---

[134] V.I. Lenin, *Imperialism: The Latest Stage in the Development of Capitalism* [1917], Detroit: Marxian Educational Society (1924) 3-8.

[135] K. Kautsky, *Nationalstaat, Imperialistischer Staat und Staatenbund* [1911], Nürnberg: Fränkische Verlagsanstalt (1915) 75.

[136] Jones (1995) 29.

[137] I. Wallerstein, 'Dependence in an Interdependent World', in Goddard et al. (1996) 177.

stein now refers to as semiperipheral countries.[138] The new label wants to stress that the international capitalist system, more than coincidentally bringing about some go-between countries, could not function without being tri-modal.[139] Both political and economic reasons are argued for this necessary tri-modality of the international capitalist system. From a political perspective, the existence of a group of semiperipheral countries is necessary to lower the disintegrating struggle between dominant and subordinated countries.[140] From an economic perspective, the ability to shift capital from a declining leading sector to a rising sector is seen as the only way to survive the effects of cyclical shifts in the loci of the leading sectors. However, in order to avoid a severe economic crisis in capitalist countries, there must be sectors able to profit from the wage-productivity squeeze of the leading sector. Semiperipheral countries provide these sectors. Chapter III will take up this idea of a system sustaining middle sector. It probes this idea for the domestic context, i.e. for multi-modal societies and inter-group conflict.

On the whole, Dependencia analysis since the 1970s has broken with the traditional determinist assessment of politico-economic development processes. The Leninist anticipation of imperialism as the highest but latest stage of capitalism has been given up. Politico-economic exchange characteristics among industrialized and other countries have been centered. However, processes of international organization are referred to in a rather pessimistic vein. Both in the case of supranational and intergovernmental organizations, distribution fights are still reviewed as an intrinsic constituent.

Section 4. An Integrated Perspective

A Non-Ideological Political Economy of Conflict

A non-ideological, integrated perspective is needed when embarking on a political economy of conflict prevention today. In a neutral way, such a perspective borrows from political economy's major schools aspects that are still relevant today, and feeds them into an integrated model. In order to arrive at an integrated model, it may also need to go beyond these schools. At first sight, the horizontal inequality approach (h.i.-approach) promises to be such a model. An integrated perspective needs to clarify the systematic place of each school in a comprehensive political economy of conflict and conflict prevention. This chapter has reviewed classical political economy for moments and degrees of internalization of conflict into economic operations. That is why Marx's political economy represented a final step. At the end of the day, Marx's political economy owns the strongest reference to economic conflict, and a clear direction of influence between the economic and political spheres, where economic rules determine politics. Fig. 1.5 visualizes the above findings. The

[138] J. Galtung, 'Structural Theory of Imperialism', in in *Journal of Peace Research*, Vol. 8, No. 2 (1971) 81-117.

[139] Wallerstein (1996) 178.

[140] Ibid.

specific objective of this investigation made that Marx was discussed from the perspective of Keynes, rather than the other way round. Needless to say that such proceeding is at odds with the history of political economy, which above all requires chronological order. Had things been for such a history, in more than one aspect Marx could have been investigated with close reference to the liberal school in political economy. That is also where Marx stands historically. Not only once Marx has been considered a 'prisoner of the ideas of his classical authorities'.[141] Defining features, such as the limited role of government, or a consideration of financial questions at a level subordinate to that of the 'real relations of production', move Marx and the classical liberals close to each other. They also separate both schools from Keynes.[142]

Fig. 1.5: Conflict and Non-Conflict Economies

School:	Liberal Economics	Keynesian Economics	Marxian Economics
Relationship between Economic Individuals:	Competition	Underemployment Equilibrium	Exploitation
Relationship between Economics and Politics:	Detachment Politics ↔ Economics	Means and Ends, Politics → Economics	Infrastructure and Superstructure, Economics → Politics
	Non-Conflict Economies	→	Conflict Economies

There can be no misunderstanding that the sequence of discussions in this chapter does not assign preference to any of the three schools of thought. In that sense, our investigation had to be as neutral as possible. An essential part of such neutrality was that a critical perspective has been spared for later parts of this book. As it is, the above investigation provides a scaffold for the evolving economic paradigm and h.i.-approach in present conflict debates. Finally, any effort to assign Adam Smith,

141 Walker (1971) 373.

142 For the relationship between Marx and the classical liberals see also S. Bell, 'Ricardo and Marx', in *The Journal of Political Economy*, Vol. 15, No. 2 (1907) 112-117; V.W. Bladen, 'The Centenary of Marx and Mill', in *The Journal of Economic History*, Vol. 8, Supplement: The Tasks of Economic History (1948) 32-41; G. Dworkin, 'Marx and Mill: A Dialogue', in *Philosophy and Phenomenological Research*, Vol. 26, No. 3 (1966) 403-414; P. Garegnani, 'Value and Distribution in the Classical Economists and Marx', in *Oxford Economic Papers*, New Series, Vol. 36, No. 2 (1984) 291-325; B. Shoul, 'Karl Marx and Say's Law', in *The Quarterly Journal of Economics*, Vol. 71, No. 4 (1957) 611-629; G.S.L. Tucker, 'Ricardo and Marx', in *Economica*, New Series, Vol. 28, No. 111 (1961) 252-269.

John Maynard Keynes and Karl Marx to a subsequent progress story would experience severe limitations in political biases that have always exerted their influence on the economic substance. For example, in Marx and Keynes a labour theory of value led to ultimately different assumptions about the future course of 'capitalism'. A falling rate of profit, and falling schedule of the marginal efficiency of capital respectively, have been co-determined by important non-economic factors. Those factors are partly rooted in scientific focus, i.e. where Keynes and the liberals ignored the challenges of technological change. To some other extent, those biases are rooted in political predilection. In Keynes, a technocratic perspective of the managerial class led to optimistic assumptions about the long-term course of the economy. Marx's sensibility for the fate of the working class eventually brought closer the idea of economic decline.

The Politico-Moral Economy of Conflict Prevention

In yet another sense, the three schools are subject to a rank order. When moving from Smith to Keynes and from Keynes to Marx, not only do we identify increased degrees of internalization of conflict into economic operations. We also observe an increasingly moral perspective that has been applied to those economic operations. Compared to political biases that have exerted their influence on the economic substance, those moral biases might weigh even stronger for the assignment of conflict to the economy. Normally, economics is not supposed to judge a particular state of the economy by applying a moral perspective. For example, it does not consider whether economic conflict could be justified by virtue of some prevailing factors, e.g. the existence of horizontal inequalities. However, more than in the other two schools, a complementary moral lens has been guiding to Marxian economics. It comes to the fore in Marx's dwelling upon patterns of exploitation and alienation. Comparable to the political economy of conflict, Keynes occupies the middle rank in a politico-moral economy of conflict. Keynes was concerned with moral questions. For example, he called Moore's *Principia Ethica* the most important book he ever read. It propelled him, throughout his life, to place his economic work in a larger quest for justice, ethics and beauty.[143] In contrast, liberal economists felt no need to consider moral features, because economic operations were deemed to be untainted by conflict.

At the same time, it is important to stress that these moral lenses are truly intuitive. They don't live up to the level of ethical theories. They don't theorize an ethical economy of conflict prevention, nor do they endeavor to do so. For example, there is a lot of moral impetus in Marx's political economy. But it is also most intuitive. Given the precepts of his superstructure rationale, Marx even had all the theoretical means at hand to argue that a spelled out ethical theory could only be a reflection of the economic infrastructure, i.e. it could only be ideology. Thus, it made no sense to engage in it. Nonetheless, the more neutral and comprehensive a moral per-

---

[143] R. Skidelsky, *John Maynard Keynes: Fighting for Freedom, 1937-1946*, New York: Viking (2000); A. Carabelli and N. Vecchi, 'Where to Draw the Line? Hayek and Keynes, on Knowledge, Ethics, and Economics' in *European Journal for the History of Economic Thought*, Vol. 6, No. 2 (1999).

spective is, the more it usually complies with an ethical theory. One would think that such a theory is less prone to be exploitable for a particular view of the economy. It will probably separate from the realm of political economy. In fact, this is also what seemingly happened with the political economists, besides Marx. While the classical liberals did not engage in a politico-moral economy of conflict, they developed some of the most remarkable ethical theories that are still valid today. For example, Adam Smith wrote his *Theory of Moral Sentiments*.[144] Only coincidentally, this book seemed to support political liberalism. Here, social organization is reflected as the outcome of human action but not necessarily of human design. An unplanned social order is regarded as far more complex and functional than a planned social order. A prime reason for Smith to assume this view was his belief in a moral sense that tells people what is right and wrong, essentially by means of feelings of sympathy. Just as the 'invisible hand' created beneficial social patterns out of people's economic actions, it too did so by means of these sympathy-guided moral actions. Furthermore, John Stuart Mill designed utilitarianism as an ethical system to center people's natural interests, e.g. interests of wealth maximization. Compared to deontological ethical theories, utilitarian theories establish a liberal view to ethics, where people are given the chance to follow up on their utility functions. In some sense, it forms another ethical counterpart to a liberal approach concerning the economic and political spheres.

From these remarks one may be tempted to conclude that a political economy of conflict is frequently inseparable from moral implications, but also that it is by definition free although complementable by congruent ethical norms. Especially, utilitarianism would seem to offer an ethical theory that clearly separates from classical liberal pondering of economic conflict, and so from any other political economy, such as the h.i.-approach and evolving economic paradigm in conflict debates today. In a word, prima facie political and ethical economies of conflict prevention would seem to comprise different pairs of shoes, complementary but separate. As the book proceeds, it will make clear that this comprises too narrow a view. There is ample reason to distinguish between economics and ethics as disciplines with clear scientific profiles. However, in the practical business of applying economics to such issues as conflict, moral *and* ethical implications encroach upon the economic substance of our thought. It is almost unavoidable that they do so. This is particularly true for utilitarian norms. Intimately, these norms seem to be tied to liberal political economy. But it was possible that an opposite ethical theory centering moral sentiments à la Adam Smith could also be tied to this school. Just as utilitarianism does not own a privilege for a liberal approach to political economy and conflict, it may comprise an ethical implication of all various economic models of conflict, including the h.i.-approach. This being said, we shall see very soon that the ethical implications of any political economy of conflict may not be downsized to a politico-moral economy of conflict and conflict prevention. Acknowledging those ethical implications means applying a truly integrated perspective.

---

[144] A. Smith, *The Theory of Moral Sentiments*, London: A. Millar, A. Kincaid and J. Bell (1759).

CHAPTER II

THE HORIZONTAL INEQUALITY APPROACH

A systematization of the horizontal inequality approach (h.i.-approach) in present conflict debates evolves on the basis of the previous chapter. Traditional assumptions as to the ethnic, racial and religious nature of group conflict have been partially abandoned in the realm of this approach. Instead, various politico-economic features are highlighted. The present chapter targets a number of key premises of the h.i.-approach, so as to prepare the ground for a series of critiques. Originally proposed by Oxford scholar Frances Stewart, the attractiveness of this approach stems from two points, i.e. from the integrated approach it offers and from the feedback that approach has solicited on the part of the international community. One may imagine the size of this feedback by weighing the following fact. During these last years, the concept has been invoked repeatedly at the United Nations.[1] Keynote speeches on the root causes of conflict have been linked to horizontal inequalities.[2/3] As a latest contribution, the UNDP *Human Development Report 2005* devotes special attention to horizontal inequalities.[4] This is quite remarkable for an academic concept, which has thus impacted on long-term conflict prevention strategies.

The integrated approach that characterizes the h.i.-approach made it necessary to reexamine political economy's three major schools. The h.i.-approach integrates aspects of all these schools into one comprehensive political economy of conflict. Different from other conflict models, it may not be related to one school only. Common aspects include economic substance as well as a number of general grounders. Reference to such grounders does not overthrow a basic premise of this first part. According to this premise, the political economy of conflict required exploration in sound economic terms. Only that way, one may avoid economic shallowness, which

---

1 The author has sought to analyze this concept in two previous works, particularly as for its application through the United Nations system. See R. Bredel, *Long-Term Conflict Prevention and Industrial Development: The United Nations and its Specialized Agency, UNIDO*, Leiden and Boston: Martinus Nijhoff Publishers (2003); R. Bredel, 'The UN's Long-Term Conflict Prevention Strategies and the Impact of Counter-Terrorism', in *International Peacekeeping*, Vol. 10, No. 2 (2003) 51-70.

2 See K. Annan, Address to the Seventeenth National Convention of the Arab-American Anti-Discrimination Committee, Arlington, Virginia, USA, 12 June 2000; K. Annan, Address to the Fourth International Conference of New and Restored Democracies, Contonou, Benin, 7 Dec. 2000; K. Annan, Address to the Foreign Policy Association, New York, 21 March 2001; K. Annan, Cyril Foster Lecture at Oxford University, 19 June 2001; K. Annan, Address at University of Oslo, Norway, 20 August 2001.

3 The link between these academic and practical approaches has been the World Institute for Development Economics Research in Helsinki, which is a part of the United Nations University, but has been involved in joint research activities with the Queen Elizabeth House at Oxford University of which Frances Stewart is the Director. See W. Nafziger and F. Stewart and R. Väyrynen (eds.), *War, Hunger and Displacement: The Origins of Humanitarian Emergencies*, 2 Vol., Oxford: Oxford University Press (2000).

4 UNDP, *Human Development Report 2005: International Cooperation at a Crossroads: Aid, Trade and Security in an Unequal World*, New York: Oxford University Press (2005).

often results when political will politicizes major schools in political economy. General grounders carry the economic substance laid out in those schools, as well as in the h.i.-approach. A profound analysis this approach designs a number of propositions.

Section 5. Main Propositions

Five propositions are designed to systematize the h.i.-approach in present conflict debates. For convenience purposes, all five propositions are put ahead. Concretely, they are the following ones:

1. Conflict is a matter of organized groups.
2. Conflict groups are primordial.
3. Symbolic factors beget stereotyping, economic factors beget conflict.
4. Economic deprivation is relative.
5. Conflict perpetuates group leadership and class structures.
6. Conflict remains internal.

Each proposition is weighed and examined against the backdrop of political economy's three major schools. To the extent that they help explaining the h.i.-approach, this analysis includes their general grounders.

Proposition 1: Organized Group Conflict

A rather common assumption today is that conflict is not primarily a matter of individuals randomly committing violence against each other. Conflict normally involves some sort of groups that engage in organized group conflict. Generally, any conflict paradigm that lays stress upon the influential role of groups in conflict is relevant, in as much as it helps removing a bias of neo-classical development economics. The latter has primarily been concerned with the role of individuals. For example, when making economic development policies the case for conflict prevention, there has been a lot of talk about how global welfare may lower potential for conflict. However, the issue of global welfare has simply been treated in relation to the sum total of individuals in a given society. The only task accepted was how welfare gains could be distributed evenly among those individuals. Much less attention has been paid to the influence social groups possess over individuals.

The h.i.-approach seeks to reverse this bias. It, therefore, rejects development thinking in the tradition of neo-classical welfare analysis. It also discards recent efforts to correct the latter by ways of an approach that exceeds a prime focus on income disparities. A major underlying assumption on which neo-classical welfare economics has proceeded is that there is no such thing as an independent community interest apart from the interest of the individuals comprising the community.[5] Chap-

[5] K. Klappholz, 'Value Judgments in Economics', in *The British Journal for the Philosophy of Science*, Vol. 15, No. 58 (1964) 106.

ter V will deal with this point at length. Here, we only need to concede the common root of neo-classical welfare analysis and political economy's earliest school, i.e. classical liberalism. This common root may not include the economic cures classical liberalism deemed sufficient for achieving social welfare, i.e. the price mechanism. However, it is certainly valid for both theories' sharing of one major grounder. This grounder contends that besides the actual satisfaction of wants, applicable ways of progressing their satisfaction are necessarily *individual*. As discussed, the individual-centered approach found expression in a microeconomic advance to macroeconomics. It also suspended a concern for non-economic competition, where individuals jointly fight for a redistribution of economic resources. Even if there was indeed an equilibrium problem in society, and potential for conflict increased, for classical liberals this still did not change the fact that no conflict occurred, because conflict lacked the necessary means. Commonly, those means are provided in processes of group building and group mobilization. Most symptomatic of this grounder still today is Adam Smith's statement according to which individuals advance their want for an economic utility alone, *rather than want it altogether.*[6]

The common root of neo-classical welfare analysis and classical liberalism as regards an assessment of primary stakeholders in conflict serves to separate the h.i.-approach from classical liberalism. According to Frances Stewart, individualist thinking 'neglect[s] a vital dimension of human well-being and social stability: that is the group dimension.'[7] Obviously, this first proposition finds good support with reality. Recent conflicts have been ethnic, racial and religious. All these comprise different types of group conflicts. But did they also imply an economic dimension? Eventually, the more one accepts the centrality of groups in conflict, this may also tempt to reject the h.i.-approach. On balance, this argument does not involve a real challenge to the h.i.-approach. Perfectly in line with their own extension on group theory, proponents of the h.i.-approach have no problem to agree that all these conflicts were indeed ethnic, racial, religious, etc. At the same time, they will assert that those symbolic variables are only the surface, which does not explain away the economic underbrush of conflict.

Proposition 2: Primordial Groups

From the perspective of the h.i.-approach, like from the perspective of some earlier conflict paradigms, conflict is linked to organized groups for whom violence is a means of their self-articulation. However, when highlighting the group component, one also needs to clarify the way conflict groups are rooted in the context of social life. One may expect to find some disagreement between earlier conflict paradigms and the h.i.-approach at this point precisely.

Two main answers are conventionally provided to the above question, each of which assumes an extreme view. According to one answer, sometimes labeled *pri-*

6 A. Smith, *An Inquiry into the Nature and Causes of the Wealth of Nations*, Dublin: Whitestone (1776) Book I, Ch. 7.

7 F. Stewart, 'Horizontal Inequalities: A Neglected Dimension of Development', in *Queen Elizabeth House Working Paper Series*, No. 81 (2002) 2.

mordialism, conflict groups are a cultural given, a quasi-natural state of being, determined by one's descent and with, in the extreme view, socio-biological determinants.[8] This belief has gained momentum with the series of ethnic, racial and religious conflicts in recent years. According to an opposite *neo-liberal* angle, group boundaries are fluid and membership in conflict groups is determined only by individual choice. Obviously, the latter angle has a lot in common with a liberal approach to political economy. The question is, which side the h.i.-approach fit in with.

Almost naturally, one would relate economic pondering of conflict to the neo-liberal angle. This angle forces us to grasp of conflict groups as free-of-choice collections of people, who unite for the purpose of some economic goals. However, rather than using the term conflict, the liberal concept of competition seems to capture the relationship between these and other groups. Such groups occur in specific occasions where individuals deem corporate behavior to serve their interests in an efficient way. Corresponding economic goals comprise the production of some market and non-market goods and services, rather than some crude category of economic distribution fights. Evidently, these groups can be more or less formal, depending on whether agreed and written rules existed or not. However, at the end of the day this distinction does not touch upon conflict groups in some real sense. Alternatively, one could move to the Marxian conception of groups, which is also economic in nature, and likely to be more applicable to the subject. After all, it revolves around two distinct economic conflict groups, i.e. bourgeoisie and proletariat. At the same time, this means moving away from extreme positions as regards the nature of conflict groups. Before that, the primordial angle may be weighed for the h.i.-approach.

According to the primordial angle, economic conflict groups would be thought of as culturally given, quasi-natural, determined by one's descent and, in the extreme view, characterized through socio-biological determinants. Accepting this angle implies operating closely to conflict paradigms that traditionally extol on the ethnic, racial and religious nature of conflict. Eventually, there wouldn't be much scope for disagreement between traditional conflict paradigms and the h.i.-approach. And yet, advocates of that approach stress precisely the primordial nature of economic conflict groups. They insist that symbolic factors in conflict (ethnicity, racial origin, religion, etc.) feature an economic underbrush.

Criticists not generally opposed to the h.i.-approach will argue that economic factors in conflict are certainly a reality, but that they relate to different conflict groups and cases of conflicts. There are some conflict groups that are more primordial, e.g. ethnic groups, and others that are less primordial. Therefore, economic factors in conflict should be assigned to groups that are less primordial, and probably located somewhere between the neo-liberal and primordial extremes. Economic factors might particularly represent the goals of raging political parties and workers unions, thus being in line with the Marxian model. For such criticists, both categories of

[8] W. Douglas, 'A Critique of Recent Trends in the Analysis of Ethnonationalism', in *Ethnic and Racial Studies*, Vol. 11, No. 2 (1988) 192-206; M. Banks, *Ethnicity: Anthropological Constructions*, London: Routledge (1996).

conflict groups, i.e. ethnic and economic groups, comprise archetypes, but that is exactly why they should never be mixed up.

Fig. 2.1: Conflict Groups According to Different Paradigms

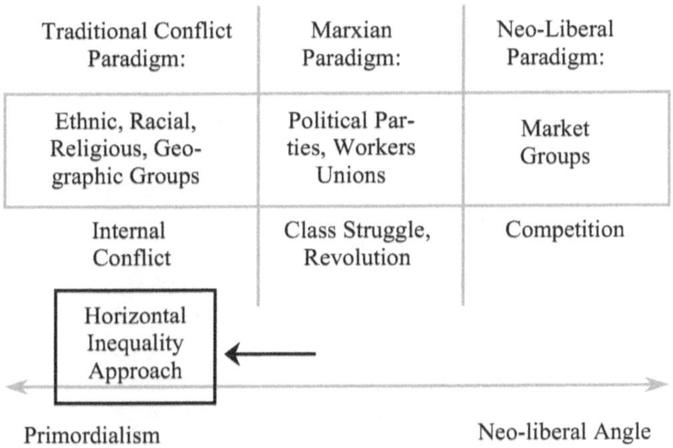

At the end of the day, the h.i.-approach serves to sharpen a debate as to whether conflict is about symbolic or economic factors, or possibly about a combination of both. As far as this approach is concerned, the latter is considered correct. The relationship between both groups of factors leads over to a third proposition implicit in the h.i.-approach. At this junction, one only sees the difference between economic groups that fall under the primordial and neo-liberal angles. Conflict groups under the primordial angle are not characterized through an efficiency function, whereas this is what characterizes economic groups competing in free market economies. They do not exist to remove market failures,[9] but for the sake of a claims function, which aims at advancing the claims of members for power and economic resources.[10] They do not act as providers of public goods, but as sheer pressure groups. Only these economic groups may account for conflict groups in some original sense.

Proposition 3: Culture and Economy

Superficially, the answer why economic conflict groups should be considered as primordial as ethnic and other symbolic groups has been most simple. According to the h.i.-approach, symbolic and economic conflict groups are *identical*. This was already implied when we alluded to the economic underbrush of ethnic, racial, religious and other conflicts. A more complicated question is how this must be seen to

9 P. North, *Institutions, Institutional Change and Economic Performance*, Cambridge MA: Harvard University Press (1990) 25.

10 F. Stewart, 'Groups for Good or Ill', in *Oxford Development Studies*, Vol. 24, No. 1 (1996).

work technically. After all, the traditional idea of conflict seems to require a decision as to whether conflict is economic *or* symbolic. A third proposition of the h.i.-approach evolves in the face of this dilemma. It contends that 'symbolic factors beget stereotyping, while economic deprivation beget conflict.' In order to understand this proposition, one is bound to consider how conflict evolves.

A widely shared belief in present scholarly debate is that conflict is in some way 'constructed'. The constructed nature of conflict is considered to harmonize perfectly with assumptions about the primordial or 'non-constructed' character of conflict groups. While conflict is in a way manufactured, the persons behind such manufacturing are in many cases group leaders, who find group mobilization a powerful mechanism when following up on their private goals. When manufacturing conflict group, leaders will often adopt a strategy of reworking historical memories to engender group identity.[11] Symbolic factors, such as ethnicity, religion, and race and geographical origin, are all likely to be exploited in this process of instrumentalizing group identities by abusive political will. Symbolic factors are deemed to exert the highest potential for conflict, because they are most closely associated with the group's own primordial nature, and therefore with dividing lines that define the in-group and out-group, or enemy respectively. Overall, these factors have been referred to as those that concern the communal identity of groups.[12]

According to the h.i.-approach, the above rationale describes only one side of the whole story. The constructedness of conflict and crucial role of symbolic factors in this regard have been accepted. At the same time, proponents of this approach assert that 'neither the constructedness nor the instrumentality of ethnicity can be explained unless we are prepared to see it as an independent as well as a dependent variable in human affairs.'[13] This is meant to say that symbolic factors would rarely work in the absence of underlying economic factors for conflict. Precisely speaking, economic factors are expected to play a crucial role both for group leaders and group members. Concerning the first, economic factors are present in the form of personal *greed*. As for the latter, economic factors are deemed to express crucial *grievances*. Symbolic factors only become acute where group leaders try to exploit group identities as a powerful mechanism in their competition for power and economic resources. Therefore, rather than advancing legitimate claims of their group, group leaders are suspected to act within their private interests. As for ordinary group members, symbolic factors are conceded as a mobilizing force, however, mainly in the late stage of evolving group conflict. In a manner symptomatic for such thinking, Frances Stewart has pointed out that for the emergence of group conflict, a degree of similarity of circumstances among members of a group (ethnicity, region, religion) is in many cases not enough to bring about group mobilization. This is the point

---

11 F. Stewart, 'Crisis Prevention: Tackling Horizontal Inequalities', in *Queen Elizabeth House Working Paper Series*, No. 33 (2000) 4.

12 E. Azar, 'The Analysis and Management of Protracted Social Conflict', in J. Volkan et al. (eds.), *The Psychodynamics of International Relationships*, Vol. 2, Lexington: D.C. Heath (1991) 93.

13 D. Turton, 'War and Ethnicity: Global Connections and Local Violence in East Africa and Former Yugoslavia', in *Oxford Development Studies*, No. 25, Special Issue: War, Economy and Society (1997) 84.

where economic grievance factors join in.[14] In many cases, group identities and economic situation will coincide in the first place, as the result of continuous suppression and discrimination in the past. For this precise reason, the h.i.-approach has taken so much pride in stressing that economic conflict groups are just as primordial as symbolic conflict groups. Most illustrative of this synergetic relationship between symbolic and economic factors in the case of group members is the following verdict: 'Men may and do certainly joke about or ridicule the strange and bizarre customs of men from other ethnic groups, because these customs are different from their own. But they do not fight over such differences alone. When men do, on the other hand, fight across ethnic lines it is nearly always the case that they fight over some fundamental issues concerning the distribution and exercise of power, whether economic, political, or both.'[15]

Fig. 2.2: Mono-Causal Conflict Theories

Paradigm:	Realist Group Conflict Theory	Social Identity Theory	
Conflict Factors:	Economic Factors	Symbolic Factors	
Affiliated Theories:	Economic Development Hypothesis	Symbolic Racism, Social Representations, Self-Identity and Role Theory	↓ Explanation of Conflict

Obviously, the dual concept of greed and grievances, as both apply to group leaders and group members, must also reject another centerpiece of the liberal model developed in chapter I. According to this centerpiece, economic conflict is an unlikely thing to occur. Mainly for two reasons: Firstly, conflict will usually lack the necessary means, i.e. provided in individuals who desert to cooperative behavior; secondly, it will normally be *uneconomic*. The latter has been deemed clear to any stakeholder in any type of economic situation, again, for two main reasons: First of all, any behavior threatening to disrupt regular supplies of goods and services will be at odds with a reality of increased economic exchange. Early, the free trade principle has been referred to as a principle 'which shall act on the moral world as the principle of gravitation on the universe - drawing men together, thrusting aside the antagonism of race, and creed, and language, and uniting us in the bonds of eternal

[14] Stewart (2000) 4.

[15] A. Cohen, *Two-Dimensional Man: An Essay on the Anthropology of Power and Symbolism in Complex Society*, Berkeley: University of California Press (1974) 94.

peace.'[16] A second liberal argument revolves around the direct costs involved in the financing of conflict.[17]

An analysis of the h.i.-approach concedes the highly integrative power of this approach with regard to factors in conflict that have mostly been treated in isolation. This does not mean to endorse the h.i.-approach. A rather exclusive focus on economic factors has previously been present in theories observing David Campbell's Realist Group Conflict Theory, having set forth that conflict is about 'real' issues.[18] A deviating focus on symbolic factors has been found in Henry Tajfel's Social Identity Theory, and others the like.[19] A glimpse of a more integrated approach has been Edward Azar's theory of protracted social conflict. Apart from symbolic factors, this approach considered social grievances, poor governance and international economic dependencies.[20] However, it established this menu of conflict factors with little attention to their interplay (Fig. 2.2). Quite uniquely, the h.i.-approach has developed the relationship between different conflict factors to the point that these factors virtually *demand* each other. With this relationship, we move away from a pattern of observation where each factor had a direct link to conflict, also providing that it was a sufficient precondition for conflict to evolve. The ultimately comfortable thing about such proceeding has been related to the possibility of invoking an infinite number of factors, for one could always be sure that one or the other factor would work. Different from that, the h.i.-approach assigns conflict factors to a *linear model*, with each factor accounting for a necessary although non-sufficient precondition for conflict (Fig. 2.3). In doing so, it integrates key doctrines of critical realism, as they oppose the liberal model and associate with elements of Keynesian economics. Thus, it rejects a prominent feature of the individual-centered approach, which is to separate each individual into a number of non-communicating cells, with no exchange among the set of motives each of them carries along. According to liberal doctrines, economic behavior is guided by pure self-interest. Other aspects of people's personality that could be necessary to arrive at a motive of action have been neglected. In a group context, such aspects realistically include aspects of people's symbolic identity.[21] Beyond linking economic and symbolic factors through a linear

16 R. Cobden, *The Political and Economic Works of Richard Cobden* [1846] 6 Volumes, London: Routledge (1995) Vol. 3, 362-363.

17 D. Ricardo, *On the Principles of Political Economy and Taxation* [1817], Cambridge: Cambridge University Press (1951) 186.

18 D. Campbell, 'Ethnocentrism and Other Altruistic Motives', in D. Levine (ed.), *Nebraska Symposium on Motivation, Vol. 13*, Lincoln: University of Nebraska Press (1965) 283-311.

19 H. Tajfel (ed.), *Differentiation between Social Groups*, London: Academic Press (1978).

20 E. Azar, *The Management of Protracted Social Conflict: Theory and Cases*, Aldershot: Dartmouth (1990) 7.

21 We reiterate L. v. Mises (1957) paradigmatic words: 'When they distinguished between purely economic motives and other motives, the classical economists referred only to the acquisitive side of human behavior. […] The approach of Classical economics appears highly unsatisfactory from the point of view of modern subjective economics. Modern economics rejects as entirely fallacious also the argument advanced for the epistemological justification of the Classical methods by their last followers, especially John Stuart Mill. According to this lame apology, pure economics deals only with the 'economic' aspect of the operations of mankind, only with the phenomena of the production of wealth 'as far as those phenomena are not modified by the pursuit of any other object.'[21] […] Modern economics traces all human actions back to the value judgments of individuals. It never was so foolish […] as to

model, the h.i.-approach puts in context different economic factors. As for these factors, academia has so far applied a rather rigorous distinction between interest-based (greed) and fact-based (grievance) conflict.[22] In practice, the concept of greed has found much favor with the World Bank.[23] The United Nations tend to focus on a grievance account of conflict.[24] Too often, the quest was for greed *or* grievance factors in conflict.

Fig. 2.3: Linear Model of Factors in Conflict

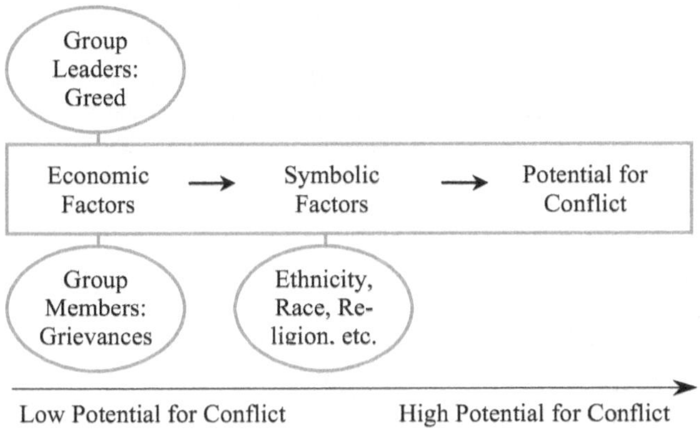

Proposition 4: Relative Deprivation

Once greed and grievance factors in conflict are no longer thought of as incommensurable, one can analyze their functioning. This brings up a fourth proposition of the h.i.-approach, which stipulates that 'economic deprivation is relative.' As for greed factors, there is little room for misunderstanding as to how these factors gain economic impact once their role in conflict is accepted. For group leaders driven by greed, conflict comprises an efficient way of following up on private economic interests. Often they advocate for an allocation of economic resources which is disproportional, both in view of other groups as well as their own group. In contrast, the concept of grievance allows for a number of interpretations as to how economic grievances spur conflict. Some of these interpretations merit a closer look, because they provide important entry points for separate structural and cultural critiques of the h.i.-approach, thus impacting on the social economy of conflict and conflict prevention.

believe that all that people are after is higher incomes and lower prices. [...] the term well-being [...] does not refer only to concerns commonly called egoistic but comprehends everything that appears to an individual as desirable and worthy of being aimed at.'

22 L. Reychler, 'The Art of Conflict Prevention: Theory and Practice', in W. Bauwens and L. Reychler (eds.), *The Art of Conflict Prevention*, London and New York: Brassey's (1994) 1-21.

23 P. Collier, 'Economic Causes of Civil Conflict and their Implication for Policy', Washington DC: World Bank (2000).

24 UN Secretary-General, 'We the Peoples: The Role of the UN in the 21st Century', (A/54/2000) 27 March 2000.

The h.i.-approach offers an interpretation of economic grievances that differs essentially from another economic school of thought. This school is commonly known as 'economic development hypothesis', and has long been considered preeminent.[25] In a nutshell, the difference between both interpretations of economic grievances can be described as follows. From the perspective of the h.i.-approach, conflict is caused by economic grievances that exist as economic inequalities between groups, rather than as poverty per se. The latter assumption is integral to the economic development hypothesis. Correspondingly, if a whole society was uniformly impoverished, there would be despair, but no motivation for group mobilization and conflict. Even if group leaders hoped to use group mobilization in an attack on the established order, they would find it difficult to secure sufficient response among their followers, if there were no underlying economic inequalities that put the group at a disadvantage compared to other groups.[26] The relative rather than absolute economic situation is seen to motivate riotous behavior of groups. Two popular expressions to capture these deviating interpretations of economic grievances are the concepts of *relative deprivation* and *absolute deprivation.*

To make this point even more clear, consider the following graphical distribution of economic assets between two groups A and B (Fig. 2.4). A focus on economic assets rather than incomes respects that especially in developing countries control over agro-based assets, e.g. access to or ownership of land, is often an important means of securing income, although also an end in itself. Therefore, imagine one hundred percent of economic assets divided between both groups is AB in the below chart.[27] The percentage share of group A is measured in the direction AB, and that of group B in the direction BA. Any point such as Y_1 or Y_2 reflects a particular percentage division of economic assets between the two. X features the case that shares are in equilibrium. In absolute numbers, the portion currently owned by group A is a_1, measured in vertical direction. Group B's absolute portion is b_1. Quite obviously, A's portion is below that of B. According to the concept of relative deprivation, it would be in this case, as well as for any $a_n < b_n$, that group A felt deprived, simply because group B was better off. At the same time, this was completely independent of how wealthy group A was in *absolute* terms, i.e. whether it was seriously impoverished or doing just fine. As part of the same logic, group A would now consider to go into conflict, as a means of achieving a redistribution of economic assets. From the perspective of group A, such a redistribution aimed at a level of economic welfare equal to b_1, in the below graph comprising a_2 or above. However, in line with the precepts of Pareto optimality, providing that the poor cannot be made any better without cutting into the affluence of the rich, this surplus could only be gained at the expense of group B, the welfare level of which consequently moved down to b_2.

---

25 L. Siegelman and M. Simpson, 'A Cross-National Test of the Linkage between Economic Inequality and Political Violence', in *Journal of Conflict Resolution*, Vol. 21 (1977) 105-128; M. Hardy, 'Economic Growth, Distributional Inequality, and Conflict in Industrial Societies', in *Journal of Political and Military Sociology*, Vol. 5 (1979) 209-227; E. Weede, 'Income Inequality, Average Income, and Domestic Violence', in *Journal of Conflict Resolution*, Vol. 25, No. 4 (1981) 639-653.

26 Stewart (2000) 5.

27 A similar model has been developed in A. Sen, *On Economic Inequality*, Oxford: Oxford University Press (1973) 17-18.

Clearly, this implied a percentage distribution of economic assets Y_2 that presents a mirror-image of Y_1. In fact, this might well be the result in societies where conflict is the driving force behind change. However, ideally the cutting point of Ab_n and Ba_n always falls together with X, for any given level of economic asserts groups A and B own (e.g. Ab_3 and Ba_3), also excluding conflict in the first place.

Fig. 2.4: Relative Deprivation

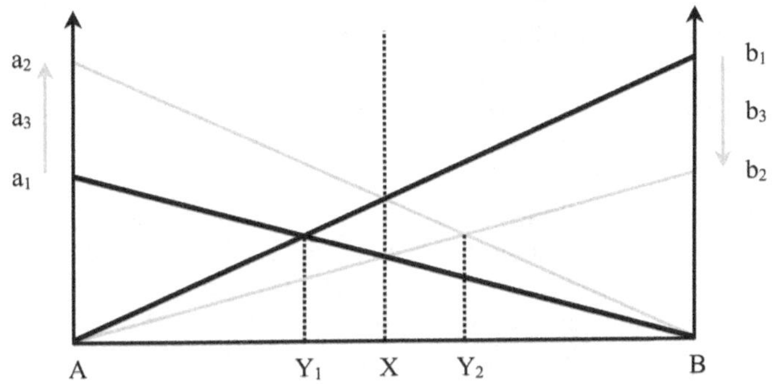

But why should economic grievances work according to the mechanisms of relative deprivation at all, rather than according to the concept of absolute deprivation, where a fixed level of deprivation of economic assets a_1 or a_2 elicits conflict (Fig. 2.5)?

Fig. 2.5: Absolute Deprivation

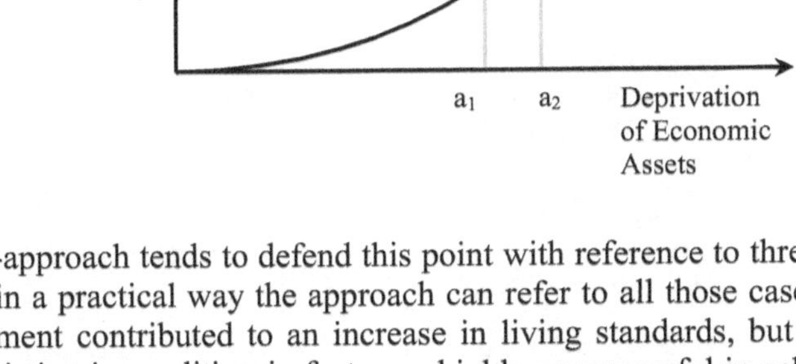

The h.i.-approach tends to defend this point with reference to three main arguments: Firstly, in a practical way the approach can refer to all those cases where economic development contributed to an increase in living standards, but did nothing to remove existing inequalities, in fact, was highly unsuccessful in achieving a reduction in potential for conflict.[28] Secondly and more generally, the economic is established as a level playing field where the possessions of individuals and groups are by definition subject to inter-personal and inter-group comparisons.[29] Economic grievances are seen to comprise nothing else but a special case of this general pattern. In as much as those comparisons are accepted, the h.i.-approach confirms, partially, a basic tenet of neo-classical welfare economics. Surely, a focus on inter-group rather than on inter-personal comparisons keeps such correspondence within certain limits. Thirdly, in search for an appropriate role of the economic development hypothesis, patterns of absolute deprivation (poverty) are considered relevant, to the extent that they focus on the relative situation.[30] Apart from that, a rather limited role of absolute grievances in conflict presents a key principle.

Criticism of the concept of relative deprivation from the side of proponents of the economic development hypothesis has been rather unconvincing.[31] By far more interesting are the challenges posed by a traditional ally of neo-classical welfare economics. Being economic utilitarianism, this ally has been concerned with the dilemma of equating the utility functions of individuals. The basis of this challenge is as follows: Both economic utilitarianism and the h.i.-approach involve a tendency to deal with economic value in a non- or pre-market sense. Both relate the fact of something being an economic asset to the direct usefulness of that thing for individuals and groups. Conversely, the absence of that good is tied to the immediate suffering or deprivation that results from it. Therefore, both concepts appear to approve of a concept of economic value that focuses on 'value in use', rather than on value in exchange, or exchange value. This may be seen as yet another common grounder, a rare occasion though that the h.i.-approach and liberal models overlap. Chapter I has dealt with economic value as exchange value. Such value materializes in the sphere of market circulation. It also dealt with aspects of the generation of economic value, i.e. Marx's and Keynes' labour theories of value. In contrast, the concept of value in use has originally been coined by Adam Smith. In fact, beyond economic utilitarianism a dealing with utility functions has always remained present in neo-classical welfare economics, thus living a life below the surface of market economic operations.

Having established this common basis of economic utilitarianism and the h.i.-approach, the announced challenge may be tackled directly. In order to get an idea of this challenge on the part of economic utilitarianism, one needs to focus on indi-

---

28 E. Muller, 'Income Inequality, Regime Repressiveness and Political Violence', in *American Sociological Review*, Vol. 50, No. 1 (1985) 47-61; E. Muller, 'Income Inequality and Political Violence: The Effect of Influential Cases', in *American Sociological Review*, Vol. 51, No. 3 (1986) 441-445; E. Muller, 'Inequality, Repression, Violence: Issues of Theory and Research Design', in *American Sociological Review*, Vol. 53, No. 5 (1988) 799-806.

29 T. Gurr, *Minorities at Risk: A Global View of Ethnopolitical Conflict*, Washington DC: United States Institute for Peace Press (1993).

30 Stewart (2000) 5.

31 J. Hartman and W. Hsiao, 'Inequality and Violence: Issues of Theory and Measurement in Muller', in *American Sociological Review*, Vol. 53, No. 5 (1988) 794-799; E. Weede, 'Income Inequality and Political Violence Reconsidered', in *American Sociological Review*, Vol. 51, No. 3 (1986) 438-441; B. London and T. Robinson, 'The Effect of International Dependence on Income Inequality and Political Violence', in *American Sociological Review*, Vol. 54, No. 2 (1989) 305-308.

vidual utility functions. Because individual utility functions are what economic utilitarianism is all about. At the same time of appreciating individual utility functions, economic utilitarianism has resulted in increased awareness that people possess different utility functions. Applied to the above terminology, this means that levels and qualities of economic assets which individuals consider satisfactory can deviate essentially. This is quite an achievement, for a distinct feature of economics has often been to treat economic needs as inherent in human beings, and therefore as universal rather than as individually and culturally owned. For example, it is for this reason that those working within needs theory consider it appropriate to generalize across cultures and across societal levels from the inter-personal and the family to the international.[32] Instead of highlighting people's needs, economic utilitarians embrace the concept of wants to stress that innate wants are probably confined to basic food, shelter and the like. All the rest, economic wants particularly, individuals are seen to develop in the course of life, or in some cases they don't.[33]

Superficially, economic utilitarianism thus poses the following challenge to the h.i.-approach. On the one hand, evidence of relative deprivation could be irrelevant, simply because it corresponded with the varying utility functions of individuals and groups. On the other hand, it could be a misunderstanding that broad-based economic justice lowers potential for conflict, also because utility functions deviate.

In order to probe the substance of this challenge, the utilitarian model requires relating to the concept of relative deprivation. Therefore, imagine the following modification to the previous setting, which considers the distribution of a given total of economic assets between two persons or groups A and B.[34] Again, one hundred percent of economic assets divided between both persons-groups is AB in the below chart (Fig. 2.6). As before, the percentage share of person-group A is measured in the direction AB, while that of person-group B is measured in the direction BA.

Fig. 2.6: Utilitarianism's Weak Equity Axiom

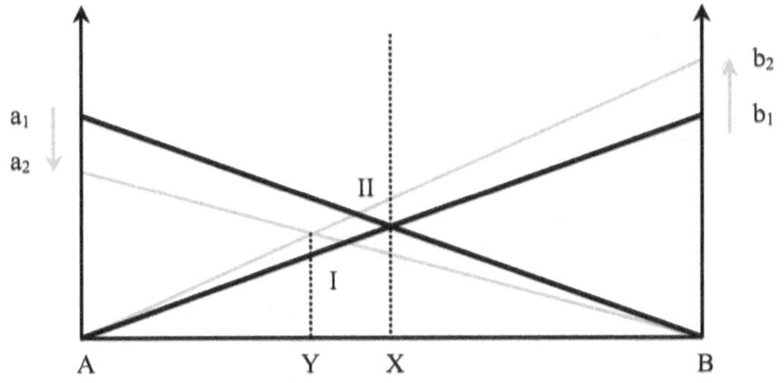

[32] J. Burton, *Violence Explained: The Sources of Conflict, Violence and Crime and their Prevention*, Manchester: Manchester University Press (1997) 35.

[33] A.F.v. Hayek, *Studies in Philosophy, Politics and Economics*, London: Routledge and Kegan Paul (1967) 314.

[34] The following model modifies an income-based model in Sen (1973) 17-18.

Let us assume now that, different from the previous scenario, the shares of A and B are indeed in equilibrium, meaning that they correspond to X. Also in absolute terms a_1 and b_1 are on par. However, assume now that in application of the precepts of individual utility functions, A's marginal schedule, meaning a minimum stock of economic assets A considers satisfactory, is exactly two thirds that of B. In absolute numbers, it will be equivalent to a_2 in the graph, whereas that of B requires b_2. Therefore, in the present situation a_1b_1, A is above its marginal schedule, while B is left distinctly below its own.

In line with the doctrines of relative deprivation, the present circumstances are in line with a situation where no potential for conflict exists. If group A and group B consider the amount of economic assets the other group owns, they will have no reason to feel deprived. However, from the perspective of economic utilitarianism a completely different picture applies. In line with the concept of deviating utility functions, the latter would recommend a transfer of economic assets from A to B, with the new optimal point being Y. It would even do so, if person-group A was already poorer than person-group B, but still above its marginal schedule of a_2. The utilitarian rule of distribution has found expression in the *weak equity axiom*. Applied to conflict groups, this axiom implies the following: Let group A have a lower level of utility or welfare than group B for each level of economic assets. Then, in distributing a given total of economic assets between both groups, the overall goal to avoid conflict must lead to provide group B with a higher level of economic assets than group A. The message for the h.i.-approach contained in these remarks is clear. Relative deprivation is irrelevant for the determination of potential for conflict, because in many cases it will correspond with the deviating utility functions of individuals and groups. For the same reason of deviating utility functions, expectations that broad-based economic justice lowers potential for conflict are mistaken.

Recent empirical analysis suggests that, under certain circumstances, agents agree to a perpetuation of income inequalities and other economic differences.[35] Still, how compelling is this challenge to the h.i.-approach on the part of economic utilitarianism really? After all, the h.i.-approach may well endorse the idea of deviating utility functions. Particularly, because an integral part of this idea is that individuals *develop* their utility functions, rather than own a stable set of innate needs. The same idea of individuals and groups developing or assessing their economic needs is part of the concept of relative deprivation. However, at the same time such assessments are seen to happen *relative* to other individuals and groups. Thus, person-group A will always take into regard the economic situation of other persons and groups B, C, etc. Despite integrating the liberal concept of wants, economic utilitarianism has paid no systematic attention to the mechanisms according to which individual utility functions evolve. Also, the related concept of inter-personal comparisons has been reserved for academic pondering, rather than applied to the stakeholders. According to this concept, academia compares inter-personal welfare levels to determine a situation of maximal economic welfare. A lack of attention to the evolution of utility functions may well lead to the assumption that economic utilitarianism proposes

---

[35] S. Freeman, 'Equilibrium Income Inequality among Identical Agents', in *Journal of Political Economy*, Vol. 104, No. 5 (1996) 1047.

only another version of absolute deprivation-centered research. Certainly, deviating from the traditional concept of absolute deprivation, levels of deprivation that constitute a motive for conflict are acknowledged to be different for different individuals. Still, economic utilitarianism assumes these levels of deprivation to be constant for each individual over times. Different from that, an essential component of the concept of relative deprivation is that utility functions and economic needs are reassessed whenever there is an occasion to do so. That is also why conflict prevention poses a never-ending task.

Another shortcoming of economic utilitarianism refers to the following fact. On the one hand, everything has been done to reach down to the level of individuals, and their deviating utility functions respectively, while before there was only the species that counted. However, on the other hand there was seemingly no way back from the isolated individual to the influences of groups on individual behavior at given times. While analyzing the liberal utilitarian model of distribution, our use of the terms person and group was not very sharp, always suggesting that both could be used interchangeably. In fact, there is no real group theory in economic utilitarianism, and it would have been appropriate to stick to the functioning of individuals therefore. However, for the purpose of bringing the h.i.-approach and economic utilitarianism into a discussion with each other, this point was neglected periodically. Different from economic utilitarianism, the h.i.-approach has no problems explaining why person A_1 will supposedly gather with other individuals A_2, A_3, A_n, when assessing its economic needs relative to person B. The h.i.-approach does so on the basis of its group theory. Thus, the actual assessment is seen to take place in the context of symbolic dividing lines. Taken alone, these symbolic dividing lines would not be sufficient to result in group conflict. But they explain why individuals, who assess their economic situation in a *relative* manner, join the earlier developed context of group mobilization and group conflict, instead of provoking private distribution fights.

Proposition 5: Horizontal and Vertical Inequalities

From the perspective of the h.i.-approach, conflict groups are attracted to conflict, because they feel relatively deprived vis-à-vis other groups. Two important questions remain to be clarified, if this is really the case. By answering these questions, our analysis moves toward a presumably fifth proposition of the h.i.-approach, stating that 'conflict perpetuates group leadership and class structures.' Before analyzing how group members develop grievances as a function of evidence of relative deprivation, group leaders were said to be motivated by greed rather than by crucial grievances. Even more than grievances, greed is bound to develop relative to the economic situation of other individuals and groups. Otherwise, there was no reason to be greedy. However, different from grievances, the notion of greed implies that a person motivated by greed desires goods he or she could also do without. Otherwise, this person may not be labeled greedy. That is why this label actually implies a moral statement. As a matter of fact, in many cases group leaders have been observed to be better off economically than ordinary group members. But here comes the first question then: Why would group members turn against other groups rather than against their own leaders, if the whole issue with conflict was about inequalities in the distribution of economic assets? More technically speaking, why would their focus be on horizontal inequalities rather than vertical inequalities?

Both terms have found entry into the h.i.-approach. The term vertical inequalities defines economic inequalities between group leaders and group members. As such, it is easily understandable. It pays tribute to the hierarchical structures group leaders and members are normally assigned to. However, here the second question joins in: Why should inter-group conflict carry the label of horizontal inequalities? After all, deprived and privileged groups are also conceivable through a hierarchical relationship. On the one hand, vertical inequalities are traditionally associated with a from-bottom-to-top pattern of measuring social inequalities. Preferentially by taking people's incomes, this pattern assigns a rank to each individual in society, irrespective of group memberships, so as to arrive at a picture of domestic income disparities. From the perspective of the h.i.-approach, such proceeding should be restricted to intra-group scenarios, thus reserving the label vertical inequalities for these kinds of inequalities. On the other hand, as an opposite label to capture inter-group inequalities, the term horizontal inequalities, should be understood against the background of Marxian-style pondering of group conflict. Chapter I made it clear that a defining part of Marx's grasping of antagonist groups was in terms of classes and social layers. In the context of social life, these classes and layers were part of a vertical structure. Conflict was a matter of proletarians raising their hands against bourgeois suppression. They would do so as capital accumulation proceeded and supposedly produced, in the direct ratio of its own energy and extent, a relatively redundant population of labourers, or 'industrial reserve army'. It was also mentioned that Marx justified the occurrence of this industrial reserve army, or accelerated relative diminution of the variable constituent of capital, with reference to technological change patterns. Ultimately, he stated that the more productiveness develops, the more it finds itself at variance with the narrow basis on which the conditions of consumption rest.[36] As a direct consequence of this initial effect on the consumer power of the working class, vertical inequalities would be so great as to result in a social revolution, and eventually in the decline of capitalism.

As opposed to Marxian insight into the functioning of group conflict, the term horizontal inequalities in the h.i.-approach abandons the class-like or vertical character of conflict. It does so by ways of establishing a clear lingual distinction. The basis for this distinction relates to the assumed primordial nature of conflict groups, i.e. to groups that are defined by symbolic dividing lines. The primordial nature of conflict groups is also employed to answer why intra-group vertical inequalities don't cause conflict, i.e. why group members turn against other groups rather than their own leaders. From the perspective of the h.i.-approach, groups are not formed in order to advance economic goals. Rather, group members address economic goals in a common way, because even before they are tied together through symbolic factors and particular loyalties. The Marxian understanding foresaw that any mental factor or aspect of group loyalty only develops in direct ratio of the economic infrastruc-

---

[36] K. Marx, *Capital Volume Three: The Process of Capitalist Production as a Whole* [1893], in Marx and Engels (1975-2005) Vol. 37, Ch. 15, I.

ture for conflict. The fact that Marx signified a situation of alienation as the common mental state of the proletariat, even before capitalism had brought about an industrial reserve army, does not change this broader picture. Chapter I also made it clear that, strictly speaking, Marx did not restrict aspects of alienation to the working class. Also the capitalist class presented moments of self-estrangement, which it was yet granted to be at ease with.[37] Conversely, for the h.i.-approach symbolic factors and other group loyalties precede common economic goals. This assumption implies the aforementioned consequence: As symbolic factors and group loyalties tend to be particularly marked in relation to group leaders, economic distribution fights will rarely target the economic situation of group leaders. Rather, they will be launched against other groups. Taken together, minor roles of intra-group and inter-group vertical inequalities justify proposition 5: 'Conflict perpetuates class structures and group leadership'.

Fig. 2.7: Inequalities According to Marx and the H.I.-Approach

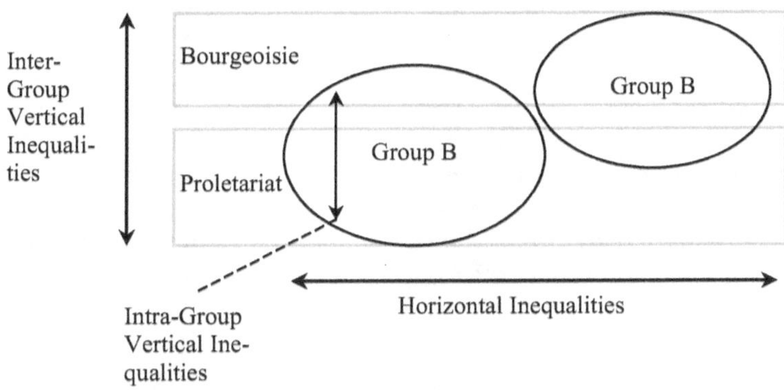

The fact remains that groups are separated into vertical factions, i.e. leaders and followers. Therefore, different combinations of horizontal and intra-group vertical inequalities may still influence processes of group mobilization and potential for conflict, depending on whether these inequalities are strong or not. Judging from the above analysis, one would assume that particular combinations of strong and weak horizontal and vertical inequalities present the same consequences with regard to potential for conflict. More precisely, if potential for conflict is strongly determined by existing horizontal inequalities, such potential should be high no matter whether strong horizontal inequalities coincide with weak (a_1) or strong (a_2) vertical inequalities.

37 K. Marx and F. Engels, *The Holy Family or Critique of Critical Criticism* [1845] in Marx and Engels (1975-2005) Vol. 4, Ch. 4.

Fig. 2.8: Types of Inequalities and Potential for Conflict

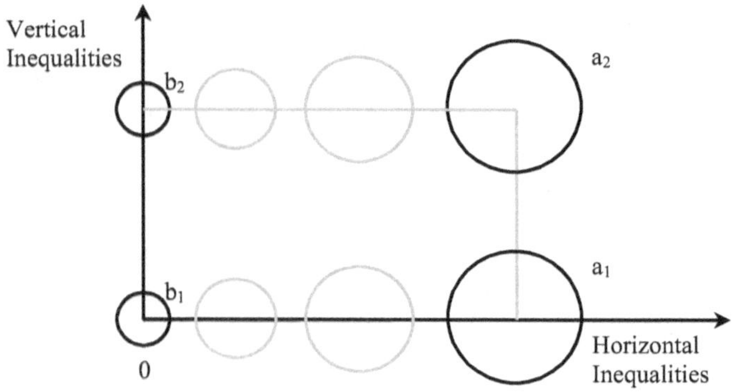

Vice versa, potential for conflict should be moderate in both cases that weak horizontal inequalities come together with weak (b_1) or strong (b_2) vertical inequalities. In fact, in many cases this is not what happened. Rather, the combination of horizontal and vertical inequalities was such that the existence of weak or strong vertical inequalities influenced potential for conflict in a decisive way. The highest potential for inter-group conflict occurred where strong horizontal inequalities coincided with certain patterns of weak intra-group vertical inequalities. Again, this brings up the question whether group members who suffer from economic grievances might turn against their leaders rather than other groups, especially when intra-group vertical inequalities are strong.

Fig. 2.9: Systematically Increased Potential for Conflict

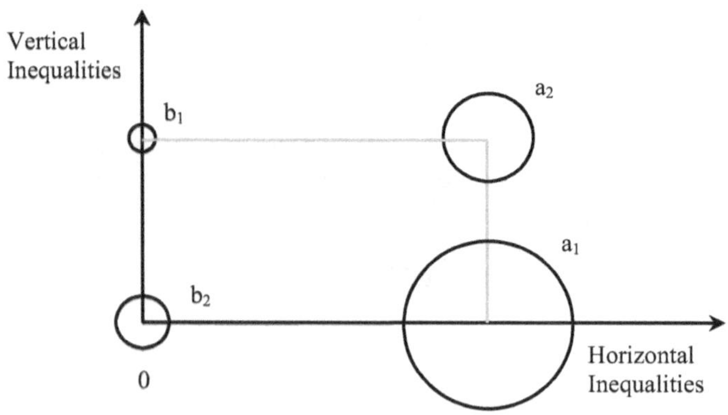

The h.i.-approach tends to give an *optimistic* explanation for the mitigating influence of strong intra-group vertical inequalities on potential for inter-group conflict. This explanation is believed not to compromise the approach's primordial group theory, implying that group loyalties are so strong as to prevent subversive action against greedy leaders. According to this optimistic explanation, it is said to be realistic that intra-group vertical inequalities reduce potential for inter-group conflict, simply because *group cohesion* is more difficult to achieve where intra-group inequalities are strong.[38] There has been no systematic weighing of the case that vertical inequalities could avoid inter-group conflict merely as a consequence of rebellion within the group. Instead, these inequalities are merely considered as an impediment on the way of mobilizing the group against other groups.

How plausible is this assumption on the part of the h.i.-approach? First of all, it is reasonable that intra-group vertical inequalities don't reduce potential for inter-group conflict, if conflict groups are thought of in terms of modern armies. Modern armies are the standard example of groups that achieve group cohesion and mobilization by building on strong vertical inequalities. This point is integral to the modes of operation of those groups, which are based on power and control. One or a group of dominant actors determine what the rest of the group will do. Although those orders typically reflect the interests of those with power, they enforce them by threats of various types, which may be backed up by norms so that the threats need rarely be used.[39]

Clearly, there are limitations of considering these modes of operation for primordial conflict groups. Therefore, how do leaders of those groups normally keep under control group members in the presence of strong vertical inequalities? After all, groups that are defined by symbolic traits normally lack an infrastructure comparable to the one of modern armies. Their infrastructure is not rooted in society as a whole. Quite plausibly, successful control will include a combination of economic incentives and symbolic features. More technically speaking, such success will depend on reinforcing cooperation-based and economic incentive-based modes of operation. As for the first modes, group members usually share into riotous goals if group leaders manage to sell the symbolic nature of conflict, while hiding their private economic interests. However, in these cases the symbolic card may weigh even stronger if intra-group vertical inequalities are pronounced, i.e. as a result of group leader charisma. Thus, cooperation-based modes may be ruled out when considering factors that divert attention from the economic privileges of group leaders, also resulting in a focus on horizontal inequalities. So much the more, economic incentive-based modes of operation need to join in.

Under normal circumstances, economic incentive-based modes give meaning to behavior in market economies. However, they can also be stretched to conflict groups operating in a non-market context. In all cases, they imply norms of delivering economic rewards and penalties to group members, depending on whether they contribute to group objectives.[40] In cases of strong intra-group vertical inequalities, group leaders will need to convince group members of great economic rewards from inter-group conflict. These economic rewards or incentives need to exceed benefits

---

38 Stewart (2000) 13.

39 J. Heyer, 'Group Behaviour and Development', in *WIDER Working Paper Series*, No. 161 (1999) 8.

40 Ibid.

from a redistribution of economic assets within the group, eventually at the cost of group leaders. The same argumentation can be applied to the h.i.-approach in conflict debates, when defending its provisions. The same argument also reveals the conceptual distance between the h.i.-approach and the Marxian model of group mobilization. With the h.i.-approach, we are bound to consider those variables that get group cohesion underway. Since group leaders assume a decisive role in this process, there is always a moment of overcoming some motives against conflict. Strong intra-group vertical inequalities can provide such a moment. Processes of group mobilization in Marx couldn't be more different. At the same time of expediting a focus on inter-group rather than intra-group vertical inequalities, the Marxian model could safely neglect problems associated with the first. The assumed *law-like* character of developments renders these problems inadequate. In line with the precepts of historical materialism, conflict relies on a law expressing the increasing misery of the proletariat, which itself relies on a law quoting a falling rate of profit. The latter comprises a supposedly irreversible trend line within the development of capitalism. Chapter I explained that in bringing about a social revolution, proletariat and bourgeoisie are assigned a role they don't control and yet cannot escape. The capitalist class, on the one hand, cannot exist without constantly revolutionizing the instruments of production. The working class, on the other, carries a revolutionary role to the extent that this role is not in excess of the current state of economic conditions effected by both classes. Its revolutionary consciousness or mental preparedness lacks any anticipatory moment. While all this can be seen as emanating from detailed economic analysis in Marx, it also corresponds to an ungrounded grounder, which has no equivalent in the h.i.-approach. Chapter V deals with this grounder in systematic depth, thus accelerating a debate on historicism. It contrasts this grounder with a manufacturing or social engineering type of approach to the economy that applies to the h.i.-approach.

A final remark rounds off this section. For there is so much emphasis on horizontal and intra-group vertical inequalities in the h.i.-approach, to what extent is this approach justified in excluding a concern for inter-group vertical inequalities? The main reference point for this exclusion is the perceived symbolic nature of conflict groups today. This nature also implies that conflict is not about class structures and social layers, although it is still about economic issues. Per se, this assumption is certainly valid. But isn't it also true that in the context of social life symbolic groups are often just as vertically assigned as classes were in the past? Therefore, does the notion of horizontal inequalities imply more than new terminology applied to similar kinds of groups? More precisely, does it also involve a re-definition of social hierarchies and opportunity structures? In the end, there could be a mitigating effect of strong inter-group vertical inequalities on potential for conflict, which is just as great as or even greater than the one from strong intra-group vertical inequalities. Regime repressiveness is a keyword in this context. An ability of group leaders to mobilize discontent depends on whether they can mobilize the necessary resources for conflict. In hindsight, high regime often repressiveness hindered the efforts of group leaders to mobilize their members. Those cases are dealt with soon as chapter III and IV move to aspects of hidden conflict.

Proposition 6: Internal Conflict

A final proposition of the h.i.-approach can be dealt with briefly. To a large extend, this proposition is entailed in the above discussion. It provides that, beyond being created within national boundaries, conflict has a tendency to stay internal. Past approaches frequently went from domestic to international scenarios. They either indicated that conflict only becomes a reality at the international level. Among others, this was the approach of Keynes' shifting-of-conflict thesis. Alternatively, international conflict provided an intensified version of domestic conflict. That was basically the idea behind the highest-stage-of-capitalism thesis developed after Marx. Chapter I has analyzed both theses. In contrast, the h.i.-approach responds to a particular need today, which is to go back from international to domestic scenarios. Thus, it goes hand in hand with a present trend at the international policy level. Increasingly, international organizations are discovering the status of groups within society as a target for interventions. Such debate involves a partial revision of past extension on the principles of national sovereignty and non-interference in internal affairs. Hence, it centers a new category of interventions, which are humanitarian interventions. Those interventions target particular threats that mark a change over prevailing threats during the Cold War period, i.e. interstate conflict and the confrontation of nuclear superpowers. Those threats are civil conflict, genocide, terrorism, etc. In a word they are internal conflicts.

Section 6. Towards Interventionism

In as much as they apply the h.i.-approach, international organizations seek to give direction to their long-term conflict prevention strategies. In order to define development interventions on the basis of this approach, the h.i.-approach requires translation into concrete economic indicators for group conflict. Particular variables need to be identified that measure economic inequalities, both horizontal and vertical ones. In principle, there are two methods of making the h.i.-approach operational, as well as to found interventions for conflict prevention: A first method is mainly quantitative in nature and pursued in econometrics. A second more qualitative approach captures in a descriptive manner situations that are likely to erupt into conflict. International organizations need to decide which approach to follow. For that, a clear separation of advantages and disadvantages of both methods is crucial.

Quantitative and Qualitative Indicators

Econometric analysis has investigated potential for conflict in relation to particular macro-economic variables. Among those variables most carefully considered are measures for economic decline, income inequality and inflation: Firstly, economic decline is commonly measured by a country's gross domestic product (GDP). Increased potential for conflict has been associated with cases where negative GDP growth was more than episodic, and the outcome of long-term politico-economic decay. As a variable to operationalize the h.i.-approach, measures for economic decline are rather inadequate, given the fact that we want to capture aspects of relative as opposed to absolute deprivation. Secondly, potential for conflict is more likely to be identified by means of monitoring income inequality. Normally measured by gross national product (GNP) per capita and the Gini index, income inequality is generally suited to account for economic discrepancies. However, it has been mentioned already that the h.i.-approach includes reservations against development thinking in the tradition of neo-classical welfare analysis, which often applies a narrow focus on income disparities. Thirdly, inflation, normally measured by annual changes in the consumer price index, may serve to cover some changes in the distribution of incomes, since it is indicative of an unresolved conflict over income claims, which the government has not been able to accommodate. Thus, some proponents of the h.i.-approach have suggested that the more rapid the inflation, the more discontented the population, and the greater the likelihood of conflict.

The h.i.-approach understands well the limitations of a pattern of research that deals with the economic side of conflict 'in some objective sense'. Quantitative research tends to hide important dimensions of the economic causes of conflict. For example, approaches focusing on economic decline and GDP rates contribute to an economic and social conditionality that promotes growth, efficiency and poverty reduction. However, while considering the over time dimension of economic deprivation, they ignore the group comparative dimension of conflict, and the impact of inter-group inequalities particularly. Also, as a measure of inequality income inequality may not correspond to the type of inequalities relevant for conflict. In general, income distribution schemes provide a vertical measure of inequalities. As Frances Stewart has stated correctly, they take 'everyone in society from top to bottom and measures their incomes and the consequent inequality. What is needed for our analysis is a horizontal measure of inequality which measures inequality between groups, where groups are defined by religion-ethnicity-class-region, according to the most appropriate type of group identification in the particular society.' In several countries, high income inequality has been present without leading to large-scale conflict, mainly because other factors prevailed. In example, widening income gaps were accompanied by an absolute improvement of living conditions, or regimes suppressed conflict.

Political factors, i.e. political power, are seen to join the below matrix as ends, but also as an important instrument for the achievement of economic power. Apart from being a goal in its own right, broad-based political participation of disadvantaged groups provides a first step to economic equity. In terms of interventions for the prevention of conflict, it also provides a way of dealing with the economic causes of conflict. A more narrow states agenda and reliance on the self-improving potential of the market when dealing with the economic sources of horizontal differentiation, are likely to appear in the later stage of industrialization. This can be said without endorsing the liberal model. In the later stage of industrialization, the market tends to take a larger role and government decisions are less discretionary and more rule-based.[41] Within the economic category, control over economic assets is an end in itself, but again it is also a means of securing income. As for all categories, the

[41] Stewart (2000) 6.

relevance of a particular element will vary according to different societies. This point has been stated correctly. For example, the allocation of housing under the social category is generally more important in industrialized countries. Access to land under the economic category is of huge importance in developing countries, where agriculture accounts for most output and employment.[42]

Fig. 2.10: Stewart's Matrix of Differentiation among Groups

Symbolic Factors		Politico-Economic Factors			
		Political Participation	Economic		Social Access and Situation
			Assets	Employment and Incomes	
ethnicity	Elements of Categories	government ministers	land	incomes / government employment	education
religion		parliament	human capital	private employment	health services
class		civil services	communal resources, incl. water	elite employment	safe water
region		army	minerals	rents	housing
conflict tradition		police	privately owned capital/credit	skilled	unemployment
		local government	government infrastructure	unskilled	poverty
		respect for human rights	security of assets against theft and destruction	informal sector opportunities	personal and household security

With the above matrix of differentiation among groups, propositions 3 and 4 have been rendered concrete. Both address the role of economic factors in conflict, and the importance of relative deprivation. The following structural and cultural critiques of the h.i.-approach are applied to particular propositions designed in this chapter. Main targets of chapter II's structural critique are propositions 4 and 5. Chapter IV's cultural critique is mainly directed at the precepts of proposition 3.

42 Stewart (2002) 9.

PART II

THE SOCIAL ECONOMY OF CONFLICT PREVENTION

Introduction

From Open Conflict to Hidden Conflict

A political economy of conflict culminates in the horizontal inequality approach (h.i.-approach). For international organizations, this approach promises to be a useful tool when embarking on a political economy of conflict prevention. Concretely, the h.i.-approach allows for defining long-term conflict prevention strategies. The present part argues the need to assimilate into such strategies a complementary social economy of conflict prevention. A social economy of conflict prevention pays increased attention to the interplay of economic with structural and cultural factors in conflict. The indication of a 'social economy' wishes to highlight the interplay of economic and social factors, rather than separate roles of both groups of factors in relation to conflict. A social economy of conflict prevention evolves on the basis of contemplations of the social economy of conflict. Those contemplations have the h.i.-approach as a specific target. As an economic theory of conflict, that approach assigns a certain role to cultural and some structural factors in conflict. This became clear during the preceding discussion. Thus, besides impacting on a political economy of conflict, the h.i.-approach also integrates signs of a social economy.

A comprehensive social economy of conflict focuses on a number of crucial limitations in the h.i.-approach, both as an academic concept and in practice. Those limitations are followed up on as separate structural and cultural debates. Chapter III challenges common perception concerning the interplay of economic and structural factors in conflict. Chapter IV discusses the impact of cultural factors on the economic basis of conflict. The reasons why both chapters are yet assigned to a common social economy of conflict are as follows:

Firstly, structural and cultural factors refer to the same context in which economic activity and economic conflict take place. That context is broadly social. Structural factors refer to a prime tangible feature of the social realm, i.e. the existence, position and relationship of fundamental social stakeholders. Cultural factors add individuality to that realm by means of various tangible and intangible aspects. Both structure and culture only exist where individuals socialize, i.e. where they form a social order. On the other hand, without structure and culture no social micro- or macro-cosmos can exist.

Secondly, although structural and cultural aspects surface different limitations of a narrowly political economy of conflict, they finally bring to the fore one overall limitation. A political economy of conflict experiences this limitation to the extent that it relies on the h.i.-approach. Part Two shows that the h.i.-approach fails to cater for a most important category of conflict. This category comprises cases of *hidden conflict*. Such inability has much to do with the way the concept of relative deprivation finds application within the h.i.-approach. No matter how essential the latter concept is for a correct appreciation of this approach, it has only been applied to the economic side of conflict. While its application justified one of six propositions, i.e. proposition 4, the concept of relative deprivation has not been probed for the structural and cultural sides of conflict. A narrow application damages the paradigmatic nature of the h.i.-approach. For that approach to assume a paradigmatic status in conflict debates, there is a need to consider the concept of relative deprivation in combination with structural and cultural factors. Only that way, cases of hidden conflict find integration.

CHAPTER III

STRUCTURE

The present chapter establishes a structural critique of the horizontal inequality approach (h.i.-approach). It explores circumstances under which the economic basis of this approach may not hold. This basis found particular expression in propositions 4 and 5. Thus, it consisted of the assumption that conflict evolves where worse-off perceptions loom, as the result of groups suffering from disproportionate economic grievances. The chapter shows that under particular socio-structural circumstances better-off perceptions can prevail and eradicate the ground for overt conflict. It is in these cases that hidden conflict becomes a reality.

Section 7. Better-off Perceptions

Structural circumstances that are likely to cultivate better-off perceptions include two major cases. Both have shown to hide potential for group conflict that lies with horizontal inequalities. A prime question regarding better-off perceptions concerns the owners of such perceptions. Also, what kind of social structure do they require in order to prevail over existing horizontal inequalities and worse-off perceptions? In a first class of cases, better-off perceptions are owned by the leaders of deprived groups. In a second class of cases, entire groups have been the owners of better-off perceptions. Especially, multi-grouped societies are likely to breed such perceptions. In as much as both classes of better-off perceptions concern the vertical component of social inequalities, they also force us to re-consider the interplay of horizontal and vertical inequalities in conflict, an issue the h.i.-approach has handled quite insufficiently.

Intra-Group Vertical Inequalities: Elite Incorporation

Obviously, the first class of cases of structural better-off perceptions refers to intra-group scenarios. It concerns group leaders in whom the perception prevails that they are better-off than ordinary group members. As part of the same perception, they feel less underprivileged in relation to groups that are better off in general. Why would this case be important with regard to potential for conflict? Chapter II has made it clear that according to the h.i.-approach group leaders play a decisive role in evolving group conflict. The h.i.-approach has shown to be highly concerned with the constructedness of conflict. The actors behind such constructing of conflict are supposedly group leaders, who consider group mobilization a powerful mechanism when following up on private goals. Apart from exploiting economic factors,[1] those leaders will often adopt a strategy of reworking historical memories to engender group identity.[2] In doing so, they will predominately act from greed, rather than in line with crucial economic grievances, which drive the behavior of ordinary group members. While group leaders and group members thus deviate with regard to their economic motives, both proceed within the confines of a relative deprivation-centered approach. Chapter II has argued that greed is bound to evolve relative to the economic situation of some other people. As such, it is not different form grievances. Otherwise, there was no reason to be greedy. Also, there are no general limitations as to the nature of goods people can feel deprived of. However, apart from subjecting greed and grievance to the concept of relative deprivation, we did not elaborate on the interplay of both kinds of economic factors. This happened in line with chapter II's focus on doctrines that have a place in the h.i.-approach.

Once conceding that conflict often results from economic greed, rather than being an organic outgrowth of crucial economic grievances, this ascertains two things: Firstly, it confirms the decisive role of group leaders in evolving group conflict. Secondly, one arrives, theoretically so far, at an option that group leaders will occasionally decide against conflict. Only the first point finds recognition within the h.i.-approach. The second point consults those structural better-off perceptions initially mentioned. It re-investigates how intra-group vertical inequalities influence inter-group horizontal inequalities, knowing that the latter are composed of two factions, i.e. economic grievances of group members and economic greed of group leaders. First of all, we may repeat the most essential point about the relationship between inter-group horizontal and intra-group vertical inequalities discussed with Chapter II. Hence, highest potential for inter-group group conflict has been identified in cases where strong inter-group horizontal inequalities (+HI) coincided with patterns of weak intra-group vertical inequalities (-V^{IA}I).

The following argument serves to assimilate this previous finding into the present analysis: 'Weak intra-group inequalities are indicative of group members and group leaders sharing a similar economic status. Whenever this is the case, there is no room for group leaders to develop better-off perceptions vis-à-vis their own group. Therefore, options to satisfy greed will be identified externally, and lead to inter-group conflict. Correspondingly, if intra-group inequalities are strong, and the economic situation inside the group differs greatly, group leaders might form better-off perceptions, and no overt conflict will occur.' Deviating from this somewhat straightforward argument, the h.i.-approach reviews the same evidence, i.e. weak intra-group inequalities combining with strong inter-group horizontal inequalities, from a purely *group cohesion*-centered angle. Thus, where intra-group inequalities are weak, group cohesion will be achieved more easily, because group members are likely to share into the goals of group leaders. Conversely, where strong intra-group inequalities prevail, processes of group cohesion and inter-group conflict could fail

[1] D. Turton, 'War and Ethnicity: Global Connections and Local Violence in East Africa and Former Yugoslavia', in *Oxford Development Studies*, No. 25, Special Issue: War, Economy and Society (1997) 84.

[2] F. Stewart, 'Crisis Prevention: Tackling Horizontal Inequalities', in *Queen Elizabeth House Working Paper Series*, No. 33 (2000) 4.

to materialize. However, when focusing on patterns of group cohesion we also signal our disinterest in low potential conflict, because we preserve an exclusive interest in those settings that get inter-group conflict underway. For such a lens, strong intra-group vertical inequalities will only constitute cases where those settings are absent (see Fig. 3.1). Chapter II referred to this lens as the h.i.-approach's 'optimistic explanation' of the mitigating influence strong intra-group vertical inequalities have on potential for conflict. Whoever accepts this lens, tends to betray himself about two important points.

Firstly, if vertical inequalities are merely considered an impediment in the process of group mobilization, one also ignores that intra-group vertical inequalities are suited to attract patterns of *rebellion*. Thus, inter-group conflict may only be prevented at the cost of intra-group conflict. Chapter II mentioned this point, while also stating that the primordial nature and particular modes of operation of conflict groups often avoid rebellion. In terms of this primordial nature, a common symbolic system frequently weighs stronger than economic discrepancies. Also, incentive-based modes of operation ensure that economic rewards and penalties are delivered, depending on whether group members comply with group objectives.[3] Secondly and more importantly, the group cohesion-centered approach looses track of crucial socio-economic inequalities, as they exist within groups. The critical point here is that strong intra-group vertical inequalities may indeed reduce potential for conflict. But the actual reasons for this mitigating effect may be rooted in better-off perceptions of group leaders, rather than in failing group cohesion. By failing to look at the broader set of structural preconditions within groups, the h.i.-approach ignores a important first category of hidden conflict.[4]

Fig. 3.1: Structural Model of Conflict Categories

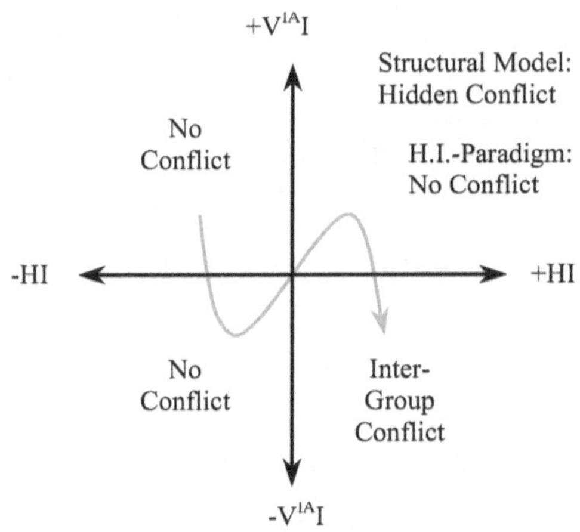

[3] J. Heyer et al., 'Group Behaviour and Development', in *WIDER Working Paper Series*, No. 161 (1999) 8.

[4] Acronyms: +HI = Strong Horizontal Inequalities; -HI = Weak Horizontal Inequalities; $+V^{IA}I$ = Strong Intra-Group Vertical Inequalities; $-V^{IA}I$ = Weak Intra-Group Vertical Inequalities; $+V^{IE}I$ = Strong Inter-Group Vertical Inequalities; $-V^{IE}I$ = Weak Inter-Group Vertical Inequalities.

Experience shows that in some African countries an informal backroom pattern of inclusiveness is far from being uncommon. This pattern relies on generous clientelist ties with minority group leaders to keep the dominant group in power. It is also in these cases that group leaders do not literally exploit the economic basis of their own group. Rather, clientelist ties subsequently add to the wealth of those leaders, thus also increasing intra-group vertical inequalities, while decreasing incentives for inter-group conflict. Especially since the end of the Cold War, power-sharing and transition to democracy are increasingly anticipated to be formally negotiated at large, inclusive peace and reconciliation conferences. Politicians are expected to attain office through open competitive elections, rather than through skillful regional and ethnic manipulation. This has blurred our picture of the existence of such corrupt practices.[5] At the same time, opportunism and willingness of minority group leaders to accept *elite incorporation* continue.[6]

From the instrumentalist view of conflict that also characterizes the h.i.-approach ('constructedness of conflict'), group leaders are more extremist than group members. They abuse group identities for their private goals. However, given that instrumentalist view, there is no plausible explanation as to why group leaders should not resort to opportunist elite incorporation, provided they deem such incorporation to suite their private interests in a better way. Especially in cases when ethnic salience is low, group leaders are likely to form inter-ethnic coalitions which above all benefit their private interests.[7]

Inter-Group Vertical Inequalities: Multi-Modal Societies and Middle Groups

In other cases, one needs to consider the conflict mitigating potential of better-off perceptions for the relationship between groups. These cases evoke yet another social structure where vertical inequalities exert their influence on existing horizontal inequalities. However, different from the cases just mentioned, those vertical inequalities concern inter-group rather than intra-group scenarios. In the first place, this may appear to inflate our understanding of vertical inequalities. It may do so particularly if we continue to apply the h.i.-approach, which supersedes the Marxian model of inter-group inequalities considered in chapter I. As for this earlier model, inter-group inequalities comprised a pattern of vertical class antagonisms, i.e. Marx famous proletariat-bourgeoisie dichotomy. In other words, a critique of the horizontal

---

5 I. Spears, 'Understanding Inclusive Peace Agreements in Africa: The Problems of Sharing Power', in *Third World Quarterly*, Vol. 21, No. 1 (2000) 105-118. For example, upon the Dergue's defeat in Ethiopia in 1991, the Ethiopian Peoples' Revolutionary Democratic Front's (EPRDF) strategy shifted, and the new regime did not consist of representatives from each of the major liberalization fronts in the country. Rather it required only the inclusion of individuals from the most prominent ethnic groups who would follow the EPRDS's lead and yet could still claim to represent those ethnic groups.

6 K. Chandra, 'Elite Incorporation in Multi-Ethnic Societies', Paper Presentation at the India and the Politics of Developing Countries Conference, Kellogg Institute for International Studies, University of Notre Dame, USA, 24-26 September 1999, 24. In Indian states Pradesh, Punjab, and Karnataka, scheduled caste elites followed a common pattern, trying to enter the Bahujan Samaj Pary by subdividing ethnic groups and therefore redefining themselves as leaders of their own ethnic groups.

7 E. Jenne, 'Political Opportunism and Ethnic Mobilization: A Triadic Model for Predicting the Ethnicization of Politics in New States', accessed at http://www.sscnet.ucla.edu/ soc/groups/scr/jenne.pdf.

inequality approach on the strength of inter-group vertical inequalities seems to run the risk of re-accommodating for the Marxian model of vertical social strata, which was ignorant to horizontal inequalities. Eventually, things could boil down to different conflict paradigms that are simply incommensurable.

For one major reason this risk is minor. The following critique centers a kind of social structure that rules out dichotomous thinking in the first place, no matter whether such thinking concerns horizontal or vertical groups. The keyword in this context is *multi-modality*. With multi-modal societies, we mean societies that are multi-grouped, that is, societies that exceed two main groups and one major dichotomy. Multi-ethnic societies are examples of multi-modal societies. Multi-modal societies are also those in which immobilizing effects occur, because particular social groups hold better-off perceptions in respect of lower strata groups, rather than worse-off perceptions in respect of dominant groups. These groups form social middle groups, e.g. ethnic middle ranks. Their tendency to make peace with existing status quo assigns a vertical rather than horizontal dimension to inequalities applying to those societies. Also, according to the idea of horizontal inequalities intergroup inequalities exclude any hierarchy or continuum. They tend to establish a sharp distinction between privileged and underprivileged groups. However, this situation does rarely apply to multi-modal societies.

Academically, the idea of multi-modal societies modifies a scenario developed by early hour structuralists dedicated to disclose the so-called imperialist underbrush of the international system after World War II. Although integrating a focus on suppressed conflict, Johan Galtung's structural theory of imperialism and Immanuel Wallerstein's World System school of thought were restricted to international scenarios. As a pattern of observation, such focus was widely in line with the circumstances of the Cold War. Where the first school set the notion of go-between nations, the latter established the concept of semi-peripheral countries. As the flipside of focusing on the status of countries in their relation to each other, these structuralist approaches were hardly concerned with the status of groups within societies.

Galtung's account of go-between nations intended to unveil patterns of *structural violence* in the international system. Later, other authors took up this approach.[8] All these approaches paid little attention to how trichotomous structures alter potential for conflict otherwise embedded in dichotomous structures. Not to mention that such being trichotomous would have been declared a pre-condition for the international system to be stable. Efforts to observe patterns of interspersing of go-between nations between center and periphery were fully focused on one major goal. This goal was to better explain the possibility of considerable distance between the extreme center and the extreme periphery. Primarily, such distance was estimated in terms of technological progress, which included means of destruction and communication. Structurally, such progress was seen to materialize in distinct positions of all three types of nations with regard to degrees of economic processing. Those degrees were considered structural in as much as they complemented each other. Go-between na-

---

8 See T.M. Shaw and M.J. Grieve, 'The Political Economy of Resources: Africa's Future in the Global Environment', in *The Journal of Modern African Studies*, Vol. 16, No. 1 (1978) 12; T. Smith, 'Requiem or New Agenda for Third World Studies?', in *World Politics*, Vol. 37, No. 4 (1985) 556.

tions would be those that exchanged semi-processed goods with highly processed goods upwards (center), and semi-processed goods with raw materials downwards (periphery). Although, to that purpose, the elites of all three nations would establish firm ties of a harmony of interest, the whole set of structural relationships was considered as one of structural violence.[9]

In a much stricter sense, Immanuel Wallerstein's World System school of thought has applied the notion of semi-peripheral countries to stress that the international system, more than coincidentally bringing about some go-between nations, could not function without being tri-modal. This is remarkable, because in an initial phase the notion of semi-peripheral countries had been used primarily to sort out whether those countries could be made the carriers of system-wide transformation, thus implying confrontation with the center states. Such confrontation was seen to depend critically on semi-peripheral countries, socialist or non-socialist ones. The touchstone of legitimacy was supposed to be with the former. The arguments for such focus on confrontation, rather than structural violence, had been collected in critical discussion with the concepts of growth, progress and development. In application to semi-peripheral countries, these concepts seemed to promise little more but the center states' willingness to achieve a relative advantage for some of those countries. A theoretical reference point for such thinking was a 'Tadpole Philosophy', which Richard Henry Tawney defined as follows: The 'consolation which it offers for social evils consists in the statement that exceptional individuals [states] can succeed in evading them [...] as though opportunities for talents to rise could be equalized in a society [world system] where the circumstances surrounding it from birth are themselves unequal.'[10] Only in late expositions of World System thinking a deviating focus comes to the fore. It centers on semi-peripheral countries as countries that keep the international system and global order functioning. Only here, the idea of a system-sustaining middle sector, or tri-modal arrangement, takes the lead. More precisely, this system-sustaining middle sector was now considered to provide for a group of countries that think of themselves as a sector better-off than the lower sector, rather than as worse-off compared to the upper sector.[11]

Besides focusing on multi-modal societies rather than international scenarios, our analysis deviates from Wallerstein's World System school of thought in two important ways: Firstly, for that school economic inequality between core, semi-periphery and periphery states were predominately caused politically, i.e. by power differentials. Raúl Prebisch, another structuralist and former Executive Secretary of the United Nations Economic Commission for Latin America and the Caribbean, did not consider semi-periphery states in a systematic manner. However, by means of what is nowadays known as the Prebisch-Singer thesis, he designated market structures as

---

[9] J. Galtung, 'Structural Theory of Imperialism', in *Journal of Peace Research*, Vol. 8, No. 2 (1971) 104.

[10] R.H. Tawney, *Equality* [1931], New York: Capricorn Books (1961) 108-109. Quoted in I. Wallerstein, 'Semi-Peripheral Countries and the Contemporary World Crisis', in *Theory and Society*, Vol. 3, No. 4 (1976) 466.

[11] I. Wallerstein, 'Dependence in an Interdependent World', in C. Goddard et al. (eds.), *International Political Economy: State Market-Market Relations in the Changing Global Order*, London: Lynne Rienner Publishers (1996) 178.

the root cause of inequalities in the world system.[12] Thus, he focused on economic operations as the key cause of inequalities. Thus, he also came up with the concept of import substituting industrialization. Secondly, Wallerstein's theory was openly Marxist. Approving his theory implies endorsing one particular school in political economy, i.e. Marxian political economy.

Before returning from this brief excurse into the early structuralist roots of multi-modal thinking, one should add the following. Tri-modal and multi-modal thinking may easily be transferred from international to domestic scenarios, because here such thinking originated. It did yet without a focus on hidden conflict. Another all-distinguishing feature concerns the fact that these initial attempts were heavily pre-occupied with middle class phenomena, i.e. vertical inequalities in a more classical sense. Compared to such preoccupation with middle classes, this analysis focuses on middle groups that are mostly primordial. For example, in a context focusing on the developing world, the term middle class has found entry into analysis of processes of de-colonization, where it has also been studied for the limited role of certain middle groups in violent nationalist movements, i.e. their cooperation with the colonial powers.[13] At the same time of centering middle class phenomena, it has been acknowledged early on that multi-modal structures are more difficult to observe where they are not hedged around by means of primordial distinctions, i.e. visible and consensual racial, ethnic or geographical dividing lines.[14] For this is certainly true, the present investigation is in a much more comfortable situation. In yet another sense, it is so. Earlier multi-modal thinking had to bother with one issue complicating the life of those eager to make the semi-periphery the carrier of system-wide transformation and confrontation with the center. That issue was the competition existing *between* semi-peripheral countries, which were obviously many for an angle investigating the 'world system'. Almost naturally, such competition, essentially for scarce resources, would divert attention from conflict with the center. Therefore, a prime question concerned the conditions under which semi-peripheral countries would favor a strategy of collective transnational syndicalism, as a result of fears that they may lose out in a game of each on his own.[15] Against their will, which was for system-change, early structuralists thus came across another version of hidden conflict. Compared to that, an investigation focusing on domestic scenarios will rarely face middle strata comprising competing middle groups. It neither has to bother with cases of middle sector competition, nor must it profit from them, i.e. in terms of evidence for vertical structures that suppress open conflict.

Better-off perceptions can have a substantial impact in multi-modal societies. The h.i.-approach reveals an inability to cater for important structural factors in conflict, given the limited number of relative deprivation scenarios it recognizes. Chapter II made it clear that those scenarios are essentially designed to reflect dichotomous relationships, i.e. differentials in economic assets between two groups A and B (Fig.

---

12 UNECLAC, *The Economic Development of Latin America and its Principal Problems*, Lake Success: UN Dept. of Economic Affairs (1950).

13 I. Wallerstein and M. Hechter, 'Social Rank and Nationalism: Some African Data' in *The Public Opinion Quarterly*, Vol. 34, No. 3 (1970) 360-370.

14 Galtung (1971) 104.

15 Wallerstein (1976) 470.

3.2). While debating fragmentation[16] and polarization indices,[17] Frances Stewart occasionally mentions that 'it seems plausible that in highly fragmented societies group differences are less salient personally and politically than in societies where there are a small number of large rivalrous groups.'[18] However, this insight has mainly been related to the symbolic side in conflict, i.e. to religious groups. It has hardly been considered for the economic side, also meaning that better-off perceptions have played no role.

Fig. 3.2: Bi-Modal Model of Relative Deprivation

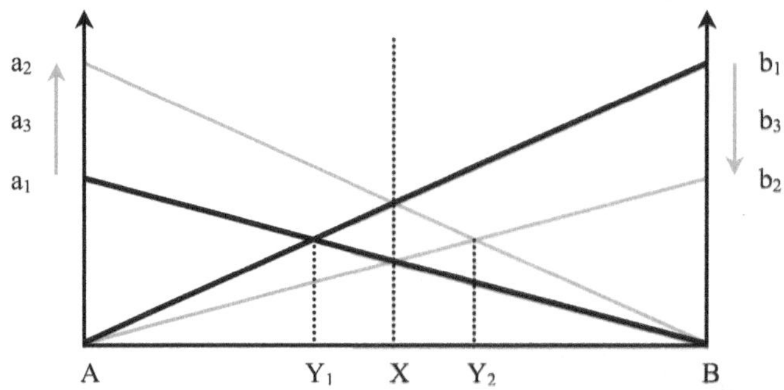

An exhaustive review of the issue of relative deprivation requires factoring in a template for multi-stakeholder scenarios. Graphically, such factoring in can be visualized in two ways. In both cases, a group C joins the economic distribution fight between groups A and B. Often, such proceeding will require extension to four, five and even more groups. For presentational purposes, this analysis sticks to trichotomous structures. A first way of capturing these kinds of structure is presented in Fig. 3.3, which basically comprises a mirror image of Fig. 3.2. Rather than only capturing groups within a trichotomous structure, it also suggests that the set of relationships within this trichotomy is linear. In that sense, newly assigned group C, which comprises the worst-off group, will mainly feel deprived in respect of middle group A, rather than bother with the comparative economic status of best-off group B.

The latter kind of perception could apply to group A. However, according to the idea of better-off perceptions, practically, this is not the case. This aspect of possible and actual perceptions of relative deprivation can be made even clearer by means of a second model sketched in Fig. 3.4. The model evolves by flipping axis AB in Fig. 3.3 vertically, thus offering a bird's view perspective on the earlier model. In the absence of any absolute component (a_n, b_n), the model captures divisions of economic assets between groups A and B.

---

16 C. Taylor and M.C. Hudson, *The World Handbook of Political and Scientific Indicators*, New Haven: Yale University Press (1972).

17 J. Estaban and D. Ray, 'On the Measurement of Polarisation', in *Econometrica*, Vol. 62, No.4 (1994) 819-851.

18 F. Stewart, 'Horizontal Inequalities: A Neglected Dimension of Development', in *Queen Elizabeth House Working Paper Series*, No. 81 (2002) 12.

Fig. 3.3: Multi-Modal Model of Relative Deprivation I

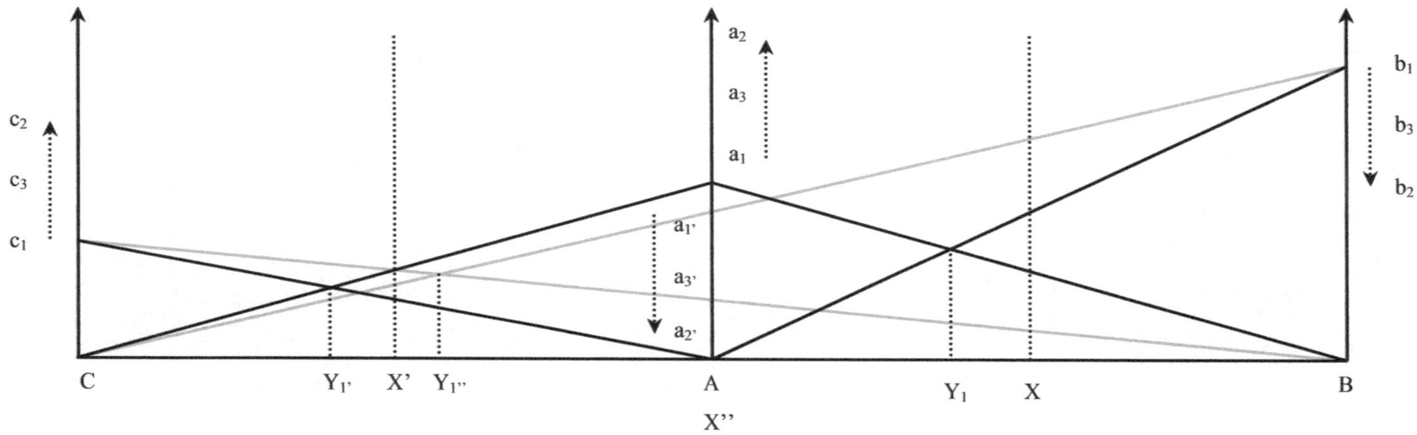

Thus, it retains equilibrium point X and point Y_1, which marks the proportional deviation from equilibrium in the comparative economic situation of both groups. One further designs the structural relationships between groups A and C as well as B and C as evens of equal length, consequently deriving triangle ABC. Within this triangle another triangle XX'X'' marks the case that divisions of economic assets among the three groups are in equilibrium. Only in this case, triangle XX'X'' is isosceles. Naturally, any economic discrepancy > 0 between the worst-off and middle group, as well as the middle and best-off group, e.g. $Y_1Y_{1'}Y_{1''}$, must result in increased economic discrepancies between the worst-off and best-off groups, thus distorting the triangle.

Fig. 3.4: Multi-Modal Model of Relative Deprivation II

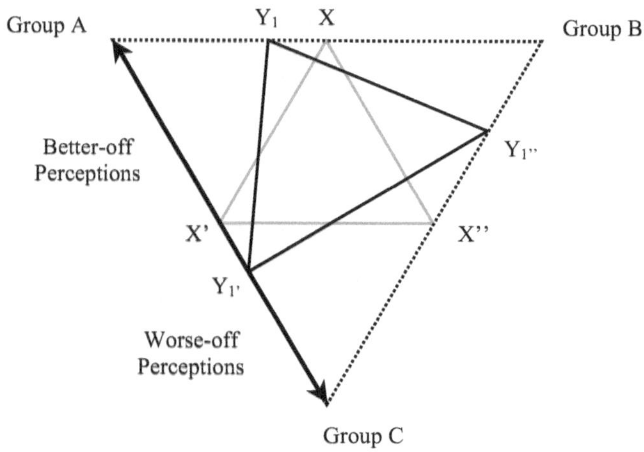

In the fist place, such increased discrepancies would seem to suggest isolated attacks of group C on group B (case 1), rather than similar attacks on group A (case 2), because group B is where group C could get the most out of redistribution conflict. This would also seem to be more likely than group A attacking group B (case 3). Alternatively, groups A and C could target group B's economic privileges in a joint manner (case 4). In yet another case, group C decides to attack both group A and group B at the same time (case 5). Any of those five *reference cases* seems more likely than four other groups of cases, one of which comprises cases of hidden conflict. Obviously, a second group, where the stimulus for conflict is to come from dominant groups (cases 6, 7, 8, 9, 10), comprises a series of *redundant cases*. The h.i.-approach acknowledges correctly that in very special cases conflict occurs, because privileged groups fear that underprivileged groups could demand more resources. However, apart from not building on multi-modal structures, these cases are rather questionable, to the extent that aspects of structural violence have been more efficient for maintaining the privileged status of dominant groups. According to a frequently observed phenomenon, dominant group B will rely on means such as *re-*

gime repressiveness, rather than go into open conflict with groups A and C, or any of them.[19] The corresponding behavior of group A foresees patterns of *domination within domination* when dealing with group C. For example, in India's South Gujarat region and other occasions, groups of urban informal sector workers have been observed for using the weakened position of groups arriving from rural areas to discharge their frustration, therefore giving rise to similar patterns of domination.[20] In return, the silent behavior expected and even demanded from those 'aliens' from rural areas contributed to the fact that no large-scale conflict occurred.[21] In yet other cases, regime repressiveness and domination within domination may actually come together.

Besides the reference and redundant cases, a number of *improbable cases* can be designed. According to these cases, upper and lower strata could, for example, unit against the middle stratum for a shift that moves the lower stratum up and helps the upper stratum to keep the middle stratum at a distance (case 11). Alternatively, the middle stratum could decide to go into conflict against the upper stratum, while simultaneously attacking the lower stratum, in a struggle to keep this stratum within its established confines (case 12). In yet another case, the stimulus for conflict could come from the lower stratum and target the better-off group in next reach, i.e. the middle group. Increasingly conscious of its own disadvantaged position, the latter joins in the fervor and takes up the case with the upper stratum. Eventually, that stratum turns conflict into a spiral by addressing the original source of conflict, i.e. the worst-off group (case 13). While all these cases are rather improbable already, a fourth group comprises a series of cases that are logically possible, however, practically absurd (cases 14 to 21). The list of cases presented in Fig. 3.5 is long but certainly not exhaustive.

Only after this fourth group, cases of *hidden conflict* are considered, if we take the h.i.-approach as a precedent. Cases of hidden conflict are certainly different from any of the reference cases mentioned. So are they from the redundant and improbable cases. Needless to say that this also applies for the group of absurd cases. However, for the following reason they could be linked to cases of structural violence considered under the group of redundant cases. According to the present definition, hidden conflict is linked to better-off perceptions of middle groups, e.g. to better-off perceptions group A holds in respect of group C's worse-off economic situation. In as much as this is the case, hidden conflict is at variance with aspects of regime repressiveness, as far as the relationship between middle groups and best-off groups is concerned.

---

19 E. Muller, 'Income Inequality, Regime Repressiveness and Political Violence', in *American Sociological Review*, Vol. 50, No. 1 (1985) 47-61; E. Muller, 'Income Inequality and Political Violence: The Effect of Influential Cases', in *American Sociological Review*, Vol. 51, No. 3 (1986) 441-445; E. Muller, 'Inequality, Repression, Violence: Issues of Theory and Research Design', in *American Sociological Review*, Vol. 53, No. 5 (1988) 799-806.

20 J. Scott, *Weapons of the Weak: Everyday Forms of Peasant Resistance*, New Haven: Yale University Press (1990).

21 J. Breman, *Footloose Labour: Working in India's Informal Economy*, Cambridge: Cambridge University Press (1996) 234.

Fig. 3.5: Tri-Modal Societies and Conflict

Reference Cases:

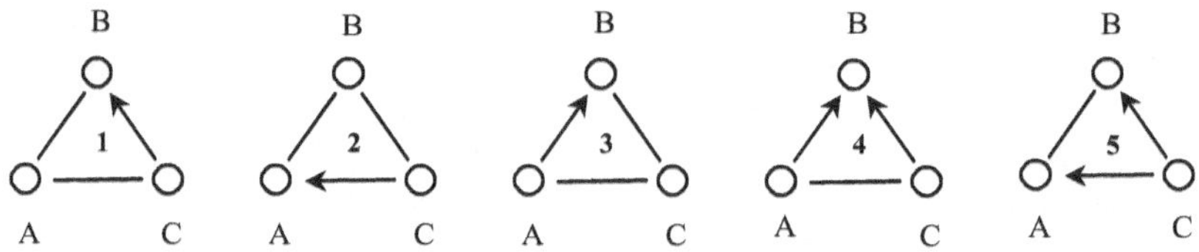

Redundant Cases:

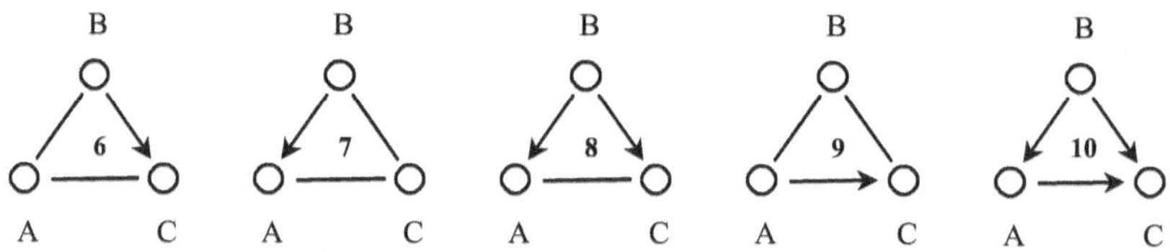

Improbable Cases:

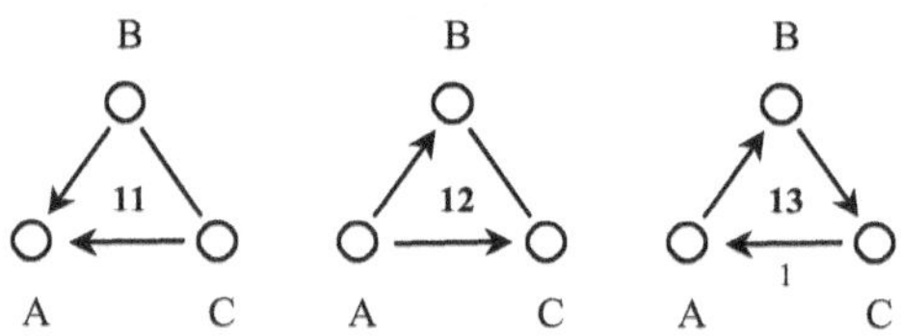

Absurd Cases:

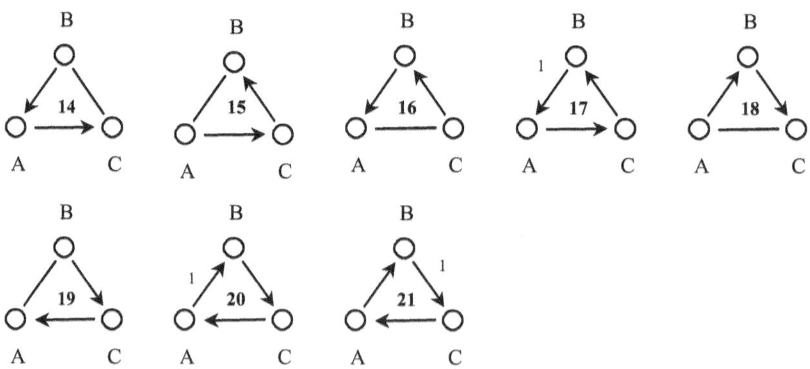

Then again, for the flipside of better-off perceptions of middle group A are still worse-off perceptions of group C, some patterns of domination within domination on the part of the middle group are necessary to keep group C down. These patterns may combine with aspects of regime repressiveness that best-off group B applies to the lower stratum. In the end, this case only reasons common sense. If both the center group and the semi-peripheral group have no interest in conflict, it should be very difficult for peripheral groups to get conflict underway. The resulting situation will be one of hidden conflict.

An entirely different question is the following one: The fact that hidden conflict is at odds with the identified reference cases does not preempt per se that the latter are not going to prevail in reality. Therefore, how can we sustain the practical relevance of cases of hidden conflict against the reference cases? After all, posing a question like that means going astray of the main point this analysis seeks to move forward. Therefore, an analysis of hidden conflict cannot pretend to replace a reality of conflict that frequently converges with the identified reference cases. It merely stresses that a thorough account of conflict exceeds the sum total of open conflict situations captured by those reference cases. Certainly, there are some arguments as to why one or the other reference case does not apply under particular circumstances; eventually, also unveiling a case of hidden conflict. For example, cases of concerted attacks of middle and worst-off groups on the established privileges of best-off groups (case 4) can be questioned, in as much as worst-off groups have been skeptical of joining violent movements with middle groups, because they feared that economic gains from conflict will not spread as far as them.[22] Also, isolated attacks of worst-off groups on the established order (case 5), or either group better-off (cases 1 and 2), may rarely succeed, because they lack the necessary opportunity structure provided in cooperative middle groups. In these and other cases, aspects of regime repressiveness and patterns of domination within domination may contribute to suppress overt conflict. However, in order to distinguish these cases from cases where better-off perceptions result in hidden conflict, the pertinent notion of *structural violence* should be kept. Also, different from cases of hidden conflict, cases of regime repressiveness are not dependent on societies being tri- or multi-modal. Certainly, the existence of structural violence has often led to question the meaningfulness of restricting conflict debates to a narrow set of reference cases. In that sense, the concept of structural violence and the concept of hidden conflict feed into the same criticism. The goal with both concepts is to encourage policy makers and academia to broaden their scope, so as to integrate a concern for those societies where conflict is less obvious and escapes a set of reference cases.

Multi-modality provides the ground on which better-off perceptions thrive. However, better-off perception may flourish even better where societies consist of several primordial groups, rather than featuring a trichotomous social structures. They may do so, particularly under conditions where those groups are assigned to a *continuum* with gradual discrepancies regarding their economic situations. While such continuum has been recognized before,[23] a systematic exploration of mitigating effects on potential for conflict has been rare. A defining characteristic of such structural continuum is that economic gaps vanish, although economic differences between society's lowest order (group C) and highest order (group B_3) are sizeable. Society becomes a breeding place for hidden conflict in these cases, because it takes less for better-off perceptions to prevail than for perceptions of relative deprivation to develop.

---

22 Wallerstein and Hechter (1970) 370.

23 Galtung (1971) 104.

Fig. 3.6: Hidden Conflict in Tri-Modal and Multi-Modal Societies

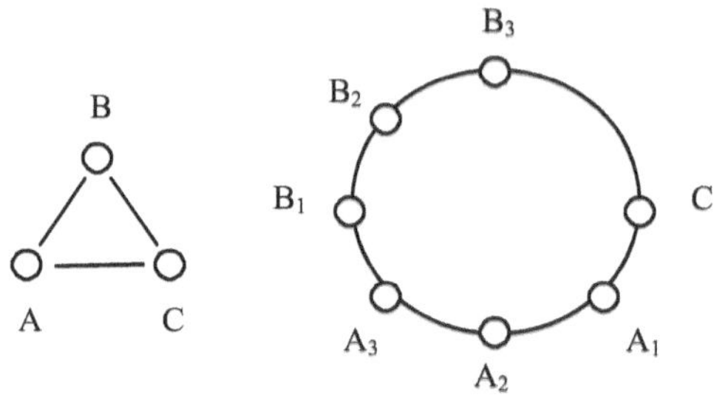

With the last remarks concerning multi-grouped societies, the present investigation has reached its end. Before continuing our debate of hidden conflict in relation to economic and cultural factors, one can sum up the observed interacting of economic and structural factors in conflict.

Section 8. Hidden Conflict

First Part

A major premise of this investigation has been that socio-economic factors, likely to influence potential for conflict, require analysis by means of one theory of interpretation. Only that way, cases can be identified where these factors reinforce or interfere with each other. In order to be such a theory, the concept of relative deprivation requires extension to structural factors. Once this is being done, it shows that horizontal inequalities between groups can result in high and in low potential for conflict. Thus, they can result in hidden conflict. A decision as to which option shall prevail in individual cases is dependent on the existence of particular vertical inequalities. Under all circumstances, those vertical inequalities separate from the Marxian account of such inequalities explored in chapter I. Vertical inequalities in the former sense are likely to breed better-off perceptions. Concretely, such vertical inequalities and better-off perceptions have been analyzed for two scenarios, intra-group scenarios on the one hand, and inter-group scenarios on the other. In the first class of cases, leaders of deprived groups have been the owners of better-off perceptions, for example, as a result of patterns of elite incorporation on the part of dominant groups. After all, if group mobilization is largely about minority group leaders following up on private economic goals, there is no plausible explanation why those leaders should not resort to opportunist elite incorporation, provided they deem such cooperation to suite their private interests. In a second class of cases, entire social groups have been the owners of better-off perceptions. The basis for these kinds of better-off perceptions were multi-modal societies, i.e. societies composed of more than two primordial groups. Better-off perceptions have been attached to middle groups. Overall, this discovery leads to a partial revision of previous thinking. Therefore, one needs to recognize structural circumstances where no bonds exist between groups in society's lower order, circumstances where middle and worst-off groups are unlikely to join hands for a concerted attack on the established order. These circumstances also bring to the front patterns of hidden conflict.

An even application of the concept of relative deprivation to all socio-economic factors in conflict can result in reduced potential for conflict. On the whole, this fact should trigger two consequences: Firstly, there is a need to go beyond open-conflict societies. Attention must be given to the problems of societies that only superficially are non-conflict societies. Secondly, a thorough consideration of socio-economic factors in conflict leads to serious challenges on the explanatory power of the h.i.-approach in conflict debates. In various cases, other concepts ought to complement this approach.

CHAPTER IV

CULTURE

Section 9. Symbolic Factors Revisited

Beyond the Linear Model of Relative Deprivation

After the preceding structural critique, the present chapter brings forward a cultural critique of the horizontal inequality approach (h.i. approach). Both critiques were already said to be complementary in that they work on the same overall limitation of that approach, i.e. failure to cater for cases of hidden conflict. A structural critique related such failure to a narrow understanding of the concept of relative deprivation. The present socio-cultural critique evolves with a consequential application of this concept to all factors in conflict, economic and symbolic ones. At the same time, both critiques are characterized by one major difference. A structural critique was faced with the situation that the h.i.-approach basically ignores structural factors, particularly as to their interplay with economic factors. Compared to that, economic and symbolic factors have been linked, but their interplay has been explained in an unsatisfactory manner. Thus, the concept of relative deprivation has not been applied to both groups of factors. Once more, such deficiency puts at risk the paradigmatic nature of the h.i.-approach.

Initially, one has to go back to the point that gave meaning to the relationship between economic and symbolic conflict factors in the h.i.-approach. As one of six major propositions, chapter II has assigned proposition 3 to capture this relationship. Proposition 3 thus specifies that 'symbolic factors beget stereotyping, whereas economic factors beget conflict.' Chapter II has granted the h.i.-approach a major achievement in assigning economic and symbolic factors to a mutual demand relationship. Rather dogmatically, earlier debate of the root causes of organized group conflict has been divided into two main strands. A rather exclusive focus on economic factors has been present in theories observing David Campbell's Realist Group Conflict Theory, having set forth that conflict is about 'real' issues.[1] A deviating focus on symbolic factors has been found in Henry Tajfel's Social Identity Theory, and others the like.[2] As opposed to this, the h.i.-approach develops the relationship between different conflict factors to the point that these factors virtually *demand* each other. With this relationship, we move away from a pattern of observation where each factor had a direct link to conflict, also providing that it was a sufficient precondition for conflict to evolve. The ultimately comfortable thing about such proceeding has been related to the possibility of invoking an infinite number of

[1] D. Campbell, 'Ethnocentrism and Other Altruistic Motives', in D. Levine (ed.), *Nebraska Symposium on Motivation, Vol. 13*, Lincoln: University of Nebraska Press (1965) 283-311.

[2] H. Tajfel (ed.), *Differentiation between Social Groups*, London: Academic Press (1978).

factors, for one could always be sure that one or the other factor would work. Different from that, the h.i.-approach assigns conflict factors to a *linear model*, with each factor accounting for a necessary although non-sufficient precondition for conflict. Beyond confirming that economic and symbolic factors comprise necessary preconditions for conflict, their concrete interplay must be explained. A thorough account of their interplay applies the concept of relative deprivation to both groups of factors. After all, the h.i.-approach stands and falls with this concept. At the same time, one should note that symbolic factors don't form a monolithic bloc. An application of the concept of relative deprivation to symbolic factors might result in different impact depending on whether groups are ethnic, racial or religious. Such difference could influence the formation of cases of hidden conflict in a critical way.

A Synthesis Model of Relative Deprivation

Despite linking economic and symbolic factors in conflict through a concept of mutual demand, an overall implication of proposition 3 has been that organized group conflict presents two independent stages. Group-specific access to economic resources will provide the ground on which groups can be mobilized in a second stage by abusing group identities. Subject to these provisions, the h.i.-approach gives expression to a linear model of evolving group conflict. Against the same background, Frances Stewart has noted that 'a range of deprivations—economic, social and political—enable political leaders to use symbolic systems of a grouping as an effective mechanism of group mobilisation.'[3] In quoting this linear model, proposition 4 has applied the concept of relative deprivation to economic factors, and economic grievance factors particularly.

Fig. 4.1: Synthesis Model of Factors in Conflict

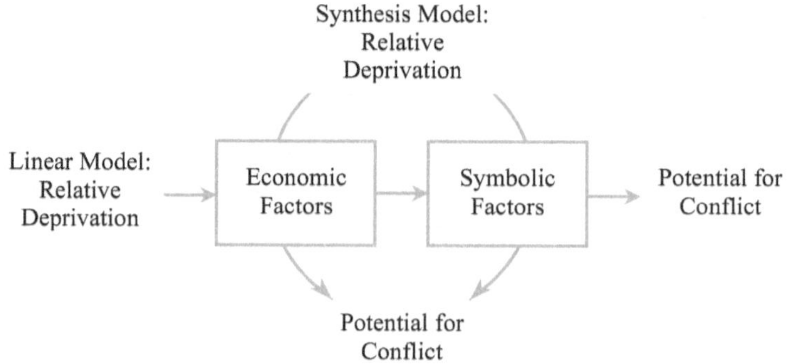

[3] F. Stewart, 'Horizontal Inequalities: A Neglected Dimension of Development', in *Queen Elizabeth House Working Paper Series*, No. 81 (2002) 9.

A key question concerning the concept of relative deprivation is why this concept should be considered for symbolic factors at all. At a first glance, it seems to comprise a purely economic concept, not really applicable to ethnic, racial and religious factors in conflict. Therefore, why would we even consider something as a *synthesis model* of relative deprivation? The concept of relative deprivation appears to be a quantitative concept, whereby a given stock of economic assets owned by group A is measured against the economic situation of group B. Conversely, differences that occur at the level of symbolic factors seem widely qualitative in nature. From a theoretical perspective, it makes no sense to say that group A is better or worse-off than group B by virtue of its ethnic root, racial origin or religious belief system, as can be done with economic differences. Certainly, doubts as to whether symbolic factors are accessible to quantitative measurement cannot mean that these factors are irrelevant. Not despite but rather because of their widely qualitative nature, symbolic differences are often so powerful tools in conflict. This is also the reason why conflict groups often apply a qualitative lens to antagonist groups, thus involving an argument of the following kind: 'The symbolic systems of these groups are utterly different from our own symbolic system. Therefore, they must be either inferior to ours (ethnic and racial systems) or wrong (religious systems).'

If, different from economic factors, groups are likely to bring themselves into a qualitative relationship with other groups as far as symbolic factors are concerned, and if there is indeed no point in measuring symbolic systems, why then would we consider a quantitative concept such as the concept of relative deprivation for symbolic factors in conflict? Above all, proponents of the h.i.-approach will ask this question.

The answer why one should do so is almost too simple if considered properly. There can be no doubt that a symbolic system cannot be quantified and weighed against others. Also, there are few doubts that the unique quality of each symbolic system has seduced groups to exaggerate the difference between themselves and other groups. However, just as one can measure the consequences when groups are put at an economic disadvantage, so are the *consequences* of discriminating groups for their symbolic identities accessible to a quantified investigation. Applied to the concept of relative deprivation, one can say that, in the second case, groups are deprived of their symbolic lives, just as they are economically deprived in the first one. Although, theoretically, no quantitative relationship or gap exists between different symbolic systems, quite frequently there are sizeable gaps in the ways how those systems are enabled to *express* themselves in reality.

Almost through the backdoor, the preceding remarks introduce an understanding of deprivation that is increasingly emphasized in development debates. Most of all, this understanding abandons the concept of relative deprivation as a purely economic concept. The most prominent advocate of an extended concept of deprivation is Nobel Price laureate Amartya Sen.[4] This extended concept means to say that we should consider the impact of deprived symbolic lives on potential for conflict when considering cases of relative deprivation. These lives may, therefore, not be assigned to an independent second stage, where they are reduced to something that can be

4 A. Sen, *Development as Freedom*, Oxford: Oxford University Press (1999).

switched on, provided crucial economic differences exist. The h.i.-approach has failed to elaborate on this point of how deprived symbolic lives influence potential for conflict.

What principal options are there when assuming that patterns of group deprivation have an economic and a symbolic side, and that both influence potential for conflict? In order to arrive at an answer to this important question, one needs to spell out the consequences when the symbolic lives of groups are deprived. In the process of doing so, one may take another start with the economic side: In search for a label for evidence of economic deprivation, we chose the concept of grievances, as it comprises all various categories of material and physical suffering of groups; in most serious cases implying malnutrition and starvation. On the other hand, when turning the attention to cases of symbolic deprivation, those tangible consequences are not really applicable. Focus must be on various aspects of groups' mental and spiritual lives. The common denominator of these aspects is that they concern the *identity* of groups, for it is in the very nature of primordial groups that they identify over habits, rituals, customs and routines, such as they stem from ethnic, religious and regional traditions. The existence of group identities must of course not imply that personal identities are fully described by group identities, from which they can deviate essentially. Also, symbolic deprivation, although intangible in the first place, can result in serious physical suffering. At this point, we only want to be aware that one deals with group identities when debating evidence of symbolic deprivation. We do so, just as one deals with grievances when considering cases of economic deprivation.

Fig. 4.2: Economic and Symbolic Deprivation

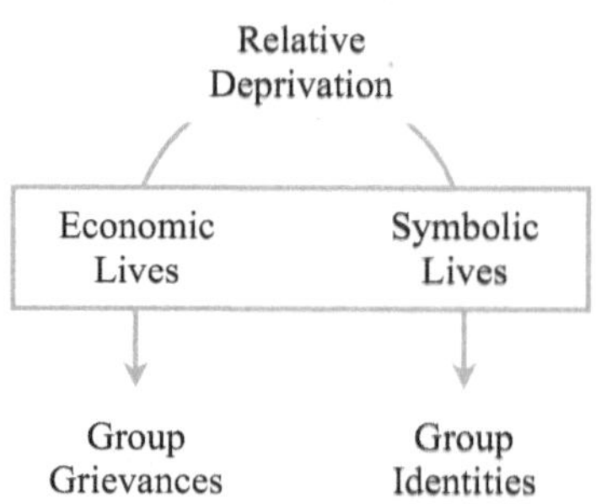

Generally, there are two main options of a synthesis model of potential for conflict that pays attention to economic and symbolic deprivation: According to a first scenario, deprived group identities could spur conflict. This has shown to be true in cases where the execution of religious freedoms and cultural rituals was objectively suppressed by other groups or, for example, in cases where languages riots occurred.[5] According to a second scenario, such deprivation may actually reduce potential for conflict (Fig. 4.3). This scenario seems more interesting, because it collides with the reaction expected from patterns of economic deprivation, i.e. waging of conflict. Obviously, this scenario is also the one that impacts on hidden conflict.

While seeking evidence for the second scenario, one could be attracted to argue with culturally ingrained patterns of conflict promulgation and conflict avoidance. On an overall level, these patterns influence potential for conflict. However, typically they are shared either nationally or regionally, and rarely identical with the symbolic identities of particular ethnic, racial and religious groups. For the same reason, they do not link up with patterns of symbolic deprivation. For example, countries like Somalia, although ethnically and religiously homogeneous, and therefore less prone to witness group-specific patterns of economic and symbolic deprivation, have been characterized by a culture of confrontation. Other countries like Fiji, although segmented in different races, and therefore generally open to patterns of economic and symbolic deprivation, have shown to possess a culture of conflict avoidance and accommodation.[6] Conflict has been abundant in the first cases, but rare in the second. Therefore, although culturally ingrained patterns of conflict avoidance can interfere with patterns of economic deprivation, and thus lower potential for conflict, they do not explain this mitigating effect from the perspective of facts of symbolic deprivation.

Fig. 4.3: Options of a Synthesis Model of Conflict

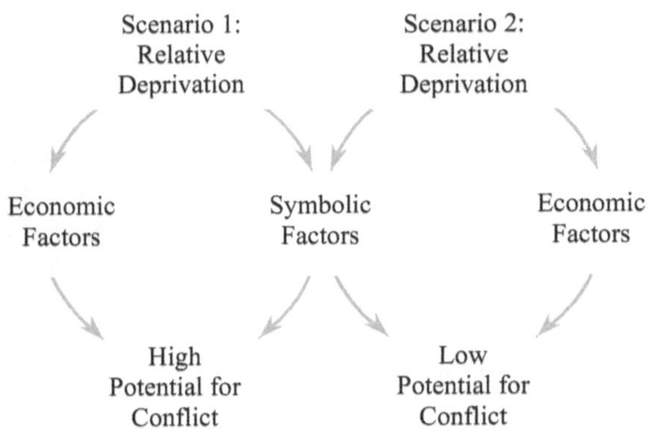

A closer look at group identities, the entry point for patterns of symbolic deprivation, approaches interferences of the latter kind, that is, scenario 2 in the above chart. Thus, the first one needs to do is to distinguish between an objective and a subjective component of group identities. Normally, the *objective* side comprises attitudes

5 A. Bamgbose, 'Language as a Resource: An African Perspective', Paper presented at the Workshop on the Role of the African Languages in Democratic South Africa, University of Pretoria, South Africa, 5-6 March 1998.

6 H.M. McFerson, 'Rethinking Ethnic Conflict: Somalia and Fiji', in *The American Behavioral Science*, Vol. 40, No. 1 (1996) 18.

such as they find expression in the use of a particular language, a special tradition, rituals, common value and belief systems, etc., always depending on the kind of primordial group under debate. In short, this side faces a range of cultural assets that impact on the symbolic life of groups. As opposed to this side, the *subjective* side of group identities means two things: Firstly, the ways groups conceive of those assets in reality; and secondly, a stable set of mental and emotional reactions related to objective group identities. Both subjective components of group identities can deviate essentially from the objective side. As for the first component, Burundi and Rwanda are good examples of situations where subjective assumptions about being a Tutsi or a Hutu continue to defy a reality of considerable intermarriage and fusion between both groups, that is, important changes on the objective side of group identities. As for the second component, one would think, for example, of those cases where people refuse a mental and emotional homecoming in aspects of their objective identity.

For the present purpose, a systematic catalogue of situations where subjective group identities deviate considerably from objective group identities is negligible. One only wants to keep in mind that objective and subjective group identities are by no means identical. This is imperative when considering cases in which group identities have been deprived. On a broader scale, the functioning of such deprivation may answer to what extent symbolic and economic deprivation interfere. At this preliminary point, it is suggested that just as group identities have an objective and a subjective component, so do incidents of identity deprivation require contemplation for an objective and a subjective side. In both cases, one will find a different impact on potential for conflict associated with economic deprivation.

Section 10. No Clash of Civilizations

Aspects of objective identity deprivation are manifold, depending much on the kind of primordial group considered. Exemplarily, they are entrenched in restrictions to exercise religious freedoms, use native languages, publicly present cultural symbols, etc. In many cases, objective identity deprivation will spur potential for conflict and, therefore, augment the momentum in patterns of economic deprivation. To what extent does this also apply to aspects of subjective identity deprivation, which are different although inseparable from the objective side? Quite frequently, there is a different outcome.

In any case, objective aspects have to be translated into a subjective concept in order to matter to individuals and groups. If individuals and groups did not absorb of the fact that their symbolic lives were deprived, there was no point in talking about identity deprivation; at least not if such deprivation is supposed to influence potential for conflict. This might sound almost too philosophical, for presumably where the symbolic or cultural self-expression of groups is objectively deprived, there will be enough reason for these groups to internalize such deprivation. However, some general emphasis on the fact that, strictly speaking, merely the subjective side opens a window on patterns of identity deprivation reasserts the importance of considering this side. Such emphasis is in line with a principal premise of this investigation as well as the h.i.-approach. According to this premise, all deprivation, symbolic or economic, is bound to be relative deprivation. This also means that patterns of deprivation include a strong perceptional or subjective component, in such that groups feel economically and symbolically deprived where they are disadvantaged compared to other groups, rather than deprived in absolute terms. From all of this, we can draw a preliminary conclusion: As long as subjective identity deprivation must be considered as a direct translation of incidents of objective identity deprivation, potential for conflict should increase where serious discrepancies in the cultural self-expression of groups occur. We might, therefore, complete our discussion of how symbolic and economic deprivation interfere, for symbolic deprivation could only enhance the momentum in economic conflict factors. Also, economic and symbolic deprivation will often go hand in hand, i.e. as a prolongation of ethnic, racial, and religious discrimination. Hence, the h.i.-approach would have been right when reducing symbolic factors to something that can be switched on, where group leaders wage conflict on the strength of economic discrepancies. Literally speaking, the h.i.-approach would have only forgotten to pay thorough attention to the symbolic side in conflict, but at long last feature the same result.

Self-Denigration and Ethnic Depression

Deviating from the above preliminary conclusion, there are circumstances under which one can reasonably expect subjective identity deprivation to interfere with the momentum in economic deprivation. The subjective side in identity deprivation is essentially more than assigned as a mental and emotional processor of incidents of objective identity deprivation. One has to be prepared that beyond and besides mental footprints from episodes of ethnic, racial and religious suppression, as well as the emotional short-term reactions they provoke, subjective identity deprivation integrates a core *long-term* effect on the state of mind of affected groups. Scholarly research shows that subjective identity deprivation results particularly in patterns of self-denigration on the part of groups, also suppressing overt conflict in a critical manner.

Long-term patterns of subjective identity deprivation need to be looked at in detail. What do we mean when we talk about self-denigration, and under which circumstances does it occur? Quite clearly, self-denigration means a situation where groups demean their native identities and turn passive as the result of a process in which they are continuously being told and demonstrated that they are inferior to others. Correspondingly, self-denigration is not the despair that may be temporarily induced by disappointments, miss-achievements or, in our case, the result of two or three incidents where groups have been deprived of freedoms that give impact to their symbolic lives. As for circumstances under which self-denigration occurs, there has been a lot of talk about cultural hegemony, and the preponderant influence of one culture over other cultures respectively. However, patterns of cultural hegemony are normally identified and criticized at an overall level, e.g. they are attached to concerns about globalization. For example, a related criticism has been the supposedly devastating influence of 'McWorldism' on indigenous cultures. Turning this criticism into a joke, Harrison Jones, former chairman of the company, once stated that in our present world the 'Coca-Cola Company is like an elephant's ass. You throw a rock in any direction and you're likely to hit it.' However, such overall criticism is hardly ever fine-tuned to the problems of suppressed ethnic, racial and religious groups within societies, although self-denigration can be a consequence in either case. Certainly, elements of cultural hegemony can also be brought down to the level of individual societies, for example, in cases where authors have identified a neo-colonial spirit. However, rather than considering cultural export patterns, especially those that are sometimes deemed to be associated with the West, the present chapter is concerned with group identities in multi-grouped societies. It is concerned with societies that meet the precondition of internal economic and symbolic deprivation.

Fig. 4.4: Subjective Identity Deprivation

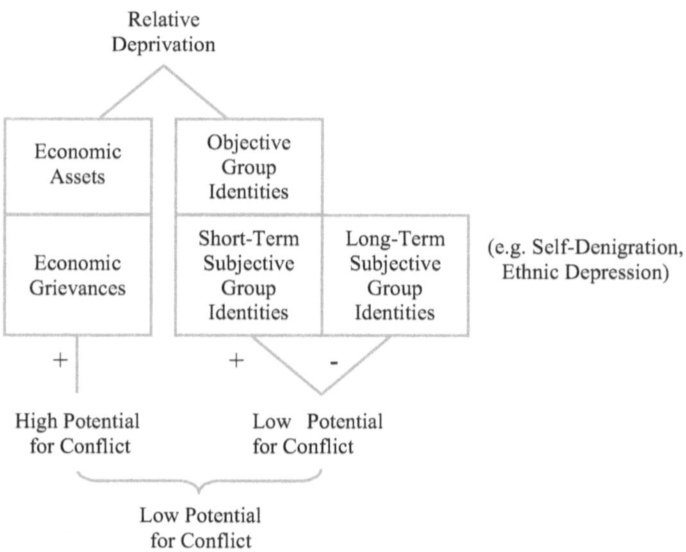

Frequently, the identities of underprivileged groups are embedded in a national identity framework. At given times, this framework is more dominant than crude patterns of Westernization. Usually, the national identity framework is identical with the most powerful group, namely, a group that is ultimately real in terms of size and physical presence. Under such circumstances, there are *exclusive* and *inclusive* identity aspects of minorities and underprivileged groups.[7] Inclusive aspects are those that overlap with the dominant identity framework. Exclusive aspects comprise elements of deviation from this framework, for example, the use of a particular language, execution of distinct religious rituals, and others more. For underprivileged groups, the exclusive rather than inclusive aspects will be a means of self-identification, and a tool for preserving original group identities. Dominant groups will frequently deprive these identities under a roof of national unity. Beneath the surface,

---

[7] F.M. Deng, 'Identity in Africa's Internal Conflicts', in *The American Behavioral Science*, Vol. 40, No. 1 (1996) 47.

calls for national unity serve to enforce the political and economic interests of those groups. Nevertheless, the body of present politico-economic research on aspects of identity deprivation tends to ignore that for dominant groups patterns of identity deprivation have a genuinely symbolic function, which could be even more important than the politico-economic dimension. Social comparison theory has suggested that in frequent cases dominant groups only manage to secure their own group identities by stereotyping others for aspects of their exclusive identity.[8] Therefore, even if a minority group disregarded its own group identity, and even if it did not own any economic interest, it might still be punished and deprived of its objective group identity, because that way the dominant group achieves self-esteem.

In the given situation, subjective identity deprivation and self-denigration, the opposites of self-esteem, occur if minority groups internalize such stereotyping on the part of dominant groups. In a North American context the effects of racism on self-confidence in black groups have been devastating occasionally. The mechanisms in place were the ones mentioned above, thus resulting in a deeper understanding of the fact that 'when the real difficulties are compounded by the fears engendered by centuries of white propagandizing that white is smarter, the result can be immobilization.'[9] In a Latin American context, 'indigenous persons internalised the stereotypes and stigmas imposed on them by the dominant sectors, and resorted to self-denial and self-denigration in order to become accepted.'[10] Comparable patterns of self-denigration have been reported for other parts of the world.[11] For example, Teenek Indians in Mexico, have been observed for considering themselves as 'less than nothing', 'stinking', 'dirty Indians', and 'ugly idiots' and so and so forth.[12]

In view of processes of stereotyping and patterns of self-denigration, the idea that group identities are always suited to mobilize riotous behavior requires rethinking. This idea comprises a main premise of the h.i.-approach, portraying group identities as something that can be switched on in a second stage of evolving group conflict. It shows that group identities are quite frequently a source of reduced self-esteem vis-à-vis dominant groups, and associated with feelings of inferiority, depression and lethargy. In point of fact, *ethnic depression* is a well-observed phenomenon in clinical psychology.[13] Certainly, patterns of submissiveness and giving in to dominant groups provide an extreme case. But so does the opposite case of identity-related fervor and group mobilization. Both extremes have been analyzed systematically

---

[8] L. Festinger, 'A Theory of Social Comparison Processes', in *Human Relations*, Vol. 7, No. 1 (1954) 7-40; H. Tajfel (ed.), *Differentiation between Social Groups*, London: Academic Press (1978); H. Tajfel and J. Turner, 'An Integrative Theory of Intergroup Conflict', in W. Austin and S. Worchel (eds.), *The Social Psychology of Intergroup Relations*, Monterey: Brooks and Cole (1979) 33-47; H. Tajfel, 'Social Psychology and Intergroup Relations', in *Annual Review of Psychology*, Vol. 33 (1982) 1-39.

[9] R.J. Herrnstein and C. Murray, *The Bell Curve*, New York: Free Press (1994) 187.

[10] R. Stavenhagen, 'The Return of the Native: The Indigenous Challenge in Latin America' in *University of London, Institute of Latin America Studies, Occasional Papers*, No. 27 (2002) 11.

[11] J. Hebert, 'Identifying Cajun Identity: Cajun Assimilation and Revitalization of Cajun Culture', in *Loyola University New Orleans, Student Historical Journal*, Vol. 31 (1999-2000).

[12] A. de Vidas, 'The Culture of Marginality: The Teenek Portrayal of Social Difference', in *Ethnology*, Vol. 41, No. 3 (2002) 209.

[13] E. Saez-Santiago, and G. Bernal, 'Depression in Ethnic Minorities', accessed at http://latino.rcm.upr.edu/saez.pdf.

under the labels of 'complementary differentiation' and 'symmetrical differentiation'.[14] Complementary differentiation, capturing the case of self-denigration, is the response of passivity to the dominant group asserting X, Y and Z. Therefore, if 'assertive behavior is not responded to in the same currency, but meets with submissiveness it is likely this reaction will serve to bring about more of the same from the dominant group. The dominant group will keep asserting itself over and above the dominated group, and the dominated group will continue to submit.'[15] In contrast, symmetrical differentiation captures the case of resistance and investment in conflict. Therefore, when 'the dominant group asserts X, Y and Z, the subordinate group will respond with its own X, Y and Z. It will be its own X, Y and Z though. That is, the subordinate group will use whatever resources it has to assert itself.'[16] The question remains, which option is likely to prevail in individual cases.

Racial, Ethnic and Religious Groups

If one only wanted to falsify the h.i.-approach, one could point to those actual cases where economic deprivation did not lead to large-scale conflict, eventually because a history of stereotyping and patterns of self-denigration caused that the subordinate group tolerated a situation of identity deprivation. In principal, this would be enough to demonstrate that symbolic factors in conflict are not per se such that they can be switched on. This would also provide individual cases of complementary differentiation. However, such proceeding would do nothing to clarify cases in which complementary differentiation prevails over symmetrical differentiation. For the purpose of falsifying the h.i.-approach, one could also employ a second argument, as such closely related to social identity theory. Chapter II made it clear that the h.i.-approach shares into particular doctrines of social identity theory. However, the h.i.-approach would never go so far as to suggest that symbolic factors could *prevail* over economic factors. Social identity theory does precisely that. It draws our attention to situations where people have been observed to take action that was completely counter to their economic interests. Frances Stewart herself mentions the case of Sri Lanka, where rioters burned down factories in which they worked, thereby destroying their own basis for employment.[17] This and other cases revive the idea that group identities can be a predominant factor in conflict.[18] As for social identity theory, this idea has thrived on the assumption that individuals possess over a *principal* need to identify with groups. Surely, the risky potential in a principal need for identification lies with group members who capitalize directly on conform-

---

14 Z. Bauman, 'Modernity and Ambivalence', in *Theory, Culture and Society*, Vol. 7, No. 2-3 (1990) 143-169.

15 S. Wahl, 'Cultural Hegemony, Cultural Self-Denigration, and What We Should do About it', in *Philosophical Diatribes*, Vol. 35, accessed at http://www.froyd.net/philosophy/philo35.htm.

16 Ibid.

17 F. Stewart, 'Crisis Prevention: Tackling Horizontal Inequalities', in *Queen Elizabeth House Working Paper Series*, No. 33 (2000) 9.

18 E. Azar, 'Protracted International Conflicts: Ten Propositions', in E. Azar and J. Burton (eds.), *International Conflict Resolution: Theory and Practice*, Sussex: Wheatsheaf (1986) 31.

ist behavior. Conflict could get underway, both no matter what the economic circumstances were and how irrational group leaders justified riotous goals.

Besides questioning the h.i.-approach, the above analysis also puts at stake social identity theory. It does so, to the extent that in a significant number of cases identify deprivation occurred and symbolic factors could not simply be switch on. However, apart from falsifying both investigative angles, a *constructive* approach broaches those cases in which symbolic deprivation indeed lowers potential for conflict residing with economic deprivation. In one sense, processes of subjective identity deprivation could vary, depending on whether group identities are primarily ethnic, religious, racial or other. The dividing line between religious suppression, ethnic harassment and racial discrimination is not always sharp, and stereotyping processes overlap. The ethnic cleansing in Bosnia Herzegovina has been referred to as an example where the religious factor has not sufficiently been examined.[19] There are other cases where this is equally true. However, some pertinent distinctions exist. As the stepchild of prejudice, racism often provides a category of cases in which stereotyping processes are strongest, because in addition to targeting the symbolic identity framework of groups they are based on conspicuous physical differentiation.[20] South Africa, Ethiopia and other societies provide cases of racism where the national identity framework has been most strongly identified with the dominant group. Therefore, cases of racism may also be those where coinciding economic and symbolic deprivation frequently hamper large-scale conflict, and fosters hidden conflict.

Different from cases of racism and ethnic harassment, a positive relationship has been observed between membership in suppressed religious groups and self-esteem.[21] The fact, that membership in religious groups can buffer processes of self-denigration suggests that religious role-taking in front of a transcendent deity compensates for continued stereotyping on the part dominant groups. Deviating from particular cultural habits, as they relate to ethnic and racial groups, religious activity can be defined as a set of experiences in which specific is bound with general. In other words, religion does not deal with tradition, customs or individual preferences, but with *truth*. Deviating from sciences, this will often take the form of revealed truth, in that specific mercy incidents are treated as universal revelations. In each individual case, the degree of deviation from a scientific approach depends on whether truth is being acquired in a purely sensual way, thus giving room to a system of idolatry, or read from the pages of a holy book, also implying an inherent tension that pervades all religions with holy books. This tension exists as rational thought, which is allowed to be a part of the acquisition of truth. However, no matter how truth is being acquired, essential is that religion always deals with some sort of truth, certainly with a mental backyard for doubts but no option of co-existence of different truths.[22]

---

19 M.A. Sells, *The Bridge Betrayed: Religion and Genocide in Bosnia,* Berkeley and Los Angeles: University of California Press (1996).

20 P.S. Woodward, *The Unstable State*, Boulder: Lynne Rienner (1990) 7.

21 C. Ellison, 'Religious Involvement and Self-Perception among Black Americans', in *Social Forces*, Vol. 71, No. 4 (1993) 1027.

22 L. Friesen, *Higher Thought and Lower Motives: A Programmer's Guide to the Mind,* accessed at http://209.87.142.42/y/book2/Book_027.htm.

In case symbolic deprivation happens to religious groups, this will be viewed as a rejection of truth, and not as rejection of a particular cultural way of life. Whereas racism and ethnic discrimination manipulate the me of the physical body, and censor the cultural self-expression of groups, religious suppression is viewed as a suppression of truth. Even worse, not only does the dominant group reject truth, but it also sets up its own system of truth. Whenever this is the case, a system of revealed truth must react in self-defense, so as to oppose the heretics. The sort of strife this engenders will often look as follows: Firstly, there will be interaction, because each group of believers will attempt to preach truth to the other group. It proclaims a mission of saving the world by introducing opposing beliefs to the genuine source of truth, thus redeeming the enemy from evil and leading him to a fellowship with good. Secondly, this will lead to conflict, in as much as each system of belief is offended by the holy items of the other beliefs.[23] For the same reason, it is more unlikely to witness hidden conflict in these cases that antagonist religious groups rather than competing racial and ethnic groups are involved.

Whether there will be open conflict or not still depends on the individual nature of different religious groups. It depends on whether religious groups prefer to resort to a pariah existence under the dominant identity framework, or even assimilate into that framework to become parvenus.[24] For example, early Christianity has taught that suffering can have a place in God's plan, in that it allows the sufferer to share in Christ's agony and his redeeming sacrifice. It, therefore, conferred meaning on suffering by inscribing it within an imaginary cosmic moral order, thereby dulling its pain with the salve of theodicy. As Friedrich Nietzsche occasionally states, 'not suffering, but the senselessness of suffering was the curse which till then lay spread over humanity.'[25] Early Christianity was assigned to work on the senselessness of suffering, rather than on suffering as such. In modern times, where discouragement of worldly accomplishments is less prevalent, and the concept of sin does not foster guilt and self-doubt among the faithful, conflict is more likely to be pursued for truth's sake.[26] Extremist Islamic groups attract such a view. In that sense, terrorism could comprise the opposite extreme of hidden conflict. At the same time, this must not mean that it does not include a political economy.[27] On the contrary, terrorist groups could fit the general framework of this investigation.

Figures 4.5 - 4.7 comprise graphical systematizations of the above discussion. The y-axis measures degrees of relative deprivation (RD) over time (t), both in relation to economic deprivation (ED) and symbolic deprivation (SD). The x-axis captures potential for conflict associated with both forms of deprivation.

---

23 Ibid.

24 H. Arendt, *Rahel Varnhagen: The Life of a Jewess*, London: Published for the Leo Baeck Institute by the East and West Library (1957).

25 F. Nietzsche, *On the Genealogy of Morals* [1887], transl. by H.B. Samuel, Mineola: Dover Publications (2003), Third Essay, Sec. 28.

26 N. Branden, *Honoring the Self: Personal Integrity and the Heroic Potentials of Human Nature*, Los Angeles: J.P. Tarcher (1983).

27 H. Schumann, 'Die wahren Globalisierungsgegner oder: Die politische Ökonomie des Terrorismus', in *Aus Politik und Zeitgeschichte*, No. 13-14 (2003) 24-30.

Fig. 4.5: Racial Groups and Potential for Conflict

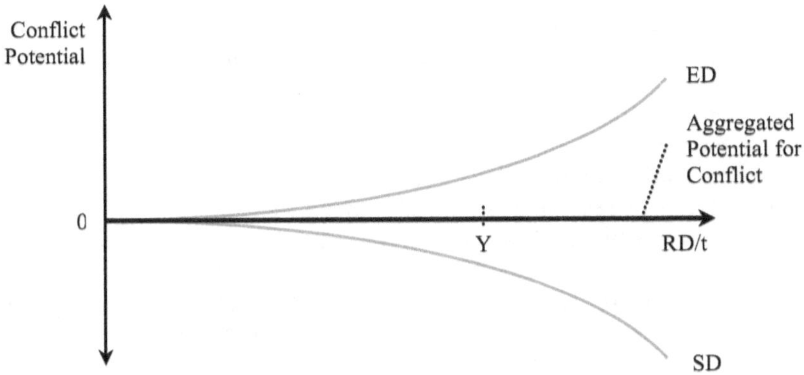

Fig. 4.6: Ethnic Groups and Potential for Conflict

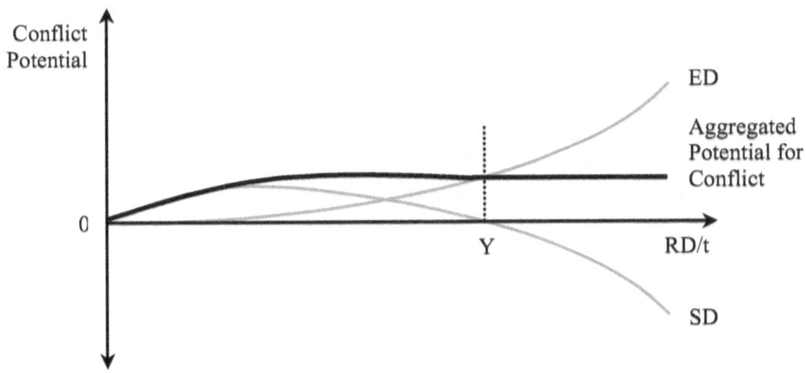

Fig. 4.7: Religious Groups and Potential for Conflict

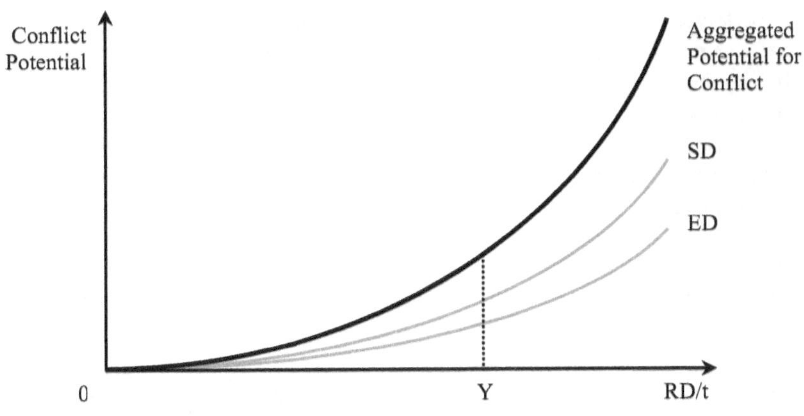

Combination of economic and symbolic deprivation allows for measuring aggregated potential for conflict. For all three kinds of primordial groups, aggregated potential for conflict presents values ≥ 0 for various degrees of relative deprivation. Apart from that, such potential varies greatly depending on group conflicts of different kinds. Deprived racial groups feature the lowest potential, while deprived religious groups own the highest potential for conflict. At deprivation point Y, the aggregated curve for racial and ethnic groups resembles a linear trend line at moderate levels, thus being indicative of hidden conflict. The aggregated curve for ethnic groups at lower levels of relative deprivation is to account for the mentioned short-term effects from subjective identity deprivation, as they are associated with symbolic deprivation in the early phase. Because subjective identity deprivation comprises a direct translation of incidents of objective identity deprivation in this phase, the curve goes up. All three curves operate on the assumption that it makes no sense to assume that aggregated potential for conflict could fall below zero. However, for non-aggregated potential of conflict associated with symbolic deprivation this is different. Here, zero numbers only reflect a neutral attitude on the part of conflict groups. Once moving into areas such as ethnic depression and self-denigration, we have to allow for values < 0, so as to make clear that identify deprivation, rather than representing a neutral attitude, can offset potential for conflict residing with economic deprivation.

As a result of assuming that group identities can be switched on in a second phase of evolving group conflict, the h.i.-approach has treated ethnic, religious and racial conflict under a common roof of cultural conflict. Consequently, there has been little attention to some important aspects of group identities. In detail, those aspects are the following ones: Firstly, group identities have been treated in a rather static fashion, with a main focus on the nature of conflict groups. As for this nature, conflict groups are assured to be primordial on account of inherited identities. Less attention has been paid to the dynamics group identities are subject to at given times; if not objectively then certainly with regard to subjective statements group members form about objective group identities. Taken together, these subjective statements provide a stable set of mental and emotional reactions. Only in a general manner, the h.i.-approach recognizes that groups are important for their members' self-esteem. Together with Akerlof and Kranton, Stewart thus acknowledges that identity aspects ought to be reflected within utility functions. These functions are acknowledged to exceed politico-economic factors and to include patterns of self-esteem.[28] However, as for the h.i.-approach problems settle in when moving to the specific case of identity deprivation. On the one hand, the approach concedes that 'unequal access to political/economic/social resources by different cultural groups can reduce individual welfare of the individuals in the losing groups over and above what their individual position would merit, because their self-esteem is bound up with the progress of the group.' On the other hand, one has been quick to ascertain that 'of greater consequence is the argument that where there are such inequalities in resource access and outcomes, coinciding with cultural differences, culture can become a powerful mo-

[28] G. Akerlof and R. Kranton, 'Economics and Identity', in *The Quarterly Journal of Economics*, Vol. 115, No. 3 (2000) 715-753.

bilising agent that can lead to a range of political disturbances.'[29] Therefore, with the h.i.-approach one lacks a systematic account of how deprived group identities may actually work against potential for conflict entailed in economic deprivation. One also misses an in-depth consideration as to how such potential may vary with different group identities, i.e. with racial, ethnic and religious groups. The above analysis may help out in this situation. It further sharpens our picture of hidden conflict.

Section 11. Hidden Conflict

Second Part

A major premise of this investigation has been that economic and symbolic factors, likely to influence potential for conflict, require analysis by means of the same theory of interpretation. Only that way, cases can be identified where both reinforce or interfere with each other. In order to be such a theory, the concept of relative deprivation must be extended beyond economic factors. Thus, it requires application to symbolic factors, namely to group identities. Economic and symbolic deprivation can interact in such form that they result in reduced potential for conflict. Another outcome of this application is a provisional explanation for why groups subject to racism are sometimes less willing to turn violent than ethnic and religious groups. Apart from repressive measures on the part of racist groups, deprivation of self-esteem tends to be strongest in these cases. In religious settings, underprivileged groups reaffirm group identities in a transcendental manner, rather than in a group-comparative way. Thus, these identities could well exacerbate the economic basis of conflict. The implication for theories combining economic and symbolic factors is that they should distinguish more clearly whether ethnic, racial, religious or other kinds of primordial groups are discussed. On the whole, the fact that interplay of economic and symbolic deprivation can reduce potential for conflict should trigger two consequences: Firstly, there is a need to go beyond open conflict societies. Focus needs to be on the constraints of societies that are only superficially non-conflict societies. Chapter III has revealed socio-economic deprivation as a complex field. In various cases, structural circumstances perpetuated inequalities, rather than led to open conflict. Economic better-off perceptions were particularly relevant in this context. The present analysis opens yet another window on hidden conflict, as a neglected category of conflict. Secondly and more generally, a thorough contemplation of symbolic factors in conflict leads to serious challenges on the explanatory power of any economic paradigm in conflict debates.

---

[29] Stewart (2002) 3.

PART III

THE ETHICAL ECONOMY OF CONFLICT PREVENTION

Introduction

Of the Scientific Profiles of Economics and Ethics

After analyzing conflict prevention and development for distinct political and social economies, we can focus on their ethical economy. Before approaching the ethical economy of conflict prevention and development, it is useful to clarify the meaning of such an economy. In a most general manner, the notion of an 'ethical economy' wishes to stress that economic pondering of conflict and conflict prevention is inseparable from ethical implications. This might surprise given the fact that, initially, an ethical evaluation of the evolving economic paradigm could seem to face the challenge of being applicable to economic pondering. In order to ensure such applicability, economics and ethics need to overlap with regard to their specific scientific profiles. If economics and ethics were *incommensurable* concerning their pondering of conflict, an evaluation of ethical implications would encounter significant limitations.[1] Besides, there may be no question that conflict can be made the object of separate ethical and economic scrutiny. A main challenge seems to be to think both of them together. The job of an ethical evaluation of the evolving economic paradigm appears to stand and fall with this exercise.

As Part Three continues, we realize that the real challenge concerning the interplay of economics and ethics is different. Thus, it is not preserved in pondering of both spheres specific scientific profile, and the extent to which those profiles are reconcilable. Part Three demonstrates that both converge in a number of ethical paradoxes of the evolving economic paradigm in conflict debates. An ethical critique of this evolving paradigm emanates directly from attempts to surface its ethical implications. Eventually, this critique must not complain about a lack of ethical norms in conflict prevention debates. An essential part the ethical economy of conflict prevention is to go beyond such a critique, and to advise on some way forward. The principal goal with such an economy is to sensitize policy makers and academia for the need to complement economic interventionism with some form of ethical interventionism. A prime target for such complementary ethical interventionism are long-term conflict prevention strategies of international organizations.

A basic premise of this book is that the horizontal inequality approach (h.i.-approach) provides a strongest economic model to impact on the evolving economic paradigm in conflict prevention debates. International organizations have come to

[1] T.S. Kuhn, *The Structure of Scientific Revolutions*, Chicago: University of Chicago Press (1962).

embrace this approach when designing long-term conflict prevention strategies. By centering the h.i.-approach, one establishes a premise that can be attacked on principal grounds. Especially when reviewing this approach for the social economy of conflict prevention, there remained a risk that proponents of the evolving economic paradigm would exit to other models in the first place. In contrast, the ethical economy of conflict prevention applies to most economic models that are granted a paradigmatic status. In that sense, an ethical economy is in a more comfortable situation than both political and social economies of conflict prevention. Any political economy of conflict prevention needs to digest the ethical critique that emanates from the sheer idea of such an economy. In line with this dictum, Part Three refers to the evolving economic paradigm in general. Time and time again, the h.i.-approach will be consulted, both because it might exemplify a particular ethical problem, or because it is increasingly prone to host such a problem. At all times, this implies seeking a compromise between specific and more general argumentation. Because it adds preciseness to debates, the first kind of argumentation is usually preferable. At the same time, one wants to avoid trade-offs that owe to too specific a debate.

An ethical evaluation of the evolving economic paradigm in conflict debates targets three different layers (Fig. 5.1). Three separate chapters are designed to deal with these layers. Ethical implications increase with each layer, as one moves from bottom to top.

Chapter V deals with value judgments. Value judgments are different from ethical norms and associated paradoxes. But they influence the questions we pose, the answers we seek and the actions we take. In terms of ethical implications, this discussion relates to the bottom layer in the below figure. The chapter starts off by identifying implicit ethical statements that primary actors form when embarking on economic conflict. These statements form primary value judgments. From there, the chapter moves on to value judgments economic models bear. This analysis applies to international organizations, to the extent that more recently their development cooperation has come to evolve on the basis of a comprehensive assessment exercise that precedes development strategies and interventions. Economic models, such as the h.i.-approach, are employed to arrive at practical assessments. Concretely, these models are integrated into particular assessment tools applied at the country level.[2]

Chapter VI moves on to strategies and interventions for development and conflict prevention. The evolving economic paradigm founds those strategies and interventions. Here, ethical norms and paradoxes become real. In terms of ethical implications, this discussion comprises the middle layer in the below figure. The chapter applies a rule initially mentioned in the preface. This rule sets that development practitioners *cannot not supply ethical statements* in conflict debates. We must follow this rule even as one engages in a purely economic discussion that superficially excludes explicit ethical norms. A prime goal is to render these implied ethical norms explicit, so as to respond to a built-in threat. Given their implicit nature, these norms leave ethics with no option to react, essentially because they are never stated explicitly. The process of rendering explicit these norms finds support from the side

[2] The *Common Country Assessment* (CCA) process of the United Nations Development Group and UN Country Teams provides a most respectable such tool.

of ethics in a line of thought that has been referred to as *ethical realism*. An ethical realism-centered angle identifies and links ethical welfarism and ethical modernism as two particularly problematic ethical norms relevant to the evolving economic paradigm. Both ethical models are originally designed. The economists-philosophers consulted in designing ethical welfarism range from quantitative and qualitative act-utilitarians, such as Jeremy Bentham and John Stuart Mill respectively, to rule-utilitarians such as R.M. Hare and different outcome moralist's like Amartya Sen. The economists-philosophers consulted in designing ethical modernism are such seemingly adverse authors as Karl Marx and Karl Popper, i.e. the formers holism, technological determinism and anti-interventionism, and the latter's piecemeal social engineering approach and technological interventionism. In as much as it implies ethical welfarism, the evolving economic paradigm culminates in a number of concrete *ethical paradoxes*. To the extent that it implies ethical modernism, that paradigm collides with a concept of autonomy for which Immanuel Kant remains the main reference.

A critique of both ethical models leads over to a debate of ways forward, especially for international organizations actively engaged in long-term conflict prevention strategies. Chapter VII broaches human rights-based approaches to development for their potential to surface ethical norms in development cooperation, in such way as to remove their ethical paradoxes. While impacting on the top layer in the below figure, it separates from economic pondering. In terms of ethical implications, it addresses the top layer in the below figure. The chapter concludes with an outline of specific requirements of a spelled-out ethics of conflict prevention. Development cooperation that also deserves the name of ethical interventionism must absorb of such an ethics.

III.1: Ethical Implications in Conflict Debates

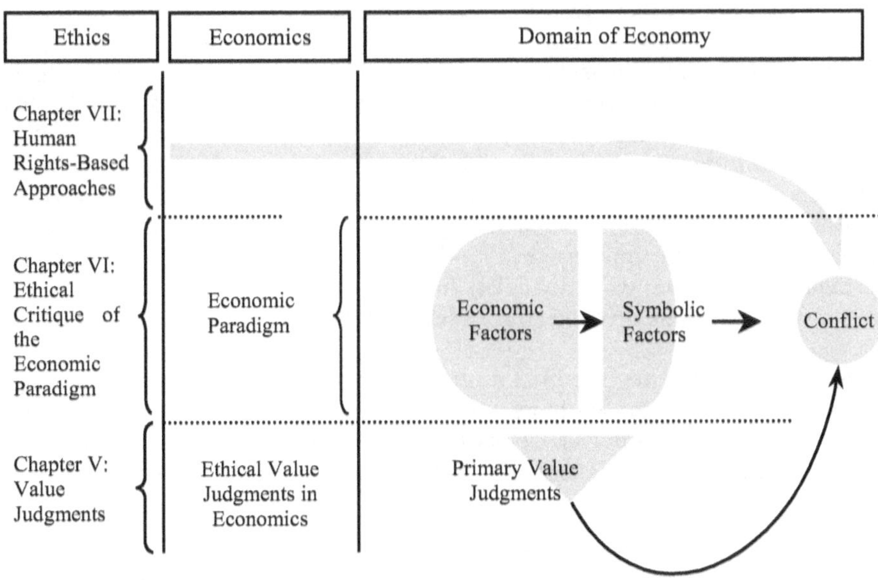

Before developing the three layers, one may return to the initial point. There, the real problem facing any ethical economy of conflict prevention seemed to be the incommensurable nature of economics and ethics. In the course of this part, economics will subsequently adopt component elements of the scientific profile of ethics. Thus, it makes sense to spell out both disciplines specific scientific profiles, especially the one of ethics. Besides sounding out the starting point of our investigation, these profiles give a taste of the considerable effort which it takes to reveal the evolving economic paradigm as a carrier of ethical paradoxes. On the face of it, the scientific profiles of ethics and economics are as follows:

The scientific profile of ethics materializes when realizing that the job of ethics is to deal with norms. Exclusively, those norms relate to human actions. A norm in the field of ethics assigns value to particular human actions, whereas other actions are dismissed. The assignment of value normally finds expression in saying that an action is 'morally good', while an action is labeled 'morally bad' where such value is missing. Different from the social sciences, ethics does not look for an *explanation* of particular actions. It is not interested in the generic causes that trigger particular behavior. Based on norms, the task of ethics is to ask what *justifies* such behavior.[3] Different form the social sciences, this involves contemplation about actual and future behavior, as well as actions that have never taken place and might never take place. Therefore, when talking about justifications this should not mislead to believe that the job of ethics is primarily retroactive. Applied to the situation of conflict, ethics allows for posing normative questions and for imposing duties on stakeholders in conflict. For sure, there is not only one ethical theory. The same evidence, e.g. the same characteristics of a given conflict, may prompt almost deviating ethical answers. It may prompt norms assigning moral *or* immoral value to associated actions. In yet other cases, identical ethical answers are derived from completely different norms and processes of justification. However, a common feature of all ethics is, firstly, that it asks for those justifications. Secondly, beyond dealing with human actions in general, ethics ties those justifications to the behavior of individuals. It, therefore, makes individuals the center of attention. Rather than appreciating of groups as primary actors, groups are always taken to comprise groups of individuals. Hence, just as stating that conflict is uneconomic, one can also say that conflict is immoral. But from an ethical viewpoint, this statement must always be traced back to the actions of individuals. Not primarily because, different from individuals, groups can rarely be held accountable in practice. Mainly, because the norms ethics applies are developed from insight into the nature of individuals in the first place, e.g. their dignity, interests and faculty. In that sense, it was rather rhetorical when the preface to this book invoked an adjustment of ethics to the realities of group conflict.

Different from the job of ethics, economics does not offer a normative theory of conflict. Neither does the evolving economic paradigm. The goal of economics is not to judge whether particular factors in conflict are just and fair. It does not consider whether a given conflict could be justified by virtue of some prevailing factors,

3 C.M. Korsgaard, *The Sources of Normativity* (with G.A. Cohen, R. Geuss, T. Nagel, B. Williams) Cambridge and New York: Cambridge University Press (1996) 9-10.

i.e. the existence of horizontal inequalities. It is true that this distinction has become blurry over and over again. More than in most political economies of conflict, a complementary moral lens has been guiding to Marxian economics. Chapter I observed this phenomenon, while dealing with the politico-moral economy of conflict prevention. Compared to that, the evolving economic paradigm appears to maintain a strictly descriptive approach. It formulates analytical judgments to the extent that causal relationships among and within different groups of factors are explored. Thus, it aims at particular economic laws. However, economic laws on the whole are not meant to be imperative. They do not profess to have binding force upon conduct. So far as they are valid, they are valid simply as generalized statements of the results that will follow from the interaction of given factors and forces. Those factors and forces are not spoken of as either moral or immoral, but only as operative in a certain direction and with a certain probability. In a word, economics does not of itself lay down any norms, as ethics professes to do, as to what we are to do and abstain from doing.[4] For example, while revolving around the dichotomy of economic and symbolic factors in conflict, the h.i.-approach applies a non-judging, vastly descriptive lens. With regard to both groups of factors, it identifies the extent to which they contribute to the motives and forces that spur groups into violent action. Therefore, it asks about factors that possess *normative strength for* riotous groups. At least not willingly, it would extend this focus on normative forces to judgments of the moral or immoral character of associated motives for conflict.

On the whole, those different scientific profiles of ethics and economics hold good in philosophy of sciences. In practice, their relationship is far more complicated. This part shows why.

---

4 W.R. Sorey, 'Ethical Aspects of Economics', in *International Journal of Ethics*, Vol. 17, No. 1 (1906) 3-4.

CHAPTER V

VALUES

The present chapter broaches the interplay between economics and ethics in conflict debates by centering values that infringe on the former. Separately, it considers value judgments for the domain of economy and for economic models that work on this domain.

Section 12. Values in the Economy

The idea that the domain of economy contains values can be put in context with the preceding analysis. There, particular conflict factors possessed *normative* strength for groups, thus motivating their acting. At least temporarily, these factors also appeared to carry values that are pro conflict. The role of economic and symbolic factors in this process was distinctly different. Economic factors accounted for the objective basis of conflict. Symbolic factors played a great subjective role. In two important ways, they served to escalate normative potential for conflict: Firstly, they represented a stage where group leaders gave explicit normative meaning to economic situations implying potential for conflict. Secondly, distortions as to the objective normative basis of conflict took place with their help. Purposely, they exaggerated the economic ground for conflict. Such manufacturing of normativity by use of symbolic means aimed at uniting the group under a common roof of conflict. However, we also saw that rarely such manufacturing would work where it lacked the economic basis of conflict.

The last chapter showed that the translation of economic normativity into a symbolic concept for conflict is sometimes more difficult. It made clear that the subjective nature of symbolic factors may well maximize normative potential for conflict in one direction. However, in a second direction the same excess of subjectivity can see the normative basis of conflict fading. Also in those cases, symbolic factor provide normative meaning; an opposite meaning though, which advises against conflict.

Primary Value Judgments

In effect, what does it mean that particular factors provide normative meaning to conflict? At the same time of realizing that economic and symbolic factors possess this kind of normative strength in conflict, a quasi-ethical lens wants to be acknowledged. Conflict parties apply this lens. In the case of economic conflict, it comes to the fore where groups feel *justified* to alter existing economic conditions, e.g. horizontal inequalities, by using force. If not explicitly, i.e. verbalized by group leaders, still implicitly they apply a quasi-ethical argument of the following kind:

A: For the current distribution of economic resources puts our group at a disadvantage, a forced redistribution is *just and fair.*

In other case, more amenable to this analysis, economic evidence does not translate into economic conflict directly. Rather, concurrent symbolic fragmentation adds a normative dimension to conflict. The corresponding quasi-ethical statement says:

B: For that other racial-ethnic-religious group is inferior, engaging them in conflict is *just and fair.*

These are just examples. Quasi-ethical statements, implicit or explicit, are manifold. Behind these statements that relate to different categories of conflict, one will find quasi-ethical theories of different complexity and degrees of reflection. More than in the case of other conflicts, we are likely to identify full-grown ethical theories when conflict turns into a religious guise. However, in one aspect all those implicit and explicit statements are equal: No matter whether a given ethical lens manages to stand a neutral examination, it remains a fact that for raging groups there is no room for doubts as to the rightness of their cause. Under all circumstances, perpetrators of conflict are committed to what they consider the morally *right* thing to do. Eventually, implicit and explicit ethical statements imply a necessary mental detour in the process of evolving group conflict (see Fig 5.1). On the whole, quasi-ethical statements are tied to the primary stakeholders in conflict. That is why they form primary ethical statements. A primary ethical statement assigns values to particular actions. Thus, they form primary value judgments in the domain of economy.

Primary value judgments don't downgrade the relevance of economic and symbolic factors in conflict - on the contrary. They do not even restrict an exclusive role of these factors, as far as the motives for conflict are concerned. One only realizes that both groups of factors are necessarily being filtered through implicit or explicit ethical statements. An analysis of these statements takes place in a highly contextual manner. So far as primary value judgments are concerned, they are fully integrated into the domain of economy.

To the extent that they are considered as pure reflections of economic evidence, primary value judgments could also be questionable. Because, how can we assume the existence of something like a purely economic situation, i.e. a situation exclusively driven by economic factors? For the most part, individual and group motives are not simply of the kind conveniently or inconveniently called economic. Economic forces do not altogether determine people's actions. As Alfred Marshall noted quite early: 'Ethical forces are among those of which the economist has to take account.'[1] Correspondingly, there must be something more genuine about ethical motives than these motives being pure representations of economic motives, representations to help the latter assume normative strength once people start to act. Two complementary aspects sustain this criticism.

On the one hand, one can question the concept of a purely economic *situation*, as a situation uninfluenced by ethical and quasi-ethical factors in the first place. Almost

[1] A. Marshall, *Principles of Economics*, London and New York: Macmillan and Co. (1890) Preface.

by definition, a situation of economic conflict rules out this option. At best, a purely economic situation seems applicable to a situation of free, equilibrated competition among suppliers and consumers, prominently emphasized in liberal doctrines. The separation of the economic sphere from political influence-taking has been a direct consequence. Possibly, such separation could also be stretched to ethical, quasi-ethical and an array of other influences. But in general, the concept of a purely economic situation does not hold much in reality.

On the other hand, one needs to pay attention to the *inhabitants* of those purely economic situations. Finally, this means turning the criticism into a review of actor behavior. The whole issue becomes one about possible limitations in the concept of homo oeconomicus, i.e. a wealth of ethical motives that supposedly co-influence economic agents. In fact, there can be doubts as to whether homo oeconomicus is indeed so rampant an egoist, or so callous an embodiment of rational choice decisions, as has been suggested. In the extreme view, economic and ethical motives could be observed for an inverted relationship, where economic motives comprise quasi-representations of ethical motives. A prevailing economic motive, such as the desire of wealth, has thus been specified as merely 'a factious desire which either arises after reflection on the facility which wealth gives for gratifying other desires or else grows upon man of business through the gradual restriction of his interests to business and its immediate results.' In that sense, the desire of wealth would need 'to be set a-going by other desires non-economic in nature.'[2] Just as the other extreme, such perception probably assumes an oversimplification, with little relevance for cases of economic group conflict. In the latter cases, individuals and groups are driven by crucial grievances, rather than wealth maximization efforts. Three main points apply to the inhabitants of those particular economic situations.

Firstly, to a certain extent the concept of economic grievances dismisses the concept of rational choice. Attached to wealth maximization models in the classical liberal tradition, those models went out to highlight the perfect rationality of individuals. Chapter I made it clear that, outside development economics, the job of disposing of the rational choice axiom has been realized most effectively by proponents of a 'critical realism'. For example, Ludwig von Mises' criticism of the rational choice axiom focused on the illusion that each individual could be separated into a number of non-communicating cells, with no exchange among the set of motives each of these cells carries along. Aspects of personality that potentially influence the rationality and egoistic maxims of individuals needed to be accounted for.[3] In a general manner, the evolving economic paradigm acknowledges this point. The necessary consequences have been drawn for the relationship between individuals' economic objectives and their symbolic identities, but not for the interplay between economic and ethical goals.

Secondly, aspects of deviation from homo oeconomicus have been studied in relation to why individuals comply with group goals. Chapter IV has referred to situations in which people have taken action that was completely counter to their own

---

2 W.R. Sorey, 'Ethical Aspects of Economics', in *International Journal of Ethics*, Vol. 17, No. 1 (1906) 8.

3 L.v. Mises, *Theory and History*, New Haven: Yale University Press (1957) Part 3, Ch. 10, II.

economic interests. This point too has found entry into the evolving economic paradigm.[4] But again, the necessary consequences have not been drawn in an ethically sensitive fashion.

Finally, in search for aspects that undermine homo oeconomicus, the quest is not for the mere existence of some ethical motives, but for their straightforward influence on the pursuit of economic goals. Few people will question the existence of such motives. However, different from situations of economic welfare maximization, their influence-taking poses important question marks when crucial economic grievances are centered. At best, one may imagine the following scenario: As with primary value judgments that are ethical representations of economic motives, ethical aspects may also be associated with other motives. Thus, there can be (quasi)-ethical motives *for* conflict that are in excess of the economic basis. For example, this is the case where violent religious groups bring forward some crude ethical theory, deemed to justify their activities. In the context of economic grievances, the non-identity of economic and (quasi)-ethical motives happens to release, in the first instance, of the need to confront economic motives for conflict with pure ethical motives *against* conflict. However, even where deviating or supplementary ethical motives were absent, we are still left with the fact that economic factors in conflict require filtering through primary value judgments in order to assume normative strength. In any case, those judgments persist as ethical overload in the economy.

Section 13. Values in the Evolving Economic Paradigm

Occupied with the dichotomy of economic and symbolic factors, the evolving economic paradigm tends to neglect value judgments in conflict. It does so, in as much as those aspects could feed into the reserve fund of normativity that spurs conflict groups into action. Only in a most general manner, the evolving economic paradigm confirms a template for normative reserve funds of conflict groups. In such general form, it must be read into the paradigm as a concern for factors possessing intrinsic normative strength for riotous groups. However, the only factors recognized are economic and symbolic factors.

The preceding section proves that economic and symbolic factors combine with primary value judgments. It further shows that ethical motives are more than pure representations of economic evidence. Thus, it elaborated a profile of economic situations and actors influenced by some sort of ethical motives. An important consequence for economic theory building is that, for the sake of ensuring an accurate account of economic conflict, it needs to include a perspective on value judgments and ethical factors. However, it is also true that so far economic theory building is free to adopt this view or not. A different point concerns those value judgments economic theory may not abandon, because they are not attached to primary stakeholders, but rather integral to economic theory itself. The talk is of those value

---

4 F. Stewart, 'Crisis Prevention: Tackling Horizontal Inequalities', in *Queen Elizabeth House Working Paper Series*, No. 33 (2000) 9.

judgments economic theory and the evolving economic paradigm integrate for the sake of *being economics* at all.

Before relating this point to present economic theory, an interesting side point concerns past economists' dealing with the issue of pure economics. We can tie this point to political economy's big schools analyzed in chapter I. In terms of those schools, classical liberalism has voted for the widest possible detachment of economics from any other segment of society. For example, in defining the object of political economy, John Stuart Mill committed his own writing to be an investigation of 'the nature of wealth, and the laws of its production and distribution'. This seems to imply a most narrow definition of economics in the first place. However, even in a laissez-faire apologist like Mill, we find advocacy for an integrated approach, as he goes on stating that any investigation of the nature of wealth involves 'directly or remotely, the operation of all the causes by which the condition of mankind, or of any society of human beings, in respect to this universal object of human desire, is made prosperous or the reverse.'[5] Responsiveness to values and other factors in economics can be observed even better in Alfred Marshall's writings. Here, economic theory has been committed to be 'a study of mankind in the ordinary business of life; it examines that part of individual and social action which is most closely connected with the attainment and with the use of the material requisites of well-being. Thus it is on the one side a study of wealth, and on the other more important side, a part of the study of man.'[6] Uncompromisingly, economics is stated to be 'on the one side, a science of wealth; and on the other, that part of the social science of man's action in society that deals with his efforts to satisfy his wants, in so far as the efforts and wants are capable of being measured in terms of wealth, or its general representative, i.e., money.'[7] Overall, economics has rarely been so confident about the extent to which economics can be pure economics. But even the classical writers understood that no clear cut dividing line existed between economics on the one hand, and a comprehensive study of man, his various motives and wants, on the other.

Economic Value Judgments

Having exposed how past writers dealt with the issue of pure economics, one can turn to value judgments vested in present economic theory. The latter might only divest itself of these judgments at the expense of quitting to be economic theory. The evolving economic paradigm is not exempted from this possible challenge. Several categories of value judgments require attention here. The present sub-section focuses on a category of value judgments most intimately related to economic theory building. It concerns judgments containing assumptions about what economic value is, the substance of all economics. Thus, it concerns economic value judgments. Mostly, those judgments are implicit, and take for granted when economists embark

---

[5] J.S. Mill, *Principles of Political Economy: With Some of Their Application to Social Philosophy* [1848], Fairfield: A.M. Kelley (1987) Preliminary Remarks.

[6] Marshall (1890) Book I, Ch. I.I.

[7] Ibid. Book II, Ch. II.I.

on their theories. In this specific context, they merit a closer look. An important question arising alongside concerns the basis of economic value judgments. How do we measure economic value, also enabling us to form economic value judgments subsequently? Occasionally, ethical value judgments have been invoked for the process of determining such value.

Usually, the economic value of any good is set by two complementary standards: Firstly, the good's relation to a certain amount of other goods, which it can be exchanged for. Secondly, its money price as a general measure of the ratio in which goods can be exchanged for each another. Both standards are part of the same economic rationale, which assigns economic value to be *exchange value*. Most economic concepts discussed in chapter I hinge on this understanding of economic value. These include the concept of the market, the concept of competition, and others more. However, once considered properly, the limits of grasping of economic value in terms of exchange value are set. In fact, the whole concept of exchange value involves a *circulus in definiendo*. For what happens when economic value is defined as exchange value is that a given good A is determined by its exchangeability for a certain amount of goods B, C, etc. Vice versa, all these goods are being determined by relation to good A. Obviously, this implies a circle. The situation only worsens if help was sought by measuring the value of all goods in terms of money, for money itself has to be valued in terms of goods. The circle actually involved in the concept of exchange value is normally hidden from us, because we are used to define the value of goods in money terms, and overlook that the value of money is by no means independent from the world of goods.

Chapter II has distinguished the concept of exchange value from another concept of economic value, which is the concept of *utility*. The concept of utility was instrumental for a clear grasp of the concept of relative deprivation, in the absence of reference to market-type economic activities in the evolving economic paradigm. At that point, it was ignored that the concept of exchange value virtually requires the concept of utility. It requires the latter to ensure that goods have an economic value independent of other goods and money as the generalized measure of the ratio of the exchangeability of goods. Therefore, what the concept of utility does is to release the task of measuring economic value from the burden of comparative measurement, or *extrinsic* valuation of goods. It promises an intrinsic valuation, in as much as 'utility' refers to the immediate usefulness of any economic good in the process of satisfying individual needs and wants. As Adam Smith hence stated, economic value as determined by the concept of utility corresponds to 'value in use'.

Several doubts have been raised against the concept of utility as an appropriate measure of economic value. They seek to ensure a role for ethical value judgments when determining economic value. Apart from a number of rather week arguments, two main angles could sustain the case of ethics. As for the week arguments, there has been, among others, criticism of utility as a term, because it is seen to suggest an ethical theory 'which we have no right to assume.'[8] Obviously, such criticism ignores that the stimulus for linking economic and ethical value judgments comes

---

[8] W.R. Sorey, 'Ethical Aspects of Economics II', in *International Journal of Ethics*, Vol. 17, No. 3 (1907) 318.

from ethics. Thus, it should not be blamed unduly on economics, which is commonly rather indifferent against ethics. In such cases, ethics is overly attracted to identify its own premises in economics; namely, a relationship close enough to state a conflict in the use of terms. Economics, on the other hand, is normally far from suggesting an ethical theory when producing economic theory. Later on, we shall see that the concept of utility *actually* implies elements of an ethical theory. However, as such this theory requires careful extraction. Therefore, not only that normally economics does not set itself for an ethical theory in its own domain, this will invalidate the second part of the argument, being that we have no right to assume an ethical theory when using utility as an economic concept. As opposed to the argument just mentioned, there are two potentially plausible arguments for a role of ethics in the process of determining economic value:

A first argument questions whether an objective standard of utility for economic goods can be attained the way economic theory does, i.e. by comparing different individuals' desire for things and by averaging their strength. It concerns the fact that value judgments are based on generalizations from *fact*, as the only standard of measuring utility in the absence of any independent ideal. Since ethics is commonly considered as a discipline that derives value judgments from independent ideals and principles, it could seem to be the logical cure for economic value judgments. A reference world of independent values could be found in Kant's assertion that for ethics it would make no difference if it was established that an action of true value had never once been performed in history; still it would be possible to say which actions carried value on account of ethical principles that measure those actions in the absence of existing fact. Unfortunately, the presented argument is straightforward only from a logical point of view. A second glance reveals serious limitations. Those limitations do not rest with restrictions to make economic entities the object of ethical value judgments. For example, one may well say that a person's consumption of violent computer games poses ethical question marks, although it is an essential part of that person's utility function. However, at all times the ethical value judgment does not invalidate the economic value judgment, which says that consumption of violent computer games can be a utility.

A most serious limitation of this first argument is the following: The indicated problem of economic value judgments only materializes where particular methodological claims are transferred from philosophy of science and conferred upon economics. Ethics participates in those methodological claims of philosophy of science. Both philosophy of science and ethics are used to express strong reservation against truth, i.e. true value judgments, that is acquired through generalization from fact. The same individual above, who consumes violent computer games to augment its utility function, may well be joined by an infinite number of other individuals with a similar utility function. Epistemologically speaking, we are still not entitled to form a generalized judgment of the kind saying 'consumption of violent computer games is a necessary element of individual utility functions'. Because, epistemologically speaking, one cannot rule out the existence or occurrence of a deviating case. While this is a rather obvious example, chosen with reference to ethics in the first place, the standard examples in philosophy of science are trickier. So, for example, in Karl

Popper's white and black swans argument, where the sheer possibility of a black swan invalidates the generalized judgment that swans are white.[9] The point is that when drawing the aforementioned conclusions, we get caught in the traps of *inductive fallacy*. A prime way out of this trap for philosophy of science has been to prescribe deductive method, where judgments are gained as conclusions from first premises and axioms. Philosophy of science arrives there at the expense of confining itself to analytical rather than synthetical judgments. Different from synthetical judgments, analytical judgments are only logically correct. The whole issue of scientific judgments becomes one of internal coherence, rather than correspondence to the outside world. The parallel recommendation for ethics has been that its judgments ought to be rooted in ideals. Therefore, David Hume remains a major proponent of the idea that ethical norms cannot be derived from descriptive statements alone.

Different from ethics and philosophy of science, economics is largely an empirical social science, although elements of deductive, apriori economic method are applied in econometrics today. To the extent that this is the case, it cannot exit to deduction. Economics' solution to the problem of induction is that it operates through *falsification*. Falsification provides a means of revising generalized statements, i.e. hypotheses, in as much as evidence to the contrary occurs. This also means that the goal of economics with concepts such as the one of utility is never for verification of its judgments. At the same time, these judgments can be considered valid as long as they have not been proven wrong. At the end of the day, it is not the practice of generalization from fact that per se causes a problem to economics. Rather, a problem would occur where economics was reluctant to revise its judgments, if this was necessary. Therefore, applied to the concept of utility, a role of ethics in economic value judgments will hardly evolve alongside methodological criticism of established economic practices, which include generalizations from fact. Thus far, ethical value judgments simply comprise a different category of value judgments.

A second argument probing ethical value judgments in the process of determining economic value evolves as radicalized version of the first argument. As such, it seeks to overcome shortcomings in the latter. The argument makes serious with the need to measure economic value intrinsically. Remember, the whole concept of utility arose in the first place to cope with the hurdles of extrinsic valuation, as they relate to the exchange value of economic goods. In so far as the concept of utility contemplates the economic value of goods as value in use, it centers the individual to which those goods are useful. This individual and its utility function constituted the 'fact' in the earlier argument. By virtue of making the individual a part of the process of determining economic value, the concept of utility partly abstracts from the good considered. However, by virtue of this reference the concept might also see vanishing its worth as intrinsic valuation of economic goods.[10] When using this point as a second argument against the concept of utility, one needs to understand the difference from the first argument. Different from this argument, the second argument seeks to remove any external reference from the process of intrinsic valua-

---

[9] K. Popper, *The Logic of Scientific Discovery*, London: Hutchinson (1959).

[10] Sorey (1907) 318.

tion, rather than only reference to fact. That way, it does not only criticize a particular quality of the reference, but the very 'fact' of there being a reference at all.

The sole purpose of this somewhat awkward argument is to renew calls for a role of ethical value judgments when measuring economic value. In as much as this is the intention, it also implies that ethics is so different a mechanism of intrinsic valuation that it can jump in where economics leaves a gap. It implies further that this difference can be spelled out clearly. However, this is also the point where the argument reveals its underdeveloped side, for it is caught, rather hopelessly, in a blurry understanding of ethics itself. After all, ethics arrives at its own value judgments only by judging situations and actions according to those ideals, which the first argument established as a *differencia specifica* over economic preoccupation with generalized facts. In summary, it shows that all valuation, economic or ethical, is necessarily *relational*. It is relational to the various systems of measurement applied. Developed by William Stanley Jevons, Carl Menger and Léon Walras, the doctrine of marginal utility has been instrumental in this regard.[11] As such, it has helped to understand that the value of a good is determined by the need for it and by its relative scarcity or abundance at any given time. This value is not determined by any intrinsic or inherent worth. At the end of the day, such thing as a purely intrinsic valuation does not make much sense at all. For the same reason, there is no case for ethics in the measuring of economic value. Ethical value judgments comprise a category of judgments distinctly different from economic value judgments. On the other hand, this must not mean that economic theory is free of ethical value judgments.

Ethical Value Judgments

A task completely different from the one above is the following. Rather than asking whether some aspects of ethical value generation can be assimilated into the process of determining economic value, there is a need to consider authentic ethical value judgments in the business of economics. This second task revolves around the ethical neutrality of economics. Max Weber was the first who introduced this task to the course of social sciences, at that time under the label of value freedom, or *Wertfreiheit*.[12] One would expect that a debate of value freedom is particularly important today, as economics professes to be, among other things, a study of the root causes of conflict. Directly, such a debate helps to clarify the evolving economic paradigm's own standing with regard to ethical value judgments.

An initial grasp on the subject considers two possible extremes. According to one extreme, economics is ethically neutral, and to be kept so under all circumstances. We may call this position the *value-exorcism-angle*. According to another extreme, economic theory is tainted by ethical biases, no matter if it agrees or not. We may call this view the *value-impregnation-angle*. The extreme of a position advocating

[11] W.S. Jevons, *The Theory of Political Economy*, London, New York: Macmillan (1871); C. Menger, *Grundsätze der Volkswirthschaftslehre*, Wien: W. Braumüller (1871); L. Walras, *Elements d'Economie Politique Pure: Ou, Théorie de la Richesse Sociale*, Lausanne: L. Corbaz & cie (1874).

[12] M. Weber, *The Methodology of the Social Sciences*, Glencoe: Free Press (1949).

value exorcism in economics can be found in Arthur Pigou's account of sciences. Therefore:

> If the 'art' of social reform is to be effective, the basis of it must be laid in a 'science'. The contribution towards the work of practice that economists aspire to make is to provide for it this foundation. Their effort, though it may well be roused to action by the emotions, itself necessarily lies within the sphere of the intellect. Resentment at the evils investigated must be controlled, lest it militate against scientific exactitude in our study of their causes. Pity however sincere and grief however real are here intruders to be driven ruthlessly away. Stirred by their appeal we have entered the temple of science. Against them its doors are closed, and they must wait without for our return.[13]

According to the value-exorcism-angle, all ethical aspects need to be excluded from the business of economics. The other extreme, stressing the value-impregnated nature of economics, is exemplarily entrenched in the following assessment:

> There is no way of studying social reality other than from the viewpoint of human ideals. A 'disinterested social science' has never existed and, for logical reasons, cannot exist. The value connotation of our main concepts represents our interest in a matter, gives direction to our thoughts and significance to our inferences. It poses the questions without which there are no answers. The recognition that our very concepts are value-loaded implies that they cannot be defined except in terms of political valuations. It is, indeed, on account of scientific stringency that these valuations should be made explicit. They represent value premises for scientific analysis; contrary to widely held opinion, not only the practical conclusions from a scientific analysis, but this analysis itself depends necessarily on value premises.[14]

This is only one example. There are prominent statements that purport the value-impregnated nature of economics.[15] As is so often the case, the truth about ethical value judgments in economics will probably lie somewhere in the middle between those extremes. A re-investigation of ethical value judgments in economics is challenged to separate those aspects that cannot be abandoned, from other aspects that enter economic discourses by chance, or as a matter of personal predilection. Only the most careful distinction surfaces ethical value judgments in the evolving economic paradigm. The following paragraphs weigh ethical value judgments at three distinct levels of economic theory building. A first level targets the questions economic theory commonly poses with regard to its investigative objects. An ensuing second level relates to ways of identifying answers to those questions. A third level concerns the means economics commonly applies in the process of arriving at proper answers.

---

13 A.C. Pigou, *Unemployment*, New York: H. Holt (1914) 10-11.

14 G. Myrdal, *Value in Social Theory: A Selection of Essays on Methodology*, London: Routledge & Kegan Paul (1958) 1-2.

15 See H. Albert, 'Das Werturteilsproblem im Lichte der logischen Analyse', in *Zeitschrift für die gesamte Staatswissenschaft*, No. 112 (1956) 437: 'dass die ökonomische Wissenschaft von mehr oder weniger versteckten Werturteilen wimmelte und dass ihren Vertretern die Einsicht in diesen Zustand und in seine Bedeutung oft fehlte. Sie meinten ein System von Wahrheiten konstruiert zu haben und boten teilweise ein System, in dem gewisse Direktiven eine dominierende Rolle spielen.'

The Nature of Economic Questions: The object of economics is the empirical field, as it consists of a wealth of economic facts and situations. As those facts are made the object of induction, they also determine the direction of any worthwhile economic investigation. However, another truism contends that in order to get answers, one must ask questions. Applied to the empirical field, this means that from a wealth of facts one needs to cut out those facts to be examined economically, for otherwise we would not get started at all. At the end of the day, this may lead to the surprising discovery that the questions one asks are influenced by extra-economic preferences and experienced urgency, that is, certain values that enter the economic discourse. Such influence-taking of values rarely concern the acts of choosing a scientific lens. It only happens once the question has been settled whether to apply an economic or other lens. As such, it challenges the ethical neutrality of economics. Certainly, at all times values only provide one factor in a range of many that influence the nature of economic questions. Factors such as ingenuity and sheer technical skill are also important manipulators. However, although there are many influence-taking factors, they don't reduce the importance of values in economics, as has been suggested occasionally.[16]

In a progressive manner, this analysis applies to the evolving economic paradigm in conflict debates. After all, why is it that we identify 'group conflict' as so important an issue that it elicits our academic attention? An issue central enough to link it to economic hypotheses such as the one stating 'that an important factor that differentiates the violent from the peaceful [societies] is the existence of severe inequalities between culturally defined groups,'[17] i.e. of horizontal inequalities? At first sight, such focus on group conflict and horizontal inequalities is well *justifiable* without a need to assume some underlying value judgments that guide one's research decisions. A particular focus on horizontal inequalities in conflict may simply emanate from the latter having previously formed a neglected dimension of development. Therefore, it may evolve in line with the principle of equilibrated research. Incidentally, the evolving economic paradigm has claimed this point. Furthermore, as the term 'equilibrated' may invoke value implications, it could easily be replaced by the dictates of comprehensive or exhaustive research. However, there are still other value implications in queries revolving around conflict and horizontal inequalities. Those value implications barely hinge on the use of particular terminology, i.e. the notion of 'inequalities'. Language only seems to mirror real ethical concern here. Such ethical concern come to the fore where conflict and horizontal inequalities are referred to as puzzling *problems*, rather than scientific questions; for example, as so real a group of problems that they deserve treatment and prescription through 'an array of actions that can be taken to correct horizontal inequalities.'[18]

A common belief today is that in conflict debates scientific pondering and a problem-centered lens are prima facie inseparable. According to such belief, they are not to be merged initially by means of certain value judgments. Those who belief that

[16] K. Klappholz, 'Value Judgments in Economics', in *The British Journal for the Philosophy of Science*, Vol. 15, No. 58 (1964) 101.

[17] F. Stewart, 'Horizontal Inequalities: A Neglected Dimension of Development', in *Queen Elizabeth House Working Paper Series*, No. 81 (2002) 3.

[18] Ibid. Abstract.

this is the case may wish to refer to an epoch, when conflict did not cause the same concerns to academics and policy makers. At that point, conflict was a defining part of the *raison d'etat* of nation states. As such, it was justified by scholars ethically inspired by their own age, i.e. the age of nationalism.[19] In a different sense, those scholars confirm the rule that scientific questions are biased by extra-economic preferences and value judgments. Back then, these value judgments converged in the *just war* doctrine. Often, this troublesome doctrine is seen to locate in pre-modern times. In that sense, it would also serve to confirm the ethical neutrality of present sciences. However, clearly such view assumes an oversimplification. It does so, in light of cases in which early modern ethics itself has contemplated conflict without a problem-centered lens. The latter could happen to a thinker of such ethical rigor as Immanuel Kant. For example, in paragraph 28 of *Critique of Judgement*, entitled 'Nature as Might', judgment is caught in aesthetical spectatorship, eventually reflecting upon the sublimity of conflict:

> For what is it that, even to the savage, is the object of the greatest admiration? It is a man who is undaunted, who knows no fear, and who, therefore, does not give way to danger [...] Even where civilization has reached a high pitch, there remains this special reverence for the soldier; [...] for the reason that in this we recognize that his mind is above the threats of danger. And so, comparing the statesman and the general [....] the verdict of the aesthetic judgement is for the latter. War itself [...] has something sublime about it, and gives nations that carry it on in such a manner a stamp of mind only the more sublime the more numerous the dangers to which they are exposed, and which they are able to meet with fortitude. On the other hand, a prolonged peace favours the predominance of a mere commercial spirit, and with it a debasing self-interest, cowardice, and effeminacy, and tends to degrade the character of the nation.[20]

Given the fact that even ethics can be discharged of a problem-centered perspective on conflict, there is no automatism that draws economics to such a lens. However, while economics in general will not escape the influence-taking of some value judgments, the evolving economic paradigm confirms a deeply problem-centered perspective on conflict. Therefore, more than in average economic pondering, its scientific questions have to be regarded as influenced by value judgments.

The Nature of Economic Answers: Just as the questions one poses with regard to an investigative object, so are the answers to those questions often influenced by value judgments, if not ethical tendency. This is especially true for those economic problems that invoke an array of competing explanations, each of them lurking to be granted the final say. The reasons for such cacophony are sometimes identified in ever-increasing degrees of complexity of the 'economic machine' itself. Thus, although one can pose clear-cut questions, one may not be entitled to clear-cut answers. More precisely, this cacophony can be thought of in terms of two particular

---

19 C. Garve, *Abhandlung über die Verbindung der Moral mit der Politik: Oder einige Betrachtungen über die Frage, inwiefern es möglich sei, die Moral des Privatlebens bei der Regierung der Staaten zu beobachten*, in Gesammelte Werke, Zweite Abteilung, Vol. VI, Hildesheim, Zürich and New York: G. Olms (1987).

20 I. Kant, *Critique of Judgement* [1790], translated by J.C. Meredith, Oxford: Clarendon Press (1952) Para. 28.

categories: Firstly, situations are plentiful where economic answers are seemingly *incommensurable*, with none of them having prevailed so far. Secondly, in other cases one is forced to choose among several solutions that are all acceptable as for their applicability to a given problem. But here comes the question which solution to grant preference to.

Some economists have preferred to root particularly the first category of cases in the *relativity* of all economic thought. Thus, it might not be value judgments that taint the substance of economic theories and make them result in incommensurable statements. According to such belief, it is not enough if one allowed 'a rational wind to blow away the illusion of theoretical certainty with which our ideological biases provide us.' At the end of the day, one was 'left with nothing but the uncomfortable knowledge that many of our theories have only relative validity.'[21] Apologists of the general relativity-angle tend to overlook the historical entrenchment of economic theory building. Most theories own strong reference to the particular economic circumstances of their time. For example, Keynes' declared goal was to show that in the succeeding twentieth century a laissez-faire approach to the economy would hardly fulfill its original promises. That is, it would fail to cater for an equilibrated and most efficient allocation of resources, which was so strongly foreseen by Adam Smith. While the example could appear to summon the general relativity of economic thought, it actually expands on the fact that different historical circumstances require backing through different economic answers. In effect, Smith's goal with a liberal political economy was not more but to illustrate that, in his own time, the laissez-faire principle was superior to the precepts of mercantilist regulation.

Once realizing that the problems of incommensurability are not about the general relativity of economic thought, but partly about ignorance to historical factors, this opens a window on evaluating economic theories according to *present* demands. Certainly, the decision for a liberal or more interventionist approach to political economy still poses a troublesome task today. Probably because in addition to value judgments that are contained in the political economists, one always brings own value judgments into such an evaluation. Keynes did not develop an explicit ethical theory comparable to Smith or Marx. Nevertheless, he was concerned with socio-economic development beyond a narrow investigation of the determinants of effective demand. So are our evaluations today. The likelihood of both kinds of value judgments even increases in the context of development debates. Development theory in the second half of the twentieth century has provided seemingly incommensurable answers to the problems of underdevelopment. In the end, these deviating answers were frequently *ideological* in nature. They were so in a rather open way, thus even going beyond implicit value judgments. To a substantial degree, this ideological nature came from the fact that development theory was almost inseparable from the issue of conflict. The standard argument of left development economist, critical of their own discipline, was that a prime goal of any development solution was the penetration of international capitalism and the infiltration of the political motives of the neo-colonial powers, as they sought to extend their allies during the

---

21 R.L. Meek, 'Value-Judgments in Economics' in *The British Journal for the Philosophy of Science*, Vol. 15, No. 58 (1964) 93.

Cold War confrontation.[22] Development economists from the right often argued that development cooperation has contributed much to politicize life in the Third World, because it has been supplied primarily to governments of recipient countries.[23] By increasing the economic and political power of host governments, their scope for patronage allegedly expanded. According to some scenarios, this even included North-South conflict.[24]

In no similar way, the evolving economic paradigm in present conflict debates is ideological in nature. But still, it provides economic answers to the problems of development and group conflict that are largely incommensurable with other theories. As a conflict theory, defining traits of this paradigm concern the importance of horizontal as opposed to vertical inequalities, and relative as opposed to absolute deprivation. A deviating focus on vertical inequalities characterizes economists in Marx's tradition. For Marx, antagonist groups were mainly composed of classes. Thus, they complied with particular social layers, which located vertically in the context of social life. On the other hand, a deviating focus on absolute deprivation scenarios is central to proponents of the so-called economic development hypothesis.[25] Furthermore, by assuming a combination of interest-based and fact-based factors in conflict, the evolving economic paradigm is challenged at two different fronts by purist conceptions that either highlight greed[26] or grievance factors[27] in conflict. All these differences cannot be explained by deviating research focus alone. Acceptance of one stance naturally involves rejection of another. In order to make sense of this cacophony in economic conflict debates, one must assume that particular value judgments are inserted in the research process. The logic of this argument evolves on the basis that none of the theoretical competitors can be falsified in the first place. This is the situation at present, and our analysis does not alter this fact. Neither does it claim the existence of only one paradigm in present conflict debates, nor does it object to other economic theories. The horizontal inequality approach (h.i.-approach) has been selected for three main reasons: Firstly, on the strength that it occupies prominent ground in conflict debates; secondly, indications that it provides for a comprehensive approach; finally, as a strong *representative* of economic theories of conflict in general. One could well argue that all these points present value judgments. But the necessity of such value judgments is just what this analysis is all about.

---

22 G. Mavrotas, 'Foreign Aid, Economic Development and the Role of the UN', in D. Bourantonis and M. Evriviades (eds.), *A United Nations for the Twenty-First Century: Peace, Security and Economic Development*, The Hague and Boston: Kluwer Law International (1996) 307.

23 P. Bauer, *Equality: The Third World and Economic Delusion*, London: Weidenfeld and Nicolson (1981) 104.

24 Mavrotas (1996) 307.

25 L. Siegelman and M. Simpson, 'A Cross-National Test of the Linkage between Economic Inequality and Political Violence', in *Journal of Conflict Resolution*, Vol. 21 (1977) 105-128; M. Hardy, 'Economic Growth, Distributional Inequality, and Conflict in Industrial Societies', in *Journal of Political and Military Sociology*, Vol. 5 (1979) 209-227; E. Weede, 'Income Inequality, Average Income, and Domestic Violence', in *Journal of Conflict Resolution*, Vol. 25, No. 4 (1981) 639-653.

26 P. Collier, 'Economic Causes of Civil Conflict and their Implication for Policy', Washington DC: World Bank (2000).

27 UN Secretary-General, 'We the Peoples: The Role of the UN in the 21st Century', (A/54/2000) 27 March 2000.

A second group of cases introduced above, diverges from a patt situation. Here, we don't fail to falsify particular theories with the consequence of setting up a situation of incommensurability, where economic theories are favored as a matter of personal predilection. On the contrary, proactively we approve of different economic theories at a time. However, once moving to the selection of specific explanatory models (x_1, x_2,...x_n) under those theories (t_1, t_2,...t_n), the question comes which theory to endorse. In most cases, the corresponding selection process will be guided by the following rationale. This rationale can be illustrated for a society's problem with horizontal inequalities. Since a situation of incommensurability shall be avoided, we may invoke tentatively that a concern for horizontal inequalities unites theories t_1, t_2,...t_n. Therefore, the following rather trivial premises and conclusions will guide the selection process:

1. The scientific community ought to seek explanations to horizontal inequalities wherever horizontal inequalities occur in a given society.
2. Society y_1 shows signs of horizontal inequalities.
3. Explanative model x_1 describes horizontal inequalities in society y_1 most sufficiently.
4. The scientific community ought to apply explanative model x_1.

The reason why explanative model x_1 of theory t_1 will be chosen in this case, although other explanative models are principally accepted as well, *justifies* from its applicability to the conditions pervading society y_1. Horizontal inequalities can be extremely diverse. The same applies to theories and explanative models that capture, describe and evaluate those inequalities. The example of horizontal inequalities fits particularly well, because also the evolving economic paradigm acknowledges that the 'relevance of a particular element varies according to whether it forms an important source of incomes or well-being in a particular society.'[28] The relevance of particular explanative models varies with it. For example, in the case of society y_1 group specific access and ownership of economic assets might form a prevailing element of horizontal inequalities. In society y_2 group specific employment and income patterns could dominate. Solutions to the problem pervading society y_1 will focus on theories dealing with natural resource allocation patterns, credit schemes, and the like. Certainly, in reality things are often not as simple. In several cases, it might be unclear which elements comprise decisive factors in terms of horizontal inequalities. This could be particularly true for large and complex societies. Therefore, while dealing with society y_1's distribution problem, should one focus on the banking and credit scoring system, patterns of natural resource allocation, or even other issues? In these cases, one is faced with a clear *problem of choice*. The selection process of particular theories and explanative models must go on. If we don't want to water down the process of identifying appropriate answers to superficial criteria, such as coincidental availability of technical skills in the scholar, we must assume that value judgments enter the selection process. A questionable type of value judgments in these situations gives scientific preference to problems that occur in the short run.

---

[28] Stewart (2002) 9.

Economic Means: The scope for value judgments in the process of finding economic answers appears gradually diminished with the evolution of an engineering approach to economics. To some extent, this approach is the logical result of the breakdown and destruction of the 'economic machine' as a scientific concept, which assumed undisputed validity for the classical economists and Marx, and with limitations also for Keynes. While the international economic order becomes ever more complex, economists have transformed their science from a holistic journey, employing a restricted number of overall concepts, such as the price mechanism, into a social engineering type of discipline. As such, economics is fine-tuned to ever smaller segments of the economy. The role of value judgments is said to be about as great or small, as it is in the work of the engineer, that is, practically a negligible one.[29] However, rather than speculating about feasible economic segments, there is a need to look into the means economists have come to embrace. The axiom of value exorcism in economics could gain ground in this course. Two developments deserve particular attention:

A first development revolves around the prevailing role of *mathematical method* in various branches of economics today. This overall development is not at all identical with the idea that, just as nature, economic reality can be subjected to quasi-physical laws. Mathematical method only participates and sometimes radicalized this verdict, so strongly rooted in political economy and classical liberal writers particularly. Chapter I occasionally went to raise the issue of econometric models in economics today. Rather than proceeding under a value-centered approach, it applied an epistemological angle.[30] A legitimate criticism evolving from this angle was the following one. Classical and neo-classical proponents of econometrics were challenged for their application of a misplaced ontology. This ontology features a view of the economic domain as a closed system and people as separable individuals. Thus, it implies an undue focus on the identification of event regularities. Proponents of econometrics were challenged for the idea that the foundations of macroeconomics are indeed microeconomic, i.e. their belief that aggregate activities can be deconstructed into individual activities, subjected to mathematical models and understood from there. As opposed to this view, critical realists focus on the socio-economic world as an open system, where the different components of the social realm are highly internally related and subject to mutual influence.[31]

Different from the epistemological angle, a value-centered approach may well arrive at the opposite conclusion. In example, by focusing on the rule of law, mathematical method may have helped to remove value judgments from the means economics applies. Therefore, what could be bad from the perspective of *truth value*, could be favorable from the perspective of *ethical value*. Nonetheless, on the other hand, there can be doubts as to whether mathematical method comprises indeed so

---

29 Meek (1964) 95.

30 T. Lawson, *Economics and Reality*, London: Routledge (1997); T. Lawson, 'Connections and Disconnections: Post Keynesianism and Critical Realism', in *Journal of Post Keynesian Economics*, Vol. 22, No. 1 (1999) 3-14; T. Lawson, *Reorienting Economics*, London: Routledge (2003).

31 S. Austen and T. Jefferson, 'Comparing Responses to Critical Realism', Paper presented at the Seventeenth Conference of the History of Economic Thought Society of Australia, Perth, Australia, 6-9 July 2004.

effective a means to guarantee value exorcism in economics. It may help to remove value judgments from our economic means. At the same time, it cannot account for the very act of installing mathematical method to economics. This act of initiation hinges on a very particular view of the economic world. It rests on ontology that features event regularities and the economy as a closed system. Rather than assuming the status of a first axiom, this act is impregnated with value judgments. For the same reason it attracts strong leadership on the one side, and harsh opposition on the other. All things told, in order to achieve value freedom in economics, the existence of mathematical method is not enough.

A second development in the application of economic means integrates mathematical method as one element of a more comprehensive set of tools. Thus, it is generally more amenable to debates about value exorcism in economics, even if the opposite should turn out to be the case. A closer look into this set of means justifies from the preceding analysis. Chapter II has elaborated on the evolving economic paradigm against this set of tools. Being neo-classical *welfare economics*, the latter underlies most development economics in one or the other way today. A brief summary of major precepts of neo-classical welfare economics identifies the place where value judgments could play a role. Therefore, as an independent branch of economics, welfare economics has supplied a tool that allows for formulating rules by which the various economic situations open to a society at any given time may be ordered and compared from the point of view of their relative desirability. Those rules come into play upon conceding that the price mechanism and other mechanisms rarely cater for an optimal economic situation.[32] A major assumption on which neo-classical welfare economics has proceeded is that there is no such thing as an independent community interest apart from the interests of individuals comprising the community.[33] This insight has led to recognize that what benefits one individual or several individuals can affect others adversely and harm even others. Two major consequences have been drawn: Firstly, focus is placed on *individual* preferences and utility functions. Secondly, *interpersonal comparisons* of utility between those who benefit and those who are harmed are applied, so as to determine which particular economic situation is most desirable for any given society.

Chapter II gave a taste of the complexity of interpersonal comparisons of utility in welfare economics. They challenge to deal with such intricate features as the weak equity axiom and others more.[34] Coincidentally, such complexity evolves as yet another challenge to the salience of mathematical method. Because, the application of such method to welfare economics has been emphasized as a straightforward means. Once more, this challenge concerns the truth-value of mathematical method, as well as its status as a value-free discipline. In welfare economics, mathematical method promises to enable 'the summary treatment of galaxies of micro-entities,' called individuals, because it 'can embrace as many individuals, and as many characteristics of as many individuals, as there are symbols.'[35] While doing so, mathe-

---

32 Meek (1964) 94.
33 Klappholz (1964) 106.
34 A. Sen, *On Economic Inequality*, Oxford: Oxford University Press (1973) 17-18.
35 J. Cropsey, 'What is Welfare Economics?', in *Ethics*, Vol. 65, No. 2 (1955) 116.

matical method is held to sum up and compare individual utility functions, rather than bound to abstract from people's idiosyncrasies. To that extent, it is held to aggregate. Evidently, the act of aggregation must not be an act of classification, for the individuality of each heterogeneous individual is to be preserved intact into the conclusions. However, if conducted in this rigorous fashion, it is only in a manner of speaking that the application of mathematical method in neo-classical welfare economics helps to solve the problem of heterogeneity. At the same time, only the latter progresses the identification of an economic situation of relative desirability. It is well known that for neo-classical welfare economics the formulation of overall welfare criteria and welfare indexes provides a way out of this trap. Such criteria and indexes employ levels of employment or patterns of income distribution, as a means of measuring social welfare. Chapter II has made it clear that this solution must lead to frictions with the evolving economic paradigm, i.e. the h.i.-approach. The latter emphasizes qualitative rather than quantitative indicators. Apart from making concessions to the original idea of welfare economics, welfare criteria have widened the scope for value judgments within neo-classical welfare analysis. Inside and outside welfare economics, mathematical method implies value judgments to the extent that it features a particular view of the world. However, once moving to actively define welfare criteria, this involves a selection process of particular criteria. The different criteria chosen so far show that value judgments have been brought in by the score.

More fundamental value judgments than those linked to the processes of applying mathematical method and welfare criteria, are related to the founding principles of individualism and interpersonal comparisons in welfare economics. Those value judgments can be spelled out concretely. At the same time, one can see whether the evolving economic paradigm escape similar judgments, eventually on account of its modifications to neo-classical welfare economics.

A most fundamental value judgment rests on the assumption that *individual* preferences and utility functions are to count. The latter has been derived from the assumption that no such thing as a primary community interest exists. Paul Samuelson was right in stating the indispensably value-impregnated nature of this assumption.[36] Where the concept of community interest is not dismissed as a senseless one, individual preferences will hardly evolve as a research focus. The Marxian approach to society's basic entities in terms of classes remains a classical example. At the same time, one needs to be clear about the difference between this and another value judgment that only shares the same conclusion with neo-classical welfare economics. From an authentically ethical angle, this other value judgment appreciates the importance of individual interests. It does so, devoid of deduction from the fact that the concept of community interest could bee a pointless one. As such, it guides the development policies of various development agencies today. It is embodied in calls to make individuals the center of international concern. Having been preoccupied with macro- and welfare indicators for more than half a century, development practitioners have discovered the striking concerns of peoples, groups within states and

[36] P.A. Samuelson, *Foundations of Economic Analysis*, Cambridge MA: Harvard University Press (1947) 223.

eventually of the single individual just recently.[37] Before, the principles of national sovereignty and non-interference in internal affairs frequently impeded such focus.

The value-impregnated nature of neo-classical welfare economics and current development policy lead to question, whether the evolving economic paradigm escapes value judgments that serve to enable a focus on the interests of individuals. Otherwise, does it even want to escape those judgments? A fundamental proposition identified for the h.i.-approach foresees that conflict is a matter of organized groups, rather than individuals randomly committing violence against each other. This assessment has led to reject development thinking in the tradition of neo-classical welfare analysis, as well as recent efforts to broaden a narrow focus on income disparities present there.[38] Both are considered to be overly focused on individuals, in the absence of attention to how group membership influences individual preferences, affects rational choice type thinking and leads to significant changes in individual welfare functions.[39] A critique of neo-classical welfare analysis gave rise to an opposite principle purporting the importance of group preferences in welfare economics, particularly when tailored to an analysis of potential for conflict. Particular proponents of the evolving economic paradigm have spared no efforts to show that often conflict is about horizontal inequalities among groups. However, one can hardly dismiss that, irrespective of its actual truth-value, any proposition establishing welfare as a function of group preferences includes a value judgment. It does so just as much as preceding opinions.

As for the radicalized, ethical version of the principle of individualism in present development policy, there are no signs of disapproval on the part of the evolving economic paradigm. The Millennium Development Goals (MDGs) of the United Nations are not rejected for the high-sounding development objectives they express, or due to a limited role in efforts to address the root causes of conflict. Rightly speaking, these goals are criticized on the strength of their repeating the same methodological bias of neo-classical welfare analysis. They are criticized for being unduly 'concerned with the *numbers* of individuals in poverty in the world as a whole', in the absence of attention to 'who they are, or where they live.'[40] As opposed to this, development policy would only move ahead by paying increased attention to how group gains or losses enter individual welfare functions. For the same reason of restricting its criticism of the Millennium Development Goals to the methodological principle of individualism, proponents of the evolving economic paradigm approve of the ethical principle of individualism they contain.

A second group of value judgments in neo-classical welfare economics is integral to the assumption that *interpersonal comparisons* form major devices for picking a situation of relative desirability. The value-impregnated nature of interpersonal comparisons relates to the practical acts of comparing individual utility functions. The results of such comparison are always somewhat arbitrary and conventional, and hardly ever testable by observation, introspection or by asking questions. Hence,

---

37 See UN Secretary-General (2000).
38 A. Sen, *Development as Freedom*, Oxford: Oxford University Press (1999).
39 Stewart (2000) 9.
40 Stewart (2002) 2.

more than once it has been claimed that interpersonal comparisons of utility may have 'no place in pure science'.[41] While this is a strong statement, this analysis is only interested in the value-related implications it carries. Those implications are clear. Neo-classical welfare economics integrates further signs of a value-impregnated tool, although it is deemed to provide a set of value exorcizing means in the first place. According to occasional conjecture, interpersonal comparisons are not at a similar rate value-impregnated, as they are unscientific.[42] But such speculation is rather unconvincing. Rather than rescuing interpersonal comparisons form value judgments, such speculation seems to comprise yet another or meta-category of value judgments.

An essential outcome of chapter II is that *intergroup comparisons* rather than interpersonal comparisons matter when determining social welfare functions. Intergroup comparisons would seem to be even more crucial when employing social welfare as an indicator of potential for conflict. A related recommendation of the h.i.-approach reasons a shift from interpersonal comparisons to intergroup as well as intra-group comparisons. The basis of this recommendation are two fundamental assumptions. A first assumption stresses membership in primordial groups as an important element of people's lives. A second assumption dwells upon the importance of group-specific horizontal inequalities and their conceptual cousin, i.e. the principle of relative deprivation. Chapter II employed both assumptions against neo-classical welfare economics and economic utilitarianism. It did so, to the extent that both have done much to center the individual, with no way back to how groups influence individual behavior.

The evolving economic paradigm cannot ignore that interpersonal comparisons are partly relevant. They are important to the extent that individual welfare functions are being *developed*, rather than given in the first place. This point comprises another clear outcome of chapter II. Neo-classical welfare analysis and economic utilitarianism normally take utility functions as a given. Beyond that, utility functions are seen to *deviate* for each individual. Economic utilitarianism's 'weak equity axiom' is based on this assumption. The emergent nature of welfare functions serves to question the necessity of such deviation. Chapter II showed that only this assumed emergent nature manages to remove a serious challenge from the h.i.-approach and evolving economic paradigm, entailed in economic utilitarianism. According to this challenge, relative deprivation could be irrelevant in terms of potential for conflict. It could be irrelevant, in as much as it corresponded to the deviating welfare functions of individuals and groups. For the same reason, expectations that broad-based economic justice lowers potential for conflict could be mistaken. At this point, we can sharpen the earlier argument: Therefore, once accepting that welfare functions are being developed, one is also forced to recognize that the acts of comparison from which those functions evolve are necessary the work of individuals. By definition, groups don't compare. Only the individual group member does. Group-consciousness of specific welfare levels only materializes as a second step in this process.

[41] L.C. Robbins, *An Essay on the Nature and Significance of Economic Science*, London: Macmillan (1948) 139.

[42] Klappholz (1964) 105.

However, for no other reason but due to the necessities of *epistemological individualism* interpersonal comparisons remain meaningful. As such, they are meaningful at the level of the primary actors, rather than at the level of academic pondering about welfare. The latter assumption characterizes neo-classical welfare analysis.

The preceding debate of interpersonal and intergroup comparisons results in a number of conclusions. Generally, there is no reason to assume that intergroup comparisons are less tainted by value judgments than interpersonal comparisons. The evolving economic paradigm demonstrates a certain understanding of this problem, particularly when contemplating appropriate measures that capture horizontal inequalities among groups. Thus, it states that when measuring horizontal inequalities

> we need, as far as possible, a *descriptive* measure rather than *evaluative* one [...] Of course, any description involves evaluation – so that we cannot arrive at a completely value-free description. Our aim is to measure HI as 'objectively' as possible. Where different measures involve some element of valuation, then in principle (data and time allowing) we should try different descriptive measures to see whether we get robust results.[43]

For the evolving economic paradigm, the critical question with values is not about implementing a sharp distinction between value-free and value-impregnated means in economics. Rather, one needs secure the necessary awareness that value judgments are sometimes inseparable from those economic means. The question is to what extent value judgments can be removed in each individual case. There are no economic means that are prima facie ethically neutral as opposed to others. Ultimately, a Max Weber dictum also applies to this paradigm, which thus seems to comply with a writer who 'does not unwittingly (or just to be clever) deceive his readers concerning the absolute heterogeneity of the problems.'[44] Those problems come together in the intricate challenges of description and prescription. More than Max Weber, the evolving economic paradigm appears to accept that, their absolute heterogeneity notwithstanding, description and prescription are often inseparably intertwined in reality. In concrete cases, the main task is not about preserving their semantic difference, but to separate the descriptive from the prescriptive elements. In effect, this very practical problem goes beyond the means economics applies. It relates to all three levels discussed in this sub-section, i.e. the questions, means and answers economics employs.[45]

---

43 Stewart (2002) 11.

44 Weber (1949) 20.

45 For some early writings on the issues of economic value, values in economics, as well as the relationship between economics and ethics see C.E. Ayres, 'Moral Confusion in Economics', in *International Journal of Ethics*, Vol. 45, No. 2 (1935) 170-199; A.P. Becker, 'Some Philosophical Aspects of Economics', in *Philosophy of Science*, Vol. 15, No. 3 (1948) 242-246; K.E. Boulding, 'Some Contributions of Economics to the General Theory of Value', in *Philosophy of Science*, Vol. 23, No. 1 (1956) 1-14; R.G. Collingwood, 'Economics as a Philosophical Science', in *International Journal of Ethics*, Vol. 36, No. 2 (1926) 162-185; G.R. Geiger, 'The Place of Values in Economics', in *The Journal of Philosophy*, Vol. 27, No. 13 (1930) 350-361; F.H. Knight, 'Intellectual Confusion on Morals and Economics', in *International Journal of Ethics*, Vol. 45, No. 2 (1935) 200-220; F.H. Knight, 'Abstract Economics as Absolute Ethics', in *Ethics*, Vol. 76, No. 3 (1966) 163-177; J.J. Spengler, 'Have Values a Place in Economics?', in *International Journal of Ethics*, Vol. 44, No. 3 (1934) 313-331; R.G. Tugwell, 'Economics and Ethics', in *The Journal of Philosophy*, Vol. 21, No. 25 (1924) 682-690.

At the end of the day, the reality of the indicated problem requires defending against a cure that has been proposed occasionally, but does not help much in practice. This cure may be referred to as the *logical case for value freedom* in economics. Straightforwardly, this case can be developed from a discussion in the previous sub-section. Under the label of inductive fallacy, philosophy of science told us there that universal judgments of the kind saying 'all swans are white' are invalid. They are invalid because they are bound to generalize from a restricted number of empirical observations, while the existence or occurrence of a deviating case cannot be ruled out under all circumstances. The parallel recommendation for ethics was that true ethical value judgments cannot be derived from descriptive statements alone. Applied to the problem of removing value judgments from economics, this allows for formulating the logical case for value freedom. Therefore:

> if true value judgments cannot be deduced from descriptive statements, then descriptive statements, the basis of economics, ought to be value-free (or non-prescriptive) by virtue of the fact that true value judgments cannot be deduced from these statements. Ergo, economics is value-free.

The logical case for value freedom in economics turns philosophy's inductive fallacy argument against ethics, where the latter identifies value judgments in economics. The logical case for value freedom has found application to all three levels of economic theory building analyzed above, that is, the questions, means and answers economics employs.[46] However, what seems to reason a compelling case in the first place, reveals serious limitations once considered properly. We may only focus on the two most striking limitations.

A first limitation is integral to the assumption that the problem of value judgments in economics can be dealt with forthwith at a logical level. Obviously, the logical case refuses to consider the problem at the appropriate level, which is the practical level. A simple but consequential reply is to stress that economists will not abstain from inserting value judgments into their analysis, because, logically speaking, prescriptive statements cannot be derived from descriptive statements. Also, value judgments are not going to be removed from existing economic theories given this fact alone.

A more serious limitation relates to the fact that the logical case for value freedom in economics only accounts for *true* value judgments. Indeed, those judgments cannot be deducted from descriptive statements. Apart from that, the logical case provides no criterion to distinguish between bad and good judgments. Therefore, applying the logical case means overlooking that value judgments can be more or less valid in ethical terms. A prescriptive statement or norm to kill is clearly inferior to a prescriptive statement or norm to prevent conflict. However, according to the logical case, a logically correct but bad prescriptive statement must be judged as superior to a logically wrong but good prescriptive statement.

With the evolving economic paradigm one is safe against the myths of a logical case for value freedom in economics. While seeking to remove value judgments

---

[46] Klappholz (1964) 99-110.

from its means, especially the h.i.-approach remains aware that a completely value-free description cannot be guaranteed. Certainly, in terms of the three levels applied, the paradigm can be accused of shortsightedness with regard to the extent to which value judgments have entered its own contemplations. However, what if in the end ethical implications of the evolving economic paradigm went beyond implicit value judgments? What if it was, in one way or the other, pregnant with ethical norms or even related to an entire ethical theory?

CHAPTER VI

ETHICS

Section 14. Development Cooperation

Technical and Ethical Imperatives

Proving the value-impregnated nature of economic theory is a straightforward task. A more difficult job is to substantiate a link with ethical norms. Because, what would it mean to say that the evolving economic paradigm was in some sense pregnant with ethical norms? Despite initial guess, it meant that this paradigm went beyond value-concessions to a strictly descriptive approach. It implied that the paradigm was only superficially about causal relationships between groups of factors in conflict, i.e. about economic and symbolic factors. In the end, it could contain elements of a normative ethical theory, of which moments of prescriptiveness only presented a poor picture. Generally speaking, two options of such an imperative theory can be thought of.

In one case, the evolving economic paradigm was normative in that, unwillingly, it provided some of those factors and forces that drive groups of people with ethical meaning. Applied to the case of conflict, it exceeded neutral assumptions about the extent to which individual factors possess normative strength for riotous groups. Thus, it extended those assumptions to judgments of the moral and immoral character of particular motives for conflict. Ultimately, this implied the adoption of an ethical statement similar to the one taken on by conflict groups that feel morally justified to alter existing economic conditions by using force. In modification of the primary value judgments they form, this ethical statement provided:

> A: For the current distribution of economic resources in society *x* puts group A at a disadvantage, a forced redistribution is *just and fair*, if group B refuses to reallocate existing resources.

Most serious limitations of such undertaking relate to the nature of the disputed good. Under exceptional circumstances only, policy makers and academics will sympathize with a forced redistribution of economic resources. Theoretically, this could be the case where horizontal inequalities were extreme, long-lived and resistant to change. In the Marxian order of things, vertical inequalities were constitutive of a social revolution carrying the moral imperative 'proletarians of all countries, unite!' For technical reasons, it must be even harder to assign a normative component to conflict where the disputed good were cultural declivities. The concept of cultural dominance is a blurry one and cannot be measured to similar extent as economic inequalities. Chapter IV has explored a number of solutions to the intangible nature of cultural declivities by dwelling upon cases of identity deprivation, e.g. evidence of reduced self-esteem. However, because cultural declivities are largely intangible, liaising with an ethical statement is almost impossible, although they often provide the basis for primary value judgments of conflict groups. Theoretically, this ethical statement took shape as follows:

> B: For cultural group A suppresses group B's cultural freedoms, i.e. racial-ethnic-religious identity, it is *just and fair* for the latter to go into conflict.

Both a precarious moral structure, particularly in the realm of religious terrorism, and a preoccupation with the economic basis of conflict rule out this ethical statement for the evolving economic paradigm. Also the first ethical statement has no justification in this paradigm. If one was still sought to identify moments of a normative ethical theory in the latter, this might be possible in broad terms in relation to political economy. As for the relationship between economics and ethics pictured there, that paradigm participates vaguely in the Smithian rather than Marxian order of things. After all, it was Adam Smith who set two standards for economics in its relation to ethics: Firstly, in deviation from mercantilist doctrines, ethical norms were to be derived from the physical rather than vice versa.[1] He, therefore, began with economic reality, investigated the laws and regularities inherent in it, and only after that, at the end of the story, announced that these laws and regularities were just or moral. Both, Marxian political economy and the evolving economic paradigm would probably subscribe to this first standard. However, Smith secondly described those economic laws as just, not so much because they conformed to some pre-existing scheme of morality, but rather because they were natural, i.e. because they were necessarily inherent in the prevailing set of socio-economic relationships and manifested themselves objectively, automatically and independently of people's will.[2] Such easy-handedness with regard to the moral qualities of economic reality hinged much on the liberal equilibrium model and the price mechanism. Both serve to eliminate any moment of conflict from economic operations in the first place. For sure, such easy-handedness would not find much overlap in Marxian political economy, i.e. its politico-moral economy. Nor will it find much overlap in the evolving economic paradigm. From the distinct position of that paradigm, the conceptual distance to Marx's revolution imperative is probably wider, than to Smith's doctrine concerning the normativity of economic fact. However, in the absence of a concrete ethical statement in this paradigm that morally rationalizes people's economic motives, elements of a normative ethical theory must be sought on different grounds.

In a second case, the evolving economic paradigm could be normative on account of particular *interventions* it prescribes for achieving conflict prevention. Those interventions could emanate straightforwardly from the importance of particular factors in conflict. In this case, the paradigm was observed for an implicit conflict prevention strategy. Having devoted so much attention to the conflict-building potential of horizontal inequalities, this strategy needed to factor in a set of policies that supposedly 'correct' horizontal inequalities. As a matter of fact, although this part has

---

1 To be sure, such epistemological revolution has been trimmed at suspending anticipations of the world as a moral order, rather than at eradicating value judgments from economics.

2 R.L. Meek, 'Value-Judgments in Economics' in *The British Journal for the Philosophy of Science*, Vol. 15, No. 58 (1964) 90.

been kept rather short, the horizontal inequality approach (h.i.-approach) culminates in some sort of policy advice, or so-called 'affirmative action'. In Frances Stewart's words this means that

> horizontal inequalities ought to be an important consideration in development thinking [...] Horizontal Inequalities should be part of development policies for *all* societies, not just those currently, or have recently been, in conflict. [...] Where horizontal inequalities are found to be large policies are needed to correct them [...] I have called these policies affirmative action.[3]

Relevant policies to correct horizontal inequalities are supposed to locate in the political, economic and social fields. In so far as relevant policies are namely related to those fields, the evolving economic paradigm includes a distinct category of imperatives. Apart from being among others economic, these imperatives are *economical*, or convenient, in as much as they establish a quasi-causal relationship between the root causes and interventions for conflict prevention . Therefore, conflict prevention is considered to be about some neat affirmative or corrective action. It is about a number of *technical imperatives*. Obviously, technical imperatives are more complex than technicalities. But they refer to empirical conditions that can be transformed with time and effort in such manner as to accommodate for conflict prevention goals. For the same reason of a focus on empirical conditions, it appears that the evolving economic paradigm does not bother with ethical imperatives, when considering appropriate interventions for conflict prevention. However, ethical imperatives may still have trickled in these technico-empirical discussions. They may have done so, not so much by way of explicit inclusion, but as per what these discussions abstract from. Thus, while discussing the liberal school in political economy, chapter I occasionally highlighted two options of scientific abstraction. At least on first approximation, there are only these two: Either we consider something, for example conflict prevention, *as not* having or requiring a particular dimension, i.e. an ethical dimension. Alternatively, we observe it *not as* assuming or requiring this dimension.[4] In the first case, we deal with a precisive mode of abstraction. The latter case provides for a non-precisive mode. While the first case specifies certain actual characteristics *as absent*, certain actual characteristics are merely *absent from specification* in the latter.[5] Applied to the issue of meaningful interventions, this distinction creates two main options:

In a first case, the evolving economic paradigm went so far as to claim that conflict prevention strategies only needed to address the economic root causes of conflict. Thus, they needed to correct horizontal inequalities, without a concern for other aspects of conflict prevention. As part of the same rationale, ethical impera-

---

3 F. Stewart, 'Horizontal Inequalities: A Neglected Dimension of Development', in *Queen Elizabeth House Working Paper Series*, No. 81 (2002) 34.

4 See Aristotle, *Physics* [ca. 350 BC], Oxford and New York: Oxford University Press (1996) 193b22-36; Aristotle, *Metaphysics* [ca. 350 BC], Cambridge MA: Harvard University Press (1969-73) 1077b23-1078a29.

5 R.T. Long, 'Realism and Abstraction in Economics: Aristotle and Mises versus Friedman', Paper presented at the Austrian Scholars Conference No. 10, Ludwig von Mises Institute, Auburn, USA (2004) 6.

tives were completely *redundant* of conflict prevention strategies. For sure, elements of precisive abstraction capture the relationship between economic and symbolic factors in that paradigm. These elements also apply to interventions that are deducted from this presumed relationship. Chapter II made it clear that both groups of factors have been assigned to a linear model, where symbolic factors rarely provoke conflict in the absence of underlying economic factors. One cannot repeat frequently enough that the goal of chapter IV has been to question the foundations of this approach. It did so, by designing a synthesis model of factors in conflict, which focuses on rather than abstracts from symbolic factors. Above all, such abstraction came to the fore in the view that symbolic factors can be 'switch on' in the process of mobilizing groups, whereas normally things are more complex. However, as for the relationship between economic and ethical factors, there are no indications of precisive abstraction in the evolving economic paradigm. This also applies to the parallel relationship between economic policy advice and ethical imperatives. Therefore, in the absence of related indications, one may treat this case as not applicable to this paradigm.

In a second case, the evolving economic paradigm only *abandoned* an ethical lens from its own particular research focus. In this case, it did not treat ethical imperatives as irrelevant with respect to interventions that augment conflict prevention strategies. However, if this case was fully applicable to the evolving economic paradigm, one should expect that such non-precisive abstraction had been made explicit. One should expect that paradigm to have isolated from the broader picture of conflict those particular aspects it focuses on. In order to facilitate such perception, the h.i.-approach should have been identified as one of several approaches to deal with conflict. In the absence of such remarks, this second case may not be the one most applicable either.

At the end of the day, there might be another option besides the two just mentioned, which both concern the relationship between technical and ethical imperatives. The evolving economic paradigm takes shape with this third option. Methodologically, this option approaches Spinoza's simple but compelling statement *omnis determinatio est negatio*, i.e. all distinction is negation.[6] According to this option, abstraction is not as simple that it either results in the redundancy or temporary abandonment of ethical imperatives from interventions in conflict. The point is the following: Directly as a result of not including explicit ethical imperatives, the evolving economic paradigm may lead to a number of implicit ethical imperatives. Eventually, this point leads back to the initially established rule that *one cannot not supply ethical statements* when debating. Here is the point to make thorough use of this rule. In order to better understand this third option, all three options relating technical and ethical imperatives to each other can be assigned to yet another translation:

As for the case of precisive abstraction, the relationship between both kinds of imperatives is the following. Ethical imperatives are held to be redundant of conflict prevention strategies. Technical imperatives are supposed to suffice. As a consequence, economic development becomes *synonymous* with ethical progress in the

6 B. de Spinoza, Letter to J. Jelles on 2 June 1674.

domain of conflict prevention. Given this synonymy, we might have done better to remove all ethical language. Why not stating 'economic development is synonymous with conflict prevention' in this case? Why maintaining a link to something, i.e. ethical progress, that is arguably irrelevant in connection with conflict? A truly technical imperative unaffected by ethical language states: 'Interventions to correct horizontal inequalities ought to be a prevailing type of interventions in conflict prevention.' The reason why a link to ethics is still necessary owes to the fact that, willingly or unwillingly, we preserve a template for the moral side of conflict, even though ethical imperatives are consider practically irrelevant. Thus, we remain accountable to this side. There is a need to reconcile both groups of imperatives. The expanded statement above, establishing the synonymy of economic and ethical progress, pays reference to this fact.

As for the case of non-precisive abstraction, the relationship between technical and ethical imperatives is completely different. Here, ethical imperatives are simply abandoned from conflict prevention strategies. Thus, technical and ethical imperatives are considered *irreplaceable* through each other. So much the more, they are valid in their own right. In terms of progress towards conflict prevention, economic development and ethical progress comprised different pairs of shoes, both relevant. The irreplaceable nature of technical and ethical imperatives was matched by different sciences, i.e. the social sciences and ethics.

A third case of the relationship between technical and ethical imperatives applies to the evolving economic paradigm. Generally, this option has to do with the status of that paradigm as a paradigm. From the very beginning, this analysis referred to the evolving economic paradigm as a *paradigm*, rather than theory or discipline, with all the implications of scientific paradigms in philosophy of science.[7] Scientific paradigms force to think of different theories in the same research context, e.g. in the context of conflict sciences. The h.i.-approach was set up as such a paradigm to establish a lingual equivalent to its touching upon other branches of conflict sciences. Thus, as a paradigm it extends both to economic and cultural studies of conflict. So far as this paradigmatic nature also extends to ethics, it requires further analysis. Generally, the paradigm-centered approach forces to conceive of technical and ethical imperatives in terms of their commensurable or incommensurable nature. It does so, rather than leaving things at the level of synonymies or the irreplaceable nature of different imperatives. A sequence of points deepens this assessment.

Superficially, an extension of the evolving economic paradigms to the field of ethics could be established with reference to the formers supposed 'instrumental' nature. According to Frances Stewart, 'taking action to reduce group inequalities may be the most efficient way of achieving other objectives.'[8] However, rather than making economic and ethical interventions commensurable, this instrumental nature contemplates side effects of interventions targeting horizontal inequalities on a limited number of macro-indicators, i.e. gross-national unemployment and poverty levels. The goal has been to show that group-centered interventions to reduce horizontal inequalities exceed the context of groups. Supposedly, they unleash a substantial

[7] T.S. Kuhn, *The Structure of Scientific Revolutions*, Chicago: University of Chicago Press (1962).

[8] Stewart (2002) 4.

portion of their impact at the level of society as a whole. On the whole, the instrumental nature of such interventions concerns an inner-economic and purely technical debate.

Secondly, on a more general level the instrumental relationship between group-specific and gross-national gains is representative of a founding aspect of the evolving economic paradigm. The consequences of this aspect are felt most clearly in relation to ethics. As for representatives of that paradigm, there is a willingness to link the group level with the national level. However, both are linked insufficiently with society's smallest entities, i.e. the individual. The h.i.-approach stresses that individual welfare gains must not be jettisoned, and that the group dimension is added to the individual dimension, rather than supposed to replace it. At the same time, one needed to be prepared that the promotion of group equality could be 'at the expense of' individual welfare gains. In a word, there might be 'substantial trade-offs between individual and group goals.'[9] There can be no question about the reality of such trade-offs. Most likely, such trade-offs involve the welfare functions of individuals of better-off groups. However, apart from that the group-centered approach is indicative of a deficient elaboration of the concept of individuals. The evolving economic paradigm distracts from the individual not so much by neglecting its welfare function. It does so, to the extent that it makes individuals the *passive object* of discussions, especially when debating appropriate interventions. According to this concept of interventions, one is prone to ask what can be done *for* individuals, rather than installing them as dynamic actors who execute interventions on the basis of intrinsic norms. With the evolving economic paradigm, one is prone to consider how the capabilities of individuals can *be* enhanced. Only ethics centers individuals in a manner that their capacities are employed in a proactive manner. No waiting for enabling empirical conditions is accepted. Thus, ethics seeks to benefit from a pool of normativity intrinsic to individuals when debating behavior in conflict.

Thirdly, once before this analysis stressed that the stakeholdership of individuals in the course of their lives comprises an irreducible fact. This earlier context contemplated the meaningfulness of interpersonal comparisons in welfare economics. The actual meaning of such comparisons was deducted from the requirements of epistemological individualism. It was argued that individual and group welfare functions are being developed, rather than given in the first place. Acceptance of this fact leads to recognize that the acts of comparison from which welfare functions evolve are necessary the work of individuals. By definition, groups don't compare. It is always individual group members who do so. Consciousness of group-specific welfare levels only evolves as a second step in this process. As opposed to this earlier debate, the present point concerns elements of normative rather than epistemological stakeholdership of individuals. It concerns their proactive participation in interventions that augment conflict prevention strategies. As for the evolving economic paradigm, aspects of precisive or non-precisive abstraction rarely characterize the relationship between technical and ethical imperatives. This becomes clear only now. Their relationship is entrenched in a passive approach to individuals. In short,

---

9 Ibid. 5-6.

the relationship between technical and ethical imperatives in the evolving economic paradigm must be thought of as follows:

> Although they are not identical with each other, economic development is an authentic *representative* of ethical progress in the domain of conflict prevention.

This relationship is deducted forthwith from the evolving economic paradigm's passive approach to individuals.

Fourthly, the implications of this relationship are felt insufficiently when concentrating on the supply side of interventions. For different reasons, development policies sometimes ignore that interventions are not goals in themselves. There is a need to center the *demand side* or beneficiaries of interventions, also implying that the passive approach to individuals is not simply taken as a given. There is a need to rediscover the individual, unbiased by its membership in primordial groups. Only this way, the evolving economic paradigm may be appreciated correctly. Only that way, its technical imperatives are evaluated as to whether they encroach duly or unduly upon particular persons traits. However, once different personal traits are being distinguished, technical imperatives reveal as a two-sided sword:

On the one hand, technical imperatives and interventions are indispensable of conflict prevention goals. They serve to address individuals through their *empirical person*. In as much as this empirical person concerns people's basic needs, experienced wants and utility functions, it requires recognition. To the same extent, the passive approach is straightforward. Technico-empirical interventions are designed to meet the set of empirical motives each individual carries along, e.g. economic grievances they experience. For those interventions to exert their influence in a causal manner, individuals are anticipated to be subject to causal affection. Causal affection provides a core expectation of any technico-empirical discussion benefiting from the fact that individuals are, among others, driven by empirical motives.

On the other hand, if technical imperatives are defined without attention to their legitimate claim over particular personal traits, they become questionable. Thus, they might encroach upon other personal traits, above all upon people's *moral person*. They run the risk of exploiting that individuals are, among others, driven by empirical motives. While extending their causal and passive approach, they also prevent a proactive approach to conflict prevention. An active approach materializes together with ethical imperatives that are directed at the primary stakeholders in conflict. It anticipates the proactive absorption of those imperatives, rather than a passive collecting of the benefits of technical imperatives, which development practitioners transfer. As part of a proactive, in example, ethical approach, individuals execute self-responsibility in the domain of conflict prevention. Concessions to the execution of self-responsibility are integral to the evolving economic paradigm. According to one of its founding principles, men do not fight over cultural differences alone. When they 'fight across ethnic lines it is nearly always the case that they fight over some fundamental issues concerning the distribution and exercise of power, whether economic, political, or both.'[10] Before individuals bring their moral person into play, they are allegedly driven by empirical motives in cultural affairs, i.e. concerning their ethnic, racial, religious identities. Empirical motives are seen to have a decisive influence on their *cultural person*. On the whole, this assumption may still be correct. The account of hidden conflict developed in chapter III and IV hardly serves to release individuals from the realm of passivity. However, at all times there ought to be awareness of the implications of such thinking.

Hypothetical Imperatives

Although technical imperatives and empirical motives might encroach upon people's moral person, they cannot result in the complete dissolution of that moral person. As chapter V mentioned before, we do own a template for the moral side of individual and group behavior in conflict. And so do the primary stakeholders in conflict. Even if this template should only come to the fore in quasi-ethical statements, which conflict is filtered through, thus realizing a mental detour. Therefore, rather than dissolving people's moral person, one can observe quite frequently a process where technical imperatives *self-transform* from pure technical imperatives into deficient ethical imperatives. The resulting imperatives Immanuel Kant used to call 'hypothetical imperatives'.[11] Most important about this process of self-transformation is the reaction it permits in the beneficiaries of interventions. In the worst case, primary stakeholders went to internalize those hypothetical imperatives. Thus, they came to follow empirical motives in their ethical affairs. Technical imperatives became authentic *representatives* of ethical imperatives. A prime assumption while developing this scenario is that conflict parties will not dispose over a system of explicit ethical statements to rationalize conflict. As one example, religious terrorism tends to integrate such a system. Certainly, compared to these cases, threats from deficient ethical imperatives, i.e. hypothetical imperatives, are a mere farce.

The evolving economic paradigm requires deeper analysis for a threat to host deficient ethical imperatives that comprised pure technical imperatives in the first place. The following two sections deal with two complementary questions. Just as the evolving economic paradigm might be working for the rise of hypothetical imperatives in conflict prevention, section 15 shows that ethics itself has occasionally facilitated such a process. The corresponding line of thought in ethics is called *ethical realism*. Two distinct models under ethical realism are subsequently developed as ethical welfarism and ethical modernism. In an effort to render explicit particular ethical implications of the evolving economic paradigm, the section further applies founding aspects of both models to this paradigm. Section 16 moves on to a detailed critique of those implications. It considers whether technical imperatives that underlie interventions for economic development are indeed sufficient in terms of ethical

---

10 A. Cohen, *Two-Dimensional Man: An Essay on the Anthropology of Power and Symbolism in Complex Society*, Berkeley: University of California Press (1974) 94.

11 I. Kant, *Groundwork for the Metaphysics of Morals* [1785] transl. by T.K. Abbott, in Abbott T.K., *Kant's Critique of Practical Reason and other Works on the Theory of Ethics*, London: Longmans and Green (1879) Sec. 2.

principles on which society can rely with conflict prevention. Eventually, this section focuses on a number of ethical paradoxes that are set to derive from deficient hypothetical imperatives.

Both sections ahead are held to confirm a trend that seems to entail the last sequence of points. Therefore, only on first approximation the evolving economic paradigm could carry its name on account of a pivotal role of economic factors in conflict. In a yet deeper sense, it could comply with such a paradigm. So far, a tendency to reduce conflict prevention strategies to technical imperatives and economic interventions only appears to allow for a causal and convenient approach. Ultimately, such narrow focus on technical interventions could also serve to identify the evolving economic paradigm as an *economical* paradigm.

Section 15. The Evolving Economic Paradigm and Ethical Realism

Ethics itself has occasionally facilitated a process where technical imperatives self-transformation into ethical imperatives. In the case of the evolving economic paradigm, this process does not constitute an act of active borrowing from ethics, i.e. the precepts of ethical realism. Ethical implications of that paradigm comply with their name. They are implicit rather than explicit. When seeking to surface those ethical implications, we are responding to a process of implicit self-transformation. The threats attached to this process are greater than explicit reasoning could be. Above all, because the latter tends to remove an option for ethics to react when technical imperatives encroach upon people's moral person. An analysis of the precepts of ethical realism singles out two explicit technical-ethical imperatives that can be read into the evolving economic paradigm, i.e. ethical welfarism and ethical modernism. The ground for those imperatives couldn't be broader than in cases that the characteristics of an ethical situation were determinable in like manner and with a similar degree of certainty as those of scientific objects. Indeed, ethical realism compels to conceive of the core job of ethics in terms of observations of moral facts. Those moral facts are considered as the protons of ethics. From ethical realism, it is only a small step to stating that the demands of an ethical situation concur with those of a benign economic situation. So much the more, the idea of moral facts requires careful analysis.

Moral Facts

Ethical realism evolves with the assumption that the core job of ethics is about collecting moral facts. This assumption must be understood in direct relation to sciences. Most generally speaking, the ethical realist comprises a category of moral agent who has absorbed of a sizeable challenge to ethics from the side of natural sciences and the social sciences. Our moral agent is eager to react to this challenge. In detail, said challenge comprises the use of objective methods when dealing with scientific facts. 'Armed with the distinction between facts and values,'[12] sciences seem to imply that there cannot be *ethical knowledge* in a strict sense of the word, because objective scientific methods cannot be applied to values. Therefore, in reacting to this challenge, our moral agent feels compelled to advocate for an extension of causal and empirical methods from the natural and social sciences to ethics. According to the ethical realist, any bifurcation between facts and values falsely denies parity of scientific reasoning with respect to so divergent domains of inquiry as are sciences and ethics. Both are believed to support knowledge claims.[13]

While this would indicate an improvement to the scientific status of ethics in the first place, the picture appears to have worsened instead. Rather than rescuing ethics, the latter might actually not survive its methodological adaptation. That is, ethics could be irrelevant to the extent that it was doomed to loose its core object quite together with the old methodological ballast. Before, this object consisted of a category of truly ethical questions. What remains of ethics after its methodological adaptation could thus be comprehendible within a purely scientific discourse, led by such disciplines as neuro-sciences, psychology and economics, to mention only some. In this utterly uncomfortable situation, our moral agent is anxious to re-emphasize the unbroken validity of ethics. Therefore, for ethical realism it is not despite but rather because of its methodological adaptation that ethics cannot be substituted through (social) sciences. The basis of this assertion has been the positing of the existence of moral facts. Those moral facts are deemed to assume two qualities, firstly, to be scientifically observable, and secondly, to be genuine moral facts.[14]

Elements of ethical realism are not restricted to modern ethics. The goals of ethical realism bring back to mind a line of thought developed during the early period of enlightenment, which sought to link politics, ethics and sciences in an effective manner. By taking Descartes' *Les Passions de l'Ame* and *Le Traité de l'Homme* as a basis, this line of thought applied mathematical principles both to politics and ethics. From the present perspective, these attempts of philosophers, such as Charles Irénée Castel de Saint Pierre, appear hopelessly over-ambitious. Because they were executed in an almost amateur-like manner, they also attracted the notion of 'pseudo-

---

12 C.M. Korsgaard, *The Sources of Normativity* (with G.A. Cohen, R. Geuss, T. Nagel, B. Williams) Cambridge and New York: Cambridge University Press (1996) 47.

13 R. Werner, 'Ethical Realism', in *Ethics*, Vol. 93, No. 4 (1983) 679. See also R. Werner, 'Ethical Realism Defended', in *Ethics*, Vol. 95, No. 2 (1985) 292-296.

14 The debate on ethical realism, or as it is also labeled moral realism, features a variety of contributions, all revolving, in one way or the other, around the fact-centered, objective, empirical, descriptive, scientific, 'about the world', ontological, anti-relativist or truth-value containing status of ethical judgments. Besides Richard Werner's ethical realism, which forms the basis of this analysis, those contributions include, among others, B.W. Brower, 'Virtue Concepts and Ethical Realism', in *The Journal of Philosophy*, Vol. 85, No. 12 (1988) 675-693; B.W. Brower, 'Dispositional Ethical Realism', in *Ethics*, Vol. 103, No. 2 (1993) 221-249; H.S. Fries, 'The Method of Proving Ethical Realism', in *The Philosophical Review*, Vol. 46, No. 5 (1937) 485-502; A. Gilbert, 'Moral Realism, Individuality, and Justice in War', in *Political Theory*, Vol. 14, No. 1 (1986) 105-135; S. Hook, 'A Critique of Ethical Realism', in *International Journal of Ethics*, Vol. 40, No. 2 (1930) 179-210; J.C. Klagge, 'Moral Realism and Dummett's Challenge', in *Philosophy and Phenomenological Research*, Vol. 48, No. 3 (1988) 545-551; P. Railton, 'Moral Realism', in *The Philosophical Review*, Vol. 95, No. 2 (1986) 163-207; G.F. Schueler, 'Modus Ponens and Moral Realism', in *Ethics*, Vol. 98, No. 3 (1988) 492-500.

cartesianism'.[15] Just like modern ethical realism, they were focused on a fundamental revision of previous thinking. Previous thinking was often restricted to achieving ever-greater degrees of persuasiveness for the social sciences and ethics. Different from such thinking, the new goal was not so much to persuade as to know. As for political sciences, one may recall the startling attempts of William Petty's 'political arithmetic' and Sébastien Vauban's *Dime Royale*. As for ethics, Saint-Pierre's application of Descartes' *idées claires et distinctes* sought to rescue rather than relinquish a whole discipline by bringing it methodologically on par with sciences. At all times, the scientific status of politics and ethics hinged on one additional criterion. For both, this criterion marked the way from a merely logical to a scientific discipline. Obviously, the talk is of the need to provide scientific statements with justification in empirical evidence. Ultimately, the empirical approach contributed much to establish the prevalence of politics as opposed to ethics.[16] All things told, this early movement comprises a legitimate forerunner to present tendency to accelerate the loss of autonomy of ethics, such as it could characterize the evolving economic paradigm.

The adversary of ethical realism nowadays is *ethical internalism*. In fact, ethical realism has not only been proposed in order to accept a challenge from sciences. It also seeks to overcome ethical internalism, which is criticized for failed compliance to empirical scientific standards. From the perspective of ethical internalism, for reasonable reports of moral commitment on the part of individuals, one does not need to posit the existence of moral facts. It is sufficient to look into the psychological set, that is, moral sensibilities of individuals to report on moral commitment.[17] In concrete cases, the sources of moral commitment can be diverse. On the one hand, they are entrenched in particular emotions, such as compassion. On the other hand, they employ pure practical reason, i.e. ethical self-legislation. For ethical realism, the entirely internal nature of both sources provides the entry point for a critique of ethical internalism. More narrowly, it is stressed that:

> at this time it does not seem likely or even possible for us to have hard empirical evidence which could establish ethical internalism. We simply do not have the means to climb into another's conscious experiences to determine if their report of moral observation is a result of fact or feeling.[18]

In other words, ethical internalism leaves it open whether real moral commitment occurred. One can borrow from a basic distinction, which Immanuel Kant established, to illustrate this point. According to this distinction, ethical internalism does

---

15 M.L. Perkins, *The Moral and Political Philosophy of the Abbé de Saint-Pierre*, Genève and Paris: E. Droz, Minard (1959); M.L. Perkins, 'Civil Theology in the Writings of the Abbé de Saint-Pierre', in *Journal of the History of Ideas*, Vol. 18, No. 2 (1957) 242-253; M.L. Perkins, 'An Unpublished Letter from Saint-Pierre to Daguesseau', in *Modern Language Notes*, Vol. 70, No. 2 (1955) 110-113.

16 As Saint Pierre put it in C.IC. de Saint Pierre, *Annales Politiques de Feu Monsieur Charles-Irenée Castel, Abbé de Saint Pierre*, Londres: s.n. (1758): 'It was only when I compared the usefulness of books about morals with that of sound laws and institutional arrangements that I was forced to give preference to political sciences rather than moral philosophy' [author's transl.].

17 G. Harman, *The Nature of Morality*, New York: Oxford University Press (1977).

18 Werner (1983).

not clarify whether a moral action was really sought 'from duty' or only 'in accordance with duty', for example because of fears of punishment. At the same time of sharpening a critique of ethical internalism, this critique further illuminates ethical realism's own commitment to sciences. This commitment is empirical, in as much as it installs methodological tools such as reliance on empirical evidence to ethics. Explicitly, moral observations are limited to those cases where 'an opinion is formed as a direct result of perception.'[19] Next, this must bring up the question what kind of preconditions direct perceptions pose on the side of those moral facts that want to be observed. To the extent that those moral facts are taken for real, ethical realism must assume the existence of some new entities, which ethical internalism does not need to do. With a strictly empirical lens, one only observes morally right and wrong actions. The question is whether this lens is also applicable to moral facts that embody 'moral rightness' and 'moral wrongness'. Obviously, this would be absurd. In order to arrive at moral facts, ethical realism needed to swell ontology. Therefore, in what way does ethical realism formulate an ontological commitment?[20]

The answer to this question is composed of purely *negative* argumentation, as far as ethical realism is concerned. It actually redefines the status of perceptions in sciences. Ethical realists thus assert that objective observations are always the result not purely of the way the world is, but partly of one's own background beliefs. From the perspective of ethical realism, there are no 'immaculate perceptions'.[21] There are no absolute facts in sciences, which is not supposed to mean that we create facts and that everything is culturally relative. The same argument that limits the objectivity of sciences and discards pure empiricism, has been considered good enough to draw positive conclusions for the existence of moral facts in ethics. In reality, the argument fails to consider the ontological status of moral facts in any proper sense. Ethical realism tells us that 'the wrongs of morality are as real and legitimate a part of our experience as are the protons of science.'[22] In the end, objective moral facts barely survive the act of their proclamation. Rather than proving the possibility of ethical knowledge by presenting concrete moral facts, which could not work given their nebulous ontological status, ethical realism defects to a most general category of moral facts. Those general moral facts are called *ungrounded grounders*. Ungrounded grounders are about as general as first premises in sciences, for example, the premise that the world exists:

> Ethical inquiry, like all other inquiry, begins with its own presuppositions and [...] these presuppositions are among our ungrounded grounders. This, in part, is what characterizes ethical inquiry as objective and distinguishes it from matters of taste. I *know* that pain and anguish are intrinsically bad and worthy of avoidance. I have no idea what could convince me, including divine visitation, of the goodness of pain and anguish (this is not to say that pain and anguish are not, at times, extrinsically good). I *know* that pleasure and happiness are intrinsically good and worthy of pursuit. Again, I have no idea what could convince me

---

19 Ibid. 653.

20 For a critique of ethical realism, see also B.C. Postow, 'Werner's Ethical Realism', in *Ethics*, Vol. 95, No. 2 (1985) 285-291.

21 Werner (1983) 679.

22 Ibid.

of the intrinsic badness of pleasure or happiness (which, again, is not to say that they may not be, on occasion, extrinsically bad).[23]

All things told, there are two options how ethical realism may exceed a limited number of ungrounded grounders. Taken alone, those ungrounded grounders constitute a meager reservoir of moral facts and ethical knowledge. More precisely, those options are ethical welfarism and ethical modernism. Both options are originally designed here. They permit us to proceed to a number of explicit technical-ethical imperatives that can be probed for the evolving economic paradigm as an ensuing step. Beyond improving the ontological basis of ethical realism, both options factor out the most serious shortcoming of pure ethical realism, which is the following:

As a result of its thin ontological basis and desertion to a category of ungrounded grounders, ethical realism entails a tendency to neglect the action-guiding and justificatory components of moral observations. For the purpose of proving that ethical knowledge is possible and that ethics can be on par with sciences, ethical realism overly focuses on the status of moral observations. It is obsessed with the epistemological status of such observations, while neglecting their genuine *function*. Ethical realism 'explains how the objective descriptive meaning of such utterances is possible by providing an account of how moral facts are possible.'[24] However, it ignores that an important function of moral observations is to enable concrete ethical imperatives. Those ethical imperatives are action-guiding in people's daily life. Beyond that, moral observations found ethical norms by which concrete actions and imperatives can be evaluated and justified. Justifications as they occur to ethical realists are fully focused on the scientific standard rather than ethical strength of moral observations. Ultimately, the goal to discover ethical knowledge reveals as a prime obstacle for the identification of concrete ethical knowledge.

Both previously mentioned models share into the scientific spin of ethical realism. According to this spin, causalities and moral facts are to count in ethics. Different from ethical realism, they also provide answers to the task of identifying concrete ethical imperatives and norms. However, besides the fact that those imperatives and norms are rather technical-ethical, they shrink the process of proactive argumentation that should be a part of their identification and justification. At a glance, both models deviate as follows: The first model, to be developed as ethical welfarism, installs empirical nature as a prime moral fact to form the sole basis of all ethical imperatives and norms. More precisely, it focuses on people's natural interests. The second model, to be developed as ethical modernism, goes beyond that point. Rather than deducting the basis of ethical imperatives and norms from aspects of the empirical nature, it identifies both within that nature itself. By dwelling upon development laws of history, it suspends a need to contemplate norms for individual behavior.

---

23 Ibid. 676.
24 Ibid. 663.

Ethical Welfarism[25]

For the sake of determining moral facts, it may not be the best thing to climb into people's minds and intentions. Scientifically, such internal observations only provide weak evidence. Ethical welfarism transforms this earlier revealed precept of ethical realism into a positive doctrine. Thus, the best proof of a good character is held to relate to observations of good actions.[26] While it is always safer to judge people's actions rather than mindsets, this is even more true for the physical consequences of those actions. In particular cases, we may then say that action A was morally right and action B was morally wrong, because it had this or that consequence.[27] However, in all those cases one is also bound to say why one action is morally right, whereas another is not. In other words, we need to specify a criterion which morally right actions have to be conformable to. *Consequentialism* alone does not serve that purpose (Fig. 6.1). As an ethical welfarist one is challenged to observe a moral fact here.

A prime moral fact applicable to the given situation comprises individuals' natural interests. Those interests are linked to and rationalized by the utility principle. In Jeremy Bentham's founding definition, the utility principle comprises:

> that principle which approves or disapproves of every action whatsoever according to the tendency it appears to have to augment or diminish the happiness of the party whose interest is in question: or, what is the same thing in other words to promote or to oppose that happiness. I say of every action whatsoever, and therefore not only of every action of a private individual, but of every measure of government.[28]

Bentham's reference to happiness is partly misleading and should not be taken to theorize a strictly eudemonistic concept of utility. For Bentham and most classical utilitarians, a hedonistic line is central in giving impact to people's interests. This line emphasizes the intrinsic goodness of pleasure and fundamental worth of avoiding pain.

---

25 The term ethical welfarism is chosen so as to to distinguish this strand from related notions such as welfare analysis, welfarism or welfarist utilitarianism. At the same time it: (a) ensures a general lingual connection with economic pondering on welfarism; (b) signals partial distance from classical welfare analysis, which provides the traditional economic account of welfarism; (c) makes clear that the strand developed here comprises an ethical strand in the broader domain of welfare-related economic thought; (d) elucidates that this stance adopts elements of a very particular line within utilitarian thought. The labels of welfarism and welfarist utilitarianism have been applied to capture ethical theories that absorb of other aspects of utilitarianism. See particularly A. Sen, 'Utilitarianism and Welfarism', in *The Journal of Philosophy*, Vol. 76, No. 9 (1979) 463-489; P. Foot, 'Utilitarianism and the Virtues', in *Mind*, New Series, Vol. 94, No. 374 (1985) 196-209.

26 J.S. Mill, *Utilitarianism*, London: Parker, Son and Bourn (1863).

27 For a pertinent critique of consequentialism, or how to be a nonconsequentialist, see E. Anderson, *Value in Ethics and Economics*, Cambridge MA: Harvard University Press (1993); E. Anderson, 'Reasons, Attitudes, and Values: Replies to Sturgeon and Piper', in *Ethics*, Vol. 106, No. 3 (1996) 538-554. For a related critique of nonconsequentialism see N.L. Sturgeon, 'Anderson on Reason and Value', in *Ethics*, Vol. 106, No. 3 (1996) 509-524.

28 J. Bentham, *An Introduction to the Principles of Morals and Legislation*, London: Printed for T. Payne (1789) Ch. I.

Fig. 6.1: Versions of Utilitarian Theories

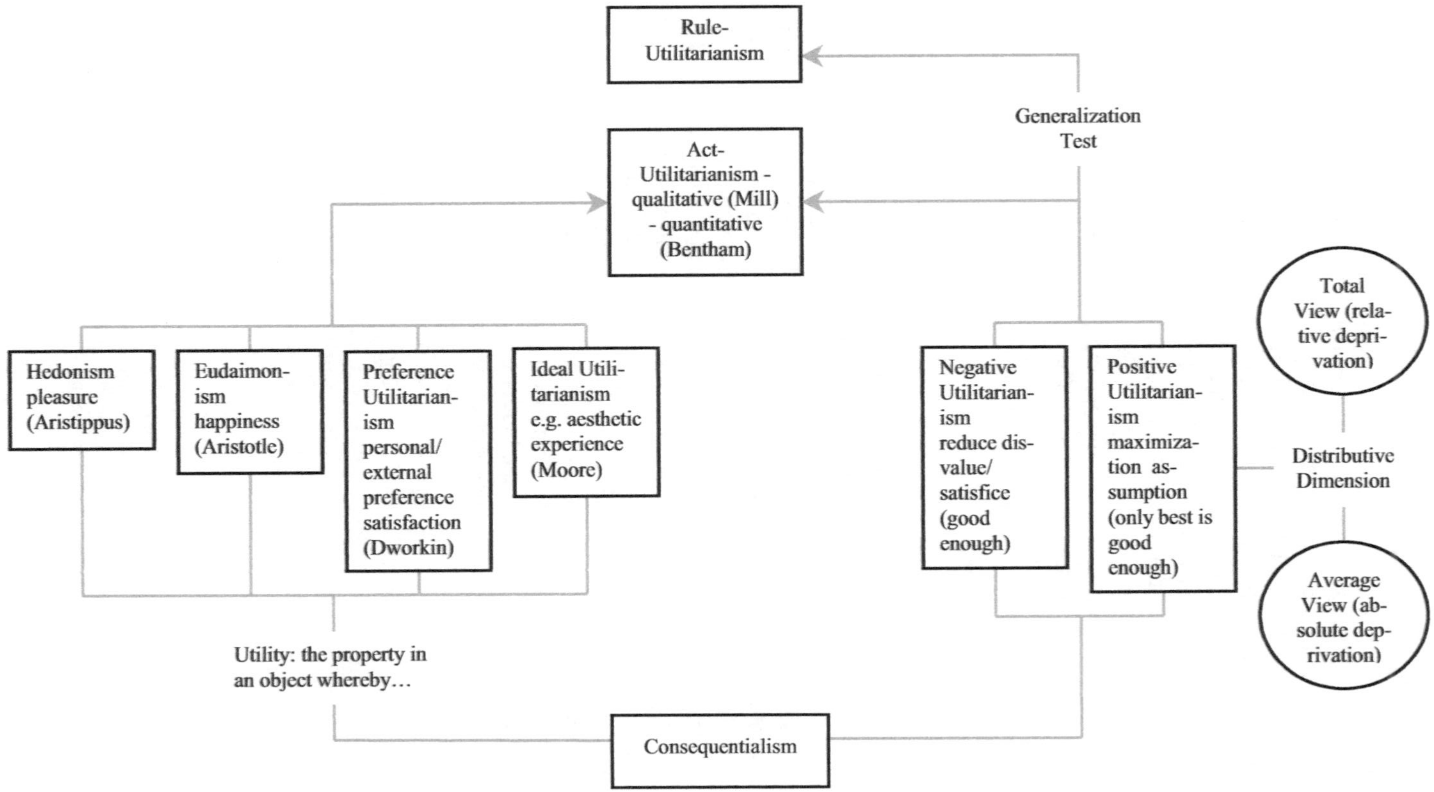

Thus, Bentham declared: 'Nature has placed mankind under the governance of two sovereign masters, pain and pleasure. It is for them alone to point out what we ought to do, as well as to determine what we shall do [...] They govern us in all we do, in all we say, in all we think: every effort we can make to throw off our subjection, will serve but to demonstrate and confirm it. In words a man may pretend to abjure their empire: but in reality he will remain subject to it all the while. The principle of utility recognizes this subjection.'[29] In the first place, the utility principle seems to do little more but to provide yet another ungrounded grounder. In actual fact, it makes serious with those ungrounded grounders. Ethical welfarism establishes the utility principle as the *only* moral fact by which to measure the consequences of moral actions. In other words, it takes this principle as the only source of ethical value and normativity of a particular action.[30] That particular action was morally right in as much as it contributed to a more of pleasure. For the same action, it would not have been enough that its intention was for a more of pleasure. It was morally right only because it achieved real progress with such pleasure. The reason why Bentham spoke more conservatively of a moral action's 'tendency' rather than actual power to augment the utility function of a party owes to the action-guiding or in-situ component of the utility principle. After all, this component makes ethical welfarism superior to abstract ethical realism, which is only concerned with the scientific status of moral facts. Therefore, in reality we have to assess the utility-augmenting, or, which is the same, ethical characteristics of an action before moving towards that action. This anticipatory moment brings in uncertainties as to the actual consequences of an action. Of course, from an ethical evaluator's perspective there is no need to emphasize tendencies. All consequences are clear once the job of an ethical evaluator gets underway. On the whole, Bentham's utilitarianism is more focused on the evaluative component of the utility principle. But he also knew about the in-situ component, which comes to the fore in his dwelling upon tendencies.

Ethical Welfarism and Act-Utilitarianism: While starting with pure consequentialism, we have subsequently climbed the left side of the center quadrangle in the above figure. Thus climbing the ladder of moral facts represented in the utility principle, we have stopped at such distinct points as hedonism, the philosophical ancestor of the pleasure principle, and eudemonism, i.e. Aristotle's theorizing of happiness as a prime ethical good.[31] By now, it is also clear why ethical welfarism provides for an elaborated version of ethical realism. Besides referencing to the utility principle, ethical welfarism leads to what is customarily called act-utilitarianism in ethics. Both, ethical welfarism and act-utilitarianism combine particular moral facts with consequentialism, i.e. the idea that actions are justified by their consequences.[32]

---

[29] Ibid.

[30] For an exemplary debate of pros and cons of actual consequence utilitarianism see M.G. Singer, 'Actual Consequence Utilitarianism', in *Mind*, New Series, Vol. 86, No. 341 (1977) 67-77; J. Temkin, 'Actual Consequence Utilitarianism: A Reply to Professor Singer', in *Mind*, New Series, Vol. 87, No. 347 (1978) 412-414; M.G. Singer, 'Further on Actual Consequence Utilitarianism', in *Mind*, New Series, Vol. 92, No. 366 (1983) 270-274.

[31] Aristotle, *Nicomachean Ethics* [ca. 350 BC], London: Penguin Books (2003) Ch. 10.

[32] In the endless literature on act-utilitarianism Peter Singer and John L. Mackie have voiced prominent support and opposition respectively. See P. Singer, 'Is Act-Utilitarianism Self-Defeating?', in *The*

However, while ethical welfarism and act-utilitarianism sometimes come very close, there are also important differences. A series of points illustrates those differences and further specifies ethical welfarism. Major differences are rooted in the particular methodological approach ethical welfarism inherits from ethical realism.

Firstly, the difference between both concepts is not per se about a plus of methodological stringency in ethical welfarism. It is not about a scientific as opposed to non-scientific approach to ethics. John Stuart Mill, a main proponent of the liberal model in chapter I, has been a major advocate of act-utilitarianism. Too much, Mill has been concerned with the logical status of ethics in order to justify such a distinction. In short, his thinking was devoted to the amenability of the whole of human conduct to the authority of logic.[33] More narrowly, the difference between ethical welfarism and act-utilitarianism is about those moral facts both approve in the process of augmenting consequentialism by substantial ethical norms. As for ethical welfarism, the limits of those moral facts are fixed by the scientific doctrine that moral observations ought to be limited to cases where 'an opinion is formed as a direct result of perception.' In a word, moral facts have to be empirically observable. Apart from the pleasure principle, some practical forms of eudemonism comprise valid moral facts. As previously mentioned, both have sometimes been used interchangeably. This trend can be observed particularly well in Bentham, where happiness often stands for pleasure. Occasionally, this is also the case in Mill. At the same point where classical utilitarian theories invoke the pleasure principle, there is a lot of talk about preference satisfaction and welfare today. Ronald Dworkin's dealing with preferences in terms of personal and external preferences provides a prototype in this context.[34] The details of this debate are beyond the scope of this analysis. The old pleasure principle is sufficiently broad to embrace those debates. Overall, it leads to the same consequences. Different from that, a number of imperfect moral facts cannot be assimilated into ethical welfarism. Those imperfect moral facts include G.E. Moore's dwelling upon aesthetical experience as a utility, as well as any other form of ideal utilitarianism.[35] The major difference of such moral facts concerns their non-empirical nature, and the problems they pose to a methodological approach to observation in terms of direct perception.

Compared to ethical welfarism, act-utilitarianism accommodates for some non-empirical interests and aspects of ideal utilitarianism. As in the case of ethical welfarism, this may be seen as a result of particular scientific doctrines. For example, in terms of particular scientific doctrines, Mill's philosophy subscribed to an extension of the province of logics from pure syllogizing or deduction to induction. It did not define scientific principles according to the requirements of induction in the first

---

Philosophical Review, Vol. 81, No. 1 (1972) 94-104; J.L. Mackie, 'The Disutility of Act-Utilitarianism', in *The Philosophical Quarterly*, Vol. 23, No. 93 (1973) 289-300.

33 J.S. Mill, *A System of Logic, Ratiocinative and Inductive: Being a Connected View of the Principles of Evidence, and the Methods of Scientific Investigation*, London: J.W. Parker (1843).

34 R. Dworkin, *Taking Rights Seriously*, Cambridge MA: Harvard University Press (1977).

35 See H. Rashdall, *The Theory of Good and Evil: A Treatise on Moral Philosophy*, Oxford: Clarendon Press (1907); G.E. Moore, *Principia Ethica*, Cambridge: Cambridge University Press (1903).

place.[36] According to such view, induction was considered to be as much entitled to be called reasoning as the demonstrations of geometry. Therefore, the office of logics was to supply a test for ascertaining whether or not inductive assertion was well grounded. To the same extent as it was logical, this test could not be empirical. As *ars artium*, or the science of science itself, logics were deemed to be not the same thing with knowledge. Rather, it was seen as coextensive with the field of knowledge. Thus, it was not confined to various branches of mathematics. In Mill's words:

> Logic is the common judge and arbiter of all particular investigations. It does not undertake to find evidence, but to determine whether it has been found. Logic neither observes, nor invents, nor discovers; but judges.[37]

In opposition to William Hamilton's logic of consistency, Mill's system of logic professed to conform to a *logic of truth*.[38] Just as the inductive truths of sciences required a logical test, so fell the whole of human conduct under the authority of logics. The truths of ethics, i.e. its moral facts, were considered to be the inductive truths of a science of morals. Concerning the principle of utility, Mill has dealt with the specific logical proof that could confirm its truth status as a first principle and sole criterion for ethics. Like any question of first principles, the given problem was held to be not amenable to direct proof, or empirical evidence. However, different from ethical welfarism, Mill was willing to make at least some concessions to the demands of empirical evidence. In like manner as the only proof capable of being given that an object is visible is that people actually see it, the sole evidence to proof that anything is desirable was deemed to be that people actually desire it. According to Mill, this assumption was sufficient in order to arrive at a question of fact and inductive experience. Concretely, the requested proof was held to be suppliable by practiced self-consciousness and self-observation, assisted by observation of others.[39] In contrast, ethical realism keeps rejecting the possibility of such self-observation, because in terms of hard empirical evidence it is impossible to climb into another person's conscious experiences. However, for act-utilitarians, self-observations open a window on non-empirical interests and aspects of ideal utilitarianism. Its logical rather than empirical approach integrates aesthetical and other experiences that are constitutive of our higher interests. These interests are seen to comprise genuine moral facts.

Secondly, as for ethical welfarism the scientific principle of hard empirical evidence determines those interests that qualify for moral facts, i.e. pleasure, pain and happiness. Beyond that, the principle establishes particular pleasures that succeed in the overall domain of pleasures and pains. More narrowly, ethical welfarism recognizes a number of 'real' pleasures and pains, all related to the deprivation of physi-

---

36 On the issue how Mill's logics explains the allowance of secondary principles in his act-utilitarianism see also J.M. Baker, 'Utilitarianism and Secondary Principles', in *The Philosophical Quarterly*, Vol. 21, No. 82 (1971) 69-71.

37 Mill (1843) Introduction.

38 J.S. Mill, *An Examination of Sir William Hamilton's Philosophy, and of the Principal Philosophical Questions discussed in his Writings*, Boston: W.V. Spencer (1865).

39 Mill (1863) Ch. 4.

cal empirical needs. Thus, it *radicalizes* Bentham's handling of pleasures and pains, which concurred with a quantitative rather than qualitative approach. The latter basically ignored a hierarchy of pleasures and pains. Besides a quantitative approach, Bentham still recognized pleasures and pains beyond those that are purely physical or empirical. He, therefore, located the pleasures of wealth and their opposite, the pains of privation, next to such ideal utilities as the pleasures of imagination. All of them were subjected to the same quantitative formula. Sometimes called felicific or hedonic calculus, this formula elaborated upon the value of particular pleasures and pains in terms of their intensity, duration, certainty or uncertainty, as well as propinquity or remoteness.[40] A key idea behind this quantitative formula was that complex pleasures and pains were resolvable into diverse simple ones, such as the ones mentioned above.[41] More than that, Bentham believed that beyond complex pleasures, most of our variegated motives could be reduced to basic ones. Thus, all such things as fear of God, public spirit, patriotism, general benevolence, compassion or gratitude were deemed to be interpretable as forms of pleasure.[42]

Before looking into how ethical welfarism radicalizes Bentham's quantitative categorization of pleasures and pains, one may see what a qualitative dealing would be. To no small extent, this serves to illustrate the reductionist approach ethical welfarism actually follows. Once more, Mill's version of act-utilitarianism adds a quality dimension to discussions about the ethical potential of pleasures and pains. Beyond qualifying for moral facts, Mill considered the higher faculties to be more elevated than the 'animal appetites'. With reference to the pleasures of the intellect and imagination, he always stressed that it is 'better to be a human being dissatisfied than a pig satisfied'. The hierarchy of pleasures these statements invoke were meant to constitute yet another unquestionable fact. Ultimately, the existence of those higher faculties allowed Mill to speak of moral duties at all. At the same time, his trust in a hierarchy of pleasures was all but perfect. More than once, he acknowledged that people's capacity for noble feelings are a tender plant, easily killed, not only by hostile influences but by mere want of sustenance:

> In the majority of young persons it speedily dies away if the occupations to which their position in life has devoted them, and the society into which it has thrown them, are not favourable to keeping that higher capacity in exercise.[43]

What kept Mill to his original belief was that poverty could once be extinguished by the wisdom of society. Today, this may sound like wishful thinking. It might also lead back to ethical welfarism, but it doesn't really. A good deal of realism in any version of ethical realism is not based on concessions to the hardships of life and the moral losses they imply; moral losses that are particularly associated with the higher faculties. The realism of such ethics lies with the scientific principle of hard empirical evidence. Guided by its empirical lens, ethical welfarism identifies the pains of

---

40 Bentham (1789) Ch. IV.
41 Ibid. Ch. V.
42 H.F. Pitkin, 'Slippery Bentham: Some Neglected Cracks in the Foundation of Utilitarianism', in *Political Theory*, Vol. 18, No. 1 (1990) 106.
43 Mill (1863) Ch. 2.

privation not so much as an obstacle to higher ethical behavior, but as a moral fact the satisfaction of which possesses exclusive ethical quality. Therefore, the satisfaction of such pains is not just a means that eventually frees individuals for higher ethical behavior. It is a virtual end in itself. Rather than using negative language, this point can also be put into positive language. Thus, one may emphasize the 'pleasures of wealth' rather than seeking an end to the 'pains of privation'. In either case we are asked to absorb of a moral fact. Beyond discarding a qualitative perspective on pleasures and pains, ethical welfarism radicalizes Bentham's quantitative approach, by virtue of a tendency to assign the pains of privation and the pleasures of wealth to be exclusive moral facts. Necessarily, the pleasures of the intellect are ethically insignificant to ethical welfarists. Therefore, an integral part of the scientific doctrine of hard empirical evidence is that the difference must fall between specifying something as absent, and that same thing being absent from specification. In our case, this something comprises the ethical value of people's higher faculties. Scientifically speaking, we are not allowed to attach ethical meaning to those faculties. They are indeed as if they were absent. Conversely, in as much as the pleasures of wealth comprise exclusive moral facts, economic issues gain strong ground in ethics. They do so on account of their sizeable impact on people's state of wealth and levels of deprivation they encounter, as well as the natural interests that relate to enhancing the one and to minimizing the other.

Elements of ethical welfarism can be observed as early as in the first half of the eighteenth century. Here, they were brought forward by a writer, i.e. Saint Pierre, who also framed the broader picture of early ethical realism. He did so yet before Bentham developed utilitarianism as an independent ethical system.[44] His profession combined with a distinct interest in some of the most puzzling problems of conflict of the time. Coincidentally, he coined the catchphrase of 'perpetual peace', which later engaged philosophical heavy weights like Rousseau and Kant. For sure, those later attempts were critical of the phrase's inventor.[45] For this earliest proponent of a peace movement, the key to solving large-scale conflict was the following: Europe's leaders needed to absorb of utilitarian principles in their political decisions. The reason why an issue as practical as Europe's *questio pacis*, its promises and limitations after the 1713-14 Peace Treaties of Utrecht, could gain the attention of ethics, was tied to the lingering problems of the *just war* doctrine. Thus, in the realm of the classical law of nations, defensive action in cases where one state had suffered harm from another only comprised a special case of just war.[46] The legal basis for any aggressive war emanated from the sovereignty of nation-states. It also derived from the

---

[44] C.I.C. de Saint Pierre, *Projet pour Rendre la Paix Perpetuelle en Europe*, Utrecht: A. Schouten (1713).

[45] See J.J. Rousseau, *Extrait du Projet de Paix Perpétuelle de Monsieur l'Abbé de Saint-Pierre*, Paris: s.n. (1761); J.J. Rousseau, *Jugement sur le Projet de Paix Perpétuelle de l'Abbé de Saint-Pierre*, Paris: s.n. (1782); I. Kant, *Zum ewigen Frieden: Ein Philosophischer Entwurf*, Königsberg: Friedrich Nicolovius (1795).

[46] See J.v. Elbe, 'The Evolution of the Concept of the Just War in International Law', in *American Journal of International Law*, Vol. 33, No. 4 (1939) 665-688; T. Pangle, 'Justice Among Nations in Platonic and Aristotelian Political Philosophy', in *American Journal of Political Science*, Vol. 42, No. 2 (1998) 377-397; G. Schwarzenberger, 'Ius Pacis Ac Belli: Prolegomena to a Sociology of International Law', in *American Journal of International Law*, Vol. 37, No. 3 (1943) 460-479.

principle of non-interference in internal affairs. Both points were defining parts of that law. In this uncomfortable situation, ethics was challenged to develop its own vision and recipe for peace in Europe. However, the very first of those visions and recipes was of a utilitarian guise. To the extent that it was brought forward with the same scientific spin characterizing early ethical realism, it also came close to ethical welfarism. It carries this name most properly, given the fact that it considered issues of conflict in relation to individual utility functions. In Saint Pierre's own words, it considered those issues in correlation to the principle of beneficence, or *bienfaisance*. Broad-based fellowship to this principle would realize perpetual peace in Europe, in as much as it permitted to specify technical imperatives aiming to augment the utility functions of individuals and nations. Ultimately, the ethical case for conflict prevention was about technical imperatives, adherence to which would suffice to solve the peace problem facing early modern times.

Elements of ethical welfarism are not limited to early hour peace activists. They can also be found in present conflict debates, and the evolving economic paradigm particularly. This is the question we went out to observe. Upon focusing on ethical theories that apply a scientific approach, i.e. ethical realism, this section re-arrived at economic questions. It re-arrived their via the utility principle and the 'pleasures of wealth', which are defining elements of ethical welfarism today. As opposed to this, the foregoing section proceeded under inverted premises. It came ultimately close to ethics, while searching the evolving economic paradigm for a tendency to integrate technical-ethical or hypothetical imperatives. Now, where is the crossing point of both approaches? Do we need to apply founding aspects of ethical welfarism to hypothetical imperatives associated with the evolving economic paradigm? Eventually, this would also establish that those imperatives are what they threaten to stand for, i.e. technical imperatives that self-transform into ethical imperatives. Before seeking an answer to this important question, some yet more specific aspects of ethical welfarism merit a closer look. These aspects serve to bring the evolving economic paradigm and ethical welfarism even closer to each other.

Ethical Welfarism and Ethical Compromises: So far, this analysis has climbed the ladder of moral facts representing the left side of Fig. 6.1. The question with those moral facts was about ethical criteria that impact on a core focus on the consequences of moral actions. As an overall moral fact, the utility principle has been invoked for the action-guiding or in-situ as well as evaluative or justificatory components of ethics. Ethical realism has been ultimately quiet about both aspects, given a narrow focus on the scientific status of moral facts. While progressing, this analysis has concentrated on the individual moral agent, i.e. his or her eligibility for real pleasures. Focus has been on measuring these pleasures quantitatively. Despite this quantitative lens, no absolute quantities of pleasure have been specified for each individual agent. Also, there has been no weighing whether such quantities could be in conflict with other people's qualification for pleasures. In a word, our analysis did not elaborate upon quantities of pleasure in *relative* terms. A corresponding perspective we owe to the evolving economic paradigm, given its focus on horizontal inequalities and relative deprivation. Obviously, the absolute and relative components of pleasure cannot be analyzed in separation from each other. A joint analysis of both considers the right side of Fig. 6.1.

Firstly, a conceptualization of absolute gains of pleasure which people qualify for morally can take utterly different forms. In the first place, ethical welfarism must proceed on a *maximization* assumption. This assumption underlies Bentham's felicific calculus and foresees that only the best is good enough, i.e. that an agent's greatest happiness be pursued. In this case, ethics is defined as the art of directing individual actions to the production of the greatest possible quantity of happiness.[47] A different conceptualization relates to the view that the consequences of an action ought to be *good enough*, rather than the best ones possible. In terms of pleasure gains, this means that to 'satisfice' is in many situations preferable to seeking to maximize.[48] Obviously, the impact on other people's striving for pleasure differs depending on which strand is endorsed. Certainly, there must be a greater impact if one subscribes to ethical welfarism's maximization assumption. An intimately related question concerns how the utility functions of groups and individuals can be reconciled under this condition, especially if such reconciliation is sought on ethical grounds.

Secondly, a focus on pleasure as a prime moral fact brings up a weird situation for ethical welfarism. Given such focus, individuals are captured as moral right holders, rather than as ethical duty bearers. Provided that moral rights are thought of as quantifiable and that a maximization assumption has been endorsed, ethics is challenged to equilibrate the moral rights of different agents. Of course, while doing so it must assume that those agents socialize. Similar to an economic debate about distributive justice, the task of equilibrating moral rights is challenged to reconcile the *same* moral right of different agents, i.e. their eligibility to pleasure. It is faced with this job, rather than with balancing any moral right of agent A with another moral right or duty of agent B. Applied to a classical example, the issue is not as simple as to reconcile agent A's moral right not to be lied at with agent B's moral duty to save agent A, where agent A was incurably sick and agent B knew about it. Under the premises of ethical welfarism, the moral rights to pleasure of two or several agents must face each other directly. They do so, in view of a narrow definition of moral rights in terms of moral facts, which is essential to this theory. On the other hand, this does not mean that a solution will be more difficult than in the other cases. However, the quality of that solution would seem to be different. Thus, it requires *compromises*, while ethics is normally not about compromises. In effect, the challenge to seek compromises within ethics under ethical welfarism does not only resemble an economic debate about distributive justice. It features important overlap with such a debate. After all, pleasures that are key to ethical welfarism consist of socio-economic gains. But how does ethical welfarism respond to a situation of con-

---

47 Bentham (1789) Ch. XVII.

48 A. Simon, *Models of Man: Social and Rational, Mathematical Essays on Rational Human Behavior in a Social Setting*, New York: Wiley (1957). A related angle is commonly referred to as negative utilitarianism. It focuses on the reduction of suffering and the 'least amount of avoidable suffering for all'. See E. Gurney, *Tertium Quid: Chapters on Various Disputed Questions*. London: Kegan Paul, Trench (1887). Elements of negative utilitarianism can also be found in K. Popper, *The Open Society and its Enemies*, London: G. Routledge & Sons (1945) Ch. 5. For the attribution of this view to Popper, see R.N. Smart, 'Negative Utilitarianism', in *Mind*, New Series, Vol. 67, No. 268 (1958) 542-543.

flict between individual utility functions, given the fact that it comprises an ethical rather than economic theory, and that it must operate through ethical rather than technical imperatives?

Thirdly, a first question in this situation concerns how far to take a compromise between different agents. For example, do we want the moral history of our agents, i.e. past accruing of pleasure, to enter the balance sheets? Alternatively, such balancing will only consider the present situation. Therefore, are conflicting utilities confined to the consequences of a present action, or do they include stocks of pleasure, where the agent with the higher stock is held to make the greater concessions? For example, it might be plausible that agent A, poor in terms of experienced pleasure, qualifies for a higher quantity of pleasure from the present situation than agent, who resides over a wealth of experienced pleasures. Ethical welfarism must cope with the question how far to extend the relative component, sometimes called *total view*. Given this question, it resembles an economic theory of relative deprivation. The latter elaborates economic distribution decisions on the basis of calculating stocks of assets of different economic agents. In the opposite case, ethical welfarism could remove any relative component from ethical compromises. Thus, its sole criterion was whether the sum total of pleasure from an action was enhanced, irrespective of how that pleasure distributed among various moral agents. It would then accept the famous *average view*. Eventually, ethical welfarism moved closer to an economic theory of absolute deprivation.

Fourthly, utilitarianism has sometimes responded differently to the situation of moral competition. Its solution has been to leave the concrete situation of two or more agents advocating their moral rights against each other. Therefore, a rule has been placed where act-utilitarianism and ethical welfarism approve of a cause. This cause has been to link in a straight manner individuals' natural interests with an ethical norm for action.[49] As regards those natural interests, Bentham emphasized once that 'the chain of causes and effects, are fastened to their throne.'[50] Rather than deducting norms from people's natural interests directly, a rule-utilitarian adaptation of ethical welfarism in situations of moral competition would filter the actions of each moral agent through a *generalization test*. Thus, it realized a detour where agents aimed at consequences that only benefited them. This detour needed to be applied both to the in-situ and evaluative components of ethical welfarism. Overall, this generalization test will have the following form. It will be charged upon moral agents and evaluators as a first moral principle that locates in considerable distance to any prime moral fact emphasized by ethical welfarism:

> Action *a* by moral agent A in situation *b* is morally right only and if performance of A by the class of similar moral agents will produce an optimific result.

---

49 An interest in causations and laws feeds into the scientific drive of utilitarian ethics. As such it has been stated repeatedly that the 'utilitarian position [...] show[s] its wholly external character, as resulting largely from the great advances made in physical science during the present century. The true scientific spirit finds expression in examining the laws of phenomena - in determining customary coexistences and sequences. The same spirit finds expression in utilitarian and evolutionary ethics.' N. Wilde, 'Kant's Relation to Utilitarianism', in *The Philosophical Review*, Vol. 3, No. 3 (1894) 291.

50 Bentham (1789) Ch. I.

Obviously, a rule-utilitarian adaptation of ethical welfarism and act-utilitarianism will often lead to reject actions that would have otherwise been approved.[51] For example, consider the pleasures of wealth: As a motive for action of agent A, such pleasures are optimific. As a universal rule, they are useless, if the goal is to forge an ethical compromise between the same moral right of different agents. Therefore, for the sake of securing the utility function of each moral agent in the long run, ethical welfarism is forced to consider Mill's utilitarian rule. According to this rule, the greatest amount of happiness altogether, rather than the agent's own greatest happiness is key.[52] Concretely, this rule is imposes abstinence on our agents, thus restricting their moral right to pleasure. As Mill stated: 'In the case of abstinences indeed—of things which people forbear to do from moral considerations, though the consequences in the particular case might be beneficial—it would be unworthy of an intelligent agent not to be consciously aware that the action is of a class which, if practiced generally, would be generally injurious, and that this is the ground of the obligation to abstain from it.'[53] Even Bentham considered self-government as indispensable of private ethics. An inevitable part of self-governance comprised 'duty to others'.[54] The latter implied forbearing to diminish the pleasures of others.[55]

Fifthly, beyond postulating their general existence, rules or ethical imperative that serve to accommodate for the utility functions of others must be rendered explicit. Ethical realists in the old days relied on the Golden Rule: 'Treat others as you want to be treated.'[56] Saint Pierre's internationalized version of the utilitarian rule was almost identical with the Golden Rule. Any international law was deemed to be deductible from this rule. Only those peace treaties would endure that were built on it. For sure, this was an illusion not only in the old days. Hardly ever, Europe's lead-

---

51 D.C. Emmons, 'Act vs. Rule Utilitarianism', in *Mind*, Vol. 82, No. 326 (1973) 226. On the relationship between act- and rule-utilitarianism see also J. Chandler, 'Act-Utilitarianism and Collective Action', in *Ethics*, Vol. 84, No. 1 (1973) 78-85.

52 On the rule-utilitarian elements of Mill's utilitarianism see J.O. Urmson, 'The Interpretation of the Moral Philosophy of J.S. Mill', in *The Philosophical Quarterly*, Vol. 3, No. 10 (1953) 33-39; J.D. Mabbott, 'Interpretations of Mill's Utilitarianism', in *The Philosophical Quarterly*, Vol. 6, No. 23 (1956) 115-120.

53 Mill (1863) Ch. 2.

54 Bentham (1789) Ch. XVII.

55 Debates considering the benefits and limitations of a rule-utilitarian adaptation of act-utilitarianism are manifold, and so are the labels applied to these debates. An exemplary debate concerns J.J.C. Smart's distinction between extreme and restricted utilitarianism. Smart's own vote was for extreme utilitarianism and against the promises of restricted utilitarianism, also giving rise to yet another version of radical act-utilitarianism. See J.J.C. Smart, 'Extreme and Restricted Utilitarianism', in *The Philosophical Quarterly*, Vol. 6, No. 25 (1956) 344-354; M.A. Kaplan, 'Some Problems of the Extreme Utilitarian Position', in *Ethics*, Vol. 70, No. 3 (1960) 228-232; J.J.C. Smart, 'Extreme Utilitarianism: A Reply to M. A. Kaplan', in *Ethics*, Vol. 71, No. 2 (1961) 133-134; M.A. Kaplan, 'Restricted Utilitarianism', in *Ethics*, Vol. 71, No. 4 (1961) 301-302. Without changing his own position in substantial terms, Smart later came to prefer the terms act- and rule-utilitarianism, namely after R.B. Brandthad published his *Ethical Theory*. See R.B. Brandt, *Ethical Theory: The Problems of Normative and Critical Ethics*, Englewood Cliffs: Prentice-Hall (1959); J.J.C. Smart, *An Outline of a System of Utilitarian Ethics*, Victoria: Melbourne University Press (1961). For comments on Smart's book see R.T. Garner, 'Some Remarks on Act Utilitarianism' in *Mind*, New Series, Vol. 78, No. 309 (1969) 124-128; R.G. Frey, 'Act-Utilitarianism: Sidgwick or Bentham and Smart?', in *Mind*, New Series, Vol. 86, No. 341 (1977) 95-100.

56 Mat. 7:12.

ers would strive for economic and security gains by following the Golden Rule.[57] Most likely, any rule-utilitarian adaptation of ethical welfarism entails crucial limitations.[58] Those limitations are set to occur under the in-situ component, particularly if the social milieu is not for broad-based compliance to generalization tests. However, the challenges of group conflict provide the backdrop for which ethical welfarism has been invoked in the first place, namely to reconcile individual and group utility functions on ethical grounds. A corresponding critique joins our general ethical critique of the evolving economic paradigm. This critique is laid out in section 16.

Ethical Welfarism and the Evolving Economic Paradigm: Before that, there is a need to consider the extent to which ethical welfarism and ethical implications of the evolving economic paradigm overlap. Only that way, the problems of ethical welfarism are indeed those of the latter paradigm. A synthesis of ethical welfarism and the evolving economic paradigm materializes as a series of points.

Firstly, as a conflict prevention strategy, the evolving economic paradigm gives way to interventions that correct horizontal inequalities. Apart from being among others economic, these interventions are *economical*, or convenient, in as much as they establish a quasi-causal relationship between the root causes and interventions for conflict prevention. Therefore, conflict prevention is considered to be about some neat affirmative action. It is about a number of technical imperatives. For the same reason of a focus on empirical conditions, it would seem that the evolving economic paradigm does not bother with ethical imperatives. Once having established ethical welfarism this picture changes. Ethical welfarism shows that ethics and economics can be on par in methodological terms. It does so by extending a causal and empirical approach to the domain of ethics. According to ethical welfarism, any bifurcation between facts and values falsely denies parity of scientific reasoning with respect to so divergent domains of inquiry as are the social sciences and ethics. Both are believed to support knowledge claims.

Secondly, superficially the empirical and causal approach characterizing the evolving economic paradigm could be taken to exploit the old bifurcation of facts and values, and that of economics and ethics respectively. Thus, it specified relevant interventions in the absence of ethical imperatives, rather than leaving them absent from specification. As a result, these imperatives were held to be redundant of conflict prevention strategies. Also superficially, ethical realism could seem to support the redundancy of ethical imperatives, in as much as inadvertently it abandoned its core object together with some old methodological ballast. This object comprised a set of genuine ethical questions. A more of economics would be matched by a less of ethics in conflict debates, in so far as ethics complied with scientific standards.

Thirdly, in the end the evolving economic paradigm does not touch upon ethics by ways of scientific standards. It touches upon ethics indirectly, compliant to a third way. Thus, it neither specifies ethics as redundant, nor does it simply abandon an ethical dimension from its research. A third way is entrenched in that paradigm's

---

57 Saint Pierre (1713) Part 4.

58 For some general problems of a rule-utilitarian adaptation of act-utilitarianism see, among others, G.C. Kerner, 'The Immortality of Utilitarianism and the Escapism of Rule-Utilitarianism', in *The Philosophical Quarterly*, Vol. 21, No. 82 (1971) 36-50; G.W. Trianosky, 'Rule-Utilitarianism and the Slippery Slope', in *The Journal of Philosophy*, Vol. 75, No. 8 (1978) 414-424.

group-centered approach, which involves a deficient elaboration of the concept of individuals. Hence, when debating appropriate interventions, individuals are made the *passive object* of discussions. The evolving economic paradigm rarely installs individuals as dynamic actors that are challenged to execute interventions on the basis of intrinsic norms. With the evolving economic paradigm, one is prone to consider how the capabilities of individuals can *be* enhanced. What is the promise of ethical welfarism in this regard? At first sight, ethical welfarism only comprises one of two models to improve the ontological basis of ethical realism. While insisting on the existence of moral facts, ethical realism yet resulted in a restricted number of ungrounded grounders. As for the evolving economic paradigm, ethical welfarism serves to confirm quite explicitly that paradigm's passive approach to individuals. By centering individual utility functions, it accepts those functions as exclusive moral facts. Moreover, in line with the empirical approach inherited from ethical realism, it limits those functions to a restricted number of 'real' pleasures and pains, thus feeding into an *economic* concept of deprivation.

Fourthly, earlier on the passive approach to individuals has been suspected of defining technical imperatives without attention to their legitimate claim over particular personal traits. One the one hand, technical imperatives and interventions are indispensable for conflict prevention. They address individuals through their empirical person, their basic needs, experienced wants and utility functions. On the other hand, technical imperatives threaten to encroach upon people's moral person. In the absence of efforts to give proactive definition to that moral person, this threat is only vague. However, in the realm of ethical welfarism this threat is ultimately real. Ethical welfarism provides a line of thought that addresses people's moral person *through* their empirical person, and only through that person.[59] Rather than identifying the pains of privation as an obstacle on the way to higher or ethical behavior, satisfaction of the former is assigned with exclusive ethical quality. Rather than being a means that frees individuals for higher ethical behavior, such satisfaction comprises an ethical end in itself. The pleasures of the intellect and of imagination are those that normally impact on people's moral person. For ethical welfarism, they are ethically insignificant. To the extent that the economic occupies large ground in ethics, this closes the circle to the evolving economic paradigm.

---

[59] Obviously, the problem of interferences between people's empirical and moral persons must not be confused with a completely different problem, which relates to the deviating identities of different persons. The latter problem has been addressed by John Rawls, when stating that the utilitarian approach extends to society as a whole the principle of rational prudence for one person (J. Rawls, *A Theory of Justice*, Cambridge MA: Harvard University Press (1971) 22-28). Occasionally, Rawls' objection has been called the 'separateness-of-persons' objection (D. Jeske, 'Persons, Compensation, and Utilitarianism', in *The Philosophical Review*, Vol. 102, No. 4 (1993) 541). The goal with this objection has been to indicate that society is composed of distinct persons, each with a life to lead, a point of view, and that persons cannot simply be cashed out (B. Schultz, 'Persons, Selves, and Utilitarianism', in *Ethics*, Vol. 96, No. 4 (1986) 721). The latter has been stressed particularly in rejection of Derek Parfit's view of utilitarianism, according to which one should 'focus less upon the person, the subject of experience, and instead focus more upon the experiences themselves' (D. Parfit, 'Later Selves and Moral Principles', in A. Montefiori (ed.), *Philosophy and Personal Relations*, London: Routledge and Kegan Paul (1973) 153).

Fifthly, a process that self-transforms technical into deficient ethical imperatives, becomes possible with ethical welfarism, given the latter's peculiar definition of ethical imperatives. The evolving economic paradigm and ethical welfarism join hands in asserting that individuals and groups ought to follow empirical motives in their moral affairs. As long as one focuses on this paradigm, devoid of its intellectual neighborhood in ethics, its self-transformation potential only comprises a vague threat. However, this threat increases dramatically once noting that the preconditions for such self-transformation are readily available with ethical welfarism. In this situation, it may not help that ethical implications of the evolving economic paradigm are implicit rather than explicit. Threats associated with the former are greater than those attached to explicit reasoning. Because, for ethics they remove an option to react to technical imperatives that encroach upon people's moral person.

In the end, such threat may not be underestimated. Because also with regard to procedural problems, the evolving economic paradigm and ethical welfarism are on par. A most important procedural problem concerns how to deal with the *group dimension* in economics and in ethics. Given a focus on quantifiable moral rights, and pleasure gains particularly, ethical welfarism is challenged to equilibrate the same moral right of different agents. Thus, it deviates from conventional ethical theory, which primarily balances any moral right of agent A with another moral right or duty of agent B. Overall, ethical welfarism assigns ethics with a weird task, which is the need to forge ethical compromises. It does so in substitution of traditional ethical categories, such as right and wrong. To that extent, ethical welfarism is indeed on par with the evolving economic paradigm, i.e. a horizontal equality approach to distributive justice. This approach revolves around a single good, which is the economic good.

The above synthesis of ethical welfarism and the evolving economic paradigm causes that a critique of ethical welfarism comprises a critique of that paradigm. It establishes that, to some extent, the problems of ethical welfarism are those of the latter. Before embarking on this critique, the second stepchild of ethical realism requires analysis. Being ethical modernism, this model serves to capture yet other aspects of the evolving economic paradigm, equally important to an ethical critique.

Ethical Modernism

Ethical modernism comprises a second strands to improve the ontological basis of ethical realism, as well as to factor out some of its shortcomings. As such, ethical modernism goes beyond ethical welfarism. Rather than deducting ethical norms and imperatives from aspects of the empirical nature, it identifies both within that nature itself. By dwelling upon development laws of history, ethical modernism suspends a need to contemplate norms for individual behavior. In line with the precepts of ethical realism, these laws are confirmed to be accessible to direct knowledge. Although they are politico-historical and not prima facie ethical, they also comprise moral facts of a different kind. In a nutshell, historical laws seek to adjust our ethical norms and imperatives, so as to make them conformable with impending historical changes. The connection with ethical welfarism is that ethical modernism takes historical laws to promote in one way or the other those pleasure gains that are so central to the former. The promotion of those gains lies with history heading for ever higher degrees of perfection. These are, in brief, the promises of ethical modernism. What follows is an analysis of most important premises that underlie ethical modernism. Those premises are widely unrecognized. Particularly, they are outside the scope of traditional accounts of historicism, such as the one developed by Karl Popper. We argue that the premises of ethical modernism are hardly confineable to historicism. Its harshest opponent, *piecemeal social engineering*, reveals similar principles. Ultimately, this assumption provides the basis for considering ethical modernism for the evolving economic paradigm. For that purpose, the latter is presented as a paradigm that shares important methodological doctrines with piecemeal social engineering.

An analysis of basic premises founding ethical modernism lays bare the driving forces of social change. Ethical modernism can be identified, initially, in those theories that conceive of social change in terms of historical laws; theories for which Popper has coined the term historicism. It can be identified where analysis of historicism's economic and political traits combines with an ethical lens. In ethical terms, defining features that are commonly reserved for economic and political aspects of social change show to influence historicism. More precisely, those features are anti-interventionism and (anti)-perfectionism. However, no matter whether economics, politics or ethics are considered as the carrier of historical laws, the need for a law-centered or causal historical analysis has always been felt most urgently where the root causes of conflict came under scrutiny.[60] Marx's pondering of social revolution in terms of historical materialism comprises a most prominent theory to confirm this view.

Anti-Interventionism: Marx's theory also serves to elucidate the first of two defining features of historicism, to be called anti-interventionism. According to Marx, the ultimate aim of the social sciences ought to be 'to lay bare the economic law of motion of modern society.'[61] Chapter I made it clear that for Marx this economic law mainly proceeded through patterns of technological change, i.e. the introduction of labour-saving machines under capitalism. It also showed that Marx's idea of technology change is yet not fully compatible with a system of technological determinism, as has been argued quite frequently.[62] Marx was aware that a proper account of early capitalist societies had little to do with technological change patterns. Rather, a tendency to fully develop the division of labour described those societies. Such division mainly counted on efficiency gains from improving the dexterity of labourers whose business was being reduced to one simple operation in a chain of many. In a word, for Marx the origins of capitalism lay not in a change in technology, but in a change in social relations, and the emergence of a class of property-less wage labourers.[63] We concluded by stating that a major role of technology should be confined to Marx's view of mature capitalist societies. Only here, automation comes into full swing, in that it transforms the machine from a means of transmitting hu-

---

60 K. Popper, *The Poverty of Historicism*, London: Routledge & Kegan Paul (1960) Ch. 13.

61 K. Marx, *Capital Volume One: The Process of Production of Capital* [1867], in Marx and Engels (1975-2005) Vol. 35, Preface to the First German Edition.

62 G.A. Cohen, *Marx's Theory of History: A Defense*, Princeton: Princeton University Press (1978).

63 D. MacKenzie, 'Marx and the Machine', in *Technology and Culture*, Vol. 25, No. 3 (1984) 482.

man action to the object of labor into the actual doer of the work.[64] And yet, for machines don't make history, some kind of human decision had to be in place. According to Marx, sciences, the original source of technological innovation, had to be pressed into the service of capital. In the present context, one should add that the human nature of this decision may well limit the role of technological determinism in Marx's economic theory. By no means does it weaken his broader belief in anti-interventionism. Any of those proclaimed human decisions still finds its neat place in a system of anti-interventionism. As Marx stated: 'even when a society has got upon the right track for the discovery of the natural laws of its movement [...] it can neither clear by bold leaps, nor remove by legal enactments, the obstacles offered by the successive phases of its normal development. But it can shorten and lessen the birth-pangs.'[65]

(Anti-)Perfectionism: Another defining feature of historicism refers to the fact that historical laws are considered to be linear, but rarely in a neutral direction. Either those laws are such that they subsequently perfect the social order, or they lead to its anticipated collapse. John Stuart Mill's liberal account of political economy exemplifies the perfectionist line. For the specific purpose of this analysis, his account is more interesting than Marx's historical perfectionism, or anticipation of communism. This owes to a possible connection with ethical welfarism. Also, compared to Marx, Mill's dealing with historical laws was pro-scientific. As such it is developed in ensuing parts of his already mentioned logics book. According to Popper, the laws of succession Mill exposes there are historical laws, because they seek to determine a sequence of historical events in the order of their actual occurrence. Indeed, Mill speaks of a method that 'consists in attempting, by a study and analysis of the general facts of history to discover [...] the law of progress; which law, once ascertained, must [...] enable us to predict future events, just as after a few terms of an infinite series in algebra we are able to detect the principle of regularity in their formation, and to predict the rest of the series to any number of terms we please.'[66] Moreover, the law under which history progresses was deemed to be a law of real progress. Thus, saving occasional and temporary exceptions, the general tendency would be one of improvement, a 'tendency towards a better and happier state.'[67] A connection with Mill's act-utilitarianism materializes at this junction. While the latter's succession laws also knew some cyclical elements, it is clear that the promotion of happiness in terms of pleasure gains lay with history heading for ever higher degrees of perfection.

A final reference to early enlightenment proponents of ethical realism rounds off this point. As previously mentioned, those proponents were particularly concerned with the challenges of perpetual peace in Europe. Not only that present ethical realism finds a methodological equivalent in efforts to apply Descartes' *idées claires et distinctes* to ethics there. Not only that a focus on aspects of beneficence, or *bienfaisance*, established a predecessor to the pleasure principle observed by ethical welfa-

---

64 K. Marx, *Outlines of the Critique of Political Economy* [1858], in Marx and Engels (1975-2005) Vol. 29, 5-256.

65 Marx (1867) Preface to the First German Edition.

66 Mill (1843) Book VI, Ch. X, Sec. 3.

67 Ibid.

rism. But also, where ethical welfarism is subjected to a historical perspective, earliest proponents of an ethical realism are able to supply a law-centered and perfectionist line. At that time, such a line made use of the concept of *perfectibilité*. The latter concept established the belief that the current silver age was about to enter into a golden age.[68] An essential component of such belief was that the final state of perfection was identical with a state of perpetual peace.

Besides optimistic striving, historicism also knows an anti-perfectionist line. According to this line, history may not proceed under a progress story. On the contrary, especially in the old days anti-perfectionism was an attractive option. In pre-Socratic times, Heraklit's famous notion 'everything flows' attracted fatalism. For Plato, the golden age where philosophers were kings lay all in the past, and the course of history was to deviate ever more from these glorious days, with no option to turn things around. This anti-perfectionist line is important, because it allows for a category of historical laws piecemeal social engineers rarely accept. Before developing this point, we may extend our analysis of the economic and political traits of historicism, so as to include the previously mentioned ethical lens. Eventually, this lens leads to discover ethical modernism. As was also mentioned, historicism participates in ethical modernism on account of integrating anti-interventionist and (anti-)perfectionist doctrines. It gives rise to a particular version of ethical modernism, which may be called ethical passivism.

Ethical Passivism: For economists and politicians, acceptance of historical laws can only imply the dissolution of their job, in as much as this job is proactive. As Popper states, the historicist can only interpret social development, however, nobody can change it.[69] A different consequence applies to the moral philosopher. Where history prescribes a defined course, ethics is held to discard any perspective on what *ought* to be for the sake of assumptions as to what *will* be. At the macro-level, ethical imperatives needed to be adjusted, so as to make them conformable with the impending changes. This affected the job of the moral philosopher as typically conceived. Typically, this job is to ponder ethical situations unaffected by historical circumstances and personal endeavors for universal justifications only. At the micro- or in-situ level, individual behavior still needed to accommodate for an option to be counter to the historical laws of motion. For the following reasons: Firstly, while acting individuals don't follow historical plans. Secondly, otherwise moral behavior as such rather than only particular norm-setting ethical imperatives were removed. Because, by definition moral behavior must cater for an option to fail. That is why historicism cannot subscribe to ethical determinism. However, it implies that at all times moral misbehavior will not bend the historical laws, whatever those laws are, perfectionist or anti-perfectionist laws. Under the precepts of ethical passivism, ethics is held to digest that moral behavior need not be corrected on a broader scale. Because, on the whole moral misbehavior will not change history's predestined course.

---

[68] J.E. Ringier, *Der Abbé de Saint-Pierre: Ein Nationalökonom des 18. Jahrhunderts*, Karlsruhe: G. Braun (1905) 108.

[69] Popper (1960) Ch. 17.

Ethics normally considers individuals the way they ought to be, rather than the way they are. An implication of historicism is to take them 'how they are, rather than the way they ought to be.'[70] Such being 'how they are' must not be misinterpreted as reference to natural interests. Otherwise, ethical modernism and ethical welfarism simply converged. Precisely speaking, ethical modernism disposes of any significant ethical ought by considering individuals the way they *are going to be*, rather than the way they are.

Having considered historicism, one can turn to *piecemeal social engineering* and its respective link with ethical modernism. Deviating from common belief, the difference between historicism and piecemeal social engineering was introduced by John Stuart Mill rather than Karl Popper, inexplicitly though. Roughly, the difference between both kinds of approaches is this one: Historicist approaches are concerned with the causes that produce states of society in general. Superficially, piecemeal social engineering is more limited. Thus, it is concerned with the effects of a given cause in a certain state of society.[71] Deviating from Popper, Mill considered the first category of scientific questions as superior to the second. This assumption was in line with his focus on succession laws. For Popper, the second category of inquiries is authentic of serious scientific pondering. He agrees with Mill that the methods of the natural and social sciences need to be fundamentally the same. However, he disagrees about what those methods are. Different from Mill's holistic approach and focus on laws of succession, Popper subscribes to his famous method of hypothesis, where any prognosis retains the character of tentative hypothesis. According to him, there can be corroboration of a hypothesis but never final proof, whereas falsification is always possible. In any concrete case, the question how did one find a theory relates, as it were, to an entirely private matter, as opposed to the question how did one test that theory.[72]

This point is sufficiently documented. More interesting for the purpose of this analysis is the link with ethical modernism. The idea of such a link recalls our initial hypothesis that aspects of ethical modernism are not confined to historicism, but also identifiable in piecemeal social engineering. Certainly, a link like that can only be relevant to the extent that it helps linking ethical modernism and the evolving economic paradigm, ultimately as a result of methodological doctrines that this paradigm and piecemeal social engineering share. On first approximation, it would seem that the entirely different methodological advance of Popper's piecemeal social engineering approach also rejects a link with ethical modernism. It seems to do so, in so far as it leaves behind the methodological ballast of historicism. However, once we recognize the following connection with historicism, this also establishes a first step towards the initial hypothesis.

Historicism and piecemeal social engineering don't deviate in that only the former anticipated a particular state of society. Both are inspired by a vision of the future state of society, although in concrete terms these visions may deviate. However, historicism and piecemeal social engineering really deviate about proper ways of

[70] Saint Pierre (1713) [author's transl.].
[71] Mill (1843) Book VI, Ch. X, Sec. 1.
[72] Popper (1960) Ch. 29.

reaching that social state. Historicism, on the one hand, features a largely anti-interventionist doctrine. In contrast, piecemeal social engineering implies a *proactive* attitude toward the social order. Thus, Popper also called it the 'technological approach' to social sciences. Rather than engaging into passive prophecy, the technological approach intimates steps that can be taken proactively to achieve results that also bring closer the anticipated state of society. Certainly, this proactive attitude does not mean that any result can be achieved, once it is adopted in principle. The technological approach also points out what cannot be achieved. But here as well piecemeal social engineering brings into play its own version of the second doctrine defined above. The state of society targeted by piecemeal social engineers is in all cases a state of subsequent perfection. In economic and political terms, such perfection is embodied in accumulation of wealth and power by certain groups, or the distribution of wealth and power among them.[73] This point can be formulated even stronger. The state of society targeted by piecemeal social engineers *must* be a state of subsequent perfection. By definition, piecemeal social engineering must subscribe to a progress story. Historicism only interprets social developments. Thus, it fits well with an anti-perfectionist line of thought. Different from that, the achievement of real social progress is the only self-legitimation of any piecemeal social engineer, because he is programmed to intervene and not to interpret. Polemically speaking, the piecemeal social engineer is forced, quite inevitably, to think of the goals that cannot be achieved in terms of goals that don't want to be achieved.

Of course, there are social goals of different size. However, it is rather ridiculous to think that the dilemma of successful-to-be interventions and far-reaching social goals could be solved by lending the label 'private' to such interventions. Popper occasionally does that, with the intention to distinguish these interventions from utopian and holistic interventions, which are correctly discarded as limited to the age of totalitarian planning. Overall, social interventions are public and not locked away in the private field. They are public to the extent that, when trying to assess the consequences of some proposed reform, the piecemeal technologist must do his best to estimate the effects of any measure on society as a whole, presently and in the future. Popper also had to acknowledge this point.[74] In the end, he was not successful in solving the given dilemma. So is any piecemeal social technology prone to be. Clearly, the dilemma cannot be solved ex negativo by resorting to an ever more precise definition of the utopian approach, and by leaving piecemeal social engineering undefined in this utterly import field. This can only deceive about the fact that no precise demarcation line exists. Finally, these contemplations permit to link the two most significant points about piecemeal social engineering discovered by now. Hence, one can summarize that the latter adopts a proactive attitude toward economic and political interventions, which are progress-anticipating rather than only progress-oriented. Both points establish sort of a *manufacturing style* that applies to piecemeal social engineering. This style leaves no uncertainties as to the means and ends of social development.

---

[73] Ibid. Ch. 21.

[74] Ibid.

Another step toward the initial objective of probing aspects of ethical modernism for piecemeal social engineering derives from the fact that passive and proactive elements rarely distribute exclusively between historicism and piecemeal social engineering. Just as there can be proactive elements in historicism, there are passive elements in piecemeal social engineering. Just as those proactive elements don't change the broader picture of ethical passivism for historicism, piecemeal social engineering combines neatly with ethical passivism. In the case of the latter, aspects of ethical passivism even result straightforwardly from politico-economic pro-activism. For this to become clear, one may consider first the proactive elements in historicism.

Marx held the view that although a society can neither overleap the natural phases of its evolution, 'it can shorten and lessen the birth-pangs.'[75] Provided the economic infrastructure was forthcoming, it could embark on a social revolution. Social revolutions comprise the only category of open conflict Marxian economics recognizes. Of course, all pro-activism was justified only so long as it acquiesced in impending changes and helped them along. However, it would never lead to a general change in the history's laws of motion. In line with the infrastructure-superstructure rationale chapter I considered, political pro-activism could never be corrective of the economic infrastructure. In Marx's famous words, 'the mode of production of material life conditions the general process of social, political and intellectual life. It is not the consciousness of men that determines their existence, but their social existence that determines their consciousness.'[76] At best, political pro-activism and the economic basis of conflict formed a harmonious and well-planned entity catering for a concentric attack. The essential point about Marx's historicism is that any pro-activism would be political and not ethical. While historicism locates close to ethical passivism anyway , it does so even more in light of the small window of pro-activism that has been reserved for the processes of shortening and lessening history's 'birth-pangs'.

Having said that, one can proceed to the other assumption that piecemeal social engineering also combines with elements of ethical passivism. Despite featuring elements of strong politico-economic pro-activism, it might do so in a yet increased manner. For sure, the passive elements of piecemeal social engineering are not related to interventions for politico-economic change. Despite their gradual character, these interventions bring forward a manufacturing type of approach to social development, if not history. An intrinsic part of this approach is that the place of ethics in the process of designing the future becomes rather small. Two major factors that sustain this assessment are, firstly, confidence as to a set of rather practical means; and secondly, a mode of implementing social change that is equal to administrating progress. Therefore, for piecemeal social engineers the means of social development are at hand. Occasional setbacks are not blamed on those means. Under these conditions, one can hardly expect the confines of pro-activism to be broadened. One can hardly expect piecemeal social engineers to consider ethical interventionism. In a

75 Marx (1867) Preface to the First German Edition.

76 K. Marx, *A Contribution to the Critique of Political Economy* [1859], in Marx and Engels (1975-2005) Vol. 29, Preface.

nutshell, if there is no proactive approach toward the ethical side of social development and conflict prevention in piecemeal social engineering, this must be seen unfortunately as the flipside of politico-economic pro-activism.

Most of the points elaborated for piecemeal social engineering also apply to the evolving economic paradigm. Proponents of that paradigm design technical imperatives, as an proactive though convenient way of fostering development and conflict prevention goals. Piecemeal social engineers measure social progress in terms of accumulation of wealth and power, as well as their even distribution among groups. Thus, they approve of economic factors, which are so central to the evolving economic paradigm. However, for all these reasons the motives for ethical passivism in piecemeal social engineering will also apply to that paradigm. Twice before a passive approach was pointed out, especially for this paradigm's concept of individuals. In the realm of this passive approach, one is prone to ask what can be done *for* individuals, rather than installing the latter as dynamic actors who execute interventions on the basis of intrinsic norms. With the evolving economic paradigm one is prone to consider how the capabilities of individuals can *be* enhanced. In the end, this means downgrading their normative stakeholdership in conflict prevention strategies.

The present debate of pro-activism and passivism serves to illustrate the logic that underlies this passive approach to individuals. Sheer confidence as to a set of politico-economic means and a manufacturing approach to social progress are likely drivers of the evolving economic paradigm, just as of piecemeal social engineering. Vice versa, that paradigm's acceptance of *individual passivism* helps to illustrate the consequences of *ethical passivism* in piecemeal social engineering. Obviously, ethical passivism belongs to the group of external interventions (in conflict), whereas individual passivism theorizes a resulting feature of the primary stakeholders in interventions. Graphically, the relationship between external interventions and primary stakeholdership can be pictured as follows:

Fig. 6.2: Ethical and Individual Passivism

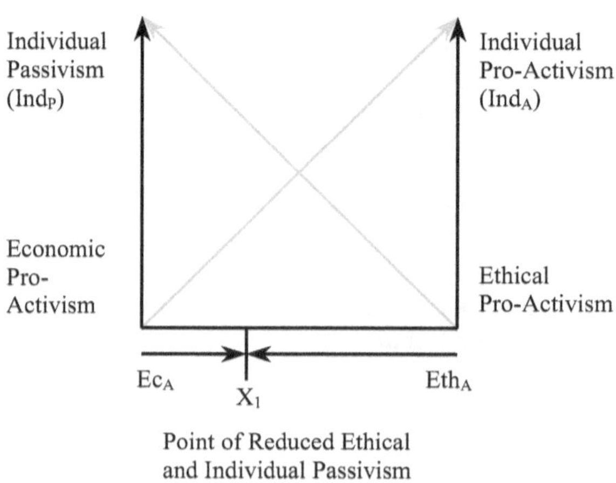

As can be seen quite easily, there are fairly direct ways from economic pro-activism (Ec_A) to individual passivism (Ind_P), and from ethical pro-activism (Eth_A) to individual pro-activism (Ind_A). Similarly, there are no direct ways from Ec_A to Ind_A, and from Eth_A to Ind_P. In the first case, the social engineer jumps in where individuals and conflict groups ideally assume self-responsibility. In the second case, individuals employ their moral person, which is by definition proactive and not passive. The clue is that in order to be discharged of individual passivism, economic pro-activism must enter into a coalition with ethical pro-activism. Although axis Ec_A-Eth_A seems to suggest that such coalition implies a compromise on both sides, this is actually not the case. Both can augment each other. There is a compromise only to the extent that economic pro-activism must be willing to dispose of deficient ethical imperatives, i.e. hypothetical imperatives. In this particular case, it needs to dispose of ethical modernism. X_1 could be pictured as a point where we have just decided to approach ethical pro-activism, i.e. as a point of reduced ethical as well as individual passivism. Certainly, for the presented situation many development economists will claim that economic pro-activism has one major goal, which is capacity building. Thus, no matter whether it aims at conflict prevention or other development goals, capacity building will be a precondition for individual pro-activism. However, often this means two things: Firstly, individuals and groups can only become proactive stakeholders once the job has been done, i.e. capacity has been built and conflict has been prevented. Secondly, capacity building goals don't remove the unholy alliance with deficient ethical imperatives that characterizes the evolving economic paradigm, both as ethical welfarism and ethical modernism. For this unholy alliance to become ultimately clear, an ethical critique of this paradigm is needed. This critique follows as a final step below.

Section 16. Critique of the Evolving Economic Paradigm

An ethical critique of the evolving economic paradigm in conflict debates goes back to the point where the need for such a critique became acute first. That point was when a simple axiom was found to capture the relationship between technical and ethical imperatives in that paradigm. According to this axiom, economic development could be an authentic *representative* of ethical progress in the domain of conflict prevention, although both are certainly not identical. Implicitly, this axiom also extended technical imperatives, as they serve to address people's empirical person, to their moral person. The present section considers a number of concrete ethical limitations and threats deriving from this axiom. Prior to that, one may repeat that the ethical implications of this axiom are indeed implicit rather than explicit. Overall, such implicitness threatens to remove an option for ethics to react to technical imperatives that encroach upon ethical imperatives.

Ethical welfarism and ethical modernism have been found to support the unholy alliance between economic and ethical progress from ethics' own side, each of them for different reason. At the same time, both versions of ethical realism have helped to surface important ethical implications of the evolving economic paradigm, as they relate to its founding axiom. A critique of these implications distinguishes between those elements that relate to ethical welfarism and to ethical modernism respectively.

The Three Paradoxes of Ethical Welfarism

Ethical welfarism centers ethical implications of the evolving economic paradigm that are broadly utilitarian. Those implications link interventions for economic development and ethical progress in the following way. In application of a vastly empirical lens, they focus on people's desire to minimize economic deprivation and to maximize economic gains in terms of moral facts. To that extent, any progress on the economic side must also constitute some sort of ethical progress. Consequently, every economic intervention for conflict prevention will also comprise some sort of ethical intervention. The latter arrangement is only being complicated by the distributive component of economic development, without which ethical progress cannot be achieved. Economic development must happen in an even way, so as to deserve the label of ethical progress. It must remove existing horizontal inequalities. A critique of these utilitarian implications of the evolving economic paradigm materializes with a number of ethical paradoxes. Straightforwardly, those paradoxes result from a moral fact- and utility-centered approach that respects the distributive component of development.

The Contingency of Moral Fact

What happens when ethical imperatives and interventions are restricted to moral facts, especially when those moral facts are held to be empirically observable, i.e. to be preserved in economic development? Certainly, for the sake of determining moral facts, one must not try to climb into people's minds. Scientifically, internal observations only provide weak evidence. In other words, once moral facts are appreciated, it is only consequent that they are limited to cases of direct perception, i.e. evidence that people's seeking of economic gains is satisfied. The actual limitations and threats of such an approach are contained in a first ethical paradox. One can show that upon giving way to a moral fact-centered approach to ethical imperatives, we are bound to bless those cases where economic development does *not* promote conflict prevention goals at a similar rate, or is even detrimental to these goals. What else would this constitute than an ethical paradox?

Firstly, by appointing empirical observations as a judge in the field of ethics, one indicates a willingness to approve of generalizations from fact, i.e. from economic evidence. In philosophy of sciences, generalizations from fact only constitute cases of inductive fallacy. From this perspective, one is not entitled to universal judgments about the empirical world, because we cannot rule out the existence or occurrence of a deviating case. This was the message we received earlier when debating economic value judgments. The present point does not concern aspects of economic value generation. It contemplates ethical value, i.e. whether such value can be derived as yet another category of generalizations from fact, that is, from economic evidence. Here, we need to engage the moral philosopher. An authoritative answer cannot merely allude to the problems of inductive fallacy.

Secondly, for the given investigative problem to materialize one initially needs to dispose of common perception concerning the difference between descriptiveness and prescriptiveness. David Hume first emphasized this difference. Thus, he claimed that ethical norms cannot be derived from descriptive statements alone. At this junction, we don't want to exploit this difference. It even prevents us from formulating a hypothesis such as the one saying that economic development could be an authentic representative of ethical progress in the area of conflict prevention. It also prevents us from considering related limitations and threats. Because in this case, economic and ethical questions are not even allowed to enter the same context. Also, chapter V made it clear that the difference between descriptiveness and prescriptiveness establishes hardly more but a logical case for value freedom in economics ('If true value judgments cannot be deduced from descriptive statements alone, then descriptive statements, the basis of economics, ought to be value-free, or non-prescriptive, by virtue of the fact that true value judgments cannot be deduced from these statements. Ergo, economics is value-free'). There is a need to criticize efforts to equate interventions for economic development and for ethical progress beyond some apriori logical argument. While true ethical norms may indeed not be derivable from fact, this does not change the 'fact' that, practically, the entities of ethics are sometimes considered in terms of moral facts.

Thirdly, generating moral facts by generalizing from economic fact raises a situation of ethical *contingency*. For the following reason: Provided one makes serious with such generalizations, who guarantees that economic development always implies effective conflict prevention? In many cases, economic development will combine with conflict prevention goals, just as the evolving economic paradigm envisages. But even a hypothetical option that both don't go hand in hand, poses too much of a risk. If not in practical terms, then certainly in terms of an ethical system which is based on moral facts. Because what would this hypothetical option mean? In the present scenario, moral facts are tied to economic development, as the only means of achieving conflict prevention. By no means, they are tied to the issue of conflict prevention directly. In this situation, evidence to the contrary would lead to a partial revision of the hypothesis that economic development begets conflict prevention. However, obviously a system of moral facts could not be adjusted as well. Because this *system of moral facts* was ultimately attached to the empirical economic basis, there was no room for adjustment, as otherwise a *system of ethical norms* would leave. In the worst case, a system of moral facts could mean that ethical approval of homo oeconomicus goes along with homo oeconomicus' obliteration. This obliteration had no chance to invoke our moral protest and ethical interventions. Eventually, this hypothetical scenario arises in close conceptual proximity to a revised doctrine of 'just war'. Preserved in the classical law of nations, the classical doctrine of just war determined a number of fairly precise cases where ethical considerations could be abandoned while engaging other conflict parties in conflict. In contrast, the present doctrine would not refer to legal statutes, which provide for some flexibility of interpretation. It would seem to comprise an instrument in the hands of the international community, unsolicited but inescapable, to measure quasi-objectively moral facts and facts of immorality. In a system of moral facts tied to economic fact, the immoral comprised no defined option with regard to conflict, except for those cases where conflict coincided with the opposite of economic development, i.e. economic retreat. As one was bound to speak of moral facts in all cases where economic development was detrimental to conflict prevention goals, it was also impossible to maintain an independent idea of ethical progress. No matter how much one tried to maintain such an idea, one was still deemed to sacrifice it. What happened was that conflict prevention goals were sacrificed without any room for argumentation, because no argumentation had been allowed for in the first place. This included particularly *proactive normative* argumentation, which is indispensable of any ethical interventionism.

In summary, the evolving economic paradigm threatens to approve of a system of moral facts tied to economic fact. In such a system, conflict prevention possesses no independent ethically qualities, because economic fact combines with any ethical ought. Conversely, if one lacked the economic preconditions for conflict prevention, one was also lacking a moral obligation to pursue conflict prevention.

Conflict as a Utility?

An empirical economic approach to ethical imperatives endorses cases where economic development does not promote conflict prevention goals, or is even detrimental to conflict prevention goals. Unwillingly, it compels to such endorsement as a *consequence* of particular premises. Different from this first ethical paradox, a second paradox shows that the evolving economic paradigm contains elements of *prima facie* endorsement of particular cases of conflict, i.e. because conflict contributed directly to the economic goals of individual stakeholders in conflict. This fairly strong statement composes as follows.

A system of moral facts, which is also latent in the evolving economic paradigm, identifies economic development as a prime utility. It designs technical imperatives and interventions for economic development, so as to achieve conflict prevention goals. The link between economic development and conflict prevention remains purely technical. An ethical lens in situations of conflict is only gained through its participation in a particular economic state, i.e. in a state of development or retreat. At the same time, one cannot repeat frequently enough how this idea of economic development providing for a prime utility is gained: Guided by an empirical lens, the pains of privation are identified not so much as an obstacle to higher ethical behavior, but as a moral fact the satisfaction of which possesses exclusive ethical quality. Therefore, the satisfaction of such pains escapes the idea of being a means to eventually free individuals for higher ethical behavior. It comprises a virtual end in itself. In as much as the pleasures of wealth comprise exclusive moral facts, economic issues gain strong ground in ethics. They do so on account of their sizeable impact on people's state of physical wealth and the deprivation they encounter, as well as the natural interests that relate to enhancing the one and to minimizing the other. After all, ethical utility functions that converge with economic utility functions could be acceptable for evaluators, i.e. for interventionists and proponents of the evolving economic paradigm. However, they are inadequate for the primary stakeholders in economic activities and conflict i.e. for the in-situ component. Such deviation requires separate consideration, both for situations of economic development and situations of economic retreat. Ultimately, this also reveals the second of three ethical paradoxes engaging the evolving economic paradigm.

Firstly, the distinction of in-situ and evaluative components is applied to a situation of economic retreat. As for the primary stakeholders in conflict, it is clear that both economic gains and conflict can be utilities. While the former comprises an end in itself, the latter could be a means to alter economic retreat. For the same reason, deprived groups often identify an ethical moment in conflict. The previous chapter included a debate of primary value judgments. Upon stating that economic factors possess *normative* strength for raging groups, it compelled us to acknowledge a quasi-ethical lens in conflict. This lens comes to the fore where groups feel justified to alter existing economic conditions, i.e. horizontal inequalities, by using force. If not explicitly, i.e. verbalized by group leaders, still implicitly they apply a quasi-ethical argument of the following kind: 'For the current distribution of economic resources puts our group at a disadvantage, a forced redistribution is just and fair.' Other cases are more applicable to the evolving economic paradigm. In these cases, economic evidence does not translate into economic conflict directly. Rather, concurrent symbolic fragmentation adds a normative dimension to conflict. A corresponding quasi-ethical statement on the part of conflict groups provides: 'For that other racial-ethnic-religious group is inferior to us, engaging in them in conflict is just and fair.' In one aspect, all these quasi-ethical statements were said to be equal. No matter whether a given quasi-ethical lens manages to stand a neutral ethical examination, it remains a fact that for raging groups there is no room for doubts as to the rightness of their case. Under all these circumstances, perpetrators of conflict are committed to what they consider the morally *right* thing to do. Eventually, primary value judgments imply sort of a necessary mental detour in the processes of evolving group conflict. At the same time, it was clear that evidence of primary value judgments hardly downgrades the relevance of economic and symbolic factors in conflict. One only realizes that both groups of factors are necessarily being filtered through quasi-ethical statements. These statements rationalize both economic gains and conflict as a means of achieving those gains.

Secondly, things are set to change dramatically, when turning to the corresponding evaluator's strand, or interventionist angle. Combined cases of economic retreat and conflict are those where any evolving economic paradigm runs the risk of extending ethical judgments from the economic evidence to the means that could seem to reverse economic retreat. The evolving economic paradigm is perfectly aware of this problem. In effect, one can only repeat that this paradigm cannot approve of conflict in cases where economic retreat endures. For the economic paradigm, conflict may never comprise a utility. However, within a system of moral facts, economic retreat and conflict set up cases where conflict prevention goals and ethical concerns are rather coincidentally not at odds. Thus, they are save of a problem that attaches to cases of economic development. Those cases could elicit ethical approval in the realm of failing conflict prevention. They give rise to situations where the first ethical paradox settles in. While the evolving economic paradigm will not back up cases in which conflict comprises an economic and ethical utility to deprived groups, any evaluator's strand might still have to face some of those implicit value judgments identified earlier. One may think especially of those that go along with a problem-centered lens toward conflict. But again, implicit value judgments have little to do with the conditionality of ethical approval. The evolving economic paradigm indicates clear disapproval where conflict seeks to be a means of adjusting group-specific economic retreat, e.g. horizontal inequalities.

Thirdly, the same distinction between in-situ and evaluative components should be applied to situations where economic development is accomplished. A second ethical paradox of the evolving economic paradigm materializes here. As for the primary stakeholders in conflict, it is a sad truth that incentives for conflict are rarely limited to an economic relief character. Too often, economic advantage from conflict exceeds those cases where deprived groups seek to release economic distress. If privileged conflict parties conceive of sizeable economic gains from conflict, they will also manage to sell conflict as an ethical utility. Apart from identifying conflict as an economic utility, those parties will apply quasi-ethical justifications to their situation of economic wealth. They will also extend these justifications to everything that serves to increase their privileges, e.g. to conflict. In terms of scale, such conflict has shown to possess an international and a domestic side.

Internationally, one may refer to doctrines such as the concept of hegemonic stability. Again, this doctrine can be identified in some aspects of international relations today. Chapter I made it clear that, in one direction, this doctrine concerns security gains from economic dominance abroad. In a second direction, economic dominance is related to power politics, and ultimately to conflict. A most prominent advocate of both doctrines has been the realist school in international relations. The common ground of both doctrines is that they are often sold under the mantle of preemptive conflict. The all-distinguishing element from approaches such as Keynes' meanwhile skeptical account of free trade and international economic interdependence concerns the relief-character striving for economic dominance assumed in the latter cases. Thus, it aimed at mitigating economic distress at home. For the same reason, such pondering rather falls into the previous category theorizing economic retreat. Marxian economics provides an even more pessimistic approach to international economic expansion. Thus, it occasionally extended on international political economy as imperialism or highest stage of capitalism.[77] Only here, conflict becomes an intrinsic attribute of dominant economic players in their relationship with developing countries.

In other cases, economic expansion combines with domestic conflict. It would exceed the capacities of this book to mention all cases in which conflict has been a powerful tool in the hands of dominant groups, rather than a means of reversing economic deprivation. As such a tool, it has either served to stabilize or to enhance economic supremacy. Also, it has taken the form of civil war, ethical cleansing, racial conflict or regime repressiveness. No matter how we name such conflict, a critical feature of the evolving economic paradigm concerns the limited attention that has been paid to those cases. Such lack of attention also includes the justificatory processes dominant groups apply, in order to install conflict as an ethical utility. Sometimes only a change of perspective is needed and conflicts, that in the first place represented the economic struggles of underprivileged groups, will be found to

[77] V.I. Lenin, *Imperialism: The Latest Stage in the Development of Capitalism* [1917], Detroit: Marxian Educational Society (1924).

constitute cases of proactive repression for the sake of economic goals. In fact, rarely the stimulus for conflict can be allocated to one side. Chapter IV identified identity deprivation as a proactive pattern of domination that causes passivity and submissiveness on the other side. Deprived groups were found to internalize the stereotypes and stigmata dominant groups imposed on them. As a result, they resorted to self-denial and self-denigration. The evolving economic paradigm has failed to consider these cases. In the purview of this paradigm, symbolic factors translate the underlying economic basis into conflict. But cultural deprivation neither just happens to groups, nor does it serve to elicit conflict in every single case. Often, there are proactive patterns behind which involve dominant economic groups. In practice, those patterns are difficult to observe, because they take the form of hidden conflict. This was a clear outcome of chapter IV. In other cases, economic expansion hides behind patterns of regime repressiveness. This was an outcome of chapter III. Once a change of perspective is applied, one also realizes that frequently enough economic and symbolic deprivation are secured through armed protection of current status quo. Alternatively, dominant economic groups allowing limited conflict to operate preserve them. An essential feature of proactive economic deprivation and cultural stigmatization is that they are rationalized to the point that they become quasi-ethical utilities in the hands of those groups.

Fourthly, the corresponding evaluator's strand considers to which extent the evolving economic paradigm is free in responding to situations where dominant groups perceive an economic advantage from conflict. To what extent is it ethically bound when those groups capitalize on and ethically rationalize conflict? For a system of moral facts, economic gains are ethical gains. However, patterns of economic dominance aggressively enforced may still not be approved. Comparable to those situations where deprived groups regard conflict as an ethical utility, the evaluator's job is to hold back with ethical approval. However, an inner conflict remains. Our system of moral facts has been tied to economic fact in the first place. In this situation, perpetrators of conflict could turn our ethical premises against us. Any economic paradigm is then forced to rely on delusive *optimism* and wishful thinking. Generally, such delusive optimism would find expression in expectations that privileged groups *will not* dare to wage conflict, only because it is indeed less likely they will compared to deprived groups.

In one sense, such optimism would rely on ballast from the classical liberal doctrine, which is still prominent among liberal scholars and politicians today, often in the context of debates on globalization. Chapter I showed that the liberal model thrives on the assumption that efforts to make economics the case for conflict are *uneconomic*. The argument that conflict will provide rioting groups with a commercial advantage has been rejected as an illusion.[78] Two main reasons have been building for this belief: Firstly, in a situation of ever-increased international economic exchange, any behavior threatening to disrupt regular supplies of goods and services normally needs to be avoided. Thus, quite early Richard Cobden referred to the free trade principle as a principle 'which shall act on the moral world as the principle of

---

78 N. Angell, *The Great Illusion: A Study of the Relation of Military Power in Nations to their Economic and Social Advantage*, New York and London: G.P. Putnam's Sons (1912) vii.

gravitation on the universe - drawing men together, thrusting aside the antagonism of race, and creed, and language, and uniting us in the bonds of eternal peace'.[79] Secondly, more relevant to the issue of internal conflict has been the financing aspect. David Ricardo was among the first to extend on the economic burden which such financing imposes on society.[80]

On balance, efforts to dismiss economic advantage from conflict are restricted to picking affirmative cases. But even if no deviating example existed and one's optimism was over and over confirmed in practice, there remains tangible theoretical inconsistency in a system of moral facts that relies on economic fact and utility considerations. Beyond delusive optimism, such a system has few things to offer for the purpose of solving the dilemma of conflict as an economic and ethical utility. To the same extent, it is trapped in a second ethical paradox.

At long last, a logical solution would be to concede that the concept of utility is deeply insufficient in terms of ethical imperatives on which any evolving economic paradigm and conflict prevention strategy can rely. However, before giving up on this concept, one may resort to a final option that could appear to rescue this paradigm. Therefore, a first reaction our discussion is likely to prompt from proponents of the evolving economic paradigm is to blame that discussion for being insufficient in a most fundamental sense. Thus, they will seek to identify a lack of consideration to the *sum total of utilities*. This sum total covers all stakeholders in conflict and not just some, such as dominant *or* underprivileged economic groups. Indeed, only a comprehensive dealing with all utility functions involved moves our discussion to a preeminent point. The ground for such a comprehensive dealing has been prepared above. It was set while debating the issue of compromises in ethics.

Ethical Compromises

While dealing with two ethical paradoxes of the evolving economic paradigm, a normally large group in conflict was temporarily neglected. This group concerns the passive elements in conflict, i.e. people that are engaged in conflict by others, no matter whether they comprise deprived or privileged groups. When lifting both ethical paradoxes, the focus was on limitations third parties are set to encounter with ethical interventions, if they endorse the evolving economic paradigm. The second ethical paradox also included a separate focus on perpetrators of conflict. Thus, it fulfilled an earlier promise to release the primary stakeholders in conflict from their role as passive object in development debates. All in all, such focus on third parties and proactive parties in conflict was straightforward, because our concern was for those aspects that might impede ethical interventions, rather than factors that demand ethical interventions anyway. Once turning to these factors, it is imperative to center the victims of conflict. Only with this group, the need for ethical compro-

---

[79] R. Cobden, *The Political and Economic Works of Richard Cobden* [1846] 6 Volumes, London: Routledge (1995) Vol. 3, 362-363.

[80] D. Ricardo, *On the Principles of Political Economy and Taxation* [1817] Cambridge: Cambridge University Press (1951) 186.

mises becomes acute. However, a *third ethical paradox* materializes just here, when considering sum totals of utility.

Firstly: A weighing of sum totals of utility and the distributive component in conflict is what the evolving economic paradigm is all about. This derives from a number of main propositions chapter II identified. In detail, those propositions are related to the group dimension, relative deprivation and horizontal inequalities in conflict. Certainly, a weighing of distributive aspects is not the privilege of that paradigm. For example, traditional welfare analysis features a major concern for interpersonal comparisons. A major assumption on which this branch of economics has proceeded is that there is no such thing as an independent community interest apart from the interests of the individuals comprising the community.[81] This insight has led to recognize that what benefits one individual or several individuals can affect others adversely and harm even others. Two major consequences have been drawn from this assessment: Firstly, individual preferences and utility functions are focused. Secondly, interpersonal comparisons of utility between those who benefit and those who are harmed are seen to determine which particular economic situation is most desirable for any given society.

Secondly: A main disadvantage of traditional welfare analysis in economic discourses could turn out as an advantage, when observing the ethical qualities of such discourses. This advantage concerns the individual-centered nature of traditional welfare analysis. In the first place, a lack of consideration to the group dimension was to provoke the protest of the evolving economic paradigm. In the absence of a community interest, the latter still insists on the existence of *group interests*. As opposed to this, ethical discourses are per se held to center the individual. This is also why traditional welfare analysis would initially seem to hold an advantage over the evolving economic paradigm, because above all to the single individual moral rights can be attached. Above all, from individuals ethical responsibility can be demanded. While this is certainly true, the present context centers justifications that apply to external ethical interventions. Particular attention goes out to the moral rights of rioting and victimized groups in economic conflict, rather than their ethical duties. Whereas ethical obligation is always individual, moral rights can be shared collectively and hence attached to groups. To that extend, the initial advantage of welfare analysis must vanish. While considering the evolving economic paradigm's sharing into ethical welfarism, this was an implicit premise we made. Explicitly, this debate included a template for shared moral rights, sum totals of utility and ethical compromises. On the basis of this template, a critique was felt to be necessary. But the critique itself was temporarily postponed. As such, it follows here. Previous points feeding into such a critique can be applied to the evolving economic paradigm directly:

An ethical approach to the utilitarian basis of this paradigm broaches relative aspects. Thus, it applies the so-called 'total view' when reconciling the moral rights of perpetrators and victims. For the sake of ensuring compatibility with the economic basis of this paradigm, the relative component must be such that both groups' moral

---

81 K. Klappholz, 'Value Judgments in Economics', in *The British Journal for the Philosophy of Science*, Vol. 15, No. 58 (1964) 106.

history enters the balance sheets. This moral history consists of past accruing of utility. Therefore, we do not want to limit ourselves to conflicting utilities arising from a present situation. There is a need to consider stocks of utility. For the present situation, these stocks imply that the agent with the higher stocks is to the make greater concessions. Quite similarly, economic distribution decisions take into regard stocks of economic assets of perpetrators and victims, who will often comprise perpetrator-victims (underprivileged groups) and victimized perpetrators (privileged groups). Furthermore, in order to ensure compatibility between the evolving economic paradigm as an economic and ethical theory, a utilitarian calculus of moral rights may not be limited to sum totals of utility in the absence of concern as to how that utility distributes among different moral agents. The latter would mean to apply the so-called 'average view', thus helping to set up an ethical counterpart to the concept of absolute deprivation in economics. However, once ethical and economic implications of the evolving economic paradigm are fine tuned to the relative component, resulting ethical imperatives are required to forge ethical compromises.

More narrowly, for the evolving economic paradigm ethical compromises come into play as follows: Since there is a tendency to grasp of moral rights in terms of economic utility functions, rioting and victimized groups seem to possess over a prime moral right. The need to forge ethical compromises results from the fact that the paradigm cannot resort to a solution that is much more common in ethics. Therefore, normally the moral right of one agent or group faces ethical duty on the other side. This duty ought to take up said moral right, thus enforcing it in practice. On the whole, this is how ethical situations are solved. In contrast, the existence of one overall moral right, i.e. economic utility maximization, leaves no option but to seek ethical compromises. Evidently, resource conflict accomplishes those cases where a compromise fails to materialize. It consolidates those cases where a compromise solution has been suspended. If not before, here at the latest ethical interventions come into play, eventually to enforce the moral rights of victimized groups. However, a key question must be whether the concept of ethical compromises is a helpful concept at all, especially to found of ethical interventions.

Thirdly: A critique of ethical compromises materializes as a sequence of points. It finally culminates in a third ethical paradox of the evolving economic paradigm.

Sub-point One: A consideration of sum totals of utility conscious to distributive aspects threatens to encounter basic limitations. A model developed by Amartya Sen illustrates those limitations. Mainly, this model has been designed to contemplate the utilitarian implications of welfarism. In order to show that problems of utility distribution enter welfarism at a very high cost, Sen uses individuals rather than primordial groups. Pertinent cases of utility redistribution have been designed according to two extremes, i.e. redistributive taxes and torture. In both cases, (x,y) and (a,b), equality in utility distribution is achieved by utterly different methods. Model (x,y) involves a rich person r and a poor person p. Different from that, model (a,b) theorizes a seemingly perverse case. Here, r comprises a dreamer whose utility function comprises a happy disposition, while p features a morose, ill and frustrated policeman getting his simple pleasures or utility gains out of torturing.

Fig. 6.3: Models of Utility Redistribution

Sen (1979)		*x* (no tax)	*y* (redistributive tax)
utilities	*r*	10	8
	p	4	7

		a (no torture)	*b* (torture of *r* by *p*)
utilities	*r*	10	8
	p	4	7

		x' (no econ. redistrib.)	*y'* (econ. redistribution)
utilities	*r*	10	8
	p	4	7

		a' (no conflict)	*b'* (*p* wages conflict upon *r*)
utilities	*r*	10	8
	p	4	7

Sen's major point concerning both models is that once we introduce a distributive component to considerations of sum totals of utility, utilitarian welfarism requires to rank *x* and *y* in exactly the same way as *a* and *b*. The point is that we cannot decide for *y* (redistributive tax) without deciding for *b* (torture):

> Welfarism would insist that the state of affairs with redistributive taxation (*y*) is better than without taxation (*x*) *if and only if* the state of affairs with the torture (*b*) is better than that without torture (*a*). Many people would, however, hold that the case involving redistributive taxation is better (i.e., *y* is better than *x*) but the case involving torture is not (i.e., *b* is not better than *a*). One is free to hold such a view only by rejecting welfarism. To discriminate between the two pairs would bring in non-utility information, which can have no role of its own under welfarism.[82]

At first glance, both cases seem to have a lot in common with two models that can be developed from the present discussion. A first model considers economic redistribution scenarios (x',*y'*) more generally, rather than redistributive taxes particularly. A second model contemplates group conflict (*a'*,*b'*) instead of torture. Similar as the original models, the evolving economic paradigm could be compelled to accept *b'* when deciding for *y'*. However, at a closer look the problem vanishes. Aspects of equality in utility distribution are being secured. For that purpose, the preceding analyses of ethical welfarism defined utility functions in a sufficiently narrow manner. While including pleasure from economic factors (x',*y'*), pleasure from conflict has been excluded explicitly. From the very outset, (*a'*,*b'*) does not comprise a valid model of utility redistribution. Thus, conflict has been analyzed as a *means* of achieving economic redistribution, rather than as a utility in itself. The whole second ethical paradox related to such being a means. The notion of 'conflict as a utility' never departed from this rule. In Sen's scenario, non-utility information has to be brought in aposteriori, so as to secure redistributive taxes without having to accept torture. Different from that, the previous distinction between ends and means ensures an inner-utilitarian debate. On the whole, the evolving economic paradigm

[82] Sen (1979) 474.

may not be subjected to another ethical paradox only because it combines attention to sum totals of utility with a focus on equality in utility distribution.

Sub-point Two: Once a focus on equality in utility distribution has been secured, it also seems to ensure the validity of ethical compromises. Pursuant to such a focus, the following situation arises: For ethical compromises to materialize, one needs to assume a *duty* of privileged groups to dispose of economic assets to underprivileged groups. Only in those cases, the moral rights of these groups can be enforced. Applied to the same graphical model chapter II developed while making sense of the concept of relative deprivation, one needs to provide normative strength to the distribution problem depicted there. Thus, for every $a_n < b_n$ an ethical imperative needs to take shape, requesting an equal distribution of economic assets between groups A and B.

Fig. 6.4: Ethical Compromises

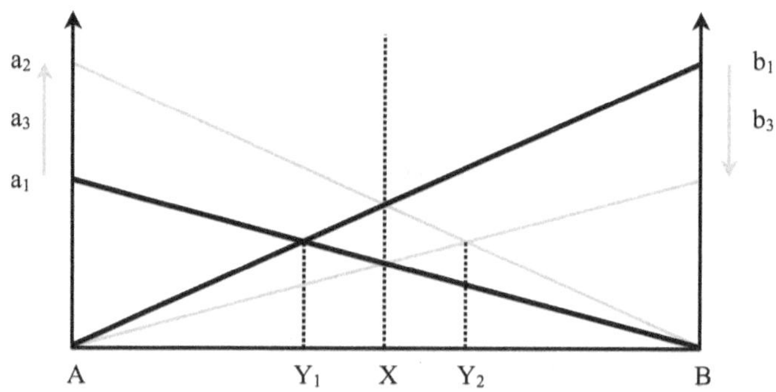

Here precisely, new problems settle in for a purely utilitarian debate. As it stands, a purely utilitarian approach lacks the means to assign normative ethical meaning to utility redistribution scenarios. As it stands, ethical welfarism is fine-tuned to the utility maximizing behavior of individual agents and groups. The consequences of any action are counted by the progress those agents and groups achieve in separation from a concern for others. Therefore, as far as it is equality oriented, ethical welfarism only manages to recognize each agent's and group's sharing into one basic endeavor, which is utility maximization. This point is not at odds with the previous point, where a focus on equality in utility distribution was just secured: Firstly, with this point we only confirmed those things that may generally claim the status of a utility, i.e. pleasure from economic gains. Perverted utilities were thus prevented from entering the balance sheet of utilities, i.e. pleasure from torture and conflict. Secondly, nothing actually impedes ethical welfarism as well as the evolving economic paradigm from considering sum totals of utility and from contemplating issues of equality in utility distribution. But they fail to mobilize the normative means so as to practically *enforce* equality in utility distribution, thus also impacting on ethical interventions.

Here and only here, *non-utility* information must be brought in. It comes into play to help overcoming a major barrier for ethical compromises. As it is, this barrier relates to the fact that the evolving economic paradigm only captures primary stakeholders in conflict as right holders, the latter being a straightforward outcome of its utilitarian approach. Ethical duties are out of scope, duties as they could eventually be imposed on those stakeholders, and privileged groups particularly. As for these groups, no duty to dispose of economic assets to underprivileged groups may materialize within a purely utilitarian debate. With no ethical compromises in sight, this paradigm is prone to operate close to a third ethical paradox. The given situation can only be helped by means of non-utility information of the following kind.

Remark One to Sub-point Two: Superficially, a rule-utilitarian adaptation of the evolving economic paradigm could seem to be the right solution. There can be debate as to whether this adaptation secured an inner-utilitarian debate in the absence of non-utility information. But even if this was the case, one cannot avoid severe limitations of such an adaptation in the context of economic redistribution conflict. As previously mentioned, a rule-utilitarian adaptation in situations requiring ethical compromises would filter the actions of each group through a *generalization test.* Thus, it realized a detour when groups aimed at consequences that only benefited them. It took the form that action *a* by group A in situation *b* was right only and if performance of A by the class of similar groups produced an optimific result. Overall, this detour needed to be applied to primary stakeholders in conflict. But it could also provide an entry point for ethical interventions. All things told, it was clear that a rule-utilitarian adaptation would often lead to reject actions that would have been approved of in the first place.[83] In order to secure the utility function of each moral agent in the long run, it imposed a duty to exercise abstinence on privileged groups, particularly in situations of scarce economic resources, thus restricting their moral right to pleasure. It imposed what R.M. Hare occasionally called level-2 decisions to limit level-1 thinking, which is immediate and purely intuitive.[84]

Apart from the fact that ethical duty is normally individual and group duty only evolve as a secondary ethical category, the signaled rule-utilitarian adaptation contains the following limitation: For sure, such an adaptation imposes restrictions on moral rights, i.e. on economic utility maximizing behavior of privileged groups. At the same time, it theorizes *prospective actions*, that is, actions that are scheduled to materialize in the future. Each actor is held to adapt his or her behavior, so as to bring it in line with a universalized version of consequentialism. Each actor is required to think the whole social milieu, rather than within the boundaries of personal and group egoisms. All of this might be helpful in solving the ethical dilemmas of upcoming distribution decisions. However, rule-utilitarianism does nothing to change existing *states of affairs*, such as they often involve an ultimately real distribution problem. Such distribution problems are urgent and they need to be solved now. Imposing future abstinence on privileged groups may hardly solve them. The whole issue becomes equal to postponing a decision, and conflict will rarely wait for that. To some extent, rule-utilitarian theorizing of prospective actions resembles the liberal debate of negative and positive freedoms mentioned in chapter I. In terms of negative freedom, the blind is not interfered by those who could afford to pay for a

---

83 Emmons (1973) 226.

84 R.M. Hare, 'Ethical Theory and Utilitarianism', in H.D. Lewis (ed.), *Contemporary British Philosophy: Personal Statements*, 4th Series, London: Allen & Unwin (1976) 124.

sight-restoring operation. Applied to rule-utilitarianism, the poor is not worse off through those who don't share their wealth. But, in terms of positive freedom, what the blind can do is significantly limited because he goes without the operation.[85] So is the poor not likely to stop redistribution fights, only because the future could see equality when distributing new utilities. Once before it was mentioned that the history of economic acquisitions ought to matter to rule-utilitarians. Only that way, present decisions can be such that underprivileged groups benefit economically. But as far as rule-utilitarianism is concerned, this only sets up a theoretical reflection on history and present status quo. It doesn't imply a proactive redistribution of already acquired economic assets. Rule-utilitarianism helps with regard to new economic acquisitions, but not in situations of existing distribution problems. Even with new acquisition decisions one could be prone to encounter sizable problems. Thus, in executing generalization tests we might end up being a Buridan's ass.[86] Trapped midway between two equally attractive haystacks, one of which we may claim, while a generalization test forbids to demand both, we might starve to death. Polemically speaking, we may even advise others to do so in our function as ethical interventionists, because as rule-converted utility maximizers we still refused to bring in non-utility information. Obviously, such information is required even to solve this rather simple problem. On a broader scale, in order enforce normatively equality in utility distribution, both acquisition and redistribution decisions are required. Effective ethical interventions cannot rely on a rule-utilitarian adaptation alone.

Remark Two to Sub-point Two: Ethical welfarism and the evolving economic paradigm need to be combined with a different outcome morality. With reference to John Rawls, Sen has stated correctly that only such a different outcome morality allows for judging existing states of affairs. It enables one to judge these states of affairs by the utility levels of worst-off groups.[87] Thus, it also permits to change them subsequently.

Fourthly: An outcome morality based on non-utility information contemplates the cure for deficient ethical compromises. Albeit such cure, ethical compromises don't escape a third ethical paradox. This ethical paradox is almost too simple to mention, but yet essential and built in as follows: Rather than criticizing ethical compromises for some specific elements, there is a need to show that such compromises are per se inappropriate. No full-grown ethics of conflict prevention may be established on their back. By definition, ethical compromises comprise no valid category in ethics.

In strict correlation to an economic discourse about distributive justice in the evolving economic paradigm, ethical compromises are fine-tuned to solve a situation of moral competition. Rather than anticipating moral competition as the struggle of different ethical norms in a given situation, such competition features the antagonism of a single moral right as it applies to different conflict groups, i.e. their eligi-

---

85 L. Crocker, *Positive Liberty: An Essay in Normative Political Philosophy*, The Hague and Boston: Martinus Nijhoff (1980).

86 For a controversial debate on this point see J. Narveson, 'Utilitarianism, Group Actions, and Coordination or: Must the Utilitarian be a Buridan's Ass', in *Nous*, Vol. 10, No. 2 (1976) 173-194; H.S. Silverstein, 'Utilitarianism and Group Coordination' in *Nous*, Vol. 13, No. 3 (1979) 335-360.

87 Sen (1979) 465; Rawls (1971) 76-77. For an analysis of John Rawls' critique of utilitarianism see D. Lyons, 'Rawls Versus Utilitarianism', in *The Journal of Philosophy*, Vol. 69, No. 18, (1972) 535-545.

bility to economic gains. Ethical compromises seek to balance this moral right. However, in the absence of ethical duty (non-utility information), no mechanism to turn right holders into duty bearers can prevent such moral right to face itself in its other form as associated with a different stakeholder.[88] The solution for ethical compromises must be to *apportion* this moral right to economic development. However, the paradoxical nature of such compromise is immediately clear.

The solution at hand is obviously the right solution. Nonetheless, it is right in an ethically deficient sense. In ethics, it is impossible to imagine that moral rights could be apportioned. Under no circumstances, moral rights are quantifiable. Moral rights can be enforced or they can fail to be enforced. They can also collide with each other, but they cannot be enforced *by degree*. However, that is exactly what a narrow utilitarian definition of moral rights in terms of moral facts forces to do. The paradoxical thing with ethical compromises is that they can only be applied to be not applied. Provided they are applied, we are forced to leave the field of ethics where we have just entered it. Our ethical discourse turns ethically deficient. On the other hand, should we still aim to maintain an ethical lens when focusing on equality in utility distribution, then we need to extend that discourse. Our ethical discourse needs to be corrected by a non-utilitarian approach. The third ethical paradox of the evolving economic paradigm is contained in these remarks.

Ultimately, as a result of the three ethical paradoxes revealed in this section one has to concede that the concept of utility is deeply insufficient in terms of ethical norms and imperatives on which any economic paradigm can rely. Ethical implications of this paradigm that hint toward a purely utilitarian approach need to be lifted and subjected to a controversial debate. A declared goal of ethical welfarism has been to rule out such a debate, for the aim has been to provide with a system of moral facts that cannot be dismissed. The first a system of moral facts would need to do is to be defined in a sufficiently broad manner. Avoidance of pain and accruing of pleasure must be defined beyond economic development goals, that is, in relation to conflict and conflict prevention directly. Obviously, this will never lead to dispose of proactive normative argumentation, the backbone of any ethical interventionism. At the same time, a certain risk remains: Even after defining conflict as a non-utility, it could be exploited as a *pre-emptive* means of avoiding future harm from potential conflict parties. Therefore, while concluding the first part of an ethical critique of the evolving economic paradigm, we have to stress as indispensable that any economic paradigm be complemented by *normative argumentation.* Only such argumentation may avoid that technical imperatives self-transform implicitly into deficient ethical imperatives. One can only repeat that the threats of such implicit transformation are greatest where normative argumentation is lacking, i.e. as a result of a system of moral facts. Because, an option for ethics to react to technical imperatives encroaching upon people's moral person vanishes in just these cases. Prime indications of such threat are the three ethical paradoxes discussed above.

---

[88] Different from that, it has been stated correctly that for a system of rights individuals have to be regarded as bearers of judgment and responsibility and not only of sensory states necessary to maximize happiness. See L.A. Mulholland, 'Rights, Utilitarianism, and the Conflation of Persons', in *The Journal of Philosophy*, Vol. 83, No. 6 (1986) 340.

Duty as Autonomy

In order to assume normative strength, ethical interventions need to go beyond a purely utilitarian approach. In order to avoid ethical paradoxes, we need to bring in non-utility information. The question is how precisely non-utility information will augment the normative basis of ethical interventions. Obviously, by taking into regard two points: Firstly, by extending ethical imperatives to the primary stakeholders in conflict. After all, any interventionism, economic or ethical, only justifies as the overcoming of an in-situ shortcoming. This shortcoming may result from politico-economic inability, reluctance to solve an existing distribution problem, i.e. horizontal inequalities, or lack of ethical commitment to do so. Any interventionism is subsidiary. It requires deduction from imperatives that are in the first place imposable on the primary stakeholders in conflict, who are thus captured as ethical duty bearers, rather than just as moral right holders. In a word, we must rule out an ethical approach that exalts fellowship to people's natural interests and intrinsic economic laws, such as utility maximization. Therefore, we must rule out ethical welfarism. Secondly, together which such imposition at the micro-level, ethical imperatives must be extended at the macro-level. As such, they can be imposed on the course of history. Thus, one needs to break with an ethical approach that prevents ethical interventionism, i.e. ethical pro-activism, by commanding fellowship to the determining influence of historical laws in social affairs. In short, one needs to break with ethical modernism, more so because ultimately fellowship to historical laws could combine nicely with fellowship to personal economic laws. It was here that a whole species of utility maximizers was prone to collapse or succeed with conflicting moral rights, depending only on whether either case was in execution of supreme historical laws. A discussion of both groups of ethical imperatives finalizes an ethical critique of the evolving economic paradigm in conflict debates.

Self-Legislation vs. Excellence

Imposing ethical imperatives on primary stakeholders in conflict means diverting attention from their being moral right holders, as well as to define their role as ethical duty bearers. It implies suspending fellowship to intrinsic economic laws. Being an ethical duty bearer requires the following: To say that someone bears ethical duties is distinctly different from any bearing of legal duties. The latter duties are enforced by law. Both in cases of international and internal conflict, international law takes over the role of sanctioning a breach in legal duties. Often, sanctions will refer to soft-law such as the *Universal Declaration of Human Rights*. In the realm of such law, interventions take the form of legal interventionism. Pertinent means employed under such interventions are diplomatic or military. The main role of legal settings is to endorse those means, e.g. by ways of a resolution of the United Nations Security Council. The case of ethical interventionism is distinctly different. Here, no codified law specifies concrete ethical duties different stakeholders bear, one of them being to limit utility maximizing behavior. Certainly, a community can establish ethical duties in a similar strict way as it imposes legal duties. But the first are of a different quality, in that they invoke a set of intangible legislation. In Immanuel Kant's words, the essential point about both is that legal behavior only needs to be in *accordance with duty*, while ethical behavior ought to happen *from duty*. In the first case, the sources of duty are externalized into codified law. In the second case, all sources of duty remain internal, meaning that they have to be enforced and sanctioned by each individual itself. Bearing ethical duty means exercising of self-legislation.

For the present purpose, the relationship between legal and ethical interventionism has illustrative character. It helps exemplifying what ethical duties are. At the same time, one must not distract from the main purpose of this investigation. Focus remains on the relationship between ethical and economic interventionism. An investigation of their relationship aims to safeguard ethical interventions from technical and economic imperatives that are so prominent today. Most commentators agree that the sources of ethical duty are internal and in compliance with some sort of self-legislation. However, it is highly controversial what these sources and concrete ethical imperatives are. For example, ethical welfarism may claim that fellowship to intrinsic economic laws, in a way, also comprises self-legislation. Indeed, the internal nature of ethical self-legislation may occasionally tempt to merge utility maximizing behavior and self-legislation, and to treat both as identical. Beyond comprising a source of moral rights, economic laws could thus assign overall ethical quality to their owner. In the end, ethical *excellence* required no adherence to ethical duties at all.

In the context of group conflict, such reasoning doesn't work. Too often it will fail to achieve conflict prevention, especially in view of the aforementioned ethical paradoxes. However, for the purpose of approaching the requirements of real self-legislation, it merits to further explore this path. Ultimately, this provides a clear picture of what real self-legislation may *not* be. Therefore, once subscribing to ethical welfarism, self-legislation is about legalizing our natural self, rather than about some sort of legislation put forward by our ethical self. In relation to the notion of self-legislation, this sets up the classical misunderstanding between *genitivus objectivus* and *genitivus subjectivus*. As for self-legislation, only the latter comprises a way of imposing ethical imperatives on our moral person, instead of demanding fellowship to natural interests. Whoever takes on the case of ethical welfarism is compelled to claim that being ethically good is 'to be good at being what you are',[89] in the absence of ethical duty.

There is an important parallel between this understanding of self-legislation and the antique understanding of human excellence. For ancient philosophers like Plato and Aristotle becoming a moral person was a matter of being guided by the way things ultimately are.[90] In essence, becoming ethically excellent was thought of as natural as growing up. Although one needed to learn virtue, this would be like learning a language, because we are human and that is our nature. Certainly, an important difference between ethical welfarism and the old Greek philosophers is that for the latter acquisition of ethical excellence and enforcement of one's moral person were goals in themselves. In contrast, ethical welfarism remains closely related to the de-

---

[89] Korsgaard (1996) 3.
[90] Ibid. 2.

mands of society, e.g. efforts to achieve conflict-free societies. Ultimately, ethical welfarism applies the antique concept of excellence in a reductionist manner. Focus is on particular pleasures, and enforcing one's moral person basically means ensuring the demands of one's empirical person. The common ground of ethical welfarism and the antique philosophers remains that theories of ethical excellence are being pursued, devoid of a concern for aspects of real self-legislation.

Real self-legislation, both for the sake of conflict prevention goals and ethical interventionism, establishes a series of requirements. As previously mentioned, such self-legislation is about capturing stakeholders in conflict as ethical duty bearers. The latter are required to define and bear certain ethical *obligations*, each of them in separation from other stakeholders. In the first place, self-legislation comprises a free act of endorsing obligations by which our freedom is being confined. In all of this, ethical obligation differs from ethical excellence in an important way. When we seek excellence, the force that ethical value exerts upon us is attractive. When we are obligated, it is compulsive. For obligation is the imposition of value on a reluctant, recalcitrant, resistant matter.[91] The old Greek understanding of excellence, although broader than the one featured by ethical welfarism, ignored the self-convincing struggle that engages people's moral person. It also ignored a possibility to fail.[92] As John L. Mackie once stressed with regard to Plato's forms: 'The Form of the Good is such that knowledge of it provides the knower with both a direction and an overriding motive; something's being good both tells the person who knows this to pursue it and makes him pursue it.'[93] Indeed, Plato's Socrates stands an indelible monument to the view that nobody seeks to do bad things willingly. In *Menon*, Socrates thus states: 'Is it not obvious that those who are ignorant of their [the evils'] nature do not desire them; but they desire what they suppose to be goods although they are really evils; and if they are mistaken and suppose the evils to be good they really desire goods.'[94] They simply fail to recognize that something is an evil. Had they had a knowledge of the real good, it would have been pursued right away.

While the Greek philosophers don't pose an obstacle to ethical interventionism, ethical welfarism could do so. Fellowship to natural interests and intrinsic economic laws are rarely sufficient in terms of ethical progress. There is a need to emphasize the *self-overcoming* nature of ethical behavior. Ethical self-legislation must be pic-

---

91 Ibid. 4.

92 Certainly, this view applies more to Plato than to Aristotle. A view commonly attributed to Aristotle is that good (for man) is identical both with happiness and with the realization of human nature. In so far as this means merely that if one realizes one's potentialities as a human being one will be happy, and hence good, the only possible source of disagreement concerns indeed a purely causal question. However, we should not forget that Aristotle began his ethical investigations with the assumption that the good for man is happiness and only subsequently, after much analysis, concluded that the best way to achieve happiness is to realize one's potentialities as a human being. See H.D. Aiken, 'Definitions of Value and the Moral Ideal', in *The Journal of Philosophy*, Vol. 42, No. 13 (1945) 337-352.

93 J.L. Mackie, *Ethics: Inventing Right and Wrong*, Harmondsworth: Penguin Books (1977) 38.

94 Plato, *Meno* [ca. 380 BC], in Plato, *The Dialogues of Plato*, transl. by B. Jowett, Oxford: Clarendon Press (1871) 77d,e.

tured as a process of self-obligation.[95] The whole issue boils down to one basic point. Thus, different from the old philosophers one does not need to grasp of virtue as an ultimate end in itself that only adds sense to our human nature.[96] An exclusive focus may go out to the social consequences of ethical behavior. But then precisely, only if we maintain an image of the obligating and self-overcoming nature of ethical behavior, pro-activism and ethical interventionism become possible, if developments are heading for the wrong direction. Ethical interventionism recognizes the impact of egoistic and shortsighted willing. Together with Kant we may claim that 'the ought pronounced by reason confronts such willing with a limit and an end - nay more, forbids or authorises it.'[97] Where we loose track of the self-overcoming traits of ethical legislation, we also remove a template for the fragile nature of ethical progress, and with it an effective option to react.

There is another reason why ethics has sometimes been reluctant to break with fellowship to intrinsic economic laws. Self-legislation has not been dismissed on principal grounds. But arguments against effective self-legislation have been gathered on liberal premises.[98] Therefore, as a free act of endorsing obligations by which our freedom is being confined, self-legislation must be obscure to any real liberal. A closest possible symbiosis of utilitarian and liberal thought has been present in John Stuart Mill's anti-interventionist model. Both have been combined in an unprecedented manner.[99] For what we mean by freedom and autonomy, Mill occasionally used the term 'character', thus specifying:

> A person whose desires and impulses are his own—are the expression of his own nature, as it has been developed and modified by his own culture—is said to have a character. One whose desires and impulses are not his own, has no character, no more than a steam engine has a character.[100]

Certainly, a reserved attitude towards desires and impulses that are not a person's own ones does not impede ethical self-legislation. The latter only needed to reflect that person's independent will. However, self-legislation that is required *socially*

95 Further on the uneasy relationship between utilitarianism and moral obligation see R. Sartorius, 'Utilitarianism and Obligation', in *The Journal of Philosophy*, Vol. 66, No. 3 (1969) 67-81; H.W. Schneider, 'Obligations and the Pursuit of Happiness', in *The Philosophical Review*, Vol. 61, No. 3 (1952) 312-319.

96 For literature elaborating on elements of a positive relationship between utilitarianism and the achievement of virtue see for example R. Crisp, 'Utilitarianism and the Life of Virtue', in *The Philosophical Quarterly*, Vol. 42, No. 167 (1992) 139-160; J. Kilcullen, 'Utilitarianism and Virtue', in *Ethics*, Vol. 93, No. 3 (1983) 451-466.

97 I. Kant, *Critique of Pure Reason* [1781/1787], translated by N. Kemp Smith, London: Macmillan (1929) Transcendental Doctrine Of The Elements, Transcendental Logic, Second Division: Transcendental Dialectic, Book II, Ch. II, Sec. 9.

98 On the relationship between utilitarianism and liberalism see D.A. Lloyd Thomas, 'Liberalism and Utilitarianism', in *Ethics*, Vol. 90, No. 3 (1980) 319-334; T.D. Campbell and I.S. Ross, 'The Utilitarianism of Adam Smith's Policy Advice', in *Journal of the History of Ideas*, Vol. 42, No. 1 (1981) 73-92.

99 For a possible consistency problem between Mill's utilitarian theory in *Utilitarianism* and account of freedom in *On Liberty* see D.O. Brink, 'Mill's Deliberative Utilitarianism', in *Philosophy and Public Affairs*, Vol. 21, No. 1 (1992) 67-103.

100 J.S. Mill, *On Liberty*, London: J.W. Parker (1859) Ch. 3.

must encroach upon the autonomous character of any self-legislation. As such, it comes to the fore in the demands of distributive justice and conflict prevention. The idea of being socially required causes that the concept of self-legislation has rarely been reconciled with liberal thought. What Mill and others did not see is that a definition of self-legislation in the above-indicated way, i.e. as a free act of endorsing obligations, only captures one side of the whole issue. To Kant, we owe a vision of negative and positive freedoms that is completely different from the earlier discussed classical and compensatory liberal account. According to this vision, positive freedom does not only harmonize with self-legislation, but actually it requires self-legislation for the sake of what Kant called *autonomy*. In view of providing ethical interventions with a normative basis, efforts to reconcile self-legislation and autonomy are not that crucial. Because, in many cases ethical self-legislation will be indispensable even though it is detrimental to people's pool of freedoms. Nonetheless, a proper understanding of their scope for reconciliation may help to adopt ethical self-legislation in place of ethical excellence. However, who could imagine exploring such scope without looking into some of the basic tenets of Immanuel Kant's ethical theory?

Kant is famous for contending that the 'autonomy of the will is the sole principle of all moral laws and of all duties which conform to them.'[101] Vice versa, the moral laws and duties which conform to them are held to be the only source for realizing this autonomy.

The first aspect of this mutual relationship is immediately understandable. It alludes to the fact that ethical duty can only materialize if practical reason renders us autonomous of natural interests. In Kant, the opposite of autonomy is a system of heteronomy. A latter system has much in common with ethical welfarism. Only with Kant, one identifies previously unnoticed aspects in ethical welfarism. These aspects relate to ethical welfarism's particular grasp on freedom. Under the premises of ethical welfarism, moral laws are hardly given of the will's own dictation, but by a desired object, e.g. by economic desires. Moral laws then turn into 'pathological laws'. Heteronymous approaches, such as ethical welfarism, are restricted to hypothetical imperatives. In the early stage of this chapter, these imperatives were linked to technical imperatives in the evolving economic paradigm. According to hypothetical imperatives, 'I ought to do A because I wish for B.' For example, 'I ought to avoid speeding up economic maldistribution and injustice, if I wish to preserve economic privileges and repress resource conflict.' In this situation of dependence on a desired object, it is Kant's categorical imperative that seeks to rescue the ethical welfarist. With Kant, he learns that 'he ought to do A, even though he does not wish for any B.' Applied to the above example this means that: 'He ought to avoid economic injustice, still although it might not trigger resource conflict.' But, practically, what does the ethical welfarist need to do in order to arrive at this insight? For the categorical imperative to materialize, Kant also prescribed a *generalization test*, which is yet different from the one rule-utilitarianism envisages. Kant's generaliza-

[101] I. Kant, *Critique of Practical Reason* [1788], transl. by T.K. Abbott, in T.K. Abbott, *Kant's Critique of Practical Reason and other Works on the Theory of Ethics*, London: Longmans and Green (1879) First Part, Book I, Ch. 1, Para. 8: Theorem IV.

tion test does not consider whether an action to progress a given interest would be self-defeating if applied as a universal rule. It goes beyond that. Kant's test is held to 'abstract from all objects that they shall have no influence on the will, in order that practical reason (will) may not be restricted to administering an interest not belonging to it, but may simply show its own commanding authority as the supreme legislation.'[102] Eventually, this test is to come up with universal laws. Only given such independence on all matter of the law, i.e. a desired object, the ethical welfarist is enabled to exercise self-legislation in line with what Kant calls freedom in the *negative* sense.[103]

For the purpose of conflict prevention, it would be sufficient to call on ethical self-legislation whenever an economic distribution problem became acute or was not yet solved. Beyond those cases, there was no mandate to impose ethical imperatives on our stakeholders. However, from a Kantian angle such gradual imposition of self-legislation would be clearly insufficient. It was so, in view of the above-mentioned second aspect of the mutual relationship between moral laws and autonomy. This second aspect concerns the fact that in Kant the moral laws and duties conformable to them are held to be the *only* source of personal autonomy.[104] Therefore, in Kant's ethical theory self-legislation is a continuously operating problem. For the present analysis, this second aspect was guiding when emphasizing the scope for reconciliation between self-legislation and autonomy, a scope hardly realized by utilitarians and liberals.

In Kant, a mandate imposing self-legislation on primary stakeholders seeks to adjust our sensible inclinations beyond situational need. This means two things: Firstly, the problem of human beings being 'unholy enough' to be seduced by pleasure to the transgression of the moral law goes beyond cases of conflict between stakeholder interests. The sensible inclinations are held to comprise constant hindrances to the fulfillment of duty.[105] Secondly, there is a proactive dimension to self-legislation in Kant's ethical theory. Such self-legislation is not only fine-tuned to preempting the seducing influences of people's sensible inclinations. The Kantian individual performs self-legislation, because only that way it may achieve freedom in the *positive* sense. Apart from the fact that the moral law expresses the autonomy of pure practical reason, it is only the moral law that gives expression to this autonomy.[106] The moral laws the Kantian individual imposes upon itself are thus called 'laws of freedom'. For the purpose of realizing an individual's positive freedom or autonomy, those laws comprise a constant preoccupation.[107]

---

[102] Kant (1785) Sec. 2.

[103] See I. Kant (1788) First Part, Book I, Ch. 1, Para. 8: Theorem IV; I. Kant, *Metaphysics of Morals* [1797], transl. by T.K. Abbott, in T.K. Abbott, *Kant's Critique of Practical Reason and other Works on the Theory of Ethics*, London: Longmans and Green (1879) Introduction.

[104] According to the same rationale, a person's freedom may not be realized on purely economic grounds, and certainly not through mere participation in free markets, free prices, consumer freedom and consumer sovereignty, as anticipated by the classical and neo-classical liberal models. For a corresponding critique of the neo-classical and other models see K. de Schweinitz Jr., 'The Question of Freedom in Economics and Economic Organization', in *Ethics*, Vol. 89, No. 4 (1979) 336-353.

[105] Kant (1797) Introduction to the Metaphysical Elements of Ethics.

[106] Kant (1788) First Part, Book I, Ch. 1, Para. 8: Theorem IV.

[107] Kant (1797) Introduction.

Kant found independent and ultimately positive aspects in the challenges of ethical self-legislation. This should not betray about the fact that a need for both emanates above all from situational demand. It emanates particularly from shortcomings of the utility principle in terms of ethical imperatives that settle conflicts of interest. The imposition of ethical imperatives on primary stakeholders in conflict is a must in the realm of three ethical paradoxes hosted by the utility principle as well as its explicit and implicit proponents, i.e. ethical welfarism and the evolving economic paradigm. Ethical duty and self-legislation are indispensable where moral rights are in conflict with each other. At the end of the day, ethical self-legislation comprises one of two mechanisms that only secure ethical interventionism.

Ethical Pro-Activism vs. Manufacturing of History

The other mechanism to assign normative strength to ethical interventions imposes ethical imperatives on history. There is a need to break with ethical approaches that prevent ethical interventions, i.e. ethical pro-activism, by commanding fellowship to the determining influence of historical laws in social affairs. Thus, one needs to break with ethical modernism. The main connection between ethical modernism and ethical welfarism is that, in one way or the other, historical laws are taken to promote basic economic goals. The promotion of such goals lies with history heading for ever higher degrees of perfection. A crucial outcome of the preceding analysis relates to the insight that ethical modernism goes beyond traditional accounts of historicism. It especially exceeds Marx's political economy. Thus, it also integrates aspects of historicism's most prominent adversary. Ethical modernism hence accommodates for Popper's piecemeal social engineering approach to history and related aspects in the evolving economic paradigm. Despite the fact that traditional historicism and this paradigm differ vastly concerning the driving forces of history, they converge in their strong anticipatory grip on the future of society, no matter what that future is deemed to be.

Historicism has been reviewed as an anti-interventionist doctrine. According to Marx, the aim of the social sciences can only be 'to lay bare the economic law of motion of modern society.'[108] Therefore, 'even when a society has got upon the right track for the discovery of the natural laws of its movement [...] it can neither clear by bold leaps, nor remove by legal enactments, the obstacles offered by the successive phases of its normal development. But it can shorten and lessen the birth-pangs.'[109] As opposed to this view, piecemeal social engineering adopts a proactive attitude toward the social order. It establishes a technological approach to social sciences.

[108] Marx (1867) Preface to the First German Edition. Popper's criticism of Marx at this point stands on a misquotation. Popper attacked the notion that there are laws of human development, and that knowing these laws enables us to predict the future course of human history. Therefore, in *The Poverty of Historicism* he quotes Marx's *Capital* as saying that the aim is 'to lay bare the economic law of motion of human society'. But Marx actually wrote that his aim was to lay bare the economic law of motion of 'modern society', or capitalism. The economic law of capitalism, Marx's theory of value, is in fact quite specific to capitalism. This misquotation was pointed out frequently to Popper and his publishers, but every few years it is reprinted with the falsification unaltered.

[109] Ibid.

Rather than engaging into passive prophecy, the technological approach intimates steps that can be taken proactively, if we want to achieve results that also move us closer to the anticipated state of society. This state is in any case a state of subsequent economic and political perfection. More than that, it *must* be a state of subsequent perfection. We found that, by definition, piecemeal social engineering must subscribe to a progress story. Historicism only interprets social developments. Thus, it fits well with an anti-perfectionist line of thought. In contrast, the achievement of real social progress is the only self-legitimation of any piecemeal social engineer, because he is programmed to intervene and not to interpret. Polemically speaking, the piecemeal social engineer is forced to think of the goals that cannot be achieved in terms of goals that don't want to be achieved. Together, a proactive attitude toward politico-economic interventions and progress-anticipation rather than progress-orientation gave rise to a *manufacturing style*, which characterizes piecemeal social engineering. This style leaves no uncertainties as to the means and ends of social development.

In the case of piecemeal social engineering, a proactive attitude toward the social order was found to combine neatly with ethical passivism. Normally, passive elements of that kind are deemed to be a privilege of traditional historicism, given its observing of a non-intervening approach. According to historicism, ethics is held to discard any perspective on what *ought* to be for the sake of assumptions as to what *will* be, this being a straightforward consequence of history defining the course of the social realm. Under these circumstances, ethical imperatives need to be such that they conform to the impending changes. The message for ethical interventionists is that there is no need to correct moral behavior. Because, on the whole moral misbehavior will not lead to changes in history's predestined course. Ethics normally considers individuals the way they ought to be, rather than the way they are. A key implication of historicism is to take them 'how they are, rather than the way they ought to be.' For different reasons, the projected role of ethics is just as meager in piecemeal social engineering. Confidence as to a set of rather practical means to administer social development serves to keep relevant interventions within narrow margins. Mainly ethical interventions are being rejected. Eventually, ethical passivism reveals to comprise the flipside of politico-economic pro-activism. A four-pronged critique of this trend re-installs ethical pro-activism to conflict prevention efforts.

First of all, we may recall a previous point. Thus, it was argued that the consequences of ethical passivism materialize in *individual passivism*. Whereas ethical passivism belongs to the group of external interventions (in conflict), individual passivism theorizes a resulting feature of the primary stakeholders in interventions. The threats of ethical passivism are only real when they are considered at the latter level. As for the evolving economic paradigm, elements of individual passivism that may result from ethical passivism only increase such passivism to maximum extent. Overall, that paradigm features a passive approach. In the realm of this passive approach one is prone to ask what can be done *for* individuals, rather than installing them as dynamic actors who execute interventions on the basis of intrinsic norms. With the evolving economic paradigm one is prone to consider how the capabilities of individuals can *be* enhanced. In the end, this implies downgrading their normative stakeholdership in conflict prevention strategies, rather than drawing on capabilities each and every human being owns of its own by virtue of being human. It was also found that for two main reasons individual pro-activism may hardly be re-gained on economic grounds only: Firstly, according to the evolving economic paradigm the social engineer jumps in where primary stakeholders fail to succeed. Individuals and groups are installed as pro-active stakeholders only after the job has been done, i.e. conflict has been prevented. Secondly, even where primary stakeholders get involved in economic pro-activism, they remain 'prisoners' to their natural interests. For both reasons, economic pro-activism cannot warrant individual pro-activism. Real individual pro-activism may only be regained on ethical grounds. Only here individuals employ their moral rather than empirical person. By definition the former is pro-active, because of the ethical self-legislation it designs. Only here we are working on people's mindsets through norms and imperatives, rather than on the economic environment for conflict prevention. Therefore, for those aspects of economic pro-activism engendered in a manufacturing approach to history to be discharged of individual passivism, they must enter into a coalition with ethical pro-activism. Hence, the evolving economic paradigm must join such a coalition. That is also why ethical passivism is so questionable.

Secondly, the last point criticizes elements of individual passivism for the restrictions they exercise vis-à-vis conflict prevention goals. However, besides achieving these goals, aspects of individual passivism also require relating to individual goals. A prime individual goal comprises people's *autonomy*, as it has been developed from Kant's ethical theory. But how could the individual ever be considered as autonomous where history was pre-determined as a whole? Either it was pre-determined in its concrete course through time, e.g. traditional historicism, or owing to a narrow set of economic drivers, e.g. evolving economic paradigm. Obviously, individual autonomy wants to be achieved with history, more precisely with those who claim to make history for others, rather than in a narrow struggle with our natural self. If people lived their natural interests in the absence of self-legislation, the result would be ethical passivism. This meant a process that *suspends* segments of individual autonomy. Individuals failed to realize a concept of positive freedom in view of capabilities that are an essential part of their human nature. At the same time, a template for individual autonomy was preserved intact. There was still an option for this autonomy to be realized in a later stage. On the other hand, if aspects of individual passivism lead to abandon a struggle with history and the makers of history, individual autonomy may not be realized in a later stage. Such an approach removes rather than suspends any segment of individual autonomy. It leads to individuals becoming the passive object of history or piecemeal social engineering. Both versions of ethical modernism annihilate at the global level the kind of autonomy we want to achieve at the individual level in a struggle with ethical welfarism.

Thirdly, part of the attractiveness of ethical modernism is that it features a progress story with regard to the subsequent moral standing of society. Where ethical progress is considered a byproduct of economic progress, and economic development deemed to be an authentic representative of ethical progress in the domain of conflict prevention, one cannot expect a major concern for people's ethical record. Where ethical imperatives are dissolvable in technical imperatives, we are tempted to applaud such self-transformation and thriving of hypothetical imperatives. However, there can be no misunderstanding that guarantees for continuous socio-ethical progress don't exist. Ethical progress is individual. As such, it wants to be achieved through individual pro-activism, i.e. self-legislation and autonomy. To the extent that this requires overcoming obstacles in our empirical nature, ethical progress also demands infinite repetition of one and the same ethical exercise, which is so exemplarily entrenched in Kant's idea of categorical imperatives designing 'practical reason'. As for this exercise, we are held to choose maxims for our actions that are suitable to become universal ethical law. However, once identified those universal maxims are only universal to the extent that they comprise everyone's duty, if he or she was put in a given situation. But they do not exceed the particular situation for which they have been identified. Any newly arising situation requires repetition of the same exercise of selecting our maxims according to their suitability as universal ethical laws. The sheer plurality of situations demanding ethical statements renders ethical progress a precarious task. If a free will constitutes the successful case of the 'property of the will to be a law to itself,'[110] then one also needs to add that this property remains preliminary.

Some fair skepticism as to the achievability of linear ethical progress in history relates to the provisional character of individual self-legislation. So why not better putting one's stakes into benign ethical effects of economic progress, especially if a serious task as conflict prevention was in jeopardy? Ethical modernists could claim that ethical pro-activism leads to a *zero-point* theory in ethical affairs.[111] As opposed to this, history may not be able to rely on a continuous start-from-scratch approach. Where do we go with ethical progress if ethical imperatives needed to be absorbed ever new, for reliance on precedents would put at risk people's autonomy? How can there be ethical progress in history if the moral history of each individual was to start from scratch every other moment? Under those circumstances, ethical interventionism might be doomed to comprise a hopeless case, since it must not build on any learning effect on the part of the primary stakeholders in conflict. More seriously, is the isolated individual ever in a position to identify proper ethical imperatives? Also, is it strong enough to execute ethical duties on their self-legislated basis?

These are serious challenges to ethical pro-activism and ethical self-legislation. However, approving them means misunderstanding the claims of a non-historical, anti-manufacturing approach to ethical progress. The latter implies the following: Firstly, by rejecting that ethical progress can be achieved en passant, while working on the economic foundations of conflict prevention, it asserts that such progress needs to be *accomplished*. It emphasizes that primary stakeholders ought to progress individually, so as to lay the foundations for ethical progress on a broader scale. This way, they may also socialize an ethics of conflict prevention. Secondly, by distinguishing morally good actions from economically good actions, a non-historical, anti-manufacturing approach to ethical progress signals that developing one's moral person must not be esteemed as a *habit*, i.e. as a custom acquired by long practice of corresponding actions. While economic progress always has a habitual component, ethical progress can not, because the thing with habits is that they are supposedly applied to routine circumstances. But as Kant stressed, if developing ones moral per-

---

110 Kant (1785) Sec. 3.

111 F. Kaulbach, *Studien zur späten Rechtsphilosophie Kants und ihrer transzendentalen Methode*, Würzburg: Königshausen & Neumann (1982) 65.

son 'is not an effect of well resolved and firm principles ever more and more purified, then, like any other mechanical arrangement brought about by technical practical reason, it is neither armed for all circumstances, nor adequately secured against the change that may be wrought by new allurements.'[112] Thirdly, apart from that there may be no question that there *can be* ethical progress beyond the individual level, and thus on a social and historical scale. But for such progress to materialize, a continuous start-from-scratch ethical approach to newly arising situations is preferable to reliance on presumed ethical qualities of economic development.

Finally, for a while piecemeal social engineering could seem to provide today's architects of historical laws. In the past, those laws were the privilege of a demiurge enlightened to design history's masterplan. At that time, actual stakeholders only executed history's masterplan, but they were not involved in designing it. Also, no distinction was drawn as to primary and secondary stakeholders. The latter, e.g. development practitioner, was acting on situations which he was a defined part of in the first place. Piecemeal social engineering and the evolving economic paradigm mark appreciable developments, in as much as they achieve maximum distance from such an approach. However, beyond defining particular social ends, piecemeal social engineers are held to prescribe the rules according to which history's game is being played. Those rules are largely economic rules. Different from the precepts of traditional historicism, these rules are executed in a proactive manner. While this can also be appreciated, a manufacturing approach toward history is the result. The latter tends to discard any perspective on what ought to be for the sake of broad-based assumptions into what will be. Apart from doing harm to the original requirements of ethical progress, exaggeration of the habitual component in economic progress must also damage the immediate goal of the evolving economic paradigm, i.e. the prevention of conflict. When 'manufacturing' historical facts, authority and control of our decisions and interventions are increased to maximum extent. With this paradigm one may feel armed against all circumstances. But conflict rarely follows routine circumstances. In the end, the evolving economic paradigm impedes a proactive attitude where, for some reason, developments are heading for the wrong direction. More recently, there have been impressive examples of such inability; for example Europe's apathy, when after almost fifty years conflict hit an economically developed region as the Balkan. Apart from institutional reasons and causes in flawed decision making, which are often quoted in such cases, apathy is to result from the false assumption that in economically developed regions conflict cannot be true, because it is suppose to be untrue.

---

[112] Kant (1797) Introduction to the Metaphysical Elements of Ethics.

CHAPTER VII

HUMAN RIGHTS-BASED APPROACHES TO DEVELOPMENT

Section 17. International Organizations

Ethical paradoxes potentially associated with a narrow economic conflict prevention agenda increase when moving into practice. Here, technical imperatives prefigured in scientific theories are actively translated into interventions. Along with them, ethical implications materialize in debatable imperatives, i.e. in hypothetical imperatives. International organizations are prime agents concerned with conflict prevention today. The horizontal inequality approach (h.i.-approach) has been endorsed in various occasions. For example, during these last years the concept has repeatedly been invoked at the United Nations.[1] Conceptually, keynote speeches about the root causes of conflict have been linked to horizontal inequalities.[2/3] As a latest contribution along this line, the *Human Development Report 2005* devotes some special attention to horizontal inequalities.[4] Also, increasingly international organizations concur with the idea of supranational players, rather than intergovernmental institutions. Thus, they take on additional responsibilities in the field of conflict prevention and development. Apart from accelerating institutional integration goals, international organizations also act as normative institutions. Hence, they accept a norm-setting role in various international fields. The latter role has increased recently, particularly in the domain of development cooperation. Thus, a rights-based approach to development has gained momentum. Ultimately, this approach extends to conflict prevention goals via the long-term role development cooperation has accepted with

---

1 The author has sought to analyze this concept in two previous works. See R. Bredel, *Long-Term Conflict Prevention and Industrial Development: The United Nations and its Specialized Agency, UNIDO*, Leiden and Boston: Martinus Nijhoff Publishers (2003); R. Bredel, 'The UN's Long-Term Conflict Prevention Strategies and the Impact of Counter-Terrorism', in *International Peacekeeping*, Vol. 10, No. 2 (2003) 51-70.

2 See K. Annan, Address to the Seventeenth National Convention of the Arab-American Anti-Discrimination Committee, Arlington, Virginia, USA, 12 June 2000; K. Annan, Address to the Fourth International Conference of New and Restored Democracies, Contonou, Benin, 7 Dec. 2000; K. Annan, Address to the Foreign Policy Association, New York, USA, 21 March 2001; K. Annan, Cyril Foster Lecture at Oxford University, UK, 19 June 2001; K. Annan, Address at University of Oslo, Norway, 20 August 2001.

3 As mentioned before, the link between these academic and practical approaches has been the World Institute for Development Economics Research in Helsinki, which is a part of the United Nations University, but has been involved in joint research activities with the Queen Elizabeth House at Oxford University of which Frances Stewart is the Director. See W. Nafziger and F. Stewart and R. Väyrynen (eds.), *War, Hunger and Displacement: The Origins of Humanitarian Emergencies*, 2 Vol., Oxford: Oxford University Press (2000).

4 UNDP, *Human Development Report 2000: Human Rights and Human Development,* New York: Oxford University Press (2000).

regard to these goals. The idea with this approach is twofold: Firstly, development interventions are seen to derive normative justification from particular human rights. Secondly, development goals are believed to promote other human rights goals, directly and indirectly.

In a way, a rights-based approach to development increases the normative role of international organizations to maximum extent. At the same time, there is a need to explore whether this approach also serves to render explicit as well as supersede the immediate ethical implications of technical imperatives and development interventions, especially those being of an economic nature. We want to analyze whether human rights remain inhabitants of a parallel world or carriers of ethical interventionism. The present section aims at preparing the ground for an answer to this ultimately important question. Section 18 then broaches an authoritative answer, thus impacting on a model for international organizations concerning the ethical economy of conflict prevention and development. The present section is divided into three parts: First follows an update on latest developments in the debate on supranationality and intergovernmentalism. An ensuing discussion relates to international organizations as normative institutions. The section finally systematizes a particular rights-based approach to development, embodied in 'Action 2' of the United Nations reform process and other initiatives.

Supranationality vs. Intergovernmentalism

The role of international organizations as intergovernmental or supranational players has been raised in a long debate between various schools in international relations. Three main schools have been at the center of this debate, i.e. a liberal, realist and Marxist school. These schools are vastly compatible with political economies major schools. The liberal school features important overlap with classical political economy. Keynes had temporarily adopted the realist school. Finally, the Marxist school evolved according to the precepts of Marx's political economy. Chapter I has analyzed these links extensively. It only remains to put the three schools in context with each other: As an earliest school, realism has been in favor of restricting international organizations to intergovernmental stakeholders. Concurrent to the emanation of patterns of Cold War-thinking it dominated the scientific study of international relations. In a military defined security arena and a reality of power seeking nation states in the 1960s, inter-governmental settings seemed compatible with the tenets of mutual deterrence.[5] Only the following decades made it clear that all forms of nationalism were increasingly at odds with an age whose technologies of transportation, communication and warfare had rendered nationalism obsolete as a principle of political organization.[6] Succeeding globalization focused on the interdependencies of national economies, thus laying ground for the upsurge of liberal theories. The liberal challenge to the realist paradigm emerged. Advocacy for supranational settings evolved under the framework of compensatory liberalism, which abandons a

5 R. McKinlay and R. Little, *Global Problems and World Order*, Madison: F. Pinter Publishers (1986) 234.

6 D. Mitrany, *A Working Peace System*, Chicago: Quadrangle Books (1966) 7.

pure laissez-faire approach. Key components of supranational thinking came to the fore in neo-functionalism. While subscribing to the view that form follows function, neo-functionalism was convinced that actors could be loyal to several agencies simultaneously. A gradual transfer of loyalties to international organizations performing most of the crucial functions was deemed likely, thus also centering supranational settings.[7] The liberal model of international organizations became a center for criticism in the late 1970s and 1980s. Marxist theories focused on the socio-economic problems of developing countries, stressing the importance of a New International Economic Order. The Brandt Commission's proposals for negotiated change became an important historical example how such criticism was taken up politcally.[8] At times, rather strange consequences were drawn from this assessment. At the extreme, an abolition of national and international forms of political organization has been anticipated. Unlike realists and liberals, Marxists did not see a major disjuncture between nation states and international forms of organization. They would rather envisage some sort of global organization based on a larger number of socialist communities, which would interact with each other to greater or lesser degree on exactly the same principles that governed international organizations.[9]

Present layouts of the international sphere render pure intergovernmental positions inadequate. With its continued commitment to the antagonist nature of domestic autonomy and international norms, realism fails to picture the complexity of the present situation. For yet different reasons, Marxists are at odds with supranational elements of the international system. An abolition of all forms of international organizations cannot hold today. Especially since the end of the Cold War, renewed optimism on the role of international organizations emerged.[10] This would also indicate the supremacy of compensatory liberal dwelling upon supranational organizations. At the same time, it would assume an oversimplification to conclude that earlier than others liberals anticipated feasible integration goals. Too close, liberal theories were related to the block-building during the Cold War to justify such an assessment.

Normative Institutions

A more feasible approach than relying on particular schools of thought is to center three basic perceptional paradigms in international relations research.[11] These paradigms have been closely related to different phases in the process of international organization after World War Two. An earliest paradigm may be called the legalist paradigm. It emerged during the process of filing of the UN Charter. As a major act of legally renewing the world order after 1945, it foresaw that analysis of statutory

---

7 E. Haas, *Beyond the Nation State: Functionalism and International Organization*, Stanford: Stanford University Press (1964) 21-22 and 47-50.

8 W. Brandt, *North-South: A Programme for Survival. The Report of the Independent Commission on International Development Issues*, London: Pan Books (1980).

9 McKinlay and Little (1986) 62.

10 V. Rittberger, *Internationale Organizationen: Politik und Geschichte. Europäische und Weltweite Zwischenstaatliche Zusammenschlüsse*, Opladen: Leske und Budrich (1994) 84.

11 Ibid. 85.

aspects provided an adequate picture of international organizations. Following the insight that investigating legal articles barely ensures a detailed assessment of international organizations, the scientific community came to concentrate on actual decision-finding processes. The descriptive paradigm in the study of international organizations was born. During the last decades, a third or normative paradigm has emerged. Since then, international organizations are no longer considered for their internal practices, i.e. for a set of cooperation- and decision-finding mechanisms. Rather, they are analyzed for their involvement in the creation of external international institutions, i.e. the formation of normative international regimes. While providing international institutions related to particular policy-fields, normative international regimes can be considered in two directions: Firstly, in the context of *creating* normative international regimes, the procreative capacity of international organizations to originate norms requires investigation. Secondly, in the context of *implementing* normative international regimes, the ability of international organizations to warrant the effectiveness of existing norms becomes crucial.[12]

Beyond 'Action 2'

The normative role of international organizations has seen an increase recently, particularly in the domain of development cooperation. Thus, a human rights-based approach to development has gained momentum. Ultimately, this approach extends to conflict prevention goals in two major ways: Firstly, via the long-term role development cooperation has accepted with regard to these goals; secondly, given the detrimental impact any conflict must have on the realization of human rights in the socio-economic field. The basic idea with a human rights-based approach to development is to provide development interventions with legal and normative justification in component elements of the international human rights system. Until today, those components are gathered in the *International Bill of Human Rights*. The latter consists of the *Universal Declaration of Human Rights*, the *International Covenant on Economic, Social and Cultural Rights*, and the *International Covenant on Civil and Political Rights* and its two Optional Protocols. Overall, the following aspects characterize a human rights-based approach to development:

Firstly, human rights-based approaches seek to exceed needs-based approaches to development. The latter approaches usually take a start in innate needs, which all individuals supposedly share by virtue of being human beings. For those working with needs theory, the assumption of needs that are innate provides the basis to generalize across cultures and societal levels from the inter-personal and the family to the international.[13] Human rights-based approaches strengthen the normative basis of development cooperation. Thus, they lift people's needs to the level of universal human rights. Once a need is looked at from the perspective of a human right, this also

---

[12] O. Young, 'Patterns of International Cooperation: Institutions and Organizations', in O. Young (ed.), *International Cooperation: Building Regimes for Natural Resources and the Environment*, Ithaca: Cornell University Press (1989) 31-57.

[13] J. Burton, *Violence Explained: The Sources of Conflict, Violence and Crime and their Prevention*, Manchester: Manchester University Press (1997) 35.

adds a legal dimension. Beyond acknowledging the existence of that need, this legal dimension implies an *obligation* to enforce that need or human right in practice. Development cooperation that addresses such a need derives prime normative strength. On the other hand, human rights-based approaches have a less comfortable basis when moving away from needs-based approach to development. This is particularly the case when the liberal and utilitarian concept of wants is embraced. Apart from other aspects, this concept has been to stress that innate wants are supposedly confined to basic food, shelter and the like. All the rest, economic wants particularly, individuals are seen to develop in the course of life, or in some cases they don't.[14] With its focus on relative deprivation scenarios, the h.i.-approach partly endorses the concept of wants. It provides that at least some needs are not absolute, both as for their existence as well as in quantity-terms. Rather, they are developed relative to other people who enjoy particular privileges. After all, a wants-centered angle could cause some problems to human rights-based approaches, because it removes the notion of innate needs. But development cooperation in the economic field is rarely motivated by wants. Also, human rights are rarely fine-tuned to particular economic desires so that they could spark a debate on their status as innate needs or dispensable wants.

Secondly, apart from specifying a human right to development, human rights-based approaches imply certain ways of implementing that right. In example, they set a number of normative principles for such implementation. One such principle is the principle of equality and non-discrimination. This principle is particularly interesting for the evolving economic paradigm, given the latter's focus on horizontal inequalities and relative deprivation. By ways of this principle, human rights-based approaches to development lend authority to long-term conflict prevention strategies that center the comparative dimension of (economic) deprivation. By ways of this principle, they also imply that these strategies are preferable to approaches that don't disaggregate, as such centering absolute deprivation or poverty in general.

Thirdly, human rights-based approaches to development ensure a role of international organizations in development cooperation that goes beyond their being service providers. Apart from defining individuals as rights holders, they identify different categories of duty bearers. For example, the *Universal Declaration of Human Rights* recognizes four kinds of duty bearers: Primary duty bearers, e.g. parents for children, teachers for students, police for crime suspects, doctors and nurses for patients, employers for employees; secondary duty bearers, e.g. institutions and organizations with immediate jurisdiction over the primary duty bearers, such as school principals, community organizations, hospital administrations, etc.; tertiary duty bearers, e.g. institutions and organizations at a higher level and more remote jurisdiction, such as NGOs, aid agencies, private sector organizations; external duty bearers, e.g. countries, institutions, organizations with no direct involvement, such as the United Nations, WTO, NGOs, etc. As *external duty bearers*, international organizations are no principal duty bearers, like states are. But it is recognized that 'as the world becomes increasingly globalised, moral duty-bearers at the international and trans-national

---

14 A.F.v. Hayek, *Studies in Philosophy, Politics and Economics*, London: Routledge and Kegan Paul (1967) 314.

level may be increasingly expected to assume a greater responsibility in the promotion and protection of human rights.'[15]

Fourthly, while not providing an enforceable legal basis, human rights-based approaches lend a strong normative dimension to the work of international development organizations. By no means, they lead to supersede those organizations' mandate, as has been stated occasionally. According to such view, a human rights-based approach 'involves abolishing the development enterprise as a neo-colonial programme of correction administered from rich to poor and replacing it with a common political project that recognises everyone's equal rights and judges the behaviour of all on the basis of how they realise or violate these rights.'[16] At most, development may be viewed as a sub-set of the process of fulfilling human rights. The overall promise for international development organizations is an increased normative framework for their work.

Fifthly, by systematically defining rights holders and duty bearers, human rights-based approaches overcome a shortcoming of many development debates, particularly in relation to long-term conflict prevention goals. Hence, they help installing individuals as ethical duty bearers. Long-term conflict prevention debates sometimes feature a *passive approach* to individuals. In the realm of this passive approach one is prone to ask what can be done *for* these individuals, rather than capturing them as dynamic actors who execute interventions on the basis of intrinsic norms. Especially with the evolving economic paradigm one is held to consider how the capabilities of individuals can *be* enhanced. In the end, this means downgrading their proactive stakeholdership in conflict prevention strategies, rather than drawing on capabilities each and every human being owns of its own by virtue of being human. The picture still worsens, given the fact that proponents of this paradigm are often driven by sheer confidence as to a set of politico-economic means and a manufacturing approach to social progress. Thus, chapter VI related those proponents closely to a piecemeal social engineering approach to development. For piecemeal social engineers the means of social development are at hand. Occasional setbacks don't lead to rethink those means. Under those conditions, one can hardly expect the confines of pro-activism to be broadened. One can hardly expect piecemeal social engineers to consider ethical interventions. Apart from downgrading the practical stakeholdership of individuals in conflict prevention strategies, this implies downgrading their normative stakeholdership. In a nutshell, if there is no proactive approach toward the ethical side of development and conflict prevention, and ethical passivism looms, this has sometimes been the flipside of politico-economic pro-activism. Human rights-based approaches to development could change this picture. They establish individuals as holders of a right to development. As right holders they are 'not supposed to be mere passive recipients but active subjects that are expected whenever possible, through their actions, discourse or legal claim, to invoke and demand their

15 C.M. Ljungman, 'Applying a Rights-Based Approach to Development: Concepts and Principles', Paper presented at the The Winners and Losers from Rights-Based Approaches to Development Conference, University of Manchester, UK, 21-22 February 2005.

16 H. Slim, 'Making Moral Low Ground: Rights as the Struggle for Justice and the Abolition of Development' in *The Fletcher Journal of Development Studies,* Vol. XVII (2002).

rights whether individually or collectively.'[17] Therefore, it is assumed that an individual is the subject of its rights as well as an active participant in their realization. This is particularly true to the extent that human rights-based approaches put emphasize on the process of achieving human rights goals. More than other development approaches, they attach as much importance to that process as to the goals themselves. However, at all times the notion of right holders, who demand their rights actively, must not be mixed up with full-grown ethical pro-activism. Such proactivism hinges on installing individuals as duty bearers. In principal, human rights-based approaches define ethical duty bearers in a sufficiently broad manner so as to include individuals as bearers of duty. Thus, they are considered as primary duty bearers. Nonetheless, mainly such primary bearing of duties comes to the fore in immediate relationships, e.g. parents for children, teachers for students, police for crime suspects, doctors and nurses for patients, employers for employees. To a lesser extent, the idea of primary duty may suite conflict prevention goals. Those goals are broad and often not assignable to individual stakeholders. Different from duty that stems from the process of implementing particular human rights, ethical duty does not define different categories of duty bearers. This could turn out as a major advantage. By definition, ethical duty is tied to each individual in like manner. Here, it is linked to essential personal traits which all human beings own by virtue of the fact that they are human beings. Prime personal traits are their rationality, autonomy and others more. Chapter VI has hence designed a concept of duty as autonomy referring to Immanuel Kant. All in all, individuals will not escape the bearing of ethical duty, nor a proactive role that arises from it, because conflict prevention goals could comprise vague duties.

Sixthly, human rights-based approaches are distinctly broader than the evolving economic paradigm. Given the fact that a whole set of normative principles[18] and rights is normally endorsed, such approaches allow for prioritization. Thus, they allow us to implement particular rights first. As a set, those rights allow for gradual implementation. In contrast, a narrow definition of rights in terms of economic rights, as it permeates the evolving economic paradigm, brought up a weird situation. Thus, it challenged to implement a specific right gradually, rather than to prioritize among various rights and principles. Overall, individuals were captured as moral right holders rather than ethical duty bearers. Similar to an economic debate about distributive justice, the task of equilibrating their moral rights was held to reconcile the *same* moral right of different agents, i.e. their right to economic gains. It was confronted with this job, rather than with balancing any moral right of agent A with another moral right or duty of agent B. Compared to standard procedures in ethics, the quality of a solution became different. Thus, it required *compromises* while ethics is normally not about compromises. In ethics it is impossible to imagine that moral rights could be apportioned. Under no circumstances, moral rights are quantifiable. Moral rights can be enforced or such enforcement can fail. They can also collide with each other, but they cannot be enforced *by degree*. Unfortunately,

---

[17] Ljungman (2004) 4.

[18] These principles are: universalism and inalienability, equality and non-discrimination, indivisibility and interdependence of human rights, participation and inclusion, accountability, and the rule of law.

this is what the evolving economic paradigm forces us to so. The paradoxical thing with ethical compromises is that they can only be applied to be not applied. Given their reliance on a whole set of normative principles and rights, human rights-based approaches to development release from this burden, provided they are indeed defined in a sufficiently broad manner.

Finally, human rights-based approaches to development are not new. In 1993, the World Conference on Human Rights took place in Vienna, leading to adopt the *Vienna Declaration and Programme of Action.*[19] But efforts to assimilate these approaches into the existing practices of international organizations have only been successful more recently. Especially, the United Nations System has sought to interlink its development and human rights mandates since the beginning of the new millennium. Early signposts of a human rights-based approach to development were the *Millennium Declaration* adopted by the UN General Assembly[20] and the 2000 volume of the UNDP *Human Development Report.*[21] Furthermore, in September 2002 the UN Secretary-General published his second report on reform of the Organization.[22] That report recalls paragraphs 25 and 26 of the *Millennium Declaration*, which resolves to strengthen capacity to implement the principles and practices of human rights at the country level. Action 2 of the reform report takes up this goal by requesting that the UN strengthens it own capacity at the country level.

> The United Nations High Commissioner for Human Rights will develop and implement a plan, in cooperation with the United Nations Development Group and the Executive Committee for Humanitarian Affairs, to strengthen human rights-related United Nations actions at the country level.[23]

The interagency plan of action *Strengthening Human Rights-related United Nations Action at Country Level: National Human Rights Promotion and Protection Systems*,[24] developed pursuant to Action 2, places focus on the role of UN country teams and emphasizes the importance of integrating human rights into all stages of UN action at country level, from post-conflict situations and humanitarian emergencies to development programming. Unfortunately, there is one misunderstanding in these efforts that is often overlooked. The focus of the aforementioned initiatives is on the development of national human rights protection systems, rather than development through a human rights lens. These efforts designate human rights as one compartment of development in a set of many. The goal is to assist in the establishment of institutions that protect human rights. A related objective is to achieve pro-

---

19 UN General Assembly, 'Vienna Declaration and Programme of Action' (A/CONF.157/23) 12 July 1993.

20 UN General Assembly, 'United Nations Millennium Declaration' (A/RES/55/2) 18 September 2000.

21 UNDP (2000).

22 UN Secretary-General, 'Strengthening of the United Nations: An Agenda for Further Change' (A/57/387) 9 September 2002.

23 Ibid. Sec. 2B.

24 UN, 'Strengthening Human Rights-related United Nations Action at Country level: National Human Rights Promotion and Protection Systems', accessed at http://www.un.org/events/action2/action2plan.pdf.

gress with codifying ratified UN human rights treaties[25] in national legislation. To a lesser extent, these efforts apply human rights to lift development work of the United Nations to a new level of normative strength. Therefore, the point of departure for evaluating human rights-based approaches to development remain those approaches lined out previous to centering current UN practices.

Section 18. Critique of Human Rights-Based Approaches

Referencing and Cultural Relativity

The application of a human rights-based approach to development and conflict accelerates a common trend today. As for this trend, juridical and moral practices increasingly govern all various aspects of social interactions outside the private room. While establishing the rule of law, this trend has a second dimension. Beyond setting particular rules and norms, those juridical and moral practices are characterized by the fact that in people's daily acting they are typically uncontroversial. For the most part, we don't ask 'why it is wrong to do X in spite of Y'. Even if one does, a standard reply will be that 'law says so'. Alternatively, one would appeal to a person's moral common sense. In both cases, one invokes a set of existing juridical and moral practices, which people normally abide by, although sometimes deviate from. A basic expectation is that when deviating from those practices, people retain an idea of their departure. In other words, they preserve an image of their wrongdoing.

From these remarks, one can draw a parallel to human rights-based approaches to development. Those approaches serve to add legal and moral dimensions to commitments that also occur under a needs-based approach. Not only that, they also project that associated legal and moral obligations are incontestable and prima facie acceptable to everyone. Thus, they transfer certain juridical and moral practices to the international sphere and the life of social groups and states. Previously, the question why state A must not harm state B would prompt the answer that this was against international law and particular soft law, i.e. the modern law of nations and the *International Bill of Human Rights*. Human rights-based approaches to development allow for expanding this legal basis. They envision that state C should cooperate in the development processes of states A and B, so as to fulfill the social and economic rights of their peoples. According to the precepts of long-term conflict prevention, the human rights basis of such development cooperation will also extend to conflict prevention goals, because indirectly development efforts will contribute to prevent

[25] These consist of the Universal Declaration of Human Rights (UDHR); the International Covenant on Economic, Social and Cultural Rights (ICESCR); the International Covenant on Civil and Political Rights (ICCPR) and its two Optional Protocols; the International Convention on the Elimination of All Forms of Racial Discrimination (ICERD); the Convention on the Elimination of All Forms of Discrimination against Women (CEDAW) and its Optional Protocol; the Convention on the Rights of the Child (CRC) and its two Optional Protocols; the Convention against Torture and Other Cruel, Inhuman or Degrading Treatment or Punishment (CAT) and its Optional Protocol; and the International Convention on the Protection of the Rights of All Migrant Workers and Members of Their Families (ICMW), the texts of which can be found at: http://www.ohchr.org/english/law/index.htm.

conflict. In most cases, some sort of vague moral stance will complement these legal stances. Human rights-based approaches also facilitate cases where an answer has been more difficult before, i.e. cases that refer to social groups within states. The principles of national sovereignty and non-interference in internal affairs have sought to manage those cases. A frequent implication was that the international community was left outside. Human rights-based approaches set up soft law that allows for a practical response also in such cases. For example, the United Nations' recently developed concept of humanitarian interventions allows for staying proactive where the principle of national sovereignty previously prevented external involvement. It now applies both in cases of internal conflict and all sorts of humanitarian disasters.

What really counts is that in most cases where domestic and international behavior require reasoning, this can be done with reference to some existing juridical and moral practices. The overall mode of justification we have become used to is a *mode of referencing*. Human rights-based approaches to development and long-term conflict prevention increase this trend. They do by ways of those characteristics identified above, i.e. through particular normative principles and defined categories of duty bearers, such as among others international organizations. At the same time of fixing the legal and moral, also the illegal and immoral have been defined. One should think indeed that this is a comfortable situation.

However, a quite illustrative exercise considers the following theoretical case. Consider that our average legal and moral agent in international affairs meets a person who, for some reasons, is unfamiliar with those universally deemed legal and moral practices. In fact, not someone who is against those practices, but rather unaware of their existence. Probably, our agent will find it hard to satisfy his partner by sticking to the old mode of referencing. The least he would need to do is to enter into some explanations. Such explanations could include that the *Universal Declaration of Human Rights* was adopted by the United Nations by means of General Assembly resolution 217 A (III) on 10 December 1948, to the end that every individual and every organ of society shall strive to promote respect for its rights, that it has been translated into 331 languages so far, etc. But also imagine the case that as a reaction to these explanations our 'outlaw' shows discontent. After all, he does not seem to agree with what he has heard. Far from feeling uncomfortable, our average legal and moral agent will probably lean back and understand that he made the acquaintance of someone who is apparently attracted by the illegal and immoral. But how would that agent react if he learned that his opponent was all but reaching out for the illegal and immoral? Rather, he also claimed to own a moral and quasi-legal stance. All of a sudden, our agent was in a situation where neither *referencing* nor *explanations* were sufficient. Actually, he was challenged to *justify* all those universally deemed legal and moral practices, both in order to maintain his moral monopoly and to dismiss notions of cultural relativity from the body of international human rights law.

These points can also be made concrete. After all, they are not as theoretical as they seem in the first place. No matter which conflict we take, recent internal conflicts, threats nuclear middle powers pose, or the growing number of terrorist activities around the world, a standard feature of conflict is that perpetrators are committing to what they consider the *right* thing. This is almost identical with saying that conflict has rarely been launched in fellowship of the immoral and illegal. Conflicting parties normally follow up on goals for which they find justification in front of themselves, although rarely in front of others. But it remains a fact that they apply some kind of moral lens. In the terminology of chapter V, they apply quasi-ethical statements and primary value judgments.

One may still say that quasi-ethical statements and justifications that appeal to violent groups rarely stand a neutral examination of legal and ethical norms. To the same extent, they may not imply a challenge to international juridical and moral practices, i.e. to universal human rights. This seems to be a strong argument indeed. But also imagine that some of those violent groups stepped back to engage in a debate of ethical norms, comparable to the aforementioned 'outlaw'. Consider, there was something like an ethical negotiation table where the usual perpetrators threw in their arguments. For example, what if the perpetrator of ethnic cleansing activities argued: 'Depriving people from other ethnic groups is in our own economic interest, because it will gain us more resources and enhance the wealth of our people. Grievance justifies my people, greed justifies me. I am a utilitarian and supporter of John Stuart Mill.' What if the perpetrator of terrorist attacks put forth: 'Attacking those civilians happens in the name of divinity. I am obeying orders that I am not to question. I am a voluntarian and admirer of Thomas Hobbes.' The average legal and moral agent, not used to justify his or her own ethical norms and human rights, might well raise his hand to demand compassion from the others, also feeling that this will earn him respect from all sides. But this is where the perpetrator of randomly committed middle power nuclear threats joins in declaring: 'Putting those threats is just and fair, because I ought to live up to the expectations of my people, so be compassionate with me. I am a follower of psychological ethics and aficionado of David Hume.'

When dealing with conflicts like the ones just mentioned, the international community normally focuses on obvious political paroles pro conflict, rather than quasi-ethical statements and primary value judgments. Racial inferiority, incredulity and the right political ideology, provide common patterns of argumentation associated with those conflicts. Indeed, perpetrators of conflict rarely voice primary value judgments openly. Often, they might not even be aware of them. However, more crucial than assessing whether conflict parties apply quasi-ethical statements would be to determine which ethical norms they *could* exploit for their purposes, or reject alternatively on the strength of missing proactive argumentation. For that purpose, our average legal and moral agent will first have to develop a clear picture of his own ethical norms. He will have to provide human rights in the development and political fields, previously deemed to be universal, with a sound ethical basis. He will need to engage in a process of ethical justification, so as to increase their normative strength. This only will avoid argumentational bottlenecks when confronted with ethical 'outlaws'.

The size of this task may well appear overburdening. Simply, because interventions in conflict are designed upon ethical assumptions, which are just as diverse as those quasi-ethical norms mentioned above. For example, humanitarian interventions, normally under the mandate of the United Nations, are often associated with a human rights-based approach, but also with a vague understanding of the ethical basis of human rights principles. If only for one time leaving behind the common mode of referencing, our average legal and moral agent could claim: 'Conflict A is against international law and the *International Bill of Human Rights*. It requires the international community to intervene, because it conflicts with the commands of human dignity. This follows from the categorical imperative and in advocacy of Immanuel Kant.'

In other cases, most applicable to this book, we are not considering a peacekeeping mandate. Rather, another type of humanitarian intervention is being centered. These interventions employ development cooperation. Thus, either development cooperation turns into the guise of a post-conflict peace-building mission. The aim of this mission will be to economically rebuild a country that has suffered from internal or international conflict. The long-term plan is to prevent conflict from recurring. In other cases, development cooperation aims at preventing conflict in the first place. We are then embarking on a long-term conflict prevention mission. In both cases, international development organizations are mobilized. When asked to specify our goals from an ethical perspective, we reply: 'Increasing the welfare level of that country or group is due in view of the commands of human dignity. By implementing people's socio-economic rights we also eradicate the core basis of conflict.' Chapter VI has brought as so far already as to note that another ethical norm and justification could imply sever ethical paradoxes in this case. Provided the utility principle replaced reference to the dignity of human beings, our argument threatens to resembled the perpetrator of ethnic cleansing activities. In the end, this only shows how deep a discussion of ethical norms would need to go in order to found a human rights-based approach to development.

The previous remarks illustrate that ethical norms are extremely diverse. Acceptance of some guiding moral practices normally blinds our view for this actual diversity. Even when recognizing a wide range of ethical norms, we still find each of them exploitable for different goals, some of which we may agree with, some of which we reject. Considering the above examples, few people will have a problem with utilitarian, voluntarian and psychological ethical norms, as long as they are employed to found human rights-based approaches to development, long-term conflict prevention strategies and post-conflict peace-building missions. However, in the processes of justifying conflict they will always evoke our moral protest. The good news is that *something* is wrong with those quasi-ethical arguments we just put in the mouth of perpetrators of conflict. The arguments could be true reflections of those perpetrator's inner thoughts and processes of self-justification. As was said before, conflict groups normally find good arguments that supposedly justify their acting. At the same time, these arguments lack real ethical strength. The core question is how to prove that, and how to bring that proof against perpetrators of conflict. In considering the importance of making this case a strong case, one goes beyond a merely intellectual exercise. We should understand that in today's world perpetrators of conflict commit their crimes in the crude believe that they are doing the right thing. The international community has not managed to defy this believe so far. Therefore, how can we challenge these believes in such way as to effect practical change, thus also preventing conflict in the first place? For sure, effective conflict prevention needs to go beyond the ethical foundations of human rights-based approaches to development. In terms of ethics, it also requires to found political human rights that are directly being violated in conflict. But to the extent that they evolve on a sound ethical basis, human rights-based approaches to development support long-term conflict prevention strategies. Thus, they also contribute to dismiss quasi-ethical arguments potentially associated with a particular category of conflict this book has analyzed as increasingly important today, thus being economic conflict.

In pre-modern times, political thinkers and policy makers were given no chance to be lazy about normative questions, or to rely on existing moral practices and human rights in the international field. Three hundred years ago, we operate against the background of an international law that, in fact, *justified* conflict. Comprising the classical law of nations, this law differed essentially from the modern law of nations. Under circumstances where war and conflict could not be banned legally, the only hope of overcoming it was to find the right *normative* arguments for peace.[26] Indeed, early modern times in Europe are much characterized along this line, but it was also a very productive time in terms of ethical interventionism. Directly, this point relates to the central doctrine of 'just war'.

Europe in the mid-17th century: The world was still following the old path of alliances and wars, when Francisco de Vitoria, a Dominican and professor of theology in Spanish Salamanca, went to revise the idea of a universal law. In the course of these revisions, a new quality of 'just wars' emerged, distinctly different from the ancient and medieval order of things. Particularly, the ancient account of *ius gentium* under Emperor Justin became challenged. In the old days, a law's universal character related to its status concerning the expression of natural rights of individuals. Its common, all-respected character was linked to that ground. In contrast, de Vitoria's version of a universal law was designed as a *ius inter gentes* or inter-national law, rather than as a *ius gentium*. A main implication was that peoples rather than individuals were targeted as beneficiaries of particular rights and laws. The consequences of this approach were especially marked in relation to the pertinent question of war and peace.[27] Beyond disposing of the ancient account of universal rights of individuals, de Vitoria's approach also implied a harsh break with medieval preoccupation concerning the requirements of a universal law: Firstly, the classical law of nations came to regulate the behavior of nation states. Secondly, while doing so it granted those states a status of full sovereignty and autonomy. Thus, it implied the principle of non-interference in internal affairs. Thirdly, as a consequence Europe's evolving nation states were rendered independent from the commanding influence of any superior authority. Throughout the middle age this authority had been provided by the conflicting aspirations of emperor and pope.

Coming back to the doctrine of 'just war', the classical law of nations integrated clear provisions concerning those categories of war that could claim to be legal. A twofold distinction was applied. Comparable to the modern law of nations, 'just war' could take the form of a lawful means in the hands of one state to sanction other nations that had harmed the former. Distinctly different from the modern law

26 F. Dickmann, *Friedensrecht und Friedenssicherung: Studien zum Friedensproblem in der Geschichte*, Göttingen: Vandenhoeck u. Ruprecht (1971) 131.

27 See J. v. Elbe, 'The Evolution of the Concept of the Just War in International Law' , in *American Journal of International Law*, Vol. 33, No. 4 (1939) 665-688; G. Schwarzenberger, 'Ius Pacis Ac Belli: Prolegomena to a Sociology of International Law', in *American Journal of International Law*, Vol. 37, No. 3 (1943) 460-479.

of nations, such defensive action only comprised a special case of 'just war'. From the sovereignty of nation states emanated the legal basis for aggressive warfare. At the same time, these kind of wars demanded non-interference on the part of the international community.[28]

The modern law of nations bans aggressive warfare, preemptive or not. However, since that law came into being it only managed to prevent those wars where aggressive states or groups were scared away from their plans by the responses of the international community. By no means, these states or groups found some ethical motives against conflict. Objectively, they were only prevented from doing 'the right thing' due to some practical reasons. Superficially, the modern law of nations, as well as international law and human rights law designed since then, have still brought the international community in a comfortable situation. But the flipside of all these comforts is that we have only become lazier about ethical questions, because written paragraphs replace normative argumentation. In pre-modern times, a reality of 'just wars' called on the scene all various ethical voices who opposed the existing legal concessions to aggressive nation states, also building the catalyst for an abundant number of peace tractates. Although the classical law of nations only constitutes a piece of history today, the various ethical norms contained in the works of writers such as Jean-Jacque Rousseau, David Hume, Immanuel Kant and others are still relevant today.

At the end of the day, we realize that existing legal and moral practices, however natural they may seem to us, need an ethical foundation. When seeking this foundation, we are neither just referencing to some ratified human rights treaties, nor do we merely give an explanation for particular legal and moral practices. We are asking what *justifies* the claims that these practices exert on us. As for the development and long-term conflict prevention agendas, there is a need to go beyond human rights-based approaches. The previous section identified essential characteristics of these approaches that further add to the common mode of referencing. Overall, human rights-based approaches to development tend to set legal obligations where previous approaches relied on stressing people's needs. They supply the principle of equality and non-discrimination, where previous approaches were forced to show that horizontal inequalities are indeed relevant. Thus, they put development interventions of international organizations on a strong normative and almost legal-like basis, by defining these organizations as external duty bearers. Last but not least, they invoke a proactive approach to individuals by highlighting process goals.

At the same time, human rights-based approaches don't clarify the ethical implications of development interventions in conflict. While this point also applies to the

---

28 According to the principle of sovereignty each state had the right to declare war provided an adequate cause justified forcible actions with their accompanying horrors and devastations. This did not exclude the possibility that both sides believed in the rightness of their causes. But can a war be just on both sides? Probably not. Still today, there is the problem of distinguishing between objective justice and subjective innocence. Some scholars have urged the dual nature of warfare. According to them 'it is essential to divide wars into their component parts therefore, giving separate consideration to the war of A against B and to the war of B against A, the two half-wars that constitute together A-B War.' I. Claude Jr., 'Just Wars: Doctrines and Institutions', in *Political Science Quarterly*, Vol. 95, No. 1 (1980) 84.

human rights-basis of political and military interventions, it does so increasingly to long-term conflict prevention strategies, given the attention those strategies have attracted recently. More generally, human rights-based approaches hardly inspire an explicit discourse about the ethical basis of development cooperation and conflict prevention. The expectation was precisely that, when centering human rights-based approaches pursuant to an ethical critique of the evolving economic paradigm. In the face of several ethical paradoxes hosted by that paradigm, these approaches seemed to promise two things concretely: Firstly, they would allow for centering ethical implications of long-term conflict prevention strategies. Secondly, upon surfacing those implications, they would also manage to dissolve their ethical paradoxes.

The above analysis identified evidence to the contrary. The prime aim of human rights-based approaches is to provide development cooperation and long-term conflict prevention strategies with a quasi-legal basis that leapfrogs intricate ethical questions automatically. Human rights in the socio-economic field are asserted to be universal. But their being universal is often mistaken to suspend ethical justifications in the first place. Thus, they are just as convenient or economical as the evolving economic paradigm. As they stand, they only offer vaguely an ethical tool to development practitioners, i.e. to international organizations and proponents of that paradigm. Ultimately, they comprise a weak remedy for those ethical problems that emanate from chapter VI's analysis. Beyond that, they hardly reveal the ethical deficiencies of primary value judgments, i.e. of those quasi-ethical statements conflict parties apply implicitly or explicitly. Hence, they also provide a weak cure for those value-related problems that emanate from chapter V's analysis. As long as the ethical implications of development cooperation are ignored, development practitioners are only running the risk of being inconsistent. Such inconsistency existed between the human rights-basis of development cooperation and the ethical implications of such cooperation. At the same time, one could be tempted to assume that ethical arguments are just as far off the motives of perpetrators of conflict, as they are off development discourses. However, once we ignore that the acting of perpetrators evolves on the basis of some quasi-ethical statements, we also ignore the need to go beyond ethical consistency in development cooperation. Apart from the material basis of conflict, i.e. horizontal inequalities, there is an implicit or explicit intellectual component, which is irreducible. This component focuses on the need to address people's mindsets.

Both tasks, i.e. ethical consistency in development interventions and confronting primary stakeholders on an intellectual level, ask for an independent ethics of conflict prevention. Such an ethics may finally see the following paradigm change fulfilled:

> Our century will appear as a time when, after three hundred and fifty years, we finally saw through Descartes. It is in our time that the collection of puzzles and problems that have collected around the Cartesian dualism of body and mind has been supplanted by those as-

sociated with what now appears to be the more fundamental Humean-Kantian dualism of *fact and norm*, which appeared only darkly and misleading in its Cartesian guise.[29]

Towards an Ethics of Conflict Prevention

A logically ensuing step of addressing the ethical economy of conflict prevention and development, gives proactive consideration to an ethics of conflict prevention. On the basis of such an ethics, ethical interventions may join on par economic interventions for conflict prevention. On the strength of such an ethics, human rights-based approaches of international organizations may assume increased normative strength, thus also justifying the existing mode of referencing. Certainly, such an ethics could fill the pages of yet another book. Ethical models suited to feed into a full-grown ethics of conflict prevention are manifold. Some of them were mentioned above. Equally diverse are the specific requirements of such an ethics. For the purpose of this book, we may only indicate those principal requirements that emanate from the previous critique. Thus, three basic requirements should be distinguished.

Firstly, from the deficiencies of ethical realism we learn that a moral fact-centered approach, fine-tuned at imitating sciences, only serves to develop an ontological interest in situations requiring ethical interventions. Different from that, an effective ethics of conflict prevention must provide *normative guidance*. It must assign ethical value to particular human actions, while other actions are dismissed and sanctioned accordingly. For some earliest ethical realists like Plato and Aristotle, moral facts were even more real than experienced fact. In a way, the real world was considered moral fact in itself. From such an extreme ontological view, it was only a small step to a world of things that is actually better than it seems. The ideal world, or world of ideas, became the real world. When subscribing to ethical realism, we are looking at a cosmos of self-sufficient moral facts, isolated from the practical human world. An ethics of conflict prevention needs to rescue the normative basis of ethics. It needs to make sure that values are not there for their own sake, and that they do not precede human contemplation about ethics. Values are there to provide guidance to imperfect human actions, and to possess normative character in this very particular sense.[30] Their whole legitimacy stems from this normative strength.

---

29 R. Brandom, Lecture in Contribution to the Discussion Group on 'Problems from Sellars' of the University of Chicago Philosophy Project, accessed at http://www.ditext.com/brandom/brandom.html.

30 Plato and Aristotle went astray of this point. For example, in posing his famous *what-is*-questions, particularly when approaching the nature of the morally good, Plato's Socrates applied an epistemological lens. The main goal was intellectual, rather than for the achievement of practical ethical advice. Contained in the exercise of identifying the good were a number of precise instructions. According to these instructions, the identification of the good had to take place in a dialectic manner, where proponent and opponent engaged in an open dialogue, almost naturally reaching joint insight in the end. This approach Plato called *maieutic*. Some scholars have been more reluctant to assign an ontological conception of values to Plato's philosophy. See, for example, R. Demos, 'Plato's Idea of the Good', in *The Philosophical Review*, Vol. 46, No. 3 (1937) 245-275. An even more radical understanding of the 'real' nature of values has frequently inspired such a view. See R. Demos, 'Moral Value as Irreducible, Objective, and Cognizable', in *Philosophy and Phenomenological Research*, Vol. 6, No. 2 (1945) 163-194.

Secondly, from the deficiencies of ethical welfarism we understand that, apart from defining ethical duty bearers, an ethics of conflict prevention contains *obligations*. This point concerns the way ethical norms normally exert their claims upon us, and the ways we try to live up to their standards. Almost by definition, those claims include a challenge, i.e. obligations that may be counter to more basic endeavors, such as economic utility maximization. Otherwise, we would not speak of ethical norms. However, the notion of having to overcome more basic endeavors, by putting in place self-legislation and acts of self-constraint, also implies an option to fail. This option requires recognition. For ethical welfarism, being guided by utility maximizing behavior means to be good at being what people are. Becoming a moral person is tied to a concept of human excellence. However, becoming excellent is considered to be as natural as growing up, is like learning a language. Obligation differs from excellence in an important way. When we seek excellence, the force that ethical norms exert upon us is attractive. When we are obligated, it is compulsive. For obligation is the imposition of value on a reluctant, recalcitrant, resistant matter.[31] Therefore, by recognizing obligations we acknowledge the self-convincing struggle that engages people on the way to achieving a moral person. We also acknowledge an option to fail. An ethics of conflict prevention ought to be designed in awareness of the possibility and impact of 'bad' willing. An ethics of conflict prevention confronts such willing by imposing ethical duty, and in cases of deviation by ways of moral sanctions.

Finally, from the deficiencies of ethical modernism we learn that an ethics of conflict prevention needs to accept the *human-made* character of conflict. Not only that, they also allude to the human nature and limitations of interventions for the prevention of conflict. A general precondition when debating conflict prevention from a normative angle is that we reject both conflict and conflict prevention as something inevitable, as kind of physical laws. Conflict and conflict prevention are the results of actions of individuals and groups. Those actions are by definition controversial, although not always reversible. Automatically, such a stance implies a number of challenges on the primary stakeholders in conflict as well as third parties, i.e. international organizations. The size of those challenges has been particularly unclear to historicists, but also, with limitations, to traditional piecemeal social engineers. When joining the historicist angle, we are inclined to say that 'history rules'. We are also tempted to leave the final judgment about conflict and conflict prevention to history. When joining the piecemeal social engineer's understanding of conflict prevention, his enthusiastically proclaimed 'economy rules' and a catalogue of economic remedies set the scene. The economic paradigm evolving from these rules elaborates a convenient or *economical* dealing with conflict and conflict prevention. Thus, it tends to prescribe a narrow set of technical imperatives and interventions. As opposed to this, the key message for an ethics of conflict prevention is that it must join but cannot wish to supersede other types of interventions, such as development cooperation and long-term conflict prevention strategies. Otherwise, it was prone to comprise just another economical paradigm.

---

[31] C.M. Korsgaard, *The Sources of Normativity* (with G.A. Cohen, R. Geuss, T. Nagel, B. Williams) Cambridge and New York: Cambridge University Press (1996) 4.

Before an ethics of conflict prevention materializes, ethics must be enabled to join conflict prevention debates. The prime goal of this book has been precisely that. As such, it has been designed as a critique of the ethical economy of conflict prevention and development. Ethics join conflict prevention debates by virtue of the potential ethical paradoxes economic strategies host, as well as the present normative restrictions of human rights-based approaches to development.

BIBLIOGRAPHY

Abbott T.K., *Kant's Critique of Practical Reason and other Works on the Theory of Ethics*, London: Longmans and Green (1879).

Adler P.S., 'Marx, Machines, and Skill', in *Technology and Culture*, Vol. 31, No. 4 (1990) 780-812.

Aiken H.D., 'Definitions of Value and the Moral Ideal', in *The Journal of Philosophy*, Vol. 42, No. 13 (1945) 337-352.

Akerlof G. and Kranton R., 'Economics and Identity', in *The Quarterly Journal of Economics*, Vol. 115, No. 3 (2000) 715-753.

Albert H., 'Das Werturteilsproblem im Lichte der Logischen Analyse', in *Zeitschrift für die gesamte Staatswissenschaft*, No. 112 (1956) 410-439.

Alexander S.S., 'Mr. Keynes and Mr. Marx', in *The Review of Economic Studies*, Vol. 7, No. 2 (1940) 123-135.

Anderson E., *Value in Ethics and Economics*, Cambridge MA: Harvard University Press (1993).

———, 'Reasons, Attitudes, and Values: Replies to Sturgeon and Piper', in *Ethics*, Vol. 106, No. 3 (1996) 538-554.

Angell N., *The Great Illusion: A Study of the Relation of Military Power in Nations to their Economic and Social Advantage*, New York and London: G.P. Putnam's Sons (1912).

Annan K., Address to the Seventeenth National Convention of the Arab-American Anti-Discrimination Committee, Arlington, Virginia, USA, 12 June 2000.

———, Address to the Fourth International Conference of New and Restored Democracies, Contonou, Benin, 7 Dec. 2000.

———, Address to the Foreign Policy Association, New York, USA, 21 March 2001.

———, Cyril Foster Lecture at Oxford University, UK, 19 June 2001.

———, Address at University of Oslo, Norway, 20 August 2001.

Appelbaum R.P., 'Marx's Theory of the Falling Rate of Profit: Towards a Dialectical Analysis of Structural Social Change', in *American Sociological Review*, Vol. 43, No. 1 (1978) 67-80.

Arendt H., *Rahel Varnhagen: The Life of a Jewess*, London: Published for the Leo Baeck Institute by the East and West Library (1957).

Aristotle, *Metaphysics* [ca. 350 BC], Cambridge MA: Harvard University Press (1969-73).

———, *Physics* [ca. 350 BC], Oxford and New York: Oxford University Press (1996).

———, *Nicomachean Ethics* [ca. 350 BC], London: Penguin Books (2003).

Austen S. and Jefferson T., 'Comparing Responses to Critical Realism', Paper presented at the Seventeenth Conference of the History of Economic Thought Society of Australia, Perth, Australia, 6-9 July 2004.

Austin W. and Worchel S. (eds.), *The Social Psychology of Intergroup Relations*, Monterey: Brooks and Cole (1979).

Ayres C.E., 'Moral Confusion in Economics', in *International Journal of Ethics*, Vol. 45, No. 2 (1935) 170-199.

Azar E., 'Protracted International Conflicts: Ten Propositions', in Azar and Burton (1986) 27-39.

———, *The Management of Protracted Social Conflict: Theory and Cases*, Aldershot: Dartmouth (1990).

——, 'The Analysis and Management of Protracted Social Conflict', in Volkan et al. (1991).

Azar E. and Burton J. (eds.), *International Conflict Resolution: Theory and Practice*, Sussex: Wheatsheaf (1986).

Baker J.M., 'Utilitarianism and Secondary Principles', in *The Philosophical Quarterly*, Vol. 21, No. 82 (1971) 69-71.

Bamgbose A., 'Language as a Resource: An African Perspective', Paper presented at the Workshop on the Role of the African Languages in Democratic South Africa, University of Pretoria, South Africa, 5-6 March 1998.

Banks M., *Ethnicity: Anthropological Constructions*, London: Routledge (1996).

Bauer P., *Equality: The Third World and Economic Delusion*, London: Weidenfeld and Nicolson (1981).

Bauman Z., 'Modernity and Ambivalence', in *Theory, Culture and Society*, Vol. 7, No. 2-3 (1990) 143-169.

Baumol W.J., 'Marx and the Iron Law of Wages', in *The American Economic Review*, Vol. 73, No. 2, (1983) 303-308.

Bauwens W. and Reychler L. (eds.), *The Art of Conflict Prevention*, London and New York: Brassey's (1994).

Becker A.P., 'Some Philosophical Aspects of Economics', in *Philosophy of Science*, Vol. 15, No. 3 (1948) 242-246.

Bell S., 'Ricardo and Marx', in *The Journal of Political Economy*, Vol. 15, No. 2 (1907) 112-117.

Bentham J., *An Introduction to the Principles of Morals and Legislation*, London: Printed for T. Payne (1789).

Bimber B., 'Karl Marx and the Three Faces of Technological Determinism', in *Social Studies of Science*, Vol. 20, No. 2 (1990) 333-351.

Bladen V.W., 'The Centenary of Marx and Mill', in *The Journal of Economic History*, Vol. 8, Supplement: The Tasks of Economic History (1948) 32-41.

Boulding K.E., 'Some Contributions of Economics to the General Theory of Value', in *Philosophy of Science*, Vol. 23, No. 1 (1956) 1-14.

Bourantonis D. and Evriviades M. (eds.), *A United Nations for the Twenty-First Century: Peace, Security and Economic Development*, The Hague and Boston: Kluwer Law International (1996).

Branden N., *Honoring the Self: Personal Integrity and the Heroic Potentials of Human Nature*, Los Angeles: J.P. Tarcher (1983).

Brandis R., 'Marx and Keynes? Marx or Keynes', in *Journal of Economic Issues*, Vol. 19, No. 3 (1985) 643-659.

——, 'Marx and Keynes? Marx or Keynes: A Reply', in *Journal of Economic Issues*, Vol. 21, No. 1 (1987) 470-473.

Brandom R., Lecture in Contribution to the Discussion Group on 'Problems from Sellars' of the University of Chicago Philosophy Project, accessed at http://www.ditext.com/brandom/brandom.html.

Brandt R.B., *Ethical Theory: The Problems of Normative and Critical Ethics*, Englewood Cliffs: Prentice-Hall (1959).

Brandt W., *North-South: A Programme for Survival: The Report of the Independent Commission on International Development Issues*, London: Pan Books (1980).

Bredel R., 'The UN's Long-Term Conflict Prevention Strategies and the Impact of Counter-Terrorism', in *International Peacekeeping*, Vol. 10, No. 2 (2003) 51-70.

——, *Long-Term Conflict Prevention and Industrial Development: The United Nations and its Specialized Agency, UNIDO*, Leiden and Boston: Martinus Nijhoff Publishers (2003).

Breman J., *Footloose Labour: Working in India's Informal Economy*, Cambridge: Cambridge University Press (1996).
Brink D.O., 'Mill's Deliberative Utilitarianism', in *Philosophy and Public Affairs*, Vol. 21, No. 1 (1992) 67-103.
Brower B.W., 'Virtue Concepts and Ethical Realism', in *The Journal of Philosophy*, Vol. 85, No. 12 (1988) 675-693.
———, 'Dispositional Ethical Realism', in *Ethics*, Vol. 103, No. 2 (1993) 221-249.
Burkett P., 'Dillard on Keynes and Marx: Comment', in *Journal of Post Keynesian Economics*, Vol. 8, No. 4 (1986) 623-631.
Burton J., *Violence Explained: The Sources of Conflict, Violence and Crime and their Prevention*, Manchester: Manchester University Press (1997).
Campbell D., 'Ethnocentrism and Other Altruistic Motives', in Levine (1965) 283-311.
Campbell T.D. and Ross I.S., 'The Utilitarianism of Adam Smith's Policy Advice', in *Journal of the History of Ideas*, Vol. 42, No. 1 (1981) 73-92.
Carabelli A. and Vecchi N., 'Where to Draw the Line? Hayek and Keynes, on Knowledge, Ethics, and Economics' in *European Journal for the History of Economic Thought*, Vol. 6, No. 2 (1999).
Carr E.H., *The Twenty Years' Crisis 1919-1939*, London: Macmillan (1939).
Chandler J., 'Act-Utilitarianism and Collective Action', in *Ethics*, Vol. 84, No. 1 (1973) 78-85.
Chandra K., 'Elite Incorporation in Multi-Ethnic Societies', Paper presented at the India and the Politics of Developing Countries Conference, Kellogg Institute for International Studies, University of Notre Dame, USA, 24-26 September 1999.
Chew S. and Denemark R. (eds.), *The Underdevelopment of Development: Essays in Honour of Andre Gunder Frank*, Thousand Oaks: Sage Publications (1996).
Chick V., *Macroeconomics after Keynes: A Reconsideration of the General Theory*, Oxford: Philip Allan (1983).
Christiansen J., 'Marx and the Falling Rate of Profit', in *The American Economic Review*, Vol. 66, No. 2 (1976) 20-26.
Christman J., 'Self-Ownership, Equality, and the Structure of Property Rights' in *Political Theory*, Vol. 19, No. 1 (1991) 28-46.
Claude Jr. I., 'Just Wars: Doctrines and Institutions', in *Political Science Quarterly*, Vol. 95, No. 1 (1980) 83-96.
Cobden R., *The Political and Economic Works of Richard Cobden* [1846], 6 Volumes, London: Routledge (1995).
Cohen A., *Two-Dimensional Man: An Essay on the Anthropology of Power and Symbolism in Complex Society*, Berkeley: University of California Press (1974).
Cohen G.A., *Marx's Theory of History: A Defense*, Princeton: Princeton University Press (1978).
Collier P., 'Economic Causes of Civil Conflict and their Implication for Policy', Washington DC: World Bank (2000).
Collingwood R.G., 'Economics as a Philosophical Science', in *International Journal of Ethics*, Vol. 36, No. 2 (1926) 162-185.
Conly G.A., 'Alienation, Sociality, and the Division of Labor: Contradictions in Marx's Ideal of Social Man', in *Ethics*, Vol. 89, No. 1 (1978) 82-94.
Crisp R., 'Utilitarianism and the Life of Virtue', in *The Philosophical Quarterly*, Vol. 42, No. 167 (1992) 139-160.
Crocker L., *Positive Liberty: An Essay in Normative Political Philosophy*, The Hague and Boston: Martinus Nijhoff Publishers (1980).
Cropsey J., 'What is Welfare Economics?', in *Ethics*, Vol. 65, No. 2 (1955) 116-125.
Demos R., 'Plato's Idea of the Good', in *The Philosophical Review*, Vol. 46, No. 3 (1937) 245-275.

———,'Moral Value as Irreducible, Objective, and Cognizable', in *Philosophy and Phenomenological Research*, Vol. 6, No. 2 (1945) 163-194.

Deng F.M., 'Identity in Africa's Internal Conflicts', in *The American Behavioral Science*, Vol. 40, No. 1 (1996) 46-65.

Deutsch K. et al., *Political Community and the North Atlantic Area: International Organization in the Light of Historical Experience*, Princeton: Princeton University Press (1957).

Dickinson H.D., 'The Falling Rate of Profit in Marxian Economics', in *The Review of Economic Studies*, Vol. 24, No. 2 (1957) 120-130.

Dickmann F., *Friedensrecht und Friedenssicherung: Studien zum Friedensproblem in der Geschichte*, Göttingen: Vandenhoeck u. Ruprecht (1971).

Dillard D., 'Keynes and Marx: A Centennial Appraisal', in *Journal of Post Keynesian Economics*, Vol. 6, No. 3 (1984) 421-432.

———, 'Dillard on Keynes and Marx: Rejoinder', in *Journal of Post Keynesian Economics*, Vol. 8, No. 4 (1986) 632-636.

Douglas W., 'A Critique of Recent Trends in the Analysis of Ethnonationalism', in *Ethnic and Racial Studies*, Vol. 11, No. 2 (1988) 192-206.

Dworkin G., 'Marx and Mill: A Dialogue', in *Philosophy and Phenomenological Research*, Vol. 26, No. 3 (1966) 403-414.

Dworkin R., *Taking Rights Seriously*, Cambridge MA: Harvard University Press (1977).

Elbe J.v., 'The Evolution of the Concept of the Just War in International Law', in *American Journal of International Law*, Vol. 33, No. 4 (1939) 665-688.

Elliott J.E., 'Marx and Schumpeter on Capitalism's Creative Destruction: A Comparative Restatement', in *The Quarterly Journal of Economics*, Vol. 95, No. 1 (1980) 45-68.

———, 'Schumpeter and Marx on Capitalist Transformation', in *The Quarterly Journal of Economics*, Vol. 98, No. 2 (1983) 333-336.

Ellison C., 'Religious Involvement and Self-Perception among Black Americans', in *Social Forces*, Vol. 71, No. 4 (1993) 1027-1055.

Emmons D.C., 'Act vs. Rule Utilitarianism', in *Mind*, Vol. 82, No. 326 (1973) 226-233.

Engels F., *The Peasant War in Germany* [1850] in Marx and Engels (1975-2005) Vol. 10, 397-482.

———, *Anti-Dühring: Herr Eugen Dühring's Revolution in Science* [1878] in Marx and Engels (1975-2005) Vol. 25, 5-312.

———, *Ludwig Feuerbach and the End of Classical German Philosophy* [1886] in Marx and Engels (1975-2005) Vol. 26, 353-398.

Estaban J. and Ray D., 'On the Measurement of Polarisation', in *Econometrica*, Vol. 62, No.4 (1994) 819-851.

Fan-Hung, 'Keynes and Marx on the Theory of Capital Accumulation, Money and Interest', in *The Review of Economic Studies*, Vol. 7, No. 1 (1939) 28-41.

Festinger L., 'A Theory of Social Comparison Processes', in *Human Relations*, Vol. 7, No. 1 (1954) 7-40.

Fichtenbaum R. and Shahidi H., 'Marx and Keynes? Marx or Keynes: A Comment', in *Journal of Economic Issues*, Vol. 21, No. 1 (1987) 467-470.

Foley D.K., 'On Marx's Theory of Money', in *Social Concept*, Vol. 1, No. 1 (1983) 5-19.

Foot P., 'Utilitarianism and the Virtues', in *Mind*, New Series, Vol. 94, No. 374 (1985) 196-209.

Foster J.B., 'Theories of Capitalist Transformation: Critical Notes on the Comparison of Marx and Schumpeter', in *The Quarterly Journal of Economics*, Vol. 98, No. 2 (1983) 327-331.

Freeman S., 'Equilibrium Income Inequality among Identical Agents', in *Journal of Political Economy*, Vol. 104, No. 5 (1996) 1047-1064.

Frey R.G., 'Act-Utilitarianism: Sidgwick or Bentham and Smart?', in *Mind*, New Series, Vol. 86, No. 341 (1977) 95-100.
Friedman M., *Essays in Positive Economics*, Chicago: University of Chicago Press (1953).
———, 'The Methodology of Positive Economics', in Friedman (1953) 3-43.
Friedrich C., 'Nationaler und Internationaler Föderalismus in Theorie und Praxis', in *Politische Vierteljahresschrift*, Vol. 5, No. 2 (1964).
Fries H.S., 'The Method of Proving Ethical Realism', in *The Philosophical Review*, Vol. 46, No. 5 (1937) 485-502.
Friesen L., *Higher Thought and Lower Motives: A Programmer's Guide to the Mind*, accessed at http://209.87.142.42/y/book2/Book_027.htm.
Galtung J., 'Structural Theory of Imperialism', in *Journal of Peace Research*, Vol. 8, No. 2 (1971) 81-117.
Garegnani P., 'Value and Distribution in the Classical Economists and Marx', in *Oxford Economic Papers*, New Series, Vol. 36, No. 2 (1984) 291-325.
Garner R.T., 'Some Remarks on Act Utilitarianism' in *Mind*, New Series, Vol. 78, No. 309 (1969) 124-128.
Garve C., *Abhandlung über die Verbindung der Moral mit der Politik: Oder einige Betrachtungen über die Frage, inwiefern es möglich sei, die Moral des Privatlebens bei der Regierung der Staaten zu beobachten*, in Gesammelte Werke, Zweite Abteilung, Vol. VI, Hildesheim, Zürich and New York: G. Olms (1987).
Geiger G.R., 'The Place of Values in Economics', in *The Journal of Philosophy*, Vol. 27, No. 13 (1930) 350-361.
Gilbert A., 'Social Theory and Revolutionary Activity in Marx', in *The American Political Science Review*, Vol. 73, No. 2 (1979) 521-538.
———, 'Moral Realism, Individuality, and Justice in War', in *Political Theory*, Vol. 14, No. 1 (1986) 105-135.
Gilpin R., *The Political Economy of International Relations*, Princeton: Princeton University Press (1987).
———, 'The Nature of Political Economy', in Goddard et al. (1996).
Goddard C. et al. (eds.), *International Political Economy: State-Market Relations in the Changing Global Order*, Boulder: Lynne Rienner Publishers (1996).
Gottheil F. M., 'Increasing Misery of the Proletariat: An Analysis of Marx's Wage and Employment Theory', in *The Canadian Journal of Economics and Political Science*, Vol. 28, No. 1 (1962) 103-113.
Gurney E., *Tertium Quid: Chapters on Various Disputed Questions*. London: Kegan Paul, Trench (1887).
Gurr T., *Minorities at Risk: A Global View of Ethnopolitical Conflict*, Washington DC: United States Institute for Peace Press (1993).
Haas E., *Beyond the Nation State: Functionalism and International Organization*, Stanford: Stanford University Press (1964).
Hamilton A., *Report on the Subject of Manufacturers* [1791], Philadelphia: Library of Congress (1827).
Hammen O.J., 'Alienation, Communism, and Revolution in the Marx-Engels Briefwechsel', in *Journal of the History of Ideas*, Vol. 33, No. 1 (1972) 77-100.
———, 'A Note on the Alienation Motif in Marx', in *Political Theory*, Vol. 8, No. 2 (1980) 223-242.
Hansen A.H., 'Mr. Keynes on Underemployment Equilibrium', in *The Journal of Political Economy*, Vol. 44, No. 5 (1936) 667-686.
Hardy M., 'Economic Growth, Distributional Inequality, and Conflict in Industrial Societies', in *Journal of Political and Military Sociology*, Vol. 5 (1979) 209-227.
Hare R.M., 'Ethical Theory and Utilitarianism', in Lewis (1976) 113-131.
Harman G., *The Nature of Morality*, New York: Oxford University Press (1977).

Hartman J. and Hsiao W., 'Inequality and Violence: Issues of Theory and Measurement in Muller', in *American Sociological Review*, Vol. 53, No. 5 (1988) 794-799.

Hartwig J., 'Trying to Make Sense of the Principle of Effective Demand', Paper presented at the Seventh Annual Post Keynesian Workshop, Kansas City, Missouri, USA, 22 June - 3 July 2002.

Hayek A.F.v., *Studies in Philosophy, Politics and Economics*, London: Routledge and Kegan Paul (1967).

———, *Law, Legislation and Liberty*, 3 Vol., Chicago: University of Chicago Press (1979).

Hebert J., 'Identifying Cajun Identity: Cajun Assimilation and Revitalization of Cajun Culture', in *Loyola University New Orleans, Student Historical Journal*, Vol. 31 (1999-2000).

Herrnstein R.J. and Murray C., *The Bell Curve*, New York: Free Press (1994).

Heyer J. et al., 'Group Behaviour and Development', in *WIDER Working Paper Series*, No. 161 (1999).

Hollan H., 'Class Antagonism, Exploitation, and the Labour Theory of Value', in *The Economic Journal*, Vol. 92, No. 368 (1982) 868-885.

Hömig H. and Meißner F.-J. (eds.), *Kritik des Absolutismus*, München: R. Oldenbourg (1988).

Holsti O. et al. (eds.), *Changes in the International System*, Boulder: Westview Press (1980).

Hook S., 'A Critique of Ethical Realism', in *International Journal of Ethics*, Vol. 40, No. 2 (1930) 179-210.

Jenne E., 'Political Opportunism and Ethnic Mobilization: A Triadic Model for Predicting the Ethnicization of Politics in New States', accessed at http://www.sscnet.ucla.edu/soc/groups/scr/jenne.pdf.

Jensen H., 'Marx and Keynes: Alternative Views on Capitalism', in *Atlantic Economic Journal*, Vol. 17, No. 4 (1989) 29-38.

Jeske D., 'Persons, Compensation, and Utilitarianism', in *The Philosophical Review*, Vol. 102, No. 4 (1993) 541-575.

Jespersen J., 'Macroeconomic Methodology: A Post Keynesian Perspective', Paper prepared for the Conference: Debating Critical Realism, Roskilde University, Denmark, 17-19 August 2001.

———, 'Keynes, the Principle of Effective Demand, and Open Systems', Paper for a Lecture at University of Iceland, Iceland, 10 October 2003.

Jevons W.S., *The Theory of Political Economy*, London, New York: Macmillan (1871).

Jones B., *Globalization and Interdependence in the International Political Economy: Rhetoric and Reality*, London and New York: Pinter Publishers (1995).

Kant I., *Critique of Pure Reason* [1781/1787], transl. by N. Kemp Smith, London: Macmillan (1929).

———, *Groundwork for the Metaphysics of Morals* [1785] transl. by T.K. Abbott, in Abbott (1879).

———, *Critique of Practical Reason* [1788], transl. by T.K. Abbott, in Abbott (1879).

———, *Critique of Judgement* [1790], transl. by J.C. Meredith, Oxford: Clarendon Press (1952).

———, *Zum ewigen Frieden: Ein Philosophischer Entwurf*, Königsberg: Friedrich Nicolovius (1795).

———, *Metaphysics of Morals* [1797], transl. by T.K. Abbott, in Abbott (1879).

Kaplan M.A., 'Some Problems of the Extreme Utilitarian Position', in *Ethics*, Vol. 70, No. 3 (1960) 228-232.

———, 'Restricted Utilitarianism', in *Ethics*, Vol. 71, No. 4 (1961) 301-302.

Kaulbach F., *Studien zur späten Rechtsphilosophie Kants und ihrer transzendentalen Methode*, Würzburg: Königshausen & Neumann (1982).

Kautsky K., *Nationalstaat, Imperialistischer Staat und Staatenbund* [1911], Nürnberg: Fränkische Verlagsanstalt (1915) 75.

Kennedy P., *The Rise and Fall of the Great Powers: Economic Change and Military Conflict from 1500 to 2000*, London: Unwin Hyman (1988).
Keohane R., 'The Theory of Hegemonic Stability and Changes in International Economic Regimes 1967-1977', in Holsti et al. (1980).
Kerner G.C., 'The Immortality of Utilitarianism and the Escapism of Rule-Utilitarianism', in *The Philosophical Quarterly*, Vol. 21, No. 82 (1971) 36-50.
Keynes J.M., *The Economic Consequences of Peace*, London: Macmillan (1919).
———, 'Defence and Development', in *The Collected Writings*, Vol. XIX: The General Theory and After, Part II, London: Macmillan for the Royal Economic Society (1973).
———, 'Let Goods be Homespun', in *New Statesman and Nation*, July 1933.
———, Letter to the *New Statesman and Nation*, 13 July 1936.
———, *The General Theory of Employment, Interest and Money*, London: Macmillan (1936).
Kilcullen J., 'Utilitarianism and Virtue', in *Ethics*, Vol. 93, No. 3 (1983) 451-466.
Klagge J.C., 'Moral Realism and Dummett's Challenge', in *Philosophy and Phenomenological Research*, Vol. 48, No. 3 (1988) 545-551.
Klappholz K., 'Value Judgments in Economics', in *The British Journal for the Philosophy of Science*, Vol. 15, No. 58 (1964) 97-114.
Knight F.H., 'Intellectual Confusion on Morals and Economics', in *International Journal of Ethics*, Vol. 45, No. 2 (1935) 200-220.
———, 'Abstract Economics as Absolute Ethics', in *Ethics*, Vol. 76, No. 3 (1966) 163-177.
Korsgaard C.M., *The Sources of Normativity* (with G.A. Cohen, R. Geuss, T. Nagel, B. Williams) Cambridge and New York: Cambridge University Press (1996).
Kuhn T.S., *The Structure of Scientific Revolutions*, Chicago: University of Chicago Press (1962).
Lawson T., *Economics and Reality*, London: Routledge (1997).
———, 'Connections and Disconnections: Post Keynesianism and Critical Realism', in *Journal of Post Keynesian Economics*, Vol. 22, No. 1 (1999) 3-14.
———, *Reorienting Economics*, London: Routledge (2003).
Lebowitz M.A., 'Marx's Falling Rate of Profit: A Dialectical View', in *The Canadian Journal of Economics*, Vol. 9, No. 2 (1976) 232-254.
Lenin V.I., *Imperialism: The Latest Stage in the Development of Capitalism* [1917], Detroit: Marxian Educational Society (1924).
Levine D. (ed.), *Nebraska Symposium on Motivation,* Vol. 13, Lincoln: University of Nebraska Press (1965) .
Lewis H.D. (ed.), *Contemporary British Philosophy: Personal Statements*, 4th Series, London: Allen & Unwin (1976).
Ljungman C.M., 'Applying a Rights-Based Approach to Development: Concepts and Principles', Paper presented at the The Winners and Losers from Rights-Based Approaches to Development Conference, University of Manchester, UK, 21-22 February 2005.
Llobera J.R., 'Techno-Economic Determinism and the Work of Marx on Pre-Capitalist Societies', in *Man*, New Series, Vol. 14, No. 2 (1979) 249-270.
Lloyd Thomas D.A., 'Liberalism and Utilitarianism', in *Ethics*, Vol. 90, No. 3 (1980) 319-334.
London B. and Robinson T., 'The Effect of International Dependence on Income Inequality and Political Violence', in *American Sociological Review*, Vol. 54, No. 2 (1989) 305-308.
Long R.T., 'Realism and Abstraction in Economics: Aristotle and Mises versus Friedman', Paper presented at the Austrian Scholars Conference No. 10, Ludwig von Mises Institute, Auburn, USA (2004).
Lyons D., 'Rawls Versus Utilitarianism', in *The Journal of Philosophy*, Vol. 69, No. 18, (1972) 535-545.

Mabbott J.D., 'Interpretations of Mill's Utilitarianism', in *The Philosophical Quarterly*, Vol. 6, No. 23 (1956) 115-120.

MacKenzie D., 'Marx and the Machine', in *Technology and Culture*, Vol. 25, No. 3 (1984) 473-502.

Mackie J.L., 'The Disutility of Act-Utilitarianism', in *The Philosophical Quarterly*, Vol. 23, No. 93 (1973) 289-300.

———, *Ethics: Inventing Right and Wrong*, Harmondsworth: Penguin Books (1977).

Malthus T., *An Essay on the Principles of Population*, London: J. Johnson (1798).

Marshall A., *Principles of Economics*, London and New York: Macmillan and Co. (1890).

Marx K. and Engels F., *The Collected Works of Karl Marx and Frederick Engels*, 50 Vol., New York: International Publishers, London: Lawrence & Wishart Ltd., Moscow: Progress Publishers (1975-2005).

Marx K. and Engels F., *The Holy Family or Critique of Critical Criticism* [1845], in Marx and Engels (1975-2005) Vol. 4, 5-211.

———, *The German Ideology: Critique of Modern Philosophy according to its Representatives Feuerbach, B. Bauer and Stirner, and of German Socialism according to its Various Prophets* [1846], in Marx and Engels (1975-2005) Vol. 5, 19-539.

———, *Manifesto of the Communist Party* [1848[a]], in Marx and Engels (1975-2005) Vol. 6, 477-519.

Marx K., *Economic and Philosophical Manuscripts* [1844], in Marx and Engels (1975-2005) Vol. 3, 229-348.

———, *The Poverty of Philosophy* [1847], in Marx and Engels (1975-2005) Vol. 6, 105-212.

———, 'On the Question of Free Trade', Speech to the Democratic Association of Brussels at its Public Meeting of 9 January 1848, in Marx and Engels (1975-2005) Vol. 6, 450-465.

———, *Outlines of the Critique of Political Economy* [1858], in Marx and Engels (1975-2005) Vol. 29, 5-256.

———, *A Contribution to the Critique of Political Economy* [1859], in Marx and Engels (1975-2005) Vol. 29, 257-420.

———, *Capital Volume One*: *The Process of Production of Capital* [1867], in Marx and Engels (1975-2005) Vol. 35.

———, *Capital Volume Three: The Process of Capitalist Production as a Whole* [1893], in Marx and Engels (1975-2005) Vol. 37.

Mavrotas G., 'Foreign Aid, Economic Development and the Role of the UN', in Bourantonis and Evriviades (1996).

McFerson H.M., 'Rethinking Ethnic Conflict: Somalia and Fiji', in *The American Behavioral Science*, Vol. 40, No. 1 (1996) 18-32.

McKinlay R. and Little R., *Global Problems and World Order*, Madison: F. Pinter Publishers (1986).

Meek R.L., 'Value-Judgments in Economics' in *The British Journal for the Philosophy of Science*, Vol. 15, No. 58 (1964) 89-96.

Menger C., *Grundsätze der Volkswirthschaftslehre*, Wien: W. Braumüller (1871).

Mill J.S., *A System of Logic, Ratiocinative and Inductive: Being a Connected View of the Principles of Evidence, and the Methods of Scientific Investigation*, London: J.W. Parker (1843).

———, *Essays on Some Unsettled Questions of Political Economy* [1844], London: Longmans and Green (1877).

———, *Principles of Political Economy: With Some of Their Application to Social Philosophy* [1848], Fairfield: A.M. Kelley (1987).

———, *On Liberty*, London: J.W. Parker (1859).

———, *Utilitarianism*, London: Parker, Son and Bourn (1863).

———, *An Examination of Sir William Hamilton's Philosophy, and of the Principal Philosophical Questions discussed in his Writings*, Boston: W.V. Spencer (1865).

Mises L.v., *Theory and History*, New Haven: Yale University Press (1957).

Mitrany D., *A Working Peace System*, Chicago: Quadrangle Books (1966).

Montefiori A. (ed.), *Philosophy and Personal Relations*, London: Routledge and Kegan Paul (1973).

Moore G.E., *Principia Ethica*, Cambridge: Cambridge University Press (1903).

Morgenthau H., *Macht und Frieden: Grundlegung einer Theorie der Internationalen Politik*, Gütersloh: C. Bertelsmann (1963).

Mulholland L.A., 'Rights, Utilitarianism, and the Conflation of Persons', in *The Journal of Philosophy*, Vol. 83, No. 6 (1986) 323-340.

Muller E., 'Income Inequality, Regime Repressiveness and Political Violence', in *American Sociological Review*, Vol. 50, No. 1 (1985) 47-61.

———, 'Income Inequality and Political Violence: The Effect of Influential Cases', in *American Sociological Review*, Vol. 51, No. 3 (1986) 441-445.

———, 'Inequality, Repression, Violence: Issues of Theory and Research Design', in *American Sociological Review*, Vol. 53, No. 5 (1988) 799-806.

Myrdal G., *Value in Social Theory: A Selection of Essays on Methodology*, London: Routledge & Kegan Paul (1958).

Nafziger W., Stewart F. and Väyrynen R. (eds.), *War, Hunger and Displacement: The Origins of Humanitarian Emergencies*, 2 Vol., Oxford: Oxford University Press (2000).

Narveson J., 'Utilitarianism, Group Actions, and Coordination or: Must the Utilitarian be a Buridan's Ass', in *Nous*, Vol. 10, No. 2 (1976) 173-194.

Nietzsche F., *On the Genealogy of Morals* [1887], transl. by H.B. Samuel, Mineola: Dover Publications (2003).

North P., *Institutions, Institutional Change and Economic Performance*, Cambridge MA: Harvard University Press (1990).

Pangle T., 'Justice Among Nations in Platonic and Aristotelian Political Philosophy', in *American Journal of Political Science*, Vol. 42, No. 2 (1998) 377-397.

Parfit D., 'Later Selves and Moral Principles', in Montefiori (1973) 137-168.

Perkins M.L., 'An Unpublished Letter from Saint-Pierre to Daguesseau', in *Modern Language Notes*, Vol. 70, No. 2 (1955) 110-113.

———, 'Civil Theology in the Writings of the Abbé de Saint-Pierre', in *Journal of the History of Ideas*, Vol. 18, No. 2 (1957) 242-253.

———, *The Moral and Political Philosophy of the Abbé de Saint-Pierre*, Genève and Paris: E. Droz, Minard (1959).

Pigou A.C., *Unemployment*, New York: H. Holt (1914).

Pitkin H.F., 'Slippery Bentham: Some Neglected Cracks in the Foundation of Utilitarianism', in *Political Theory*, Vol. 18, No. 1 (1990) 104-131.

Plato, *Meno* [ca. 380 BC], in Plato, *The Dialogues of Plato*, transl. by B. Jowett, Oxford: Clarendon Press (1871).

Popper K.R., *The Open Society and its Enemies*, London: G. Routledge & Sons (1945).

———, *The Logic of Scientific Discovery*, London: Hutchinson (1959).

———, *The Poverty of Historicism*, London: Routledge & Kegan Paul (1960).

Postow B.C., 'Werner's Ethical Realism', in *Ethics*, Vol. 95, No. 2 (1985) 285-291.

Railton P., 'Moral Realism', in *The Philosophical Review*, Vol. 95, No. 2 (1986) 163-207.

Rapkin D. and Strand J., 'Is International Competitiveness a Meaningful Concept', in Goddard et al. (1996).

Rashdall H., *The Theory of Good and Evil: A Treatise on Moral Philosophy*, Oxford: Clarendon Press (1907).

Rawls J., *A Theory of Justice*, Cambridge MA: Harvard University Press (1971).

Reychler L., 'The Art of Conflict Prevention: Theory and Practice', in Bauwens and Rychler (1994) 1-21.

Ricardo D., *On the Principles of Political Economy and Taxation* [1817], Cambridge: Cambridge University Press (1951).

———, *The Iron Law of Wages* [1817], in Ricardo D., *The Works of David Ricardo*, London: J. Murray (1881).

Ring J., 'On Needing Both Marx and Arendt: Alienation and the Flight from Inwardness', in *Political Theory*, Vol. 17, No. 3 (1989) 432-448.

Ringier J.E., *Der Abbé de Saint-Pierre: Ein Nationalökonom des 18. Jahrhunderts*, Karlsruhe: G. Braun (1905).

Rittberger V., *Internationale Organizationen: Politik und Geschichte. Europäische und Weltweite Zwischenstaatliche Zusammenschlüsse*, Opladen: Leske und Budrich (1994).

Robbins L.C., *An Essay on the Nature and Significance of Economic Science*, London: Macmillan (1948).

Rousseau J.J., *Extrait du Projet de Paix Perpétuelle de Monsieur l'Abbé de Saint-Pierre*, Paris: s.n. (1761).

———, *Jugement sur le Projet de Paix Perpétuelle de l'Abbé de Saint-Pierre*, Paris: s.n. (1782).

Saez-Santiago E. and Bernal G., 'Depression in Ethnic Minorities', accessed at http://latino.rcm.upr.edu/saez.pdf.

Saint Pierre C.I.C. de, *Projet pour Rendre la Paix Perpetuelle en Europe*, Utrecht: A. Schouten (1713).

———, *Annales Politiques de Feu Monsieur Charles-Irenée Castel, Abbé de Saint Pierre*, Londres: s.n. (1758).

Samuelson P.A., *Foundations of Economic Analysis*, Cambridge MA: Harvard University Press (1947).

———, 'The Normative and Positivistic Inferiority of Marx's Values Paradigm', in *Southern Economic Journal*, Vol. 49, No. 1 (1982) 11-18.

Sanderson J., 'Marx and Engels on the State', in *The Western Political Quarterly*, Vol. 16, No. 4 (1963) 946-955.

Sartorius R., 'Utilitarianism and Obligation', in *The Journal of Philosophy*, Vol. 66, No. 3 (1969) 67-81.

Say J.-B., *A Treatise on Political Economy: Or the Production, Distribution and Consumption of Wealth* [1803], Philadelphia: Lippincott, Grambo & Co. (1855).

Schneider H.W., 'Obligations and the Pursuit of Happiness', in *The Philosophical Review*, Vol. 61, No. 3 (1952) 312-319.

Schueler G.F., 'Modus Ponens and Moral Realism', in *Ethics*, Vol. 98, No. 3 (1988) 492-500.

Schultz B., 'Persons, Selves, and Utilitarianism', in *Ethics*, Vol. 96, No. 4 (1986) 721-745.

Schumann H., 'Die wahren Globalisierungsgegner oder: Die politische Ökonomie des Terrorismus', in *Aus Politik und Zeitgeschichte*, No. 13-14 (2003) 24-30.

Schumpeter J.A., *Capitalism, Socialism and Democracy*, New York: Harper (1950).

———, *A History of Economic Analysis*, New York: Oxford University Press (1954).

Schwarzenberger G., 'Ius Pacis Ac Belli: Prolegomena to a Sociology of International Law', in *American Journal of International Law*, Vol. 37, No. 3 (1943) 460-479.

Schweinitz Jr. K. de, 'The Question of Freedom in Economics and Economic Organization', in *Ethics*, Vol. 89, No. 4 (1979) 336-353.

Scott J., *Weapons of the Weak: Everyday Forms of Peasant Resistance*, New Haven: Yale University Press (1990).

Sells M.A., *The Bridge Betrayed: Religion and Genocide in Bosnia*, Berkeley and Los Angeles: University of California Press (1996).

Sen A., *On Economic Inequality*, Oxford: Oxford University Press (1973).

——, 'Utilitarianism and Welfarism', in *The Journal of Philosophy*, Vol. 76, No. 9 (1979) 463-489.

——, *Development as Freedom*, Oxford: Oxford University Press (1999).

Shapiro I., 'Resources, Capacities, and Ownership: The Workmanship Ideal and Distributive Justice', in *Political Theory*, Vol. 19, No. 1 (1991) 47-72.

Shaw T.M. and Grieve M.J., 'The Political Economy of Resources: Africa's Future in the Global Environment', in *The Journal of Modern African Studies*, Vol. 16, No. 1 (1978) 1-32.

Shaw W.H., 'The Handmill Gives You the Feudal Lord: Marx's Technological Determinism', in *History and Theory*, Vol. 18, No. 2 (1979) 155-176.

Shoul B., 'Karl Marx and Say's Law', in *The Quarterly Journal of Economics*, Vol. 71, No. 4 (1957) 611-629.

Siegelman L. and Simpson M., 'A Cross-National Test of the Linkage between Economic Inequality and Political Violence', in *Journal of Conflict Resolution*, Vol. 21 (1977) 105-128.

Silverstein H.S., 'Utilitarianism and Group Coordination' in *Nous*, Vol. 13, No. 3 (1979) 335-360.

Simon A., *Models of Man: Social and Rational, Mathematical Essays on Rational Human Behavior in a Social Setting*, New York: Wiley (1957).

Singer M.G., 'Actual Consequence Utilitarianism', in *Mind*, New Series, Vol. 86, No. 341 (1977) 67-77.

——, 'Further on Actual Consequence Utilitarianism', in *Mind*, New Series, Vol. 92, No. 366 (1983) 270-274.

Singer P., 'Is Act-Utilitarianism Self-Defeating?', in *The Philosophical Review*, Vol. 81, No. 1 (1972) 94-104.

Skidelsky R., *John Maynard Keynes: Fighting for Freedom, 1937-1946*, New York: Viking (2000).

Slim H., 'Making Moral Low Ground: Rights as the Struggle for Justice and the Abolition of Development' in *The Fletcher Journal of Development Studies,* Vol. XVII (2002).

Smart J.J.C., 'Extreme and Restricted Utilitarianism', in *The Philosophical Quarterly*, Vol. 6, No. 25 (1956) 344-354.

——, *An Outline of a System of Utilitarian Ethics*, Victoria: Melbourne University Press (1961).

——, 'Extreme Utilitarianism: A Reply to M. A. Kaplan', in *Ethics*, Vol. 71, No. 2 (1961) 133-134.

Smart R.N., 'Negative Utilitarianism', in *Mind*, New Series, Vol. 67, No. 268 (1958) 542-543.

Smith A., *The Theory of Moral Sentiments*, London: A. Millar, A. Kincaid and J. Bell (1759).

——, *An Inquiry into the Nature and Causes of the Wealth of Nations*, Dublin: Whitestone (1776).

Smith T., 'Requiem or New Agenda for Third World Studies?', in *World Politics*, Vol. 37, No. 4 (1985) 532-561.

Sorey W.R., 'Ethical Aspects of Economics', in *International Journal of Ethics*, Vol. 17, No. 1 (1906) 1-13.

——, 'Ethical Aspects of Economics II', in *International Journal of Ethics*, Vol. 17, No. 3 (1907) 317-329.

Spears I., 'Understanding Inclusive Peace Agreements in Africa: The Problems of Sharing Power', in *Third World Quarterly*, Vol. 21, No. 1 (2000) 105-118.

Spengler J.J., 'Have Values a Place in Economics?', in *International Journal of Ethics*, Vol. 44, No. 3 (1934) 313-331.

Spinoza B. de, Letter to J. Jelles on 2 June 1674.

Stavenhagen R., 'The Return of the Native: The Indigenous Challenge in Latin America' in *University of London, Institute of Latin America Studies, Occasional Papers*, No. 27 (2002) 1-17.

Steele G.R., 'The Money Economy: Mercantilism, Classical Economics and Keynes' General Theory', in *American Journal of Economics and Sociology*, Special Invited Issue: Money, Trust, Speculation and Social Justice, Part 2: Trust and Money (Oct. 1998).

Stewart F., 'Groups for Good or Ill', in *Oxford Development Studies*, Vol. 24, No. 1 (1996) 9-25.

———, 'Crisis Prevention: Tackling Horizontal Inequalities', in *Queen Elizabeth House Working Paper Series*, No. 33 (2000).

———, 'Horizontal Inequalities: A Neglected Dimension of Development', in *Queen Elizabeth House Working Paper Series*, No. 81 (2002).

Sturgeon N.L., 'Anderson on Reason and Value', in *Ethics*, Vol. 106, No. 3 (1996) 509-524.

Tajfel H. (ed.), *Differentiation between Social Groups*, London: Academic Press (1978).

———, 'Social Psychology and Intergroup Relations', in *Annual Review of Psychology*, Vol. 33 (1982) 1-39.

Tajfel H. and Turner J., 'An Integrative Theory of Intergroup Conflict', in Austin and Worchel (1979) 33-47.

Tawney R.H., *Equality* [1931], New York: Capricorn Books (1961).

Taylor C. and Hudson M.C., *The World Handbook of Political and Scientific Indicators*, New Haven: Yale University Press (1972).

Taylor O.H., 'Schumpeter and Marx: Imperialism and Social Classes in the Schumpeterian System', in *The Quarterly Journal of Economics*, Vol. 65, No. 4 (1951) 525-555.

Temkin J., 'Actual Consequence Utilitarianism: A Reply to Professor Singer', in *Mind*, New Series, Vol. 87, No. 347 (1978) 412-414.

Thomas Aquinas, *Summa Theologica* [1265-1274], New York: Benzinger Bros. (1947).

———, *On Human Nature*, Indianapolis: Hackett (1999).

Thurow L., 'A New Economic Game', in Goddard et al. (1996).

Trianosky G.W., 'Rule-Utilitarianism and the Slippery Slope', in *The Journal of Philosophy*, Vol. 75, No. 8 (1978) 414-424.

Tucker G.S.L., 'Ricardo and Marx', in *Economica*, New Series, Vol. 28, No. 111 (1961) 252-269.

Tugwell R.G., 'Economics and Ethics', in *The Journal of Philosophy*, Vol. 21, No. 25 (1924) 682-690.

Turnell S., 'Keynes, Economics and War: A Liberal Dose of Realism', in *Macquarie Economics Research Papers*, No. 7 (2002) 1-21.

Turton D., 'War and Ethnicity: Global Connections and Local Violence in East Africa and Former Yugoslavia', in *Oxford Development Studies*, No. 25, Special Issue: War, Economy and Society (1997) 77-94.

UN, 'Strengthening Human Rights-related United Nations Action at Country level: National Human Rights Promotion and Protection Systems', accessed at http://www.un.org/events/action2/action2plan.pdf.

UN General Assembly, 'Vienna Declaration and Programme of Action' (A/CONF.157/23) 12 July 1993.

UN General Assembly, 'United Nations Millennium Declaration' (A/RES/55/2) 18 September 2000.

UN Secretary-General, 'We the Peoples: The Role of the UN in the 21st Century' (A/54/2000) 27 March 2000.

UN Secretary-General, 'Strengthening of the United Nations: An Agenda for Further Change' (A/57/387) 9 September 2002.

UNDP, *Human Development Report 2000: Human Rights and Human Development,* New York: Oxford University Press (2000).

UNDP, *Human Development Report 2005: International Cooperation at a Crossroads: Aid, Trade and Security in an Unequal World*, New York: Oxford University Press (2005).

UNECLAC, *The Economic Development of Latin America and its Principal Problems*, Lake Success: UN Dept. of Economic Affairs (1950).

Urmson J.O., 'The Interpretation of the Moral Philosophy of J.S. Mill', in *The Philosophical Quarterly*, Vol. 3, No. 10 (1953) 33-39.

Vidas A.A. de, 'The Culture of Marginality: The Teenek Portrayal of Social Difference', in *Ethnology*, Vol. 41, No. 3 (2002) 209-224.

Viner J., 'Mr. Keynes on the Causes of Unemployment', in *The Quarterly Journal of Economics*, Vol. 51, No. 1 (1936) 147-167.

Volkan J. et al. (eds.), *The Psychodynamics of International Relationships*, Lexington: D.C. Heath (1991).

Wahl S., 'Cultural Hegemony, Cultural Self-Denigration, and What We Should do About it', in *Philosophical Diatribes*, Vol. 35, accessed at http://www.froyd.net/philosophy/philo35.htm.

Walker A., 'Karl Marx, the Declining Rate of Profit and British Political Economy', in *Economica*, Vol. 38, No. 152 (1971) 363-377.

Wallerstein I., 'Dependence in an Interdependent World', in Goddard et al. (1996).

Wallerstein I. and Hechter M., 'Social Rank and Nationalism: Some African Data' in *The Public Opinion Quarterly*, Vol. 34, No. 3 (1970) 360-370.

———, 'Semi-Peripheral Countries and the Contemporary World Crisis', in *Theory and Society*, Vol. 3, No. 4 (1976) 461-483.

Walras L., *Elements d'Economie Politique Pure: Ou, Théorie de la Richesse Sociale*, Lausanne: L. Corbaz & cie (1874).

Waltz K., *Theory of International Politics*, Reading: Addison-Wesley (1979).

Weber M., *The Methodology of the Social Sciences*, Glencoe: Free Press (1949).

Weede E., 'Income Inequality, Average Income, and Domestic Violence', *in Journal of Conflict Resolution*, Vol. 25, No. 4 (1981) 639-653.

———, 'Income Inequality and Political Violence Reconsidered', in *American Sociological Review*, Vol. 51, No. 3 (1986) 438-441.

Werner R., 'Ethical Realism', in *Ethics*, Vol. 93, No. 4 (1983) 653-679.

———, 'Ethical Realism Defended', in *Ethics*, Vol. 95, No. 2 (1985) 292-296.

West E.G., 'The Political Economy of Alienation: Karl Marx and Adam Smith', in *Oxford Economic Papers*, Vol. 21, No. 1 (1969) 1-23.

Wilde N., 'Kant's Relation to Utilitarianism', in *The Philosophical Review*, Vol. 3, No. 3 (1894) 289-304.

Wolff R.P., 'A Critique and Reinterpretation of Marx's Labor Theory of Value', in *Philosophy and Public Affairs*, Vol. 10, No. 2 (1981) 89-120.

Wolfstetter E., 'Surplus Labour, Synchronised Labour Costs and Marx's Labour Theory of Value', in *The Economic Journal*, Vol. 83, No. 331 (1973) 787-809.

Woodward P.S., *The Unstable State*, Boulder: Lynne Rienner (1990).

Young O. (ed.), *International Cooperation: Building Regimes for Natural Resources and the Environment*, Ithaca: Cornell University Press (1989).

———, 'Patterns of International Cooperation: Institutions and Organizations', in Young (1989) 31-57.

AUTHORS INDEX

Y

SUBJECT INDEX

Note: Terms and concepts associated with a particular author are marked with an acronym in brackets. The following acronyms apply to the following authors: I.K. = Immanuel Kant; J.M.K. = John Maynard Keynes; K.M. = Karl Marx; A.S. = Adam Smith.

J

K

L

M

N

O

P

R

S

Nijhoff Law Specials

50. K. Wellens (ed.): *Resolutions and Statements of the United Nations Security Council (1946-2000). A Thematic Guide.* 2001 ISBN 90 411 1722 9
51. P. Soar (ed.): *The New International Directory of Legal Aid.* 2001 ISBN 90 411 1718 0
52. C.M. Mazzoni (ed.): *Ethics and Law in Biological Research.* 2002 ISBN 90 411 1742 3
53. I. Omar: *Emergency Powers and the Courts in India and Pakistan.* 2002 ISBN 90 411 1775 X
54. M. O'Flaherty: *Human Rights and the UN: Practice Before the Treaty Bodies.* 2002 ISBN 90 411 1788 1
55. Y. Beigbeder: *Judging Criminal Leaders. The Slow Erosion of Impunity.* 2002 ISBN 90 411 1815 2
56. Marianne van Leeuwen (ed.): *Confronting Terrorism: European Experiences, Threat Perceptions, and Policies.* 2003 ISBN 90 411 1960 4
57. Ralf Bredel: *Long-term Con.ict Prevention and Industrial Development: The United Nations and its Specialized Agency, UNIDO.* 2003 ISBN 90 04 13619 3
58. Raphael Walden: *Racism and Human Rights.* 2004 ISBN 90 04 13651 7
59. Monique Leyenaar: *Political Empowerment of Women: The Netherlands and Other Countries.* 2004 ISBN 90 04 14099 9
60. Sjureur Skaale (ed.): *The Right to National Self-Determination: The Faroe Islands and Greenland.* 2004 ISBN 90 04 14207 X
61. Edward McWhinney: *The September 11 Terrorist Attacks and the Invasion of Iraq in Contemporary International Law: Opinions on the Emerging New World Order System.* 2004 ISBN 90 04 14143 X
62. B.G. Ramcharan: *The Protection Role of National Human Rights Institutions.* 2005. ISBN 90 04 14526 5
63. Chris de Cooker: *Accountability, Investigation and Due Process in International Organizations.* 2005. ISBN 90 04 14793 4
64. Peris S. Jones & Kristian Stokke: *Democratising Development: The Politics of Socio-Economic Rights in South Africa.* 2005. ISBN 90 04 14821 3
65. Roy S. Lee (ed.): *Swords Into Plowshares: Building Peace Through the United Nations.* 2005. ISBN 90 04 15001 3
66. J.A. Bovenberg: *Property Rights in Blood, Genes & Data: Naturally Yours?* 2006 ISBN 90 04 15053 6
67. Frank Hoffmeister: *Legal Aspects of the Cyprus Problem. Annan Plan and EU Accession.* ISBN 90 04 15223 7
68. Ralf Bredel: *The Ethical Economy of Conflict Prevention and Development. Towards a Model for International Organizations.* ISBN 10: 90 04 15305 5
    ISBN 13: 978 90 04 15305 9

For more titles in this series, consult our web site: http://www.brill.nl

MARTINUS NIJHOFF PUBLISHERS – LEIDEN – BOSTON

www.ingramcontent.com/pod-product-compliance
Lightning Source LLC
Chambersburg PA
CBHW031322230926
51848CB00001B/49
9789004153059